CHANGING THE SUBJECT

WOMEN'S DISCOURSES AND FEMINIST THEOLOGY

Mary McClintock
Fulkerson

FORTRESS PRESS
MINNEAPOLIS

*To my husband, Bill
and our children, Hopie and Will*

CHANGING THE SUBJECT
Women's Discourses and Feminist Theology

Author photo: Les Todd
Cover Design: Judy Swanson

The lyrics on page 239 are reprinted by permission of Clady Johnson.

Library of Congress Cataloging-in-Publication Data

Fulkerson, Mary McClintock, 1950–
    Changing the subject : women's discourses and feminist theology /
Mary McClintock Fulkerson.
      p.   cm.
    Includes bibliographical references and index.
    ISBN 0-8006-2747-4 (alk. paper) :
    1. Feminist theology.   I. Title.
BT83.55.F85   1994
230'.082 — dc20   93–31062
                                                            CIP

The paper used in this publication meets the minimum requirements of American National Standard for Information Services—Permanence of Paper for Printed Library Materials, ANSI Z329.48-1984. ∞™

Manufactured in the U.S.A.   AF 1–2747

98   97   96   95   94   1   2   3   4   5   6   7   8   9   10

Contents

5. Joyful Speaking for God:
Pentecostal Women's Performances   239

6. Christianity as Patriarchy:
Discourses of Parody and Politicization   299

Preface

This book is about gender, language, social location, and feminist theological resources for respecting difference. It is about meeting women whose struggles are for physical survival rather than for the feminist transformation of the academy. I *could* say that this book is a theological reflection on the differences between my feminist account of faith (as an upper-middle class, white woman in academic theology) and the very different postures toward Christian texts, gender, power, and reality of the poor Pentecostal women and middle-class Presbyterian housewives of whom I write. Yet I do not account for difference by simply collecting narratives of social location—stories of our different experiences. Rather, this book investigates the production of these differences; it offers strategies (beyond confessing my social location and appealing to the respective "experiences" of women) that will engender deeper respect for difference.

In this book I argue that feminist theology has failed to offer theories of language, social location, power, and gender capable of displaying difference. When it relies upon appeals to women's experience as the origin of or evidence for its claims, feminist theology cannot account for the systems of meaning and power that produce that experience. It cannot account, for example, for Pentecostal women's performance of scripture, for Presbyterian women's rewriting of the Reformed community's biblical text, for the occlusion of their capacities to recognize the sinful character of gendered arrangements, and even for the occlusions in academic feminist theologians' position.

By challenging the appeal to women's experience, I risk seeming ungrateful, which I most certainly am not. I have been formed and nourished by the writings of the feminist theologians whose thought I consider critically in this book. The work of Rosemary Radford

Ruether, Sallie McFague, Mary Daly, Elisabeth Schüssler Fiorenza, and Letty Russell has made me a feminist theologian. I also take a risk because feminist work is not well established in the academy. By criticizing the appeal to women's experience I risk being misread as offering new ammunition to those without feminist sympathies. That I cannot control, of course, but I can state what I understand this volume to be about.

This book criticizes the appeal to women's experience in a very specific sense, not in its employment in consciousness-raising groups, domestic shelters, or other settings where subjectivities of self-confidence are being formed. My target is the appeal in academic settings, where the production of knowledge itself needs to be challenged. My work attempts to deepen and radicalize the feminist appreciation of the constitutive character of social location on our realities—class, race, sexual preference. Experience is not the *origin* of theology in the sense of the evidence for our claims, but the reality that needs to be explained. I call upon feminists and all theologians to do the work of explaining by connecting their claims with the systems of discourse and social relations that produce them. Otherwise, as the trivialization of these issues into "political correctness" reminds us, the appeal to women's (or any marginalized) experience in academic systems can be trivialized and (mis)appropriated in a liberal, individualistic way, and the occlusions and possibilities that come from being located differently can be ignored.

I try to persuade readers that, in place of the appeal to experience, categories from feminist and liberationist uses of poststructuralism are useful for probing the hidden workings and commitments of the communities in which women reside—from conservative churches to academic settings. To write about poststructuralism is to start without a starting place. It is to claim to "use" analytical categories at the same time one is also claiming that language and attendant systems of power and meaning "use" subjects. Despite this contradiction, I think it quite useful to feminist theology or any theology to find more complex and interesting ways to indicate our locatedness; this is what poststructuralist discourse theory can contribute. Caught in the middle of these very processes of meaning (and the conflicts and desires that shape them), I cannot claim to be seeing it all or seeing with perfect clarity. I hope to help remove those ideals from our theoretical resources and to convince the reader that any respectable theology of fallibility requires such acknowledgment.

I invoke theological commitments in this work to evaluate both practices and theories. My commitments come from a Christian reading of creation, its God-dependence, violations of that dependence in socially displayed forms of domination, and a view of redemption appropriate to the structures of fallibility. My reading and its related themes, such as honoring the other and care for the stranger, are based on some of the organizing commitments of the feminism that has been generated in Christian communities.

There are two reasons why theological language is an important piece of the book. First, faith commitments are part of the thick reality with which feminist analysis has to deal. Many women use faith's language; women understand themselves to be liberated, redeemed, saved as well as oppressed by the God to which Christian communities witness. Second, the theological commitments in the book are mine.

I must warn the reader, however, that I defer the problem of the sign "God" as that is discredited by the endless processes of signification set in motion by accounts of poststructuralism. I contend that poststructuralist destabilizations do not have to be totalizing. They occur within existing structural arrangements for liberation critiques. I judge them to be incapable of permanently ending theological claims just as believers are permanently incapable of establishing the validity of these claims.

To some extent, this deferral is because I do not find it necessary to justify the faith claims I invoke, just as I do not argue that these claims are the only way to articulate theological commitments or feminist commitments. As a nonfoundationalist, I do not find the project of proving or defending the existence of God to be an interesting one, particularly for liberation theologies. While I do not want to argue that poststructuralism is simply a principle of finitude or fallibility (it is not), I do think a poststructuralist account of discourse rules out the possibility of claims that can be validated somehow outside of communities and their languages. Thus the real reason I bypass its challenge to theology here is that I disassociate feminist theological interests from the *kinds of communities that ask such formal questions*.

I continue to use theological commitments out of the conviction that the sign "God," like any other, is always invoked in a web of significations and embodied practices, such as academic criticism, worship, and social activism. "God" is neither a sign nor the object of a cognition that can be treated apart from a complex of other signifying practices. For myself and for the women I consider, the pertinent practices are those of resistance, survival, agape, hope—practices that *assume* God's existence rather than problematize it. I would not argue that the destabilized transcendent signifier of much poststructuralist criticism is totally other than the "God" invoked here, but I do think the sign "God" in a/theology has its meaning in a different web of sig-

nifying processes that are attached to a different community than the
ones I am interested in describing or that interest feminist theology.
The practices of my inquiry—my own and those of the women I write
about—simply assume a God who is somehow liberating or saving in
history. Although there is room for doubt or despair about where any
signs of that liberating presence may be found at any one time in the
communities I describe, there is no interest in entertaining the sign
"God" as an abstraction or probing whether its formal referent exists.
These communities simply act as if it does.

Given the contradictions entailed by being Christian and feminist
with a poststructuralist take on fallibility, I do not claim, then, that
there is a set of theological loci that is the archimedean point for our
problems. Rather I like the phrase coined by Karen Trimble Alliaume,
that as women have been told they do not resemble the savior, we are
in the process of "reassembling" that figure.

There are many people to thank. Sharon Welch has been a supporter
and conversation partner for years. I am indebted to her once again for
her careful response to the book. I thank colleagues Elizabeth Clark,
Wesley Kort, and Dale Martin in the religion department for their
careful readings of my work and Kenneth Surin, who was an early
reader. I also thank Liz for the support she provides, not just for me,
but for all women in religion at Duke. In the Divinity School, Stanley
Hauerwas has been a wonderfully prompt and enthusiastic reader of
the book. For that and much good talking I am grateful. I thank Divinity colleagues Grant Wacker, Richard Lischer, and Gilbert Greggs
for their help. Graduate students have been crucial conversation
partners—thanks especially to Meg Gandy, Karen Trimble Alliaume,
and Kelly Jarrett. I appreciate Rebecca Chopp's interest and support
and the Fortress Press readers' suggestions and criticisms.

I wish to acknowledge the women who helped me begin an ongoing search into the connections between my social location and those
of other women. (Thanks to Gil Griggs for ongoing conversations
about the differences between a search and a "tour.") Acknowledgment of Presbyterian women is of faithful women too numerous to
name; my greatest debt goes to my mother, who as my personal introduction to Presbyterian women has inspired me with great respect
for this community. Among the many people I have visited, including
women whose struggles come from poverty and realities most unlike
my own, I am grateful to Helen Lewis at the Highlander Center; to
Marie Cirillo and Tilda Kemplin of Roses Creek, Tennessee; Clady
Johnson and the other women at Binns County Community Center in
Nora, Virginia; Becky Simpson of Cranks Creek Survival Center in
Kentucky; Mary Lee Daugherty of AMERC (Appalachian Ministries

Educational Resource Center); and the folks at CORA (Commission on Religion in Appalachia).

A Younger Scholar Award from the Association of Theological Schools for 1991–1992 was enormously helpful as support for an extended sabbatical. I also benefitted from an American Academy of Religion Research Assistance Grant in the fall of 1991, which provided money for travel to archives. The librarians at the Historical Foundation of the Presbyterian and Reformed Churches, Montreat, North Carolina, and at the Office of History of the Presbyterian Church (U.S.A.) in Philadelphia, Pennsylvania, were crucial to my chapter on Presbyterian Women. I thank David Roebuck at the Hal Bernard Dixon, Jr., Pentecostal Research Center, and the faculty at the Church of God School of Theology. Thanks to my wonderfully enthusiastic editor, Michael West, and to Julie Odland for her careful editorial production work.

My family consistently refuses to consider theological things interesting. I (sometimes) thank them for that, and I dedicate this book to them.

Mary McClintock Fulkerson

Introduction

Five women

Katherine Bennett was an early twentieth-century leader of Presbyterian women's organizations. Her work for women took her around the globe with the church's Home and National Missions boards. At a time when women could not be ordained, she forged a ministry of major proportions: she visited every kind of overseas mission field, worked for Native Americans, and was appointed by Woodrow Wilson to the China Famine Fund. Bennett gave tirelessly of herself for what the church called "Women's Work for Women," traveling by mule or stagecoach or whatever means necessary. Yet a eulogist for this activist woman leader, noting that she was committed to the equal standing of women with men in the church, felt compelled to add that she "was not a feminist."

Before and after Bennett's time, countless women in traditional mainline U.S. Protestant denominations have devoted much of their adult lives to organizations committed to "women's work for women." The middle-to-upper-middle-class housewives who do this work in the Presbyterian Church U.S.A., for example, are modest. They speak of their limits, their lack of influence. "I'm just an ordinary woman, a housewife" is a common refrain in their publications. Whenever the subject of women's ordination arose in the years before it was achieved, they reassured the wider church (and one another) that, if it passed, women would not "take over" the ministry. This same organization exhorts its members to "change the world."[1]

---

[1]These are stories/anecdotes about real women, some of whom are discussed in chapters 4, 5, and 6.

1

Clady Johnson is a lean, intense woman who has lived her whole life in the coal-mining regions of Virginia. Leaving school after the eighth grade, she married, had four children, and nearly came to agree with her abusive husband, who "kept tellin' me I was no good for this, no good for that, and I honestly didn't think I was capable of doin' anything but goin' to the grocery store and raisin' children." Now Sister Johnson, a devout Pentecostal woman, speaks with great assurance about her transformation from a person who believed she could not escape her husband's abuse, to one who works with community ministries. She writes poetry and songs. She believes ardently that, despite the hardships of her life, she will always bounce back. She gives the credit to the Lord, who is the real agent in her deliverance. It is this God, the Holy Father, who dries her tears, who brings her out of the dark valleys, and who gave her the strength to leave her husband.

A sister Pentecostal who has obeyed God's call to ministry speaks of her worry about women's liberation and its seductive call to women to leave their homes and children and take jobs in the world. "I really believe that women have limitations, and I think we as women have an obligation. . . . We have to be more careful than a man." Denying that she chafes under the restrictions put upon her by her church, Sister Ruth Staples insists, "I always respect man ministers as my superiors." That is, unless a man gets in her way when it comes to preaching the gospel. Sister Staples's loyalties to God authorize her world travels and her courage and self-preservation in the face of male opposition.

Feminist theologians take aim at the religion of patriarchy. Rosemary Radford Ruether proposes a feminist critical principle that holds the Christian tradition accountable for its capacity to support or deny the full humanity of women. She speaks for countless women who deny the revelatory status of androcentric and sexist biblical texts because they fail the test. Ruether and other feminists create new liturgies for naming and celebrating the divine in relation to women's experiences, from rituals that exorcise patriarchal texts to celebrations of menarche and menopause.

Feminist theology scrutinizes doctrinal tradition as well. Ruether wonders if a male savior can save women. Mary Daly, in her early writings, defined liberating sisterhood as antichurch. She offered a philosophy of women's liberation as exercise in Methodicide, a process of liberation-castration-exorcism. One of the first theological targets for this radical operation is God the Father.

Why change the subject?

Among the unresolved theoretical and theological issues in feminism
is that of its very subject—woman. Challenges to both kinds of feminisms (theories and theologies) are directed at their implicit claims to
speak for all women, challenges not unlike those generated earlier by
feminists in relation to the false generic of the male subject. The quarrel recently has been with the generic pretensions of feminist theology's subject, a subject that invokes universality, implicitly if not
explicitly, by virtue of its appeal to "women's experience." The specificity of the race, class, and sexual particularity of this experience has
come under scrutiny. By making available other portraits of women,
their oppression, and their faith practices, womanist, Asian, African,
mujerista, and lesbian feminist theologians display the partiality and
specificity of feminist theology's subject—as white, Euro-American,
heterosexual, middle class, and privileged. As a sign of this diversity,
most feminist theologians now acknowledge their identity in their
work as well.

But what about women who are not feminists or liberationist academics? Should feminist theology articulate or take account of the experience of women, such as the Pentecostal women preachers, who
are adamantly opposed to the language of feminism and the kind of
autonomy and aggressiveness that they think it supports? What about
white affluent housewives—like my own mother—in mainline
churchwomen's groups, many of whom have dedicated much of their
adult lives to practicing their faith as "women's work for women"?
Are feminist theology's definitions of "woman" and current ways of
problematizing that subject adequate to encompass a feminist inquiry
into women like these who are outside feminist conversations? For
that matter, is there any good reason to move to such topics? Can feminist theories that challenge the subject "woman" help in posing these
questions?

I think there are good reasons for this broadening of the subject
woman beyond the respectful acknowledgment of women engaged in
other liberation struggles. The vision of feminist theology, as I understand it, is centered around liberating commitment to the "other"—
the "concrete other" (Seyla Benhabib)—a commitment that emerges
out of a particular liberationist recognition of the fracture of gender
oppression. Although feminist theology is a part of other religious
traditions as well, I interpret the commitment to agape for the other,
the "stranger," with a Christian narrative about remembering Jesus
faithfully. Its grammar guides my judgments.

In a liberation form this commitment to the other is a trope of the possibility for redemption of particular forms of social sin. As a vision of commitment to women, it comes not from a parochial absolutizing of women, but from a vision of God's realm as one of justice, one that is contradicted by social arrangements of hierarchy and domination, whether by virtue of gender, race, class, or sexual preference.[2] It is a utopian justice, always coming, for its ground is an eschatological horizon that is God's own.

To say that the vision of feminist theology is fundamentally eschatological is not to invoke the eschatological "reserve" that avoids politics but the eschatological proviso that recognizes the hegemonies that can accompany our universalizing claims. To claim that something is good for all, and to intend that claim to refer to what is the case, is precisely the form of domination/exclusion that Christians must refuse. Right relation to this God then entails resistance to concrete and present arrangements that oppress; it includes strategies toward their transformation, resistance grounded on *what might be.* Thus the vision of feminist theology is not a provincial commitment (idolatry) of women; it opens up a vision of a social humanity always capable of shifting its categories to confess and repent of its sin. It does not avoid responding to the concrete by appealing to some otherworldly standard but recognizes the possibilities of will-to-power in any concrete practice.

Attention to the "concrete other" should direct our thinking to the formation of concrete social subjects, then, rather than to particular individuals. "Concretely social" refers first to the sense in which subjects are produced out of the pernicious effects of a patriarchal and capitalist social order. Second, any liberating alternatives are social; social subjectivities created by Christian and other traditions are created that help reverse the effects of debilitating social processes on women. Third, if understood in these senses of social, hospitality to the other is not the vocation of helping, liberating the oppressed other; it is work to liberate *ourselves in relation to the oppressed other.* It is work to liberate women within feminist communities of discourse and to create affinities between feminist women and women in other communities.[3] It is in these terms that the call to feminist theology is to

---

[2]Rebecca S. Chopp offers the designation "G-d" as a sign of the ineffableness of the God of Israel, of Abraham and Sarah, of Tamar and Jesus and Mary Magdalene. It reminds us of the unspeakableness of this name and provides a temporary alternative to the problems of gendered discourse. Rebecca S. Chopp, *The Power to Speak: Feminism, Language, God* (New York: Crossroad, 1989), 32.

[3]Social subjectivity refers to a way of understanding ourselves as connected to

attend to a particular neighbor, woman, and speak to the realities of
the women who do not share feminist sensibilities.

This definition of a liberation feminist commitment to woman implies a refusal of liberal politics as a solution to difference: Liberalism is
a politics that solves gender, race, class, and sex oppressions by adding
the pertinent "other" to institutions. The failed logic of this inclusionary politics is familiar to many marginalized populations, or to
academics—African Americans and those who fill "women" slots—
all of whom have been put in the position of having to divide up the
small curricular territory assigned to the "other."

Key features of classic liberalism are the primacy of individuals, the
value of individual autonomy and choice, a state limited to the function of protecting the rights and freedoms of individuals, and a neutral
posture toward any account of the good in order to protect a plurality
of views. In contrast, the feminist social commitment to the "concrete
other" suggests the profound differences of feminist theological commitments from liberal philosophy. Feminism works with a vision of
the good that is much more than a "community" of free individuals.
Its vision of the good entails relations of mutuality that are contradicted by forms of domination that have been historically practiced on
the basis of gender, race, sex, and class. Understanding these oppressions as social sin distinguishes feminist theology even further from
liberalism, because it entails a theo/acentric ordering of the good.

Most important to the difference between visions, however, are the
terms of redress. On the liberal view the features of gender, race, sex,
and class are special interests of sorts, that need to be included in a
social order that has previously left them out. To address that, one includes representative outsiders whose freedoms were not previously
protected and negotiates successful accommodation of manageable
differences. Then one celebrates this as diversity. Basic to this story is
the essential sameness of all persons and the possibility of easy accommodation of the various (superficial) differences, since the social order
is left intact.

Clearly feminist theology has no such shallow notion of the processes required to transform deeply entrenched social sin. The test of
that, however, is its construction of the subject, where the issues of
addressing difference are located. Here I think feminist theology is less
clear. If the debilitating effects of the social processes on women are to

---

others, an understanding that is constructed for Christians out of our narratives of Jesus
and faithfulness, yet for a feminist cannot be simply identified with institutional Christianity. Feminist theologies forge ecumenical relations of other non-Christian communities around commitments to justice and the well-being of the marginalized.

be taken seriously, we must resist the notion of the free, autonomous individual, in whatever guise it may appear. We must explore the connections between subjects that go much deeper than special interests or differences that are secondary attributes to some real common humanity. In short, if feminist theology is to move into the deeper problems not even broached by an inclusionary logic, it must be rigorous in the attempt to dislodge the residual hold of liberal notions of subjects.

The clue that some version of the liberal subject still operates in feminist theology is found when our thinking implies that all women are the same. The dissent of Womanist and other liberationist women from white feminist theology indicates that assumption is operating. Other evidence that the connections have not been rendered deeply enough is that the feminist accounts of patriarchal biblical and doctrinal traditions are not subscribed to by other women — I refer here to those who claim to find good news in Christian scripture, appropriate their communities' traditions very differently from the feminist judgments about sexist texts and male-dominated symbols. Yet it is difficult to account for that with feminist biblical work.

We need help developing more fully the constructed subject, ridding ourselves of the Cartesian subject and disembodied subjectivity that underlie it. It is my view that there are ways in which the appeal to women's experience, central to feminist theological method, reproduces this universal subject. The appeal does not function to get at these connections, at least in the setting of academic discourse. To get at these connections we need to pursue the produced character of "women's experience," then we can begin to think about the scriptural texts and faith practices that are connected to differently produced women.

Our best sources to bring the social vision of feminist theology together with a non-universalizing notion of woman comes from the questions asked by feminist theorists. Extending feminist inquiries into the construction of gender to the produced character of all objects illuminates an alternative to the Cartesian subject. I offer it as a most helpful approach, a way to consider the problems and possibilities of respecting difference that does not merely add more perspectives to an unchanged social order. The originating revolutionary feminist discovery was of the constructed nature of gender. The move beyond a liberal theological politics requires extending the recognition that social codes create notions of masculinity and femininity to the socially coded character of *all* "objects." To fail to do this in feminist theory is to leave intact the liberal subject, whose unlocated character is just the basis for such false universals as "women's experience."

To fail to do this as a feminist theologian is also to stop short of a methodological practice that is profoundly theological. I refer to a practice that displays the fallible nature of all of our categories. Even though they are all we have, so to speak, these accounts and methodological categories are potential purveyors of our blindnesses, the sinful distortions that come with our own social locations. Feminist theorists who have extended the critique of gender to coded realities other than gender, such as anatomical difference, have important things to teach us about the codes that construct theologians and "ordinary believers" as well. Such radical criticism comes not out of a deconstructive urge, but out of a fundamental (undemonstrable) conviction that reality is gracious and God-given and that confession of and conversion from the support we give to the sinful brokenness of our social order is testimony to that grace.

This book proceeds under the conviction that taking seriously the challenge of feminist theory to the subject—that there is no "real woman"—is crucial to our ability to speak to the situation of the women whose realities I evoked in the opening paragraphs. I argue that an approach to difference must offer categories that take seriously the way in which subjects are constructed out of social relations that feature multiple forms of gender oppression. In doing so, however, we also recognize that our thinking about feminist theological reflection is not liberating praxis based upon women's experience, but is itself a produced cognitive practice inextricable from social relations. This means that the site of feminist theology is part of its meaning. Feminist theology as an academic discourse must be distinguished from feminist theology as a discourse in women's communities and political practices outside of the academy. My challenge is directed at some common methodological assumptions of feminist theological thinking as they function in academics that prevent us from hearing other women. But it also challenges assumptions that we know what a real woman is and that we need simply to continue to add the experiences of women who display the varieties of oppressions and emancipatory faith practices. The point is not to lose the subject "woman," but to *change the subject* in the sense that the complex production of multiple identities becomes basic to our thinking.

I do not, then, assume that feminist theology must remain solipsistic, or simply stay trapped in a circle of appeal to a "women's experience" that is white and Western and privileged. I hope that the different way of thinking about feminist theological method that I propose will *allow more access to the role of our own definitions in constructing the other, as well as make us understand that we have no access to the real outside of our power-laden constructions.* The warrants from a Christian theological vision for attending to the other, the agapic care for the stranger, are rendered more attuned to the possibilities of domination at the center of the act of love. Acknowledging the ambiguity and omnipresence of power is no excuse for succumbing to the notion that gracious transgressions of oppressive relations and oppressive orders are impossible.

Feminist theory and the subject

I argue that the way to change the subject and move from women's experience to a theological feminist analytic of women's discourse is through the logic of feminist criticism of the "politics of identity." The phrase refers to feminist practices which assume that something is common to or shared universally by all women—a nature, an essence—that allows a claim of commonality in oppression. While feminists have always recognized that, along with their gender, differences in class, race, and sexual preference characterize women, "identity politics" has assumed that the identity of "woman" was still significant enough to constitute an adequate basis for a politics (or a theology) of emancipation. It is precisely this identity "woman" that is challenged by the more radical voices in these debates. While historians have increasingly discovered the ways in which "woman" is an identity relative to historical context, poststructuralist constructionism goes further. It refutes the very notion of the natural or nonhistorical, nonconstructed character of the subject woman. These latter theories challenge the ostensibly obvious notion that women and men exist as natural subjects who are distinguished by the category of anatomical sex, a category that feminism held as a constant.

Poststructuralist feminists challenge the "natural sexed subject" by "textualizing" reality, that is, by recognizing that signifying processes constitute the objects that we consider and often reify as natural. Such challenges do not claim that "language is all there is," with their focus on meaning, nor do they deny that these categorical binary subjects, women (and men), exist as so defined. In fact, poststructuralist feminists take these subjects as historically real in that most people fundamentally accept internalized sexed identities and the oppressive and entrenched social relations that are built on them. It is just these kinds of "real men and women" that such feminist criticisms take up. Motivated by liberation concerns, these feminists employ poststructuralism for strategies of emancipation that can attend to the specifics of these constructed subject positions. They challenge the *natural*—read, uncoded—character of the categories that define such "objects" as anatomically sexed bodies, because positing categories as "natural" so often obscures power and interest.

Feminists turn to signifying, then, to argue that we cannot get at things outside the semiotic processes by which they come to have meaning. Realities are coded, socially signified, not natural. Historical practices of attaching "natural" meanings to women's bodies, white and African American alike, have allowed them to be subjected to uses perceived as natural to female reproductive organs or to "racial" characteristics.[4] Challenging ostensibly natural (uncoded) entities also confronts ideological effects or imbalances in power that are supported by categories not subject to question.

By taking this critique seriously, feminist theology stands to gain a theoretical apparatus for identifying the specifics of women's (or anyone's) oppression and liberation. It is an apparatus that brings three changes in feminist theology. First, we change from representational notions of language to accounts of meaning as a process of signifying. With the view that signifying constitutes reality, we are able to ask how "women" are constituted by signifying processes rather than defined by some natural biological reality or an inner subjectivity prior to discursive power relations.

Second, by giving up essentializing definitions of Christian (or any religious) tradition, we open up its possibilities in profoundly new ways. I look at the discourses of the women described in my opening anecdotes not simply because they are women, but because they appropriate Christian faith and biblical traditions in ways that they find life-giving. Their nonfeminist postures afford an opportunity to look at alternatives to any essentializing of Christian texts. My initial move to extend signifying to everything opens to view the subject-constituting processes of meaning. It also allows for a new way to analyze their sources in the community of faith—the second move in my argument. With a look at discourse, their communities' ways of reading the biblical text and the discourses of the social order and local place become part of the analysis. Once seen in these intertextual relations, the biblical text itself is no longer conceivable as a fixed container of meanings that are prior to the power relations in which subjects are embedded. The question of their oppressive or liberating character becomes more complex. The "texts" in the lives of the Pentecostal

---

[4]For a brief history of "gender," see Donna J. Haraway, " 'Gender' for a Marxist Dictionary: The Sexual Politics of a Word," in *Simians, Cyborgs, and Women: The Reinvention of Nature* (New York: Routledge, 1991), 127–48. On the creation and use of "race," see Henry Louis Gates, Jr., ed., *"Race," Writing, and Difference* (Chicago: Univ. of Chicago Press, 1986).

woman, the Presbyterian woman, and the liberation feminist woman
will prove to be different texts on this account.

Third, my feminist critique pursues this radical "textualization" for
the purpose of assessing the power relations in which all meaning is
embedded and for the light it sheds on the social structuring of sin.
Difference is a matter not only of the very different local processes of
meaning that construct "women," but also of mechanisms of power.
While there are hegemonic forces that oppress all women, such as the
processes of patriarchy and capitalism that reproduce forms of debilitating dependence for women, local forms of oppression alter these
forces. The particular forms of patriarchal capitalism not only personalize social sin, they also allow for a theological rubric of human desire
and its deformation in conceptions of oppression and liberation. Patriarchal oppression is never a totally negative, repressive force that
simply obliterates women or renders them utterly passive. Local
mechanisms of power help display the trade-offs, the pleasures and
constraints that come as the effects of the social sin of the formation of
capitalist patriarchy. The trade-offs make intelligible women's acceptance of their oppression. Just as there is no complete escape from its
reach, so also the possibilities of grace and the transgression of oppressive forces are never ruled out.

With the reconception of subjects, texts, and power, my proposal
for a feminist theological analytic of women's discourses will display
the very different ways that women produce meaning. These productions are sometimes liberating and qualify as good news because they
create spaces of well-being where there had been none. Women's resistances are defined by the alterations they forge in the systems of
rules that create their scripture and limit their practices. Oppressive or
liberating texts are not constants, then, but are socially activated, since
I locate resistance neither in the biblical text, nor in women's contexts,
nor in some combination of readers and textual meaning. Inasmuch as
a turn to textuality must allow for the integral relation of material or
social relations to women's practices, I identify the mark of social location and its gendered aspects on their practices with a figurative
notion of "graf(ph)ting." This coinage from botanical and literary creation signifies not only where practices are liberating, but how they
are constrained and limited as well, and it avoids separating the meanings of biblical texts from the meanings of social location and gender
definition. The interstructuring of these meanings is fundamental to
my argument that the nuance of difference is part of the very definition of women's resistance and oppression. It has implications for the
graf(ph)ted character of all theological writing, whoever its intended
audience.

My proposal to "change the subject" is based on the view that the liberation criticism of the category "woman" mandates an approach that takes seriously the location where "woman" is "produced." We must not lose the subject "woman." We must simply become more adept at changing that subject, that is, at respecting its multiple identities. Thus this is not feminism without women, as some critics of poststructuralism fear, but an attempt to increase the likelihood that agape for the other attends to the other's situation and our complicity in it.

With this theological appropriation of feminist theory, the Pentecostal woman can be read as a practitioner of faith with skills and pleasures, as well as constraints and blindnesses, rather than a subject whose oppression by hegemonic patriarchy has rendered her a passive victim. Likewise, the woman constructed of the discourses and social location of the middle-class housewife does not need to be subjected to the biblical texts and categories of the academic liberation feminist theologian, whose own subject position has important differences. This model also allows us to ask what the faith practices of the middle-class white churchwoman can teach us about God's liberating presence in her witness. It allows us to ask what the practices of the poor Pentecostal woman display about the power of gospel to challenge the dehumanizing and sexualizing processes of patriarchal capitalism.

The first three chapters of the book explore prominent patterns in liberation feminist theology to lift up certain of its commitments that support this project and to identify the elements that still potentially support a liberal inclusionary politics. This criticism is developed in chapters 1 and 2, where I explore the accounts of language, power, and gender that characterize feminist theological method and replace "women's experience" with the discursively produced subject position. Chapter 3 looks at the implications of the move to discourse for feminist treatments of scripture. I argue that what stabilizes the fundamentally open text is women's reading regimes. Their resisting readings have to be found in the intertextual relations—meanings available by virtue of their communities' rules for reading, their gendered aspects, and their own divergences from the rules as sustained and constrained by their social location.

With a theory of discourse developed in chapters 2 and 3, I then explore the faith practices of "other" women and argue for the points at which patriarchal/capitalist structures of oppression are resisted. In chapter 4 I read the practices of Presbyterian women as discourses of self-production and world-transformation that resist certain oppressive patriarchal constraints on their subject position. In chapter 5 I read

Pentecostal women ministers' call stories and worship performances, arguing that their ecstatic and bodily displays of joy produce their own registers of resistance as well. In chapter 6, I look again at the discourse of two feminist academic theologies. I redefine their resistance and embeddedness as politicizing parody, suggesting some of the occlusions that accompany the professional managerial social location of academics. In the final chapter I argue that portrayals of the "other" are beginnings of learning who we are as academic feminists and as participants in the occlusion of the "other" woman and what we might do to move to a more gracious place.

The theological warrant for respecting difference that emerges from a new definition of difference is the conviction that we need to narrate our stories in such a way that they enable the stories of the other to teach us. Identity is not something we have and then share or use as a basis from which to define the other. In fact, we discover from poststructuralism that our identity is rendered by the others it creates. Our story is not simply our internal story, it is constituted by others' stories as well.[5] The implication of this for our work is not that we should become storyless or have no identity but that our positing of story and identity should be always subject to criticism—particularly by the other it creates. Constructively, the test for our rendering is whether our story—our remembering of Jesus, if we are Christian—opens up the worth of the other.

---

[5]Wesley A. Kort, *Bound to Differ: The Dynamics of Theological Discourses* (University Park: Pennsylvania State Univ. Press, 1992), 127–28.

1 Constructing a
Chapter Feminist Liberation
Epistemology

> The feminist dream of a common language, like all dreams
> for a perfectly faithful naming of experience, is a totalizing
> and imperialist one.
>
> —Donna Haraway

When inclusion is not enough

There are two ways for feminist theology to approach differences
among women. One way recovers long-silenced women. It multiplies
the number of voices that speak for women and allows a variety of
women to tell their stories and to write theology from their own
perspective—as a white middle-class woman or a woman of color or a
lesbian, and so on. This inclusionary approach has engendered a
wealth of literature and much important dialogue. The very fact that
women's voices are multiple is preventive medicine of a sort. It blocks
the hegemony of Euro-American women's experience, as well as the
other kinds of false generic anthropologies. It is preventive, too, in its
reminder that theological definitions of the human, of human creation
as *imago dei*, have been misshapen and inadequate. In cases where one
kind of human subject has been produced as representative of all, these
definitions have been idolatrous. In light of this situation, multiplication of women's voices is a necessary strategic part of the theological
institution's confession of its participation in the cultural and reli-
giously sanctioned oppression of women (and, implicitly, of men).
Without inclusion nothing will change at all.

This first approach to differences is, however, in itself inadequate.
In addition to signifying the need for confession and transformation,

13

inclusionary practices are also, like their counterpart in the nonreligious public space of contemporary U.S. society (inclusionary or affirmative action programs), ambiguous at best in terms of their capacity to address fully the sins of the "fathers." That ambiguity is related at least in part to the fact that for feminist theology, the vocabulary of sin is employed to name the problem. From a feminist view, sin is never simply an act of an individual or numbers of individuals, but is embedded in and carried by social realities. Including more and different subjects does not provide institutional conversions for whole constructions of reality that privilege one form of the *imago dei* over another. Although a necessary beginning, inclusionary practice by itself does not get at the social formations that have supported a variety of other dominations that are interstructural with patriarchal relations. On an inclusionary logic alone, feminist theology would face the formidable task of supporting the addition of the faces and experiences of varieties of women in order to fill some endless list of the excluded, some institutional policy that reflected the *etc.* that is habitually the gesture of feminist analysis to indicate multiple differences.

This is not to say that feminist theologians line up in support of the philosophy behind an inclusionary logic as an adequate theological-philosophical option. At least the theological vision of liberation feminism does not support this outcome. Feminist liberation theologies conceive of the problem of misogyny and its social expressions as fundamentally intersected with classism, racism, and heterosexism rather than with the individualist liberal categories implied by inclusionary tactics. They point toward a second way, one that would take these social manifestations of sin with utmost seriousness, a way hinted at by feminist writings and practices of alternative educational strategies and models of education.[1]

Not all the theoretic practice of feminist theology, however, is in line with these tendencies. While certain liberation feminist insights lead us in another direction, some familiar features can be taken to

---

[1] The form of feminism for which this social sensibility does not apply is biblicist evangelical feminism, which still theorizes with inclusionary notions of the problem and solution. See, for example, Alvera Michelson, ed., *Women, Authority and the Bible* (Downers Grove, Ill.: InterVarsity Press, 1986).

The work of the Cornwall Collective and Mudflower Collective are the best known examples of liberation feminism's alternative notions for theological education. See *Your Daughters Shall Prophesy: Feminist Alternatives in Theological Education*, ed. the Cornwall Collective (New York: Pilgrim Press, 1980), and *God's Fierce Whimsy: Christian Feminism and Theological Education*, ed. the Mudflower Collective: Katie G. Cannon, Beverly W. Harrison, Carter Heyward, Ada María Isasi-Díaz, Bess B. Johnson, Mary D. Pellauer, Nancy D. Richardson (New York: Pilgrim Press, 1985).

support inclusionary philosophy. Together, these features can be read as a shorthand version of a method that still passes as academic feminist theology. These features include the appeal to women's experience as a source and a critical principle or norm, and the judgment that biblical texts can be gauged as oppressive or liberating when placed in critical relation to women's experience. For those who judge there to *be* liberating possibilities, this method also includes the application of feminist hermeneutical theories to the text that save the Bible (or parts of it) for women. As useful as they may be for some groups of women and in some contexts, these features can be construed to support a liberal inclusionary politics in an academic setting. They, or more particularly the assumptions about language and power that they imply, bear scrutiny in a move toward fuller development of the social-constructive sensibilities of feminist theology.

I will illustrate such a liberal-inflected reading of these features of feminist theological method: Feminist theology calls for official theological reflection to expand and include theologies normed by women's experience. Theology should be honest about its source in human experience. With different experiencers come different theologies, for theology expresses human experience of the divine. Human experience is the court of appeals for these expressions, and it is a universal stratum of presituational knowledge. However, given the discovery that there are multiple experiences, the need to privilege one (say, women's) over another (say, men's) is a matter of justice, a matter of letting everyone participate in the privileges of being *imago dei*.

Discussions of biblical and other historic traditions or the biblical canon itself as oppressive or liberating for women (due to their patriarchal, androcentric, and sexist character) can also be read in this liberal vein. Feminist theories of interpretation should yield favorable or liberating meanings for women. Feminist hermeneutics can support an inclusive logic because it implies that persons are individuals formed outside of social contexts. That notion goes something like this: Texts exist outside of social construction in that they express the meanings of their original authors (or situations), and they can be made to restate those meanings if properly approached. If not simply recovered, they can be read through interpretive grids. Interpretive grids are things that subjects use to get meanings from texts. What comes out at the other end of these different theories or grids when applied to texts is an interpretation.

Read in terms of its liberal possibilities, feminist method requires a plurality of subjects and a plurality of interpretations. What the vision of the good would entail according to a liberal reading is a world where we make room at the table for pluralities of subjects, whose ex-

periences of the divine represent difference. If the validity of these subjects' capacity to represent experiences of the divine continues to be
based upon experiential validation, we can imagine a table where interesting and provocative disputes ensue, but where the institutional
capacity to host the discussion and provide chairs at the table—or to
shut down the building altogether, so to speak—is the site where real
authorizing power is located. Further, those without the skills required to participate in the table discussion will, of course, not have
their experience of the divine articulated, or will have it articulated by
"experts" who represent them.

Because the route of orthodoxy (to continue my liberal reading and
its dilemma) and traditional interpretations of texts are closed off to
the feminist theologian, she is faced with the one fixed norm—the
oppressed subject who must be valorized in a theology of liberation.
Therein lies the dilemma. Because the oppressed subject continues
to be multiplied, it becomes more and more difficult to valorize
"women." The basis for feminist theology—or any theology—as an
academic discourse dissolves. Dissolution of the basis of theology is
not a bad thing for an antifoundationalist theology, that is, a theological proposal that understands the located character of all theological
discourse. But this loss is bad news for a feminist theology that understands itself as legitimated by women's experience. Finally, although the vision of the good and the diversity at the table are
somewhat energized by the debates, still the building, its ownership,
and its maintenance continue undisturbed. Since feminist theology intends a criticism and dismantling of these larger social realities, it is
definitely problematic for it to end up merely supporting appreciation
of varieties of women—those women, that is, who can afford the trip
to the table.

What I have described caricatures important and sophisticated
feminist theological positions and liberation feminist theology's basic
resonance as an antifoundationalist theology. In that sense it is a misreading. However, the possibility for this misreading suggests there is
a problem. My scenario highlights some of the intellectual categories
we have inherited as academic modernists. These categories prevent us
from being more successfully antifoundationalist and thereby better
able to acknowledge our own social embeddedness. They make it difficult for us to think about the socially coded, materially embedded
nature of realities, including ourselves as readers and believers. They
obscure the difficulties we get into when we conceive of subjects,
texts, and their locations as separate entities that can be used, applied,
and separated with impunity.

Although ways of speaking about ourselves and texts as separate entities are necessary everyday usages, the speech habits that keep us talking of our experience as women as a norm and of interpretive theories as things we may or may not use on texts are not useful in our theories. They do not help feminist theology say what it needs to say or to testify to God's implication in the differently configured realities of created life. We continue to use notions of an "I," a subject, that would appear to be unmarked by social coding—an "I," for example, not easily placed alongside the Pentecostal woman whose "I" will look, by contrast, blatantly situated with its ahistorical and supernatural (dare I say "ignorant"?) interpretive habits. We continue to refer to the embedded character of theology by grounding it in experience. We are using a category, however, whose value in the institutions of knowledge production is not conducive to the needed political analyses.

What feminist theology needs to articulate is the materially embedded way that "we" is constructed by texts and codes of our own social location. To acknowledge the coding does not render us passive toward biblical texts. But it does require recognition that the multiple processes by which we are made to see texts are in no way neutral. We must also see that these processes do not simply shape or influence the text. To put it bluntly, they "make" the texts, as I will argue. Our interpretive codes are related to the pleasures and blindnesses that attend our own construction in a sinfully broken set of social arrangements. It is imperative to feminist theology's vision that the features of our theoretic practice be defined with new connections that can render our social location as inextricably part of language, our biblical readings, and their work. These new connections are part of a theological vision of the fallibility of knowledge—a liberation doctrine of "finitude."

We must determine how academic (mostly Euro-American) feminism is a fragile graf(ph)t on an institutional plant that is both good and bad for it. Just as a plant graft is sustained by the sap-flow of a stronger sapling onto which it is grafted, we academics are en-graf(ph)ted onto and therefore sustained by the nourishment of institutional practices.[2] This relationship has been an essential part of the construction of our theoretic practice. That practice is not innocent of its larger stem, nor can it be simply plucked and moved without

---

[2] I thank Laura Donaldson for pointing me to this wonderful trope from Jacques Derrida, which she develops to link text and context in a way that signifies the material embeddedness of a reading. See Laura E. Donaldson, "The Con of the Text," in *Decolonializing Feminisms: Race, Gender, and Empire-Building* (Chapel Hill: Univ. of North Carolina Press, 1992), 52–65.

alteration—and alteration there must be before the kind of changes
that could allow respect for difference, affinity with the "other"
woman, can occur.

Although feminist theological commitments point in another direction from the liberal logic of inclusion, a direction that sustains social
critiques of the settings that produce Christians, the definition of feminist theology as based upon women's experience—even as liberating
practice based upon women's experience as a norm—does not suffice.
It is not a lack of respect for difference that is the problem. The problem is the lack of a theory of discourse that can allow for the productive character of our reflections in this case, of feminist theology as
academic practice, in order that the work they do might be inspected.
Until we are more comfortable with the fact that we do not, in a certain sense, know who or what we are as women, that our self-repre-
sentations are not intuitive graspings or knowledges reflective of our
real selves, but convergences of social codes—productions—then we
will not understand that our representations, our knowledges of
"other" women are productions as well. Once we have a way to theorize systems of discourse, we can begin to take seriously what our
way of knowing occludes, how it dissembles, and even contributes to
oppression. We can also begin to see the openings for transformation
in new ways. Feminist theology as a kind of knowledge must be
shaped by such a theory of discourse.

In these first three chapters I offer an alternative way to talk about
what feminist theology is and does as an academic system of discourse. To do so I draw from feminist liberation commitments, which
are most helpful for developing a theological position and practice capable of respecting difference and thereby attending to the problems in
feminist theology as an academic method and to the kinds of transformations of academic settings that will support that respect. My proposal for an alternative way of thinking about feminist theology will
then be displayed in consideration of a variety of "other" women's
discourses and by applying my critique to our construction as academic feminist theologians.

Theo/acentric ideology critique: plotting a
liberation epistemology

Feminist theology needs a liberation epistemology if it is to move
beyond or radicalize inclusionary strategies and respect difference.
Such an epistemology is not about the problem of how a subject
knows but about the relation between social relations, discourses, in-

terests, and oppression-liberation. Its purpose is to investigate how certain kinds of subjects are produced that make objects of others. A liberation epistemology is nothing new to feminist theology, which virtually began with something like ideology critique as feminist theologians identified formulations of Christian and secular traditions—language and ideas—as oppressive to women. My wish is to expand further this feminist recognition of the relation of interest to language and ideas and to connect them to social situations.

Put theologically, feminist theology must assume that its own theoretic practice is part of a broader institutional matrix, which requires evaluation by a theological logic of finitude and sin. Most importantly, it is a logic that ascribes finitude and sin not simply to individual subjects but also to social realities. An account of this finitude thick enough to qualify as a description of a social reality would be much too complex for my purposes here. I can, however, sketch a proposal for the relation of theological knowledge to interest and the relationship of interested knowledge to material relations, the realities of the socioeconomic and cultural-political order. That is a way of insisting that theology is socially embedded and therefore that both theology and its institutional matrix are part of the problem (confession) and possibilities for change (conversion). The capacity to identify linkages between place, interest, and knowledge—a liberation epistemology—is what makes it possible for feminist theology to identify the construction of difference and respect women as a multiple subject. An adequate conception of language and power, as I will show, is fundamental to this task.

With a review of some assumptions that are basic to a liberation epistemology, I will set the stage for a look at liberation feminist theologians' most common ways of defining and relating these crucial commitments and their unspoken assumptions.

A liberation epistemology is concerned with the relationship of social location to (1) ideology or the oppressive effects of discourse, and (2) to the possibilities for change or liberation that can be developed at a particular site. With the tools of a liberation epistemology, we are asking something like Terry Eagleton's question in his recent work on ideology about how a German population could come to participate in the Holocaust machine of the Nazis and also how a German conscript living with fellow Nazi soldiers could risk his life repeatedly to rescue Jews. Ideology, Eagleton maintains, answers the question of how so many human beings could convince themselves that a race of people were comparable to vermin and deserving of systematic extermination. Ideology accounts for this massive case of self-deception, blindness, and the accompanying legitimation of human brutality

beyond measure. Ideology also recognizes that desire pervades interest
and is essential to the complex and conflicted process of human understanding, either in the successful mystification of a situation like mur-
dering Jews or its avoidance. Such a thing as social evil cannot simply
be misinformation; it begs to be read as a complicity of pleasures and
wants, as well as fears and culpability.

A final element, at least assumed if not explained by ideology, concerns what we are shown by responses of people like the resisting
German conscript. According to Eagleton this is the hopeful fact that
ideological mystification is never totally successful, signified by this
strange ability of the draftee:

> Not to mistake the men he saw,
> As others did, for gods or vermin.

as Thomas Gunn put it. How do we account for the conditions that
support this ability to see otherwise? That, too, is the task a liberation
epistemology sets for itself.[3]

As a theological account, liberation epistemology differs somewhat
from Eagleton's account of ideology by construing ideology as social
sin. It hopes to determine how and where "remembering Jesus" as a
faithful practice, while not ideology-free, can nonetheless account for
some resistance, for some of the extraordinary abilities people display
when they struggle against oppression and for human liberation.
However, a liberation epistemology must take seriously those kinds of
socially compelling and constructing realities represented by ideology
critique, both in terms of the multiple projects ideology can take on
(justifying, occluding, legitimating, vilifying) and expecting that conflict and desire are at work in these processes. Following rehearsal of a
theo/acentric logic for this pursuit, I will formulate a set of features
drawn from ideology critique that hone the critical capacity of a theological liberation epistemology.

The crucial inquiry of a liberation theological epistemology, as
Sharon Welch says, is not, Does God exist?, but What kind of God is
to be practiced?[4] To put it another way, given that a liberating God is
to be displayed in history, liberation epistemology attends to questions
about what have been and what are the effects of faithfulness to this
God. When is that faithfulness not faithfulness, not resisting human

---

[3]Terry Eagleton, *Ideology: an Introduction* (London: Verso, 1991), xiii.
[4]Sharon D. Welch, *Communities of Resistance and Solidarity: A Feminist Theology of Liberation* (Maryknoll, N.Y.: Orbis Books, 1985), 4–5.

oppression but in fact blinding us to it? Its epistemological issues are not "*can* we know?" issues, to which proofs of God are the appropriate response. They have to do instead with the social effects and utopian possibilities of faith.

Although religious discourse itself is never a guarantee of faithful resisting practice, a negative mark of sorts can be suggested. That negative mark is something like the conditions under which creation is treated as dependent upon a gracious God. Those conditions can only be sketched, because the nature of being situated precludes specifying what actual practice of this grammar would look like—it always changes. However, in contrast to a construct of ideology such as Eagleton's, this much can be said: A Christian grammar of creation supports practices that regard human being as finite, not divine, and views finitude as including situatedness, which is to say partiality and interest. These features are potentially good and to be celebrated, or so say Christian traditions, even though we find reality fractured by unnecessary brokenness and oppression. This regard is, as I will argue, a wager, not a knowledge of an essential humanness.

Contrary to the modern theological habit of portraying finitude and its vulnerability to corruption as features of the individual subject, however, a liberation grammar of finitude must display the social character of these possibilities if it is to support analyses that get at the corporate nature of the oppression of women. For example, idolatry is acted out as sin against the neighbor, as Reinhold Niebuhr argued, and has a number of distorting effects on the self, including self-deception and alienation. On the basis of Niebuhr's account of finitude and sin, then, one might argue that sexism is oppression based upon the pridefulness or the self-aggrandizement of the male and that the social cost, the sin against the neighbor, is what women know as sexism.

What is wrong with this argument is that in the work of such modern theologians, the inexplicable move to sin occurs in the face of structures of temporality and location that characterize the finitude of the individual.[5] These structures of finitude include a temporality that

---

[5]I realize that Niebuhr is famous for recognizing the social or collective level of sin. See Reinhold Niebuhr, *The Nature and Destiny of Man*, vol. 1, *Human Nature* (New York: Charles Scribner's Sons, 1964), 177, 208–19. *Moral Man and Immoral Society* (New York: Charles Scribner's Sons, 1932) might appear to contradict my criticism, where Niebuhr considered immorality as a social phenomenon, as something other than the sum of individual sinful wills. By conceiving the structures of the individual apart from determinate social construction, however, Niebuhr separated the two in the ways I suggest. Modern theologians like Niebuhr and Paul Tillich use these categories and avoid owning up to their specificity. For a display of the maleness of this finite and vulnerable individual, see Tillich, whose analogy for the anxiety rooted in the polarity between

is embodied and characterized by eros, by desire that displays a yearning for the eternal and for the worldly as well. If we see the possibility
for sin in this structured instability of the individual, the finitude of the
male, the insecurity of that way of being in the world might then be
identified as the ground of the possibility of sin against the female as
threatening other.

A liberation account of finitude and the accompanying bondage of
sin, however, cannot be content with modern theology and such a
reading of misogyny. The notion that finitude, vulnerability to sin,
and actual bondage are abstract features of the individual subject invites an ahistorical, unsituated analysis of sexism. Conceived upon the
model of the vulnerability to threat as the individual's (male's) insecurity, this notion of finitude cannot accommodate the specifics and the
differences of women's situations. Further, in this scheme the problem
becomes one of individual and interpersonal relationships rather than
the embedded and intransigent social phenomena that constitute
gender oppression. There is no private, precoded experiencer where
anxiety might shape and construct sin. Sin is always coded and therefore located in social practice.

For a liberation feminist account, the features of limit, potential for
bondage, and potential for change must be located in the social conditions and relations of human beings that construct individuals in particular ways. In the terms of liberation theology, whole thought
systems and ongoing human practices bear the imprint of finitude, the
possibility for bondage, and actual oppression. These converge in
social interests and the practices they support, and it is there, at the
level of the social, that the oppressive effects of interest must be identified. The social reaches into or constructs the inner life of the subject.
An ideology critique of the notion that sin is the property or private
action of an individual would argue that this view functions to get the
community off the hook. The desires and pleasures that intertwine
forms of human oppression are socially coded as well.

My point, however, is not to articulate a full-fledged theological
grammar but to define faithful practice so that feminist ideology critique (or something like it) is a fundamental piece of it. Feminist theology requires that we be able to identify the social conditions that are
most hospitable to oppression and how they mark knowledge and dis-

---

dreaming innocence and desire for actualization (finite freedom as possibility for
temptation/sin) is the adolescent male's anxiety over whether to "actualize" himself sex-
ually. Paul Tillich, *Systematic Theology*, vol. 2, *Existence and the Christ* (Chicago: Univ. of
Chicago Press, 1957), 35–36.

course so as to alter those conditions. We can take this as an extension of the proscription against idolatry: the tradition itself is not an idol.

The significance of the grammar is seen in a comparison of feminist Christians' insights with an account of ideology. Something like the following might come from a use of Marxist Terry Eagleton's account of typical functions of ideology, which include legitimating or naturalizing the dominant, obscuring social relations, justifying the powerful, and negating challenges. A variety of theological formulations naturalize relationships of subordination for women. They make subordination appear ordained by God or by nature and therefore inevitable and universal. Certain traditions obscure social reality, making women (and men) believe that female subordination is for their own good. Teachings about the fatherhood of God and the revealed status of that designation, for example, legitimate male power. Accounts that divinize scripture "naturalize" the belief by making it absolute. Teachings that sponsor proper Christian behavior as self-denigration and selfless love work as ideology by providing a standard against which resistance looks like faithlessness, thereby denigrating any challenges women might put forward to their idealized position.[6]

With such judgments, feminist theology finds that a variety of formulations of the Christian tradition resemble the ideology of male domination; they are embedded in social relations of oppression. Because these formulations are part of the theological tradition, in scripture and orthodox doctrine itself, feminist theology employs one of the fundamental features of a liberation theology, the suspicion "that anything and everything involving ideas, including theology, is intimately bound up with the existing social situation in at least an unconscious way," as Juan Segundo defines a liberation theology.[7] Feminist theology thereby assumes that traditions—patterns of thinking and writing, theological or otherwise—are subject to the obscuring, pernicious effects of interest.

The need for traditions of resistance

This summary of ideological functions is helpful in fleshing out what social interest looks like. It can be taken to display the finitude and deformation of the Christian tradition itself. But there is still more to

---

[6]Eagleton, *Ideology*, 10–11.
[7]Juan Segundo, S.J., *The Liberation of Theology*, trans. John Dury (Maryknoll, N.Y.: Orbis Books, 1976), 8.

say. The iconoclasm of a theo/acentric logic must be linked with practices that make iconoclasm possible.[8] It must show the discourses—
whether part of the dominant biblical tradition or outside the religious
tradition or submerged in it or new combinations of biblical and cultural traditions—that made the critique possible. It must demonstrate
the potential gracious workings of the discourse, the accounting for
those who were not completely mystified and for those who saw differently. It must re(as)semble Christian practices of resisting evil and
sexism.[9] In short, while Eagleton's model offers us a picture of the
negative, woman-denigrating ideological workings of Christian traditions, we are not provided with an account of the specifics of interest
and knowledge as they contribute to emancipatory possibilities or to
women's simply experiencing that tradition differently, as they must.
A theo/acentric grammar requires such an account.[10]

The other side of the theo/acentric grammar, then, is the expectation that redeployment of this tradition or new forms of it can construct liberation for women as well. This is to say that the tradition as
discourse cannot be evil in itself. The missing piece in Eagleton's account of ideology is that traditions of resistance are required; we must
have communities' testimonies to occasions when evil is overcome.
Just because a feminist theo/acentric grammar requires that we acknowledge pernicious use of memories of Jesus does not mean we
must refuse to recognize how and when these traditions create conditions of resistance to sin, when honoring God does not mean creating
outsiders, but refusing conditions that brutalize the other. In this sense
I depart from feminist judgments that the Christian tradition is essentially oppressive *or* liberating. Neither option makes sense in light of
the starting point of a liberation theology, which assumes that great
wrong has been done by Christians yet is not about the business of
proving either God's reality or Christianity. It looks for the places that
do testify to a liberating God.

Finally, Eagleton's account is too formal. We must know what the
good is to which we are committed in order to judge oppressive forms
of mystification. This is so even if we can only speak of a transitional

---

[8]With the addition of a "feminine" ending (= *a*) to "theo/acentric" I indicate that the
traditional male sign of God needs disrupting. The term means God-dependent.

[9]I thank Karen T. Alliaume for the coinage "re(as)semble," which she uses to talk
about a feminist relationship to Christ. "Sewing What We Reap: Tayloring Christology," unpublished paper for my feminist theology class at Duke University, fall 1992.

[10]I use "requires" in the sene of its discursive logic. Some would argue that the condition for the display of the emancipatory effects of Christian tradition is the existence
of a redeeming God. I cannot make that claim with discourse analysis, other than to say
this reality is assumed by Christian discourse.

good, such as the resistance of gender domination in view of supporting a creation where what is God's is good, eschatologically speaking.
We must ask what a feminist theological position judges as ideological
mystification relative to this ideal that we hold for the social relations
of particular settings. The vision of feminist theology, briefly stated, is
a commitment to women authorized by a vision of God's creation as
hospitable for the well-being of all. Although the definition of well-
being can be contested, feminist theology judges that the historic conditions for women's well-being have not been realized. The work to
imagine and create them is the practice of agape for the stranger, a love
whose meaning and specific forms are yet to be fully understood.
What *is* clear about feminist theological practice is that it takes up a
calling or vocation to support the vision of God's realm as a realm of
justice in light of which social arrangements of hierarchy and domination, whether of gender relations, race, or other forms of human togetherness, must be resisted and transformed.

Five characteristics of liberationist epistemology

To define a feminist version of the impact of social location on knowledge that might further this end, I propose a provisional description
that summarizes the features of an ideal liberationist epistemology. It
is not one I attribute to all feminist theologians, but one I judge is consonant with feminist commitments. The modifier "liberationist" implies five things when applied to theology. First, the term indicates
that theology itself has ideological or oppressive possibilities. This is
simply to say that it requires a theo/acentric hermeneutic of suspicion.
In other words, when one of the features of feminist theology is recognition of the situated character of knowledge, we are to understand
that the beliefs and official discourses that constitute theological systems and define truth are not impervious to the impact of human interest in its pernicious forms. Nor are we to understand that the
opposite is necessary, that by virtue of being situated and interested, a
tradition is essentially pernicious. Knowledge is not *tainted* by interest:
it *is* interest.

Second, interests are connected to social conditions, which include
the economic, political, and civil or cultural aspects of a social formation. (It is no accident that the oppression of women could only be
taken seriously when perceived as a social phenomenon, rather than
the idiosyncratic complaint of individual women.) This means that interests are operative at levels that transcend the individual even though
they converge in individual agents and give specificity to desires that

are individuated. The trick for theological liberation epistemology is to articulate the relation between these social conditions and systems of meaning, otherwise the former is not easily applicable to theological reflection. This means that it is imperative to clarify the relations between so-called material or nonlinguistic and idea- and/or language-related entities.[11]

Third, the best way to relate social relations and systems of meaning (and thereby knowledge) in feminist theological inquiry is with a materialist rather than idealist conceptual frame. By that I mean that images of making or practice, which are key in theories that root knowledge in social relations, are central to thinking about truth and are preferable to images of disclosure or correlation in a liberation theology. Theological reflection is a "practice of the production of cognition," as Clodovis Boff puts it.[12] The production model places in the foreground the role of making and accountability in the theological task. It helps us get at what Eagleton identified as the ideological process of naturalization, although ideology itself will prove insufficient as a way to indicate this process. Contrasted with the epistemological image of vision and the implied passivity of knowers, a production model is important for attending to social location. Vision, however compelling aesthetically, too often invites a way of thinking about knowledge that is unsituated. A production model reminds us that a liberation theological perspective must examine the effects of dominant codes and systems of meaning it brings into being, those that produce it as well as those it consciously employs. This feature of liberation epistemology is one more way to link knowledge inextricably with the social relations out of which it emerges.

Fourth, by insisting on the inextricability of this relation, a liberation epistemology is not forced to accept simplistic reflection theories, where language or ideas and knowledge are the straightforward reflection of, or homologous with, the social relations (the class, race, gender) of their proponents. We must be able to see that social forces may overdetermine, or converge in multiple ways on women, so that oppressions and possibilities for emancipation are signified in women's discourses in complicated ways. Elisabeth Schüssler

---

[11]I do not want to define material as "stuff." This will be discussed in chapter 2.

[12]These materialist models are, of course, beholden to Karl Marx. Boff represents an example of a complex liberation theology, which conceives of the relation of systems of thought to oppression in a highly sophisticated manner. My critique of feminist theology is a much simpler account of some of the problematic ways of construing certain contents and their social matrix. Clodovis Boff, O.S.M., *Theology and Praxis: Epistemological Foundations*, trans. Robert R. Barr (Maryknoll, N.Y.: Orbis Books, 1987), 73.

Fiorenza calls this the multiplicative character of women's oppressions, that they "criss-cross and feed upon each other in women's lives."[13] In addition, a theological grammar of sin finds human relations—oppressed and oppressors alike—to be riddled with the complications of desire, fear, and pleasure, for which any reflection theory is inadequate. To indicate this, a complex formulation of the relation between social location and the oppressions that characterize it requires formulation in the very notions of the subject and language related to that subject.

The language–social location question leads to a (minimalist) definition of the subject and explicates how it is that finitude as the possibility for sin might be a fundamentally social phenomenon. This fifth feature of a liberation epistemology will allow us to respect the difference that attends the production of women. Theologically, I have said that one element of that project requires that the vulnerability or instability of finitude be defined in a different, more productive way than the instability of the temporality and vulnerability of the individual existent. It must be identified as social. However, the link with the individual is key to doing this successfully. To avoid a theology that simply tries to tack on social location to ideas, we must avoid a Cartesian theory of the self. Such a self is presocial; it assumes that some form of self-knowledge is basically given and reflective of the real self. Selfhood or self-consciousness is founded upon the capacity of the subject to be an object to itself, as it reflects back upon itself. As she reflects upon herself, the subject grasps her own identity. The subject has as an object of knowledge some idea or representation that is taken to be inherently true to her identity, her (deepest?) real self.

Criticism of the reflective theory of self

The common-sense notion that we have of our fundamentally trustworthy experience of ourselves, the presence to our consciousness of our own subjectivity, is not to be disputed. We do have experiences of ourselves that we must trust and that are fundamentally different from others' experiences of us. My quarrel is with the notion that our knowledge of ourselves is the essentially correct reflection, a mimesis, of our real and true selves. Not only would such an account avoid the theological wisdom that holds the self to be mired in self-deception,

---

[13]Elisabeth Schüssler Fiorenza, *But She Said: Feminist Practices of Biblical Interpretation* (Boston: Beacon Press, 1992), 114–16.

but such a view *is* the Cartesian subject. It cannot in the long run help or support a liberation feminist criticism of its own production or any other form of locatedness.

A host of criticisms have been mounted against this reflective (or intuitive) theory of the self; these criticisms insist upon the intersubjective character of self-knowledge. From a liberation perspective, the problem with the reflective theory is the leverage such a notion provides to the experiencing self, who can claim some special access that is more accurate than the social codes which present that subject to others. The self slips out of the site of social location and the accountability required by its acknowledgment.

From the perspective of a liberation epistemology, the only thing inherent in the subject's representation of itself is a relation to the multiple situational codes that give the self differential signs with which to understand. A liberation epistemology allows that the subject is coded, that even her private knowledge is constructed by signifying pocesses that make meaning in relation to other processes, and signs come only with social location. As a consequence this subject is unstable—finite (insecure)—but unstable as a social subject, just as any language roots a subject in a location and therefore roots a subject in social relations. The possibility that an ecclesial or Christian community might be understood as the necessary matrix for emancipatory or liberating moves depends upon such a view of the subject.

The theological valences of liberation epistemology

This account of liberation epistemology is not a reductive sociology of knowledge, for the normative position of a Christian grammar of finitude and sin developed as liberation theology defines it within a theological forum. Acknowledging that theoretical practices are not worthy of sacralization, that they are not absolute, is one piece of such a confession; acknowledging that this iconoclasm is *for* something, namely, to determine the social effects of systems of thought—how they oppress *and* contribute to liberation—is the other. This second piece is based on a vision of the eschatologically conceived, connected character of creation, when it is construed as God's. This liberation epistemology requires not simply a look at individual acts, but analysis of the relation of systems of thought to human liberation and oppression and the social subject under scrutiny. Its posture toward systems of meaning assumes that there is no free and safe place to stand. One cannot, in short, find a set of beliefs that will be free of the features of interest and historical embeddedness. Yet one can expect

that theo/acentric meaning, which arises out of liberating and recon-
ciling relations, does occur in such finite, always ambiguous formulations. Judged in a theological grammar, this constructionism is an
extension of the confession of grace, salvation by God alone moving
beyond it by complicating the way that individuals are subjects of salvation. Thus it is not simply a liberation theology of creation (finitude) and sin, but of redemption, in its concrete contemporary
irruptions.

The dominance of tropes of production in a liberation theological
perspective does not pose the false choice of either human agency or
divine causality. Admission of the socially constructed and potentially
ideological nature of theological discourse does not reduce theology to
a sociology of religion, as some have feared. The reason this admission
does not contradict the pursuit of the theological task is, again, because it extends to discourse, to sign systems, the critique that Christians make of everything created—namely, that it is not divine but is
characterized by finitude and, therefore, subject to potential distortion. Instead of a functionalism that explains and thereby reduces
faith's claims, the recognition of the "(absolute) degree to which theology is embedded, contingent historical practice," as John Milbank
puts it, is a basic mark of a theo/acentric grid for theological process.[14]
By adopting this view of theological discourse, I do not account for
the ultimate cause of human practice; I operate with a social conception of finitude that gestures at what cannot be caused or proved but
only witnessed to: its ultimate conditions, God's redemptive reality.

With this liberation epistemology I link the capacity to respect difference to the capacity to articulate the impress of interest on knowledge, which I hope will open to view the various forms of gender
oppression. It includes the interests of a particular culture, the impress
of ideological, blinding interest on theology, and the impress of interest in such a way that gracious and liberating meanings are possible, as
well. It means, more specifically, that interest affects subjects, but does

---

[14]Milbank is one who resists the co-optation of theological work by social theory. In
an important book that reads a constructionist account of historical reality with a theological grammar, John Milbank argues for an ecclesial social theory. He is concerned to
refute the reliance of liberation theologies, among others, on the discourses of social theories, and would likely be critical of the intertextual view I am proposing in this book. He
is adamant, however, that theological work cannot go back to a premodern situation. Theology must admit the "(absolute) degree to which it is a contingent historical
construct emerging from, and reacting back upon, particular social practices conjoined
with particular semiotic and figural codings." He refuses the ontology of violence and
autonomy that he finds in dominant social theories and argues that human making and
divine making are not mutually exclusive. *Theology and Social Theory: Beyond Secular
Reason* (Oxford: Basil Blackwell, 1990), 2.

so only as individuations of social reality. A liberation epistemology locates this individuation (initially) in language rather than in ideas or consciousness, for language is inextricably connected to social relations. The involvement of language in social relations means that we are talking about the relation of language and power, as well. To take this proposal further, to ask about theology as discourse and its connection to the social relations of a concrete situation will require more specific formulations of these suggestions, which will follow in subsequent chapters.

Feminist liberationists on interest and the tradition: language, gender, and power

I proceed now to my analysis of certain prominent features of feminist liberation theologies that carry with them implicit proposals about the relation of interest and social location in relation to knowledge. Although feminists generally support the view that theology is a liberating practice over an idealist notion of theology as the normative ideas that must be applied in different settings, or a kind of experience-based activity that is incapable of anything but increasing multiplication and arguments over suspected subjectivism, we must see if this view is supported by specifics on the relation of interest to discourse.

Some further clarification of my use of the label "feminist theology" is in order. The more accurate term would be feminist theolo-*gies*. Although women of color are challenging the first generation of feminist theologians, and evangelical feminists provide another set of voices to enrich the conversation, these are not my central focus. The category of feminist theology that I will examine is that of liberation feminism. In this analysis that term has a more specific referent than my idealized description. "Feminist theology" as I now use it refers to the literature that has been most significant in my own shaping as a Euro-American feminist; it refers to the feminist theologians for whom liberation is a most apt designation. Although abstracted from the work of individual theologians, a number of features have come to characterize liberation feminist theology. I will draw upon these features in order to sketch an account of interest and knowledge and pertinent lacunae important to respecting difference.[15] I will portray these features not only because they are characteristic of some of the

---

[15]The reproduction of these features as feminist theology is enough reason to give it attention as a circulating discourse. Such a pattern can be found in books like Pamela

"founding mothers," even if inadequate to the nuances of their writings, but also because the pattern exists as a possible misreading of feminist theology.

Feminist theology places the following convictions, supportive of a liberation epistemology, at the center of its method: (1) the central character of women's experience as source and criterion; (2) the need for a critical hermeneutics of suspicion in relation to scripture and tradition, and (3) the centrality of oppression–liberation categories. Although each has her own more nuanced account, these features appear in the work of the pioneer feminist theologians, Rosemary Radford Ruether, Letty Russell, and Elisabeth Schüssler Fiorenza, to name a few. Other writings, such as the work of Sallie McFague and the early (since renounced) work of Mary Daly, share features of this type of feminist theology, although developed somewhat differently. I will draw on them insofar as they display the exemplary positions and practices that I am calling liberation feminist theology.[16]

My description of theology as partial and limited by location, the acknowledgment that any such critical account is a social production and not a reflection of truth, requires that I identify not only a specific group of theological writings, but the context of production of feminist theology as well. The setting of production is a crucial piece of my investigation because I have indicated that inextricable relations between knowledge and its social relations are part of a liberation epistemology—a relation something like a graf(ph)t. By understanding production more broadly than the action of an individual agent, I need to clarify what I mean by liberation feminist theology by clarifying the setting that constitutes it as knowledge.

I will consider feminist theology as texts constituted by—written and used in relation to—the interests of its context of production, the contemporary North American academy. This focus does not deny that feminist theology is a practice in other settings as well, settings outside the educational production and legitimation of knowledge. It does underscore my intent to oppose the assumption that texts contain

Dickey Young, *Feminist Theology/Christian Theology: In Search of Method* (Minneapolis: Fortress Press, 1990).

[16]Sallie McFague distinguishes an additional move beyond liberation theologies in her metaphorical theology. She takes on cosmological issues as well as those of social historical liberation. See *Models of God: Theology for an Ecological, Nuclear Age* (Philadelphia: Fortress Press, 1987), 46–47. I should note that liberation is not the sole prerogative of white women; it shapes womanist theology as well, the work of African American women. My usage depends upon "feminist," which now connotes white women for its specificity, and distinguishes one typically white form of feminist theology from process feminism, or Jungian feminist theology, for example.

ideas that are somehow transportable to any situation with little change.[17] Feminist theology in the mode of texts of the academy is not the same thing as feminist theology in other settings, even when those very texts are "practiced" there. Liberation feminists are engaged in practices that empower women in pastoral settings or in social change agencies, and they raise important issues about difference. But they require responses that vary from those in academic settings and would require a different set of criteria to assess their treatment of difference. The context of production in an academic setting must be the source of criteria generated for judgments of what constitutes effective practice of the feminist vision there for respecting difference.

In this project the context of production and attendant epistemic conditions, or grid of intelligibility, of feminist liberation theological method is the institutional setting of knowledge production and dissemination, the institutional conditions in which academic theology is "embedded."[18] To ask the liberationist question about feminist theology in this setting, we must eventually investigate the grids of intelligibility of late twentieth-century academic institutions in the United States, a process I will only initiate in this book. How do such grids make it possible to acknowledge (or obscure) interest? How do these grids determine what counts as true? what counts as evidence? and what does not qualify? To define theological inquiry this way is to say that the function of feminist liberation theological method in relation to current definitions of academic theology and its institutional conditions is not a question of context secondary to a fixed constant called "theological reflection." Such a relation is actually constitutive of theological reflection.[19] Feminist theology has to ask how it contrib-

---

[17]While avoiding a simple reflection model, where ideas reflect or mirror the social relations out of which they come, I insist that the context of production has an impress on noetic practice. Respect for women's differences requires this point.

[18]The issues pertaining to this context, too frequently elided by dismissals of overly abstract, academic theology, are required by feminism's characteristic as a liberation theology. They are as important as issues of pastoral concern for difference. This setting is at stake in the conversations about theological education in some important books by feminists, which too frequently collapse the institutional–social formation issues of difference into the interpersonal issues of difference. I realize that it is the personal level where the institutional injustices converge and it is the individual who must raise them. However, they need more treatment as trans-interpersonal issues. I have in mind such important works as those of the Mudflower Collective and the Cornwall Collective (see n. 2 above).

[19]Clodovis Boff argues that theology is both autonomous and dependent, neutral and committed, and develops a number of levels and steps in the enterprise. His account of neutrality and autonomy are not naive forms, but ways to allow abstractings that are always cognizant of their mark by interest. Making another (not unrelated) point, Boff distinguishes between the real object and theoretical object: the God of theologians is

utes to the epistemic conditions of that theological institution. As a consequence judgments supporting or negating feminist theology will have to do with its capacity to identify and challenge the oppressive conditions under which knowledge is produced, a challenge shaped by its vision of liberation.

It is now time to get at those issues in terms of feminist theologians' categories for interest and knowledge. Is interest best displayed in ideas or in a variety of forms and sign systems? Is interest constituted in language or in something called social structures? How are they joined? How do patriarchal, sexist realities exist in the Christian tradition and how are they passed on? How does power—oppressive and liberating—relate to language, social location, and gender? The encompassing question here is how liberation feminist theologies understand the workings of the realities of patriarchal interest and relief from that. I begin by looking at the commitments that help explain what feminist theologians mean by "interest."

In a variety of ways, feminist liberation theology announces the principle I have identified as central to a liberationist epistemology, a conviction it shares with other liberation theologies and which it has radicalized in order to identify the situation of women as one of oppression. Elisabeth Schüssler Fiorenza confirms these liberation sentiments:

> The basic insight of liberation theologies and their methodological starting point is that all theology knowingly or not is by definition always engaged for or against the oppressed. Intellectual neutrality is not possible in a historical world of exploitation and oppression.[20]

Here she implicitly argues that theology should be biased toward the oppressed and their liberation, which is God's preferential option. In this view, liberation feminists identify the exploitation of women in patriarchal or male-dominant religions and societies as sin of the same order as racism and the oppression of the poor. Schüssler Fiorenza also makes clear here that linguistic formulations, discourse, reflection— something intrinsic to the knowledge process of theologizing—is inseparably connected with liberation and oppression, and not just actions or intentions or social systems. To understand what constitutes

---

only the latter; the God of the believer is the former. "Knowledge of salvation is no more salvific than knowledge of sugar is sweet." My distinctions are not precisely these, but they are intended to mark the need for more precision in the use of the term *theology* in feminist work. Boff, *Theology and Praxis*, 15–17.

[20]Elisabeth Schüssler Fiorenza, "Scripture in the Liberation Struggle," in *Bread Not Stone: The Challenge of Feminist Biblical Interpretation* (Boston: Beacon Press, 1984), 45.

the knowledge process, how it is situated, and how it is shaped by the
feature of location in feminist theology, we must look at the feminist
liberation methodological framework. That framework helps get at
what feminists mean by processes of oppression-liberation and the relation of language and power to gender—in short, an answer to the
question of how intellectual locatedness, as opposed to intellectual
neutrality, is identified.

Methodological proposals of feminist theologians

A good introduction to the pertinent liberation processes in feminism
is the well-known methodological proposal of Rosemary Radford
Ruether. That proposal is a correlationist method that places the full
humanity of women, or women's experience of struggle for liberation,
in correlation or critical relationship with the traditions of the historic
Christian faith. Ruether goes on to develop the method in a systematic
theology, posing the "feminist principle" in relation to each traditional
theological locus.[21] A similar method is also developed by Schüssler
Fiorenza in one stage of her work as a hermeneutical model for interpreting scripture. Calling it a "critical dialectical mode of biblical
interpretation," she broadens the correlation to a back-and-forth
interplay that includes a hermeneutics of suspicion, of proclamation,
of remembrance, and of creative actualization.[22] Schüssler Fiorenza's

---

[21]Rosemary Radford Ruether, *Sexism and God-Talk: Toward a Feminist Theology*
(Boston: Beacon Press, 1983); see chap. 1. There are interesting parallels between these
feminists' and Juan Segundo's identification of the liberation theology paradigm. However, as Schüssler Fiorenza rightly points out, Latin American male theologians never
take a radical critical stance toward scripture. Liberation concerns motivated by gender
seem to be the crucial element necessary to move to that hermeneutic of suspicion. See
Schüssler Fiorenza, "Scripture in the Liberation Struggle," in *Bread Not Stone*. I agree
with her about Segundo.

[22]This fourfold hermeneutics is of scripture. It might well be termed a feminist biblical theology, however, if that is conceivable with an open canon. The moment of suspicion is the critical test of the sexist or patriarchal nature of a text; proclamation is
opposed to historical positivism; remembrance is the reconstruction of women's
history—a "dangerous memory"; and creative actualization is the imaginative retelling
and ritualizing of biblical stories from a feminist perspective. Schüssler Fiorenza,
"Women-Church: The Hermeneutical Center of Feminist Biblical Interpretation," in
Bread Not Stone, 15–22. In her latest book Schüssler Fiorenza disassociates herself from
one version of a correlationist method, presenting a more detailed version of her critical
evaluative hermeneutics, which assumes that there is no "essential meaning in the scriptural text." *But She Said: Feminist Practices of Biblical Interpretation* (Boston: Beacon Press,
1992), 142–43. One might still say, however, that for her, justice-seeking feminist communities of deliberative, communicative practice are placed in critical relation to the
biblical text as prototype.

approach also grants priority to the principle of the struggle for justice for women, a norm for revelation that is parallel to the norm of full humanity within Ruether's model. Schüssler Fiorenza makes liberation of women the litmus test of the revelatory character of a biblical text.[23] For both theologians, the use of critical correlation is paradigmatic, the main feature of one important feminist methodological pattern.

This feminist method evokes the modern correlationist theology of Paul Tillich, yet is distinct enough that the latter helps to sharpen the definition of feminist theology. Tillich's correlation placed questions of the world and answers from the Christian faith in a mutual relation. As several feminists critical of the resulting sanguine approach to both terms would insist, however, the feminist version is a weighted rather than balanced method, and it is unsympathetic to several modern agendas represented by Tillich and his legacy.[24] Not only are the oppressed now identified as women, whose experiences, presence, voice, and gifts have been denied by centuries of male domination in the history of the Christian church and its surrounding environs, but they have become the preferential subject of God/ess's liberating action. Furthermore, the granting of a priority to scripture or "biblical religion" is a danger attendant to a Tillichian correlationist method that feminists cannot risk.[25]

Compared to prominent critical modern theological inheritors of Tillich, sometimes identified as liberal or revisionist, feminist liberation method departs by making primary the so-called contextual moment or contextual-situational dimension of theological reflection. Contextuality is typically the third of several moments in liberal-revisionist theologies. Schubert Ogden's 1972 version includes criteria of adequacy to human experience, Christian appropriateness, and practical truth. Edward Farley's includes historical memory, mediated uni-

---

[23]"The *locus* of divine revelation and grace is therefore not simply the Bible or the tradition of a patriarchal chuch but the 'church of women' in the past and in the present." Although she specifies that something more than the full humanity of women is needed, given that all we have are male models of humanity, Schüssler Fiorenza shares with Ruether the prioritizing of "women's experience in the struggle for liberation"; *Bread Not Stone*, xv. Later Schüssler Fiorenza disassociates herself from "full humanity of women," which is too abstract and universalizing; *But She Said*, 148.

[24]It is possible to criticize Tillich for not being a true correlationist. See David Tracy, *Blessed Rage for Order: The New Pluralism in Theology* (New York: Seabury Press, 1975), 46–47. See also Mark Kline Taylor, *Remembering Esperanza: A Cultural-Political Theology for North-American Praxis* (Maryknoll, N.Y.: Orbis Books, 1990), 24–26.

[25]Schüssler Fiorenza, *But She Said*, 142–43. Francis Schüssler Fiorenza, "The Crisis of Hermeneutics and Christian Theology," in *Theology at the End of Modernity*, ed. Sheila Greeve Davaney (Philadelphia: Trinity Press International, 1991), 117–40.

versal structures, and contextuality-practice. David Tracy offers a more complex correlationist model for revisionist theology that includes the religious dimension in common human experience and language, Christian texts in the historical and hermeneutical tradition, and metaphysics, to which he later adds contemporary praxis.[26] These theologies have a greater investment in rendering theological discourse intelligible to the postmodern world than in ordering theological practice around particular forms of social oppression.

Feminist theologies share with these thinkers attention to the historical tradition of Christianity, scriptural and extracanonical alike. They do not worry, however, about a philosophical moment identified as "structures of intelligibility," or "ecclesial universals," categories by which critical modern theologians justify and incorporate the knowledges of other disciplines. Even though feminists do incorporate other knowledges, the notion of "human existence in general"—or structures of intelligibility, as Schüssler Fiorenza would say—assumes an abstractness that is potentially pernicious from a liberation perspective. As Letty Russell puts the contrast, the agenda of contemporary white male theologians is to speak to the " 'cultured despisers' of the modern intellectual Western world"; as a liberation theology, feminism seeks the experience of the "nonperson."[27]

Bypassing the philosophical for the political-liberationist commitment to the marginalized, feminist theology puts its critical principle in relationship to the entire tradition. "The promotion of the full humanity of women" positioned against that history yields the systematic, sinful refusal of women's humanity; as Ruether says, "the denigration and marginalization of women's humanity" throughout history. Correlation means, then, that the notion of women's full humanity has the primary weight in the relationship with the tradition. The principle governs assessments of what is revelatory, what is of God or "of the holy" and what is not. Both Ruether and Schüssler Fiorenza have taken this correlationist principle to entail the opening

---

[26]Schubert M. Ogden, "What Is Theology," *Journal of Religion* 52 (1972): 22–40. Edward Farley, *Ecclesial Reflection: An Anatomy of a Theological Method* (Philadelphia: Fortress Press, 1982); *Theologia: The Fragmentation and Unity of Theological Education* (Philadelphia: Fortress Press, 1983). Tracy, *Blessed Rage for Order*, 43–63; *The Analogical Imagination: Christian Theology and the Culture of Pluralism* (New York: Crossroad, 1986).

[27]Letty Russell, *Household of Freedom: Authority in Feminist Theology* (Philadelphia: Westminster Press, 1987), 31. Feminist liberationists do not develop what Boff terms a "philosophical mediation." It may also be true, however, that they do not develop a socioanalytic mediation, either. Boff, *Theology and Praxis*, 1–62. Mark Kline Taylor, an exception to my claim, has taken this kind of structure and tried to make it work for feminist theology (*Remembering Esperanza*).

of the Christian canon. The former adds woman-centered stories from other religious traditions, and the latter argues that scripture is a prototype, a resource, rather than an archetype.[28] Schüssler Fiorenza refuses the uncritical appropriation of a woman's canon. She directs her attention to the notion of open-ended biblical interpretive strategies that allow women's differences to come to speech in a "multiple, polyvalent assembly of voices."[29] Whether we call it correlationist or not, the move for both feminists is an interpretive method designed to portray the entire Christian tradition in a new light.

While such judgments are more radical toward the Bible than any Latin American liberation theology, this radicality is not confined to the opening of the canon. Commitment to women in feminist theory has created the will to recover the women lost on account of male-oriented histories, what Schüssler Fiorenza calls a hermeneutics of remembrance. That commitment leads feminists to identify reality-constructions that keep women in their place, as well. This shift in definitions—from conceiving the problem as one of excluded historical subjects to thinking that it is more widely dispersed reality-constructions supporting women's oppression that must be addressed—indicates that the ideological power of definition is fundamental to liberation feminist theological thought. We must focus on the power of gender definitions in order to analyze the pernicious use of difference as that is found in the tradition's constructions of maleness and femaleness. Given the far-reaching nature of this form of questioning, any confinement of interests to particular female subjects will appear provincial. Feminist theological inquiry will not be satisfied with the "women in the Bible" or any other "addition" strategies that simply add women subjects to an existing subject matter.[30]

No part of tradition exempt from scrutiny

The radical potential in the critical hermeneutic of liberation feminism is found in its grasp of the workings of gender construction in the creation of expectations about place, proper female behavior, and female

---

[28]Schüssler Fiorenza, *Bread Not Stone*, 18–20. Rosemary Radford Ruether, *Woman-guides: Readings toward a Feminist Theology* (Boston: Beacon Press, 1985).

[29]Schüssler Fiorenza, *But She Said*, 148–51.

[30]This is an inclusive strategy, otherwise known in women's studies as the "add women and stir" approach and the least exciting. The turn to definition/construction is where feminist theology itself has an alternative to the inclusive approach to difference. Schüssler Fiorenza has recently added the criticism of binary gender to her constructionism; see *But She Said*, 115.

characteristics. These constructions are found throughout the Christian tradition. No part of the tradition is theoretically exempt from a critical sifting with the principle that prioritizes women's full humanity. Although this principle is complicated by Letty Russell, who balances women's benefit against the tradition with her appeal to Christ, she does acknowledge the need for a paradigm shift in authority for "all the authority structures in religion and society, including the claim that scripture evokes our consent to faith and action."[31] When figures such as Ruether and Schüssler Fiorenza prioritize the full humanity of women or the assembly of women's and other "nonpersons' " voices for liberation, the result is that no part of the Christian tradition is exempt from scrutiny. The entire tradition is judged potentially complicit with definitions of gender that are oppressive for women.

This critical attention to the entire tradition points toward a feminist theological insight: as Schüssler Fiorenza puts it, all theology is engaged, not neutral. This willingness to extend criticism to the entire tradition suggests that negative bias against women might be found in any part of the tradition. Feminists also find bias to have a positive aspect. While feminist attention to the negative content in the tradition may dominate many of its expressions, location is, in the first place, a condition of knowing in this understanding. The argument of historical-materialist feminism that *standpoint*, or position in the social formation, is epistemologically significant is consonant with what liberation feminists mean by the positive work of bias. Women's situation as the oppressed gives us a vantage on the failures of the system and is developed constructively in the fact that a positive bias *for* women helps to recuperate women's agency from accounts that render them invisible.[32]

Interest, then, is basically an epistemological issue. It can manifest in harm for women, but it is not confined to harm. Mary Ann Tolbert makes this clear by insisting that feminist hermeneutics has invalidated the scholarly worry over the danger of subjectivism in interpretation

---

[31]Russell complicates this with her christological understanding of the tradition as the workings of the gospel that always transcend the oppressive gender constructions of scripture. This allows her to leave scripture as canon pretty much in place. See her *Human Liberation*. She has moved a bit in her most recent work, however, although she is not willing to side with the open canon of Ruether and Schüssler Fiorenza. Instead of Schüssler Fiorenza's substitution of prototype—"a model of the past that is not binding or unchanging"—for scripture's authority in the place of an archetypal authority, Russell describes her position as one where "the idea of authority [is] rooted not just in the past but in the anticipation of God's intended future." *Household of Freedom*, 25, 33.

[32]Russell uses the phrase "standpoint dependent" in *Household of Freedom*, 30–31.

by showing that all interpretation is interested.[33] Interest is not merely a preference for negative contents about women and gender; it can be a valuing of women that makes their absence a concern and constitutes a will to recover them.

In these indications that bias can be *for* women as well as against them, we find in feminist work recognition of a number of senses in which knowledge is "interested." It is clear that no part of the Christian tradition is exempted from interest, whether pernicious or benevolent. It is also clear that specific definitions of maleness/femaleness exist that are judged to be pernicious for women. This means that bias is not simply a predilection, a negative (or positive) disposition attached to a position in the social order, but rather particular historical contents that value maleness over femaleness and define gender relations of domination or subordination. Thus interest has taken a specific shape as certain contents in the tradition. These contents include male imagery for God, a male savior, use of triumphalist and hegemonic images of divine power, as well as the use of images for women that are supportive of submissive, passive behaviors and statuses. Such examples indicate the impress of interest, with implicit use of unsophisticated ideology theory about legitimation of male dominance.

Finally, in liberation feminist writing we find a sense of interest as an orientation toward transformation. Schüssler Fiorenza carries this sense in her continued insistence that not only is the valuational, positioned nature of knowing essential to feminist theological work, it issues in praxis: academic research should be "action-oriented." As she says, "The motto for such an approach could be, 'If you want to know a thing, you must change it.' " Russell says one of feminism's definitional features is its treatment of theology as praxis, "action that is concurrent with reflection or analysis and leads to new questions, actions, and reflections"; it is for change in society.[34]

There is clearly an emancipatory character to this understanding of positionality. Schüssler Fiorenza calls liberation hermeneutics a pragmatics. One's care for the other, for women, generates a hermeneutic of suspicion and remembrance, just as patriarchal bias allows for

---

[33]Mary Ann Tolbert, "Defining the Problem: The Bible and Feminist Hermeneutic," *Semeia: The Bible and Feminist Hermeneutic* 28 (1983): 113–15.

[34]Elisabeth Schüssler Fiorenza, "Roundtable Discussion: On Feminist Methodology," *Journal of Feminist Studies in Religion* 1:2 (Fall 1985): 75. Russell, *Human Liberation*, 55–56. This point is true for feminist theology as a practice, as I will argue in my last chapter.

something like an ideological distortion of knowledge.[35] In Ruether's view, the languages of resistance that support this activist notion of interest come from biblical prophetic tradition as well as heretical traditions, other religions, and feminist theoretical traditions. The biblical critique of idolatry (which includes not simply the divinizing of maleness but the injustices perpetrated by power hierarchies), biblical traditions of God's vindication of the oppressed, biblical eschatological visions of just communities, and the biblical critiques of specifically religious ideology find resonance in all liberation feminist language of resistance. Russell contributes biblical traditions of shalom, peace and justice, and eschatological images of households of freedom. Schüssler Fiorenza offers traditions of active women disciples and a discipleship of equals around Jesus as languages to specify the interest for change.[36]

The effects of location on knowledge

We have seen that feminist theology is distinguished from modern and revisionist theologies precisely because it focuses on praxis and the social-contextual character of all theological claims, leading it to avoid such apologetic tasks as intelligibility to modern publics. Having recognized the biased character of knowing, feminist theology is clearly opposed to the cruder forms of value-free knowledge. Inherent in feminist theology from its inception is the notion that every discourse must be inspected, as we have seen, and that the standpoint of the oppressed, a marginalized social group, is granted priority. Its vision is the emergence of God's salvation in history, shalom—the social well-being of all—a vision stressed by Russell and Ruether to counteract the notion of salvation as individual and concerned with the afterlife. It is a vision that must begin with the knowledge of those who are nonpersons.

Four clues are evident regarding how this feminism understands the effect of location on knowledge: (1) that all of the tradition is finite and open to scrutiny; (2) that specific bias is identified with formulations

---

[35]Although few feminist theologians develop theories of ideology, some form of ideological repression seems to be the best way to characterize this failure of the tradition. It is a virtual false or distorted consciousness to which the tradition and reflection upon it have been susceptible on the subject of gender. See Rosemary Radford Ruether, *New Woman New Earth: Sexist Ideologies and Human Liberation* (New York: Seabury Press, 1975). Sharon Welch uses the work of Michel Foucault to think through feminist theological issues, and provides a very different case. See Welch's criticism of ideology in *Communities of Resistance and Solidarity*, 65–66.

[36]Schüssler Fiorenza, *But She Said*, 132.

that deny the full humanity of women—an ideological content; (3) that theological knowledge is a change-oriented practice; (4) that a marginalized position in the social formation should be epistemologically privileged. These points are consonant with a number of the elements of a liberation epistemology.

These clues display the terms of a liberation theo/acentric criticism in the following ways: The entire tradition is open to inspection. Interest is designated as potentially ideological or for good, and there is an implicit understanding in the standpoint position that the particular way in which interest is conveyed in relation to the tradition is related to social conditions of subjects. These agreements with a liberation epistemology suggest signs of an openness to a nonessentialist position on the meaning of a tradition, which I maintain is crucial to respect for difference. Because knowledge is located, we can extrapolate from the priority of standpoint in knowing for liberation feminists to the idea that "women" are produced in different social locations. We must logically assume that women occupy different standpoints and therefore this will make a difference in the nature of the understanding generated.[37]

We are still lacking three crucial elements, however, in a theory of theological discourse as production: (1) the link between systems of meaning and social conditions; (2) the related account of the subject's relation to the social (which concerns the issue of whether the subject is read as coded by the social linguistically or linked in a secondary, nonconstitutive way); and (3) treatments of desire and conflict, which I argued were needed to mark the kind of complexity that distinguishes social sin and ideology from rational error. These elements will yield a full-blown account of theological discourse as produced—a cognitive practice—and they are necessary to theorizing difference.

I turn now to the workings of language and subjects, and, inevitably, to power.

Language does it: gender and words

Although closely aligned to the first feminist insight into the positioned, biased character of all knowledge, the question about language, subjects, and power is distinct. The former, what I have looked

---

[37]Schüssler Fiorenza recognizes this in a continuing move toward the openness of the feminist space of interpretation, which must include not only the varieties of women's readings of scripture, but also prioritizes the "theories and strategies of feminists who speak from the experience of multiplicative patriarchal oppression." *But She Said*, 132.

for thus far, informs us of the commitment to allow for negative or positive positioning in knowledge, and a particular content—ideology—that is antiwoman. The latter has to do with how these interests actually work as processes of oppression and/or liberation. We need theories about the relationship of language to ideas, of ideas and language to social structures and the subjects they form, and of the relation of all discourse to power. Feminist theology's answers to these questions will lead to a place from which we can better assess the limitations and possibilities. In what follows I examine accounts of language, its constitutive character, and its relation to power that appear in liberation feminist theological options.

A prominent way the workings of gender bias in theological reflection or the tradition are indicated in feminist theology is with the conviction that language is more than "mere" semantics. Indeed, one cannot be familiar with feminist theology and not be aware that feminists insist on the great difference that language makes in the construing of reality for women, as the concern for gender constructions implies. Changes in the liturgies and symbol systems of the Christian community have been at the forefront of feminist concern because the gender constructions that are embedded in these languages are dominated by asymmetrical valuing of maleness and femaleness.

A conviction is not a theory, however. Feminist theologians have shared a conviction more than they have theorized that the issues pertaining to naming are issues worth fighting over. Gender and language are fundamental liberation concerns. Male gender constructions dominate Christian faith and the social languages of its environments, and the (fewer) female gender constructions found there include far too many notions of female subordination. These familiar judgments about pernicious gender content are central concerns because language creates (and is created by) reality. As Mary Daly so aptly appropriates Marshall McLuhan, "the medium is the message." A religion that names the divine "Father," attributes the role of savior to a "son," and identifies maleness as a key qualification for representational ministry throughout most of its communal life is not only saying something with negative implications for women; it is creating a reality where women *must be fundamentally marginalized*.[38] While feminists may differ over how essentially patriarchal Christian faith, its texts, and traditions are, we are fairly unified in our conviction that naming, a primary work of language, is constitutive rather than reflective of reality.

---

[38]Mary Daly, *Beyond God the Father: Toward a Philosophy of Women's Liberation* (Boston: Beacon Press, 1973; original reintroduction by the author, 1985), 13.

Some of the best illustrations of the constitutive nature of language are found in feminists' attention to liturgy, language for people, and language for God. Naming has a crucial relationship to women's sense of themselves: as Russell points out, "Those who say that this concern of women for language that is whole, positive, and inclusive is unreasonable should begin to think about what it is like to sit through years of lectures, sermons, instructions, etc., in which one is never named, even by inclusion in the pronouns used."[39] This phenomenon is well-described with Susan Thistlethwaite's coinage, women's "linguistic invisibility." Russell quotes Adrienne Rich about the "theft of language" that has occurred when women are not named.[40]

Concern with inclusive/exclusive language is also extended into attention to the clusters of imagery beyond binary gender analyzing the constructions that support relations of domination, submission, and self-hatred related to gender. Feminists such as Sallie McFague, Russell, Daly, Rita Brock, and Rebecca Chopp show that it is not simply words or definitions of maleness and femaleness that are at issue, but webs of symbolic associations connecting gender to sexuality, carnality, desire, the body, associations that create reality in pernicious ways for women. These constellations are the place where alternative sets of connections can be made that liberate instead of oppress.[41]

Gender oppression: powerful words and word-power?

The assumption that language is constitutive is a move toward explaining feminist theology's understanding of how interest functions in knowledge. We must remember that language is creative. The

---

[39]Russell, *Human Liberation*, 94.

[40]Susan Brooks Thistlethwaite, "Inclusive Language: Theological and Philosophical Fragments," *Religious Education* 80:4 (Fall 1985): 551–70. Russell, *Household of Freedom*, 45.

[41]Daly's identification of the systematic connections between theological loci saturated with patriarchal imagery is the best known. See her *Beyond God the Father*. McFague does a good job of connecting Christianity's patriarchal symbols with their supporting monarchical and militaristic metaphors of power in *Models of God*. Rita Nakashima Brock connects classic atonement imagery with child abuse and women's self-hatred in *Journeys by Heart: A Christology of Erotic Power* (New York: Crossroad, 1988). Rebecca S. Chopp is good on language in general, in *The Power to Speak: Feminism, Language, God* (New York: Crossroad, 1989). These are only a few of the works which explore the meanings in Christian tradition that help sustain women's oppression. Schüssler Fiorenza speaks not only of male language for God in scripture, but of erasure of women, images of subordination, and violence against women as constitutive of the androcentrism and oppressiveness of texts. See *Bread Not Stone*, 8–15.

gender contents of scripture, for example, do not reflect or describe reality but *create* reality in a negative (or positive) fashion. This is to say a second thing, namely that we assume language is fundamentally related to power. The very notion that language can be stolen assumes that having it—in the sense of being able to determine how language is used—is of enormous significance. As Russell says, the power of naming is that of claiming and changing reality.[42]

While the relation between power and language may appear obvious, it is not, and its importance needs to be examined. The reason the relationship appears obvious is that if language is reality-constituting—if naming me as a woman in liturgy somehow creates me as one—it is clearly powerful and has some capacity to affect the world for good and for ill. The link between language and power is crucial to feminist positions which maintain that the nature of the language of the Christian tradition is such that it renders women invisible, inculcates misogynistic attitudes, and needs remedying. The specifics of its working, however, should be explained in order to clarify the processes of liberation, oppression, and theological reflection. I have argued that systems of meaning are connected to social conditions, and it is only as such that these meanings are individuated. Thus we speak of a coded subject to ensure respect for the difference in women's social location. The relation of power to systems of meaning must also reflect the complications of conflict and desire. It is this account against which feminist proposals must be assessed.

A review of liberation feminist positions on language yields no consensus on language theory, as mentioned earlier. Indeed, feminist theology lacks language theory of great complexity.[43] Some examples of the dominant feminist treatments of language do suggest some commonalities in the way language is articulated or linked with power. A first example—an effective way in which feminist theologians connect language and power—avoids theory completely. Statements simply invoke the constitutive nature of language and are found convincing by many women. Feminists' description of the invisibility of women in "generic" language and the claim that the major traditions and their use in Christian communities are "male-dominated" are simply in

---

[42]Russell, *Household of Freedom*, 46.

[43]Rebecca Chopp's move into poststructuralist analysis is an important exception to this claim. She rejects an account of language as representation. She does not fit my account of the methodological portrait that relies upon women's experience, however, and her proposal does not lapse into the problems I am trying to elaborate. See *The Power to Speak*.

accord with the perceptions of numbers of women readers, myself included.

Thus we have a kind of appeal to common sense—the common sense of a particular constituency. In Daly's famous quote, "if God in 'his' heaven is a father ruling 'his' people, then it is in the 'nature' of things and according to divine plan and the order of the universe that society be male-dominated," we have a strong statement about the power of language and symbols. We do not, however, have a theory of language, gender, and power. We do not have an explanation of how the maleness of divine imagery gets such distribution, how it is interrelated with material realities, or why some women would not agree. We do have a claim that resonates with the way many women read their lives and the world. It is a claim that may assume the undeniable evidence of practices that have marginalized, excluded, and vilified women, but it does not clarify how the discourse itself carries out that oppression.[44]

A second example of feminist focus on language implies a view of power. It is found in feminists' work on inclusive language in scripture and liturgy, where the realities of the language are not simply inscribed in texts but re-created in recitation. To transform this major site for the reproduction of patriarchal values, feminists have created "inclusive language" lectionaries. These lectionaries strongly testify to feminist conviction about the power of language. The implied theory goes something like this: If certain subjects are not named in an authoritative tradition, or if characteristics perceived by a culture as negative are regularly associated with those subjects, then those subjects are harmed in some way, either by being undervalued or vilified.

This view of the constitutive nature of language suggests that the power of language is communicative and operates in single word units. The connection between language and social reality implied by notions of linguistic invisibility, for example, is located in signs, particularly in specific gendered pronouns and nouns. Thus, words "exclude"; words "express bias against individuals or groups." Inclusive language, on this logic, reverses the effect; it "recognizes the value of all human beings," as a manual puts it.[45] Feminists' review of the in-

---

[44]Daly, *Beyond God the Father*, 13.

[45]*Language and the Church: Articles and Designs for Worship*, ed. Barbara A. Withers (New York: Div. of Education and Ministry, National Council of the Churches of Christ in the U.S.A., 1984), 7. The language of "reflection" is prevalent in these discussions. However, the terms "inform" and "shape" are used in the same arguments. The vagueness of these last expressions makes it difficult to attribute specific language theories to those who say, as does the *Inclusive Language Lectionary*, that its use of inclu-

visibility of women agents in scripture and of the effects of the dominance of male figures are examples of a similar conviction about the kind of power language has. Appearance (or nonappearance) in language and the hearer's cognitive appropriation of that communication have a direct effect on reality and how reality is valued. The workings of harm or liberation—the specific way power is understood to work by feminists—appear to be largely cognitive.

Another example of this kind of work, notable not only for its brilliance but for the enormous amount of power granted to language in it, is found in Mary Daly's creative romance with language. After *Beyond God the Father*, she creates new gynocentric vocabularies to counteract patriarchy. Her theory of language is never stated, and it does not appear to matter to Daly whether signs reflect reality or create it. What does operate is a use of single words in the frame of a dictionary. Daly assumes that it is not only the appearance of femaleness in traditions and cultural languages that will address the oppression of women; what is needed is a linguistic revolution that valorizes women. Every term that applies to women and has negative associations is to be recuperated as a compliment. From "hag" to "witch" to "original sin" and "women's carnality," these terms are transformed by Daly into the highest praise—labels for the valorizing of a woman-centered universe.[46]

Although Daly's work is more radical in many ways than the inclusive language conversations, its affinities with the latter have to do with the accounts of language and power assumed by both. It is true that Daly insists that it is a mistake to simply make a semantic shift in vocabulary, and it would be a mistake to adduce from the implicit account of language/power that she thinks this revised language will solve the problem of patriarchy.[47] However, she offers no theoretical move to lead us to think that she has done anything but collapse power and semantics. In Daly's treatment of language we have another focus on content, the meaning of single words and phrases; we also have

---

sive language has "the intent of reflecting the full humanity of women and men in light of the gospel." "Introduction," *An Inclusive Language Lectionary: Readings for Year A* (The Cooperative Publication Association [Atlanta: John Knox Press; New York: Pilgrim Press; and Philadelphia: Westminster Press]: Div. of Education and Ministry, National Council of the Churches of Christ in the U.S.A., 1983). Nancy A. Hardesty offers a helpful study guide for churches, arguing that inclusive language communicates God's inclusive love best. *Inclusive Language in the Church* (Atlanta: John Knox Press, 1987).

[46]Mary Daly and Jane Caputi, *Webster's First New Intergalactic Wickedary of the English Language* (Boston: Beacon Press, 1987).

[47]Daly, *Beyond God the Father*, original reintroduction, xix-xx.

whole webs of patriarchal discourse identified, and the implicit assumption that a new female-affirming world is created with the invention of gyno-centered language. Like the inclusive language arguments, Daly grants great power to language; she departs by broadening those arguments to include larger networks of patriarchal discourse. She also assumes the entire self is oppressed by these systems of meaning. However, she always assumes that the content does the same work—has the same patriarchal meaning. Thus she has affinities with this account of the relation of language and gender to power as communication—the view that power is cognitive.

Among feminist theologians, the most sophisticated theoretical treatments of language are those of Sallie McFague and Brian Wren, who display the constitutive power of language by attending to its multireferential, figurative character. Like Daly, they expand the focus on words to larger configurations of language, identifying metaphors, networks of symbols, and models of thinking as they relate to gender and oppression. This moves the analysis outside of exclusive attention to gender-specific content to imagery about hierarchy and other asymmetrical notions of human relationships. When we ask how the actual process of harm or liberation occurs in language, the answer once again involves the communicative notion of the power of language. For McFague and Wren, however, making meaning is an equivocal process. They offer a different account from the (apparent) direct and univocal process of meaning in the views I have reviewed thus far. These theologians also indicate that the communicative process involves more than cognitive reception. According to McFague, metaphors operate disclosively as they shape the consciousness; they disrupt the old ways of thinking and evoke and inspire new pictures of ourselves, God, and world.[48] Wren goes further and insists that communication depends upon context and that language always makes meaning relative to power politics, to specific economic and social configurations.[49]

For these accounts with theories of figurative language, language makes meaning for whole selves, not simply the cognitive self. Emerging in work that follows the line of thought of McFague or

---

[48]Sallie McFague's work is found in *Metaphorical Theology: Models of God in Religious Language* (Philadelphia: Fortress Press, 1982) and *Models of God*.

[49]Brian Wren, *What Language Shall I Borrow? God-Talk in Worship: A Male Response to Feminist Theology* (New York: Crossroad, 1990), 61–83. Another move toward use and context as being essential to the meaning of language (never developed further, to my knowledge) is found in Thistlethwaite, who makes the point with Ludwig Wittgenstein. "Inclusive Language: Theological and Philosophical Fragments."

Wren are accounts of the imagining subject, a much richer notion
of the subject than that of the unidimensional cognitive message-
receiver. Schüssler Fiorenza and Russell speak of the imagination as
the site where oppressive and transformative language effects are located. The turn to the imagination is one that relies upon the powerful
effects of symbol, metaphor, and images. It assumes that the affective
self—the desiring self—is shaped, for good or ill, by those representations of reality that do not create the ordinary or refer univocally. In
these broader understandings of the multiple and communicative
nature of language and the multifaceted character of the imagination,
we move away from the determinist cognitivism of the earliest sim-
plistic-sounding associations of power with language. Although Russell still says that "talk can *always* hurt you," she also insists that the
power of language is multilayered by the authority invested in the
speaker, and that communication is more than language.[50]

Power is not simply the effectiveness of communication and understanding. It involves emotive, existential, and contextual realities.
McFague and Wren's positions, like those that develop the imaginative
possibilities in creating more liberating gender realities, also differ
from my earlier examples in that communication is not a direct or univocal process, whereby meaning occurs when a fixed message is sent
and received. With the idea that language is multireferential, we can
imagine that meaning might be more unstable than heretofore understood by feminists. As a consequence, the power-language relation
might be more complicated than the communicative model implies.
McFague and Wren, however, finally leave us to assume that how language affects oppression is explained by the feminist theological view
that it is the content of the Christian tradition that bears the harm and
to which attention must be given for liberation.[51] This is because the potential to connect these sytems of meaning with *our* social location (or
any) is not carried out. And the affective work of meaning is not connected with the conflict and desire which are part of deforming interest.

---

[50]Russell, *Household of Freedom*, 45–47. She is operating with the Sapir/Whorf hypothesis, which connects language, culture, and thought. But Russell's account does not
amount to much more than "shaping," a shaping that has enormous consequences.

[51]Using the work of Clifford Geertz on symbol systems, Carol Christ offers a succinct summary of what operates in this kind of work. Symbol systems shape moods and
create motivations. I do not find this view qualitatively different from the focus on content, because it is ultimately flawed at the same point, as I will argue in chap. 2. It relies
on some notion of prediscursive experience that is shaped by language, and it incurs the
idealist tendencies of this position. "Why Women Need the Goddess," in *Womanspirit
Rising: A Feminist Reader in Religion*, ed. Carol P. Christ and Judith Plaskow (San Francisco: Harper & Row, 1979), 274–75.

The possibility for a slightly different approach is found in the common practice of feminist theologians of ascribing power to language by means of semantic meanings or textual features as they are *used* against women. This suggests a complexity that is open to the important development of theories of language which maintain that *use* determines meaning. The benefit of such theories is that with them one would have to assume that words and texts have different meanings when settings change. One could not assume that female or male images have the same meanings, liberate or harm the same way, in different social locations. Once the setting is part of the meaning, the temptation to ascribe reality-constitutive oppressive power to meanings alone in the flat logic implied by inclusive-exclusive language is thwarted. The turn to the situation to account for the production of meaning invites more complex ways of thinking about power than simply asserting that certain meanings negate one's being. It suggests different systems of meaning might be connected to different social locations. More recently Schüssler Fiorenza has acknowledged that meaning is an utterance-dependent phenomenon. From statements about the rhetorical character of discourse, she creates a space for a new way of thinking about the power-language relation.[52] It is a space not yet fully filled, however.

I conclude by noting a practice common to feminist liberation theology that epitomizes the force and seriousness of the relationship among power, gender, and language. In addition to the ways feminists explain the effects of the Christian tradition as a set of practices, feminists locate much of its oppressive and liberating linguistic power in texts, especially in Christian scripture. The condensed expression that invests power in language is found in feminist claims that texts and translations are androcentric, that language is sexist, and that scripture itself is sexist and patriarchal. In the same vein, the power to liberate is ascribed to texts. Mary Ann Tolbert exemplifies this practice of relating harm and liberation to the tradition when she marvels that both liberating and patriarchal features are attributable to the same text, the Bible.[53]

This practice is important but cannot be explained by the work done on the subject. Feminists actually have a more sophisticated un-

---

[52]These theories are found in the work of literary critics, some of whom I will present in chap. 2. Schüssler Fiorenza has identified the rhetorical character of discourse before her most recent look at difference and feminist hermeneutics in *But She Said*. There is no theory of language, experience, power, and "discourse" in it, however, at least as I understand the questions that must be answered.

[53]Mary Ann Tolbert, "Protestant Feminists and the Bible: On the Horns of a Dilemma," *Union Seminary Quarterly Review* 43 (1989): 1–17.

derstanding than their theoretical comments display. Primarily con-
tent-oriented and communicative accounts of the working of language
do not adequately explain what feminists want to say about the pernicious character of the Christian tradition. The idea that most share,
that language or *processes of meaning* are constitutive rather than reflective, is an important move in the direction of such an account, but it is
not developed enough to carry the claims being made for the contents
of the tradition. The communicative explanations do not match the
views of language that suggest that language harms or oppresses and
renders invisible. Communicative accounts of language are not satisfactory for what feminism wants to say about the larger notion that
interest (conflict and desire) shapes knowledge. The relation of power,
language, and gender to oppression and liberation is crucial to that liberation epistemology.

Because of the inadequacy of these accounts of language, liberation feminism lacks a theory of interest that explicates the power-
knowledge connection. What *is* found in these treatments is the suggestion that power is a feature, not of a situation of use, but of a certain
group of scriptural and traditional texts that concern gender. It fails to
connect texts to systems of meaning that are then relative to social locations. However, this formulation is a strong statement about the significance and centrality of the gender-language-power relation.[54]

Women's experience: false universal?

A review of some important liberation feminist accounts of language
and the relation of language to power affords a better understanding of
what feminists mean by the situated character of knowledge. Although there are gaps in the explanations, the constructed character of
language and the relation of language to power in the processes of oppression and liberation are crucial pieces in the analysis of knowledge

---

[54]Two exceptions to the target of my critique about language need to be noted. First,
as mentioned earlier, Schüssler Fiorenza has recently stated that texts get their meaning
from the sites of interpretation; she has objected to my claim that she makes the move
criticized here. I want to hear more from her, however, about the pleasures and ideological workings of the readings of women in different social locations so that the promise of her move is fulfilled. I am interested in power as something that transverses
everything, as Foucault would say, and might channel certain readings, occlude or mute
others. See *But She Said*, 134–35. The other exception is Rebecca Chopp's recent work
arguing that language creates subjectivity along with the social order. I am in great sym-
pathy with her work. It does not differentiate the construction of women in different
subject positions, however. See *The Power to Speak*.

and its mechanisms of interest. To complete this account we must attend to the most familiar and final element of the liberationist epistemology of feminist theology—women's experience. The appeal to women's experience as a norm and as a resource has been virtually the centerpiece of a feminist methodological pattern, already reviewed in its exemplary form in the critical correlationist method of Ruether and (early) Schüssler Fiorenza.

It might seem that the appeal to women's experience would be the logical place to *begin* an explanation of how feminists understand the impact of interest and location on knowledge, instead of the last feature to be considered. But in fact, the effectiveness of the appeal (in the academic setting) can best be seen in relation to the themes I have just reviewed. The sign that accounts of language and power are really socially displayed—connecting systems of meaning to social location—is in the account of the subject. As the individuation of these systems the subject must be coded. A look at the appeal to women's experience will answer that.

The appeal to women's experience in liberation feminist theology should be understood first in terms of other accounts of theological knowledge in relation to which feminists are defining their project. As Ruether says, when applied to traditional Christian theology, the appeal to women's experience is explosive. The importance of relying upon women's experience in consciousness-raising groups is much in evidence in theological circles. Appeals to women's experience as a norm—in the sense of Ruether and Schüssler Fiorenza's critical principle—and as a resource—in the sense of the recovery of women in Christian past and present—have created a critical hermeneutics of suspicion and an explosion of research resulting in woman-affirming thealogies (a term "feminizing" the project of God-knowledge).

Making women a central topic in theological reflection has an important epistemic function, best seen in relation to entrenched views of theological reflection that refuse to recognize the imprint of the knower on the known. Feminists appeal to women's experience in two different conversations. First, experience is invoked against orthodox notions of Christian revelation in order to affirm the historical and constructed character of the tradition. By indicating the missing subject matter and antiwoman prescriptions in traditional sources, the feminist appeal seeks to historicize orthodoxy. The appeal to women's experience also contests a second theological position, that of liberal theology. Liberal theology prides itself on its adoption of historical consciousness and its willingness to champion modern challenges to the heteronomy of church and tradition. In this latter relation, feminist appeal exposes the androcentric character of the humanism in liberal theology.

Both orthodox and liberal theologies make the mistake of assuming their "subject" is generic; both are blind to the false universal — man — that pervades their theological reflection. It is in relation to such theological traditions that a feminist appeal to women's experience has its most powerful effect. This effect is feminists' challenge to theological failures to acknowledge the situated character of reflection, which is indicated in this use of the false universal, the subject "man." Ruether points out that what is *not* unique about feminist theology is that it is based upon experience; she insists that is true of all theology. What is unique, she maintains, is its appeal to *women's* experience in relation to a tradition of reflection that has never owned up to the maleness of its subject.[55]

Employed to contest the male subject as a false universal, women's experience displays the liberationist feminist commitment to the located character of all knowledge. Does it, however, cohere with the assumptions about language and power that go with the constitutive character of language? I have suggested that feminists make moves which imply this constitutive character but do not satisfactorily explain it. It is in the appeal to women's experience that I locate the failure to explain it. Saying that language is constitutive defines knowledge as interested and embedded in human experience. There is no experience, no knowledge, outside of language. In short, the feminist move to support the constitutive character of language is a move in the direction of a liberation epistemology that should connect the social location of theological claims with the subject. I have argued that linkage requires the coded subject, or the linguistic construction of the subject, otherwise stated as the refusal of a Cartesian consciousness that has some noetic ability prior to the codes that give it meaning. We must ask, then, if women's experience refers to just such a prelinguistic knowledge.

The answer to this question is complex because feminists understand "women's experience" in at least two different ways. Feminist theologians frequently insist that this phrase does not invoke private or personal experience, the kind of subjectivist appeal that is ultimately individualist. By rejecting individualist or private experience, however, may we also infer the refusal of a prelinguistic experience that would underwrite a *nonsituated* theological warrant? Feminists do not say. The opposite of private or personal in these disclaimers is not

[55]Ruether, *Sexism and God-Talk*, 12–13.

discursive or linguistic—therefore inevitably social—but a notion of women's experience that is decidedly liberation-oriented. As Letty Russell puts it, it is not just female (biological) or feminine (cultural) experience that is claimed but "the feminist (political) experience of those advocating a change of society to include both women and men as human beings, created in God's image to participate with God in the fashioning of new creation." Or as Schüssler Fiorenza has it, the appeal is to the experience of women's struggle for liberation—*feminist* experience. A defense of a similar sort is found in feminist theory. Criticizing the criticism of the essentialism in "women's experience," Tania Modleski says, "but surely for many women the phrase 'women's experience' is shorthand for 'women's experience of political oppression,' and it is around this experience that they have organized and out of this experience that they have developed a sense of solidarity, commonality, and community."[56]

Two versions of women's experience

This first version of women's experience is a social-constructionist account with debts to such thinkers as sociologists Peter Berger and Thomas Luckmann, according to whom society provides interpretive grids and commitments that give shape to experience.[57] With its liberationist commitment, however, these feminist appeals to experience are better described as feminist standpoint theory, for they imply that the position of oppression gives women (the subject) a special vantage on reality, something the sociology of knowledge does not entail.[58] Those without power see best the structures that keep them in place and the illusory views of the advantaged. The advantaged continue to read social reality through the grid of their own interests, interests that obscure the effects of their advantage on others. In secular feminist

---

[56]Letty M. Russell, *Household of Freedom*, 17–18. In *Bread Not Stone*, Schüssler Fiorenza is adamant that this is not a universalizing category; women's experience is "embedded in culture and religion" and must be criticized, *But She Said*, 149. Tania Modleski, *Feminism without Women: Culture and Feminism in a "Postfeminist" Age* (New York: Routledge, 1991), 17. This feminist version of "women's experience" is articulated by Christ and Plaskow as well in their introduction to *Womanspirit Rising*, 5–9.

[57]Peter L. Berger and Thomas Luckmann, *The Social Construction of Reality: A Treatise in the Sociology of Knowledge* (Garden City, N.Y.: Doubleday, 1966). Letty Russell uses this account; see *Household of Freedom*, 30–31.

[58]Ruether sees this standpoint as exposing the male "mystification" of authority; she uses sociology of knowledge with some Marxist appeals. Ideology, however, is a deforming of ideas that seems to operate in a determinist fashion to directly effect the elitist privilege of the powerful in social reality. *Sexism and God-Talk*, 17, 27–29.

theory, feminists with Marxist commitments develop standpoint theory, which provides some specificity to the potentially problematic category "experience."[59] It may not tell us all we need to know about interest and language, but this use of experience moves away from experience as a universalizing category.

A second version of the feminist appeal to women's experience conflicts with the idea that language has constitutive power. Feminist theologians also appeal to women's experience when they intend to refer to what has been ignored and "almost entirely shut out of theological reflection in the past," as Ruether puts it. This kind of appeal would make no sense if it only referred to feminist experience. It is, however, in Ruether's formulation of revelation that the language-experience problem is brought to the fore and we find how it is that experience can be understood as both located, and used in a problematic prelinguistic sense at the same time.

Ruether's account incorporates an appeal to experience not simply to correct a secular historian's male bias, but to provide a notion of revelation as well—since the task of marking theological reflection with its positioned nature is complicated doubly, given the fact that some relationship to God is implicated in this kind of knowledge. She defines experience as the mediation of self, world, and the divine; it is codified in symbols and tradition.[60] On this basis, women's experience is granted the mediating role for feminist theology. However, it is more precise to say that the notion "experience" functions as a more encompassing category than the symbol system, for it must mediate the divine and the self as well as the linguistically constructed worldly events.

There is an inconsistency in these uses of women's experience. In fact, some conflicts may not be resolvable. One of the uses of women's experience is at odds with the understanding of language as constitutive of reality. In the first case, where the appeal is used to support a standpoint theory, an interpretive grid presents (constructs) reality. This does not deny the insight that language situates, and it implicitly avoids the positing of prelinguistic understanding. According to this notion of "feminist women's experience," one could argue that the account of sexist texts and traditions is relative to (in the sense of constructed by) the systems of meaning that construct feminist "experience." This would help us save the appeal to women's experience

    [59]Nancy C. M. Hartsock, "The Feminist Standpoint: Developing the Ground for a Specifically Feminist Historical Materialism," in *Feminism and Methodology: Social Science Issues*, ed. Sandra Harding (Bloomington: Indiana Univ. Press, 1987), 157–79.
    [60]Ruether, *Sexism and God-Talk*, 13, 12–46.

from the charge that this account of sexist language and scripture is adequate for a universal woman and the nature of her oppression and liberation. It would avoid the idea that something common to all women is being claimed. Women other than feminists would not be implicitly invoked, and we could assume their readings of texts are different simply because their location and the systems of meaning that construct them are different.

The form of appeal to women's experience exemplified in Ruether's account of revelation, however, is problematic, for experience mediates revelation and the external realities of location. This use entails a notion that experience is a medium that represents in the sense of miming, or making present realities of the divine and the realities of being a woman. The notion of experience underlying this formulation implicates women's experience in a realm prior to language and its specificity where all (women) meet the divine. To show that, let me explore the claim a moment. The appeal to revelation as something mediated by experience entails the convergence of the *external* as mediating, because symbols codify the experience of the divine and of the self and world, with the *self-evidential*, because experience confirms that these symbols no longer renew, or confirms that they are oppressive. This account of revelation perpetuates an inner-outer dualism: Experience is linguistic in the symbols and intuitive in the confirmation.

If my reading is correct, then this kind of appeal to women's experience as norm for feminist theology has affinities with the experiential expressivism which has been identified with the aspects of liberal theology that are negative precisely because they assume this prelinguistic realm of experience. Experiential expressivism is a theological type that defines symbols and doctrines and other forms of determinate traditions as the expression of human experience of the divine. These traditions mediate two phenomena: human experience and its intersection with the divine. This view assumes an inner human experience that is prelinguistic and shared by all humanity.[61]

The appeal to intuitive and freeing self-authenticating subjectivity has been powerful in some form or other since Descartes. In this case what is added is a twentieth-century development of the notion of

---

[61]George Lindbeck, *The Nature of Doctrine: Religion and Theology in a Postliberal Age* (Philadelphia: Westminster Press, 1984), 31–32. For an excellent criticism of the feminist appeal, see Sheila Greeve Davaney, "The Limits of the Appeal to Women's Experience," in *Shaping New Vision: Gender and Values in American Culture*, ed. Clarissa W. Atkinson, Constance H. Buchanan, and Margaret R. Miles, Harvard Women's Studies in Religion Series (Ann Arbor: UMI Research Press, 1987), 31–49.

experience—that which focuses on the self-authenticating testimony of immediacy, or internal experience. What is authenticated by internal experience is received as experiential data in the form of the impingement of external reality upon one's consciousness.[62] These two uses of experience are exactly what we find in Ruether's definition of experience and revelation. We have a subject who is constituted by social codes—the external mediation of experience as symbolic tradition—but who is also a consciousness free of language, a "private" subject as well that authenticates what is received.

The problems attendant with this latter use of experience are important for feminist appreciation of the "other." The appeal to experience can be a colonializing incorporation of the other in its experiential expressive form, even though it seems to work in feminist theology to deny the ahistorical character of revelation. While the authority of experience did have liberating effects in an Enlightenment setting, and it does suggest the historical and located character of religious traditions, it does so in a clumsy way that courts falsely universalizing claims. The prelinguistic realm of experience is the site for claims about commensurate experience; it is the place where those with the power to produce knowledge can claim a common religiousness or a common identity as human. When women's experience is used as a warrant for a claim, this implicitly grants that experience the status of a universal shared consciousness. It can thereby sponsor the accounts of oppressive and liberating texts and traditions as what women will/should find liberating and oppressive. This claim is at odds with the use of feminist women's experience, which could at least claim the located character of its judgment regarding sexist texts and go on to explore the conflicts and desire that are inextricable with power and meaning.

Self-authenticating subjectivity is hardly adequate to the commitment to social location feminists seek. Experiential expressivism as a type is an awkward fit at best (and George Lindbeck is a strange ally for my criticism, which is a feminist one). If an appeal to experience is problematic in the way I have just indicated, however, it is because the insights into language, power, and situatedness in this strand in feminist theology are not consistently carried through in relation to the appeal to women's experience. The particular form of cognitive oppression and liberation that is identified by feminists is not invalid. It is not, however, the only way that the constitutive nature of language

---

[62]Raymond Williams, *Keywords: A Vocabulary of Culture and Society*, rev. ed. (New York: Oxford Univ. Press, 1976, 1983), 126–29. See Joan Scott's critique of the use of experience in "The Evidence of Experience," *Critical Inquiry* 17:1 (Summer 1991): 773–97.

and the embeddedness of language in power can be theorized. It certainly cannot be maintained as a description that repects the postures of women in other social locations. If we took these particular "sexist texts" and contents and their pernicious working to be adequate to the work of patriarchy in all women's lives, we would have to assume that women who do not agree with such accounts are lobotomized by distorted discourse. Even an account that explains divergence by assuming women do not know how they are oppressed cannot be satisfied with the implication that women are rendered utterly passive as readers of the tradition. Without an account of instability, of desire and pleasure associated with language and power, we are even more at a loss to account for other women.

This is not to say that one cannot appeal to "women's experience."[63] Rather, it is to say that the judgment is relative to the site or conditions of the appeal (which, of course, most feminists have started to say more frequently). An appeal to women's experience is one thing within the context of a women's consciousness-raising group or other interpersonal setting. It is another thing altogether in an argument where certain rules about what counts as a legitimate warrant apply and where experience functions as the source of incorrigible data. In the site where theological knowledge is produced, the context of the academy, incorrigible data may well qualify for what counts as true, but intuitive women's experience will not likely be recognized even by such rules. An appeal to incorrigible data is necessarily *not* effective as part of a liberation epistemology.

Feminist theology must articulate new rules for the academy, not the least of which is a liberation epistemology that opens up interest in terms of power and location and the productive character of all other academic knowledges. Feminists' appeal to women's experience of the second sort courts an appeal to an evidence that we cannot scrutinize as we could if it were developed in accord with feminists' assumption that language is constitutive and articulated in terms of power and the systems of meaning that make it relevant to a particular social location.[64] Thus it will not be able to insist upon the produced character of

---

[63]One possibility, not explored here, is that pursued by Teresa de Lauretis, who uses Peircean semiotics to recover the term "women's experience." This is not unlike what I will do in chap. 2 with discourse. The point is to enlist a theory of signification in order to avoid the prediscursive mental space of Cartesian consciousness. See "Semiotics and Experience," in *Alice Doesn't: Feminism, Semiotics, Cinema* (Bloomington: Indiana Univ. Press, 1984), 158–86, 211–15.

[64]This does not preclude the use of "male" and "female" realities, as Susan Bordo insists, as an absolute academic law; but it does focus us on the "messier, more slippery, practical struggle to create institutions and communities that will not permit *some*

other academic knowledges. The feminist appeal funds an account of power—being named is determinate of one's being. Thus there is no question that the ability to scrutinize this evidence is important. One's class location might have an important effect on the account of language and power that made sense of one's oppression. Feminist theology can afford to explore a more adequate account of the constitutive nature of language and its embeddedness in power, one with more openness to other forms of harm.

Summary

With this survey of the insights of feminist theology that radicalize the critical hermeneutic of liberation theologians, we see that interest, language, and power are crucial to feminist theologians' analyses. These concerns inform feminists' analyses and indicate why feminist reflection could never be simply reduced to enlightened rationality. The answers of feminist theology to the question of *how* interest and location are embedded in knowledge, however, are incomplete. I conclude that the ambiguous nature of the appeal to women's experience in feminist liberation theology is problematic because it leaves open the possibility that "universal women's experience" is the warrant for identifying these forms of oppression and liberation.

Thus far I have identified basically three ways liberation feminists understand the effect of location on knowledge: (1) the insistence that all of the tradition is open to scrutiny, (2) the identification of specific bias with formulations that deny the full humanity of women, and (3) a will for change. I judge, however, that the inconsistencies that appeared along the way show that these are not sufficient to constitute a theory of located knowledge which can truly appreciate the difference in women's social locations. Despite the potential in some of its work, feminist theology does not adequately display three elements crucial to such a theory: (1) the link between systems of meaning and social location, (2) the coded subject, and (3) treatments of desire and conflict.

The gesture toward an account of language as constitutive is a correct impulse. The notion of the "sexist text" says that power is fundamental to language. This is also a fundamentally correct impulse. However, the inconsistent grasp of the located character of "women's

---

groups of people to make determinations about reality for *all*." "Feminism, Postmodernism, and Gender-Scepticism," in *Feminism/Postmodernism*, ed. Linda J. Nicholson (New York: Routledge, 1990), 142.

experience" shows that what is really going on in liberation feminist theology is an awareness of certain contents and ideas that are harmful to women's health. In short, what I find in the feminist theologians' treatment of the power of language is not, after all, an account of the constitutive character of language, one that explicates the discursive construction of all experience. Instead, feminist accounts can be taken to invoke an account of experience that is prior to language and therefore not subject to scrutiny with regard to its own location.

This means that as feminist theologians we are not able to display the relation of language and power to gender liberation and oppression, particularly when that means to show the impress of *its own location* on our formulations—certainly a necessary condition of speaking to a variety of locations. This is seen most decisively in the appearance of an uncoded subject assumed in the appeal to women's prelinguistic experience. The appeal to women's experience may signify the constructed nature of theology, but it does not yet portray how theology is the production of a cognitive practice. In sum, there is not an account of language, gender, and power in the liberation feminist theology I have inspected that is adequate to a thorough version of the located character of knowledge and to the project of institutional conversion.

To move ahead with feminist insights, we are faced with two issues with regard to the question of how interest is understood by relating language and gender and power in a more comprehensive fashion. The first problem is that of *language and its constitutive character* and how language situates the subject. Of the tendencies in feminist theologies, the appeal to "feminist" or located linguistic experience is the more promising for resolving this problem. Attention to the problem of language-constituting location leads to the second issue identified in this analysis, that of *the formulation of power*, inadequately presented here as a cognitive process, which works by effacing or symbolically obliterating (or affirming) women while ignoring conflict and desire. We need an adequate theory of language to situate women, which means we must ask how this is related to systems of meaning and the social relations that constitute and are part of the production of oppressive and liberating power.

In the next chapter, I will pursue a theory of discourse that takes up the first of these problems by offering an alternative to "women's experience." This theory will shed more light on what is at stake in the problematic appeal to subjects and texts that are conceived in modern ways, that is, as unlocated, prelinguistic experiencers who are able to escape the impress of interest or social sin.

2
Chapter

Feminist Theology: Language, Power, and Gender Reconsidered

> More than words . . . is all you have to do to make it real.
>
> — Extreme

> Let us not, therefore, ask why certain people want to dominate, what they seek, what is their overall strategy. . . . Rather than ask ourselves how the sovereign (patriarchy) appears to us in his (its) lofty isolation, we should try to discover how it is that subjects are gradually, progressively, really and materially constituted through a multiplicity of organisms, forces, energies, materials, desires, thoughts, etc. We should try to grasp subjection in its material instance as a constitution of subjects.
>
> — Michel Foucault

I argued in chapter 1 that feminist theology has an inadequate account of the relation of interest and location to knowledge, a problem that affects its capacity to reflect upon its own location and upon the difference in women's social locations. For an adequate account I must develop feminists' insights into the <u>constitutive power of language</u>, along with accompanying accounts of the nature of oppression and liberation. This means that a theory of language and power must move beyond the cognitive process that characterized much of the discussion of sexist discourse. The theory must provide an alternative to the use of the experiential-expressive version of feminist theology's appeal to women's experience.

Feminist poststructuralism: an apology

The feminist theory with the most to contribute regarding the problems with experiential appeals combines liberationist concerns with use of poststructuralist views of language. Other types of feminist theory, particularly liberal and radical or cultural feminism, still depend upon the experiential warrant to make their arguments and elaborate their visions.[1] In this chapter I draw from feminist thinking that employs poststructuralist discourse theory for liberation interests. Discourse theory, which understands language as a (but not the only) signifying process that constructs rather than represents reality, will allow me to sketch an alternative to the experiencing subject of feminist theology. That alternative is the discursively constructed subject position.

The view that discourse constructs subjects brings with it a way of thinking about the work of language to oppress and liberate different from that implied in feminist liberation theologies. It will offer a way to think about the constitutive nature of language and power that is more nuanced to the distinctive and located character of women's situations—the systems of meaning that constitute them—than that found in liberation feminist theological accounts. This alternative—an analytic of women's discourses—provides access to different forms of gender oppression and liberation. It also exposes more serious problems in the experiential expressivism manifested in feminist theological method. It is incomplete as the offering of an analytic for women's faith practice, however, without exploration of an alternative to the sexist or liberating text. Chapter 3 will complete my analytic by proposing the account of biblical texts that results from the turn to signifying processes and the implication of this analytic for processes of liberation and oppression.

First, some clarifications are in order. *Poststructuralism*, as distinguished from the more widely used term *postmodernism*, refers to a theory of language, of which the most well-known example is the

---

[1]The appeal to women's experience still figures in some Marxist and socialist feminisms. Standpoint theory, the feminist materialist position of Nancy Hartsock, is a case in point. Some of the more recent versions of such theories use poststructuralist work, however, and are not identified with the appeal in the same way as liberal and radical-cultural feminisms are. This may be because these latter two contain views of the essential subject, either "neutral" in the case of liberalism or "woman" in the case of radical-cultural feminism. Such a view does not lend itself easily to totally constructionist accounts. For a helpful account of different types of feminist theory (not including poststructuralist feminism), see Alison M. Jaggar, *Feminist Politics and Human Nature* (Sussex, England: Harvester Press; and Totowa, N.J.: Rowman & Allanheld, 1983).

practice of deconstruction. Postmodernism, a cultural logic, is typically associated with aesthetics, but often used loosely to refer to a host of reactions to the modern. The issue of women and respecting difference — the problem of the false universal — has to do with the constitutive character of language for "experience." Therefore the label *postmodern* is not a helpful way to identify my analysis, except to say that poststructuralism is a refusal of a view of language (and, by extension, a subject) typically identified with the modern.[2] Thus my critique is not directly postmodern, nor is it directly allied with Jacques Derrida, given the use of the term *theology* in deconstruction for the very language/knowledge practices I am criticizing. My aims are unabashedly liberationist and theological, a term that I will assume can work more transgressively than simply as an exemplary metaphysics of presence.[3]

With these qualifications, is it possible to "use" poststructuralism for liberationist theological purposes? I think it is, but an apology is in order for what may appear an eclectic proposal. Although long past its prime in France where it originated in the 1960s, poststructuralism was picked up by English-speaking literary and cultural theorists in the 1970s and is still important in feminist theory. One reason for the feminist appropriation of poststructuralist theory is that the use of gender and women's experience to identify patriarchy in the 1970s has produced claims about the universality of phallocentrism — claims that

---

[2]The term *postmodernism* is used broadly; frequently, it includes some form of poststructuralism. See Jean-Francois Lyotard or Fredric Jameson for theorists of the postmodern and Jacques Derrida, Jacques Lacan, Julia Kristeva, and Michel Foucault for poststructuralism. See "Introduction" in *After Philosophy: End or Transformation?* ed. Kenneth Baynes, James Bohman, and Thomas McCarthy (Cambridge, Mass.: MIT Press, 1987), 1–18, for an overview of the linguistic turn and its various forms: poststructuralism, postanalytic philosophy, hermeneutics, and critical theory. Regarding the epistemic aspects of the modern, see Timothy J. Reiss, *The Discourse of Modernism* (Ithaca, N.Y.: Cornell Univ. Press, 1982). The relation of the term *modernism* to aesthetics is, of course, entirely different.

[3]In Derrida's works and other poststructuralist writings, the term *theological* stands for practices grounded in the "transcendental signified" (meanings that are fully present and self-enclosed), for which the sign "God" is considered exemplary. See Jacques Derrida, *Of Grammatology*, trans. Gayatri Chakravorty Spivak (Baltimore: Johns Hopkins Univ. Press, 1974), 49–50; *Position*, trans. Alan Bass (Chicago: Univ. of Chicago Press, 1981), 19–20; *Writing and Difference*, trans. Alan Bass (London: Routledge and Kegan Paul, 1978), 136. There are several accounts of the relationship between Derridean poststructuralism and theology, the practice of religious reflection: Mark C. Taylor, *Erring: A Postmodern A/Theology* (Chicago: Univ. of Chicago Press, 1984); Kevin Hart, *The Trespass of the Sign: Deconstruction, Theology and Philosophy* (Cambridge: Cambridge Univ. Press, 1989). In contrast to Taylor's death-of-God account and the negative theology account of others, Hart (p. xi) offers an account of deconstruction as "an answer to the theological demand for a 'non-metaphysical theology.' "

are unnuanced with respect to the complexities of race, class, and other identities. "Women" is simply not a universal state of victimization, as women of color and so-called Third World women testify.[4] Euro-American feminists have begun to respond in self-critical ways as the deleterious effects of their universalizing claims are exposed. This process has been aided by the radical undermining of unities made possible by poststructuralism and by a recognition of the exhaustively coded (or textual) nature of reality.

The Euro-American feminist self-critical posture generated by poststructuralism has not gone unremarked. Susan Bordo calls it "gender scepticism," the suspicion of gender as a false universal. Gender scepticism casts a hypercritical and nuanced eye on the differently nuanced meaning of "woman" through history. A typical book, in fact, bears the question "Am I That Name?" regarding "women" as its title.[5] Some feminists raise concerns about what they see as an extremist reaction of self-criticism. Tania Modleski warns of the disappearance of women from feminism, a tendency she observes when the employment of poststructuralism in its deconstructive form appears to aid the conservative backlash against women in culture and the wider social formation of the '90s.[6] Another feminist points out a certain irony in poststructuralism's ostensible correction of Cartesianism. If the sin of the dualism in the Cartesian subject was the idealizing of a "view from nowhere"—the essence of male rationality—the movement of poststructuralism is hardly an improvement, the argument goes. Poststructuralism, with its valorization of multiplicity, indeterminacy, and heterogeneity, continually displays the instability of any text or any subject. Poststructuralism thus funds the "view from everywhere." An erasure of the body is effected when poststructuralism works to celebrate difference and multiplicity. This, Bordo warns, is a

---

[4]Such writers as Chandra Mohanty, Trinh T. Minh-Ha, and Gayatri Chakravorty Spivak employ poststructuralism to expose the colonializing effects of white feminists' use of "women's experience" to investigate "Third World women."

[5]Susan Bordo, "Feminism, Postmodernism, and Gender-Scepticism," in *Feminism/Postmodernism*, ed. Linda J. Nicholson (New York: Routledge, 1990), 133–56. Denise Riley, *Am I That Name? Feminism and the Category of "Women" in History* (Minneapolis: Univ. of Minnesota Press, 1988).

[6]Tania Modleski, *Feminism without Women: Culture and Feminism in a "Postfeminist" Age* (New York: Routledge, 1991). Modleski brings together the conversation and debate in a helpful way, even if she does not probe the real possibilities of feminist poststructuralist criticism. The use of poststructuralism has been controversial in all the fields where it has been employed: in feminist historical work and philosophy, as well as in feminist cultural and literary studies (domains in which it is most prominent). Feminist historian Joan Scott, for example, has been highly criticized for her use of poststructuralism.

dangerous bypassing of the realities of bodied limits—of always being somewhere and constrained.[7]

These warnings are well heeded and will shape my use of poststructuralism. Whether it depends upon appeals to women's experience or not, the generative context of feminist theory is commitment to the liberation of women along with conviction of the dominance of patriarchal power in contemporary and past social arrangements.[8] The specifics of these claims about feminism are clearly contested in this wave of criticisms of essentialist tendencies in the use of "woman." I will assume, however, that continued self-identification with the term *feminist* indicates a theorist who understands change as the point of theorizing and has the entrenched social forms of male hegemony as a target. The givens of late twentieth-century life are still textured by asymmetries of power and resources that are based on gender as well as class and race. A view from everywhere can never get at such realities. Such a context, as Bordo and Modleski warn, dictates a careful use of poststructuralism.

Moreover, my analysis is a theological reading of the convergence of interest and knowledge, one that views these issues with the grammar of theo/acentric finitude. Thus my agenda for this debate is somewhat more complicated than negotiating loyalty to feminism with the risks of literary theory. Poststructuralist accounts of language help theologians display the embeddedness of readings and practices in networks of meaning (and, by implication, power). My theo/acentric grammar of social finitude focuses on forms of oppression, the possibilities for liberation in those situations, and the way in which traditions of faith are a guiding rubric. The benefit of poststructuralism to these liberation-theological interests is not its potential to defer meaning forever or undermine unities endlessly. The benefit is rather its ability to expose the kind of finitude and danger that attend our transitional unities. This merits elaboration.

I have in some sense misspoken when I refer to the "use" of poststructuralism as if it were a hermeneutical choice that I, a free subject, take up and utilize as one of a number of hermeneutical options. As Jane Tompkins points out, poststructuralism is not one of a number of methods that one can pick up and put down at will. Rather a poststructuralist account of language shows how "I" am used by a signi-

---

[7]Bordo, "Feminism, Postmodernism," 136–45.

[8]For a helpful, brief definition of *feminist* that highlights the political commitment, see Toril Moi, "Feminist, Female, Feminine," in *The Feminist Reader: Essays in Gender and the Politics of Literary Criticism*, ed. Catherine Belsey and Jane Moore (New York: Basil Blackwood, 1984), 117–32.

fying process already operative. It dissolves the discrete "objects" of subjects, texts, methods, and interpretations into "a single, evolving field of discourse." This dissolution of everything into discourse or "textuality" does not mean that we cannot posit unities, such as subjects and texts, but that we must take account of the embedded, constructed, and political character of the "objects" that emerge. According to structuralism (semiotics and poststructuralism alike), the authorizing of any particular discourse, text, or signifying process does not come from its referents or its origins, as Wesley Kort points out, but from the discourse itself.[9]

What literary theory says with regard to the unavailability of extradiscursive foundations for knowledge has resonances with a theo/acentric grammar. There is a theological logic that leads to a parallel agreement that theological knowledge is nonfoundational as well. The "must" comes from the logic of a grammar which not only requires that entities be accorded a nonabsolute status, but that they be employed to honor the created goodness of the "neighbor." It is this embeddedness in processes of meaning that helpfully evokes what Christians mean (or ought to mean) by situatedness and finitude.[10]

A theological analysis carried out by way of the inescapability of the signifying processes or social codes that construct us all is able to portray three features of a liberation theological grammar of finitude. (1) Compared to the notion that language represents or corresponds to reality, it is better suited to display the bondage of sin and how that bondage is enmeshed in those specific processes. (2) Liberating transgressions of that bondage can be identified in the discursive possibilities of the situation, rather than in a freedom external to a situation. (3) The constitutive, embedded character of subjects suggests that Christian perspectives are distinctive, yet not universalizable. They are distinctive because they create subject positions not available to others; conversely, Christians literally are not in the position to articulate hegemonic accounts of "human experience." These three aspects of the constitutive character of codes do not legitimate Christian theologizing but neither can they disprove it. While feminist theologians have not displayed these convictions with language theory, it is

---

[9]Jane Tompkins, "A Short Course in Post-structuralism," *College English* 50:7 (November 1988): 733. Wesley A. Kort, *Bound to Differ: The Dynamics of Theological Discourses* (University Park: Pennsylvania State Univ. Press, 1992), 30–36.

[10]One cannot say here that what poststructuralists mean by the "différance" that makes distinctions possible *is* the Christian principle of finitude. The former is not a principle or a theory. See Jacques Derrida, "Différance," in *Margins of Philosophy*, trans. Alan Bass (Chicago: Univ. of Chicago Press, 1982), 3–27. Tompkins explains "différance," "A Short Course," 739–47.

high time that we, for whom language is such a constitutive reality, did so.

Employment of poststructuralism as an account of language (meaning) has served a number of feminists outside of theological conversations well. As a move away from representational views of language, poststructuralism allows them to identify and destabilize the practices that fall prey to the naturalizing of discourse.[11] It allows the destabilizing of subjects and texts, which will be exactly the two moves feminist theology needs in order to advance toward a position that can respect difference. By recognizing the textual or coded nature of all of reality, we can perceive its conventional or made character, then look at the existing forms of unity granted texts and subjects and the systems of meaning that create them, and discover their cracks and occlusions in order to press the possibilities for change. We may, as it were, pose new kinds of "objects" or unities whose liberating character will have meaning only in relation to the positions they challenge. We will not expect these "objects" to escape the fragility and risks of their location, however; they, like any other, cannot be absolutized.

We should look now at the emergence of the notion that everything is textual—"a single, evolving field of discourse," as Tompkins puts it, in order to show how subjects are not stable sites of meaning. Feminist concern with the existent situations of gender oppression will move the analysis to a question that poststructuralism by itself does not answer. We need to know how specific meanings are produced for a feminist analytic that will enable more radical questioning of the things which constitute gender oppression and liberation. For that I will theorize discourse as a communicative event that can occur even with the destabilized subject, woman. Because my question concerns the possibilities for liberation, we must understand these two seem-

---

[11]As indicated in the earlier discussion, naturalization is one of the functions of ideology. It occurs when the assumptions of a community or social order are allowed to remain invisible as assumptions, making them appear true and beyond question. Beliefs are naturalized when they seem to reflect the very order of things; for example, views that woman has "natural" domestic duties suited to the "natural" fit of her body and nature to the needs of the child. One of Derrida's first targets for deconstruction was the prioritizing of speaking over writing, as he exposed the fallacy of the assumption that the presence of the speaking subject grants transparency to the "real meaning." In the denaturalization of the assumption that spoken language provides the full presence of meaning, poststructuralism goes far beyond sociology of knowledge; it requires a skeptical posture toward the assumed transparency of any form of discourse, the investigator's as well, not simply the belief systems of a social order. For feminists, the naturalization of discourse is inimical, for the possibilities of sustaining the status quo and its oppressions lie first and foremost in the assumption that the beliefs that support women's subordination or the unnaturalness of the homosexual are "transparent to the real." Derrida, *Of Grammatology.*

ingly contradictory things: how the subject does not control meaning and also how change occurs through the processes of meaning . . . how subject woman "produces" emancipatory meanings at the same time that sexist ones are produced "over her head," so to speak.

In what follows I will argue that an understanding of language as an unstable process of signifying is helpful to feminist thinking about the conventional nature of reality. Reality is coded or textual, rather than constructed out of nonsemiotic terms like empirical objects and experience or consciousness. Poststructuralist criticism helps in rethinking three domains that are operative in feminist theologians' inadequate treatments of language, gender, and power: (1) the theory of language as representation; (2) the Cartesian/experiencing subject; and (3) the relation of power to discourse. As we move out of modern ways to conceive the three domains, alternative possibilities will emerge for conceiving women as producers of meaning and of the workings of power.

From representing to signifying

The linguistic turn incorporates a variety of kinds of language theory, all of which are aimed at undermining the Cartesian and Kantian notions of the subject with their unlocated and prediscursive (transcendentally grounded) consciousness. The most important shift in language theory for feminist analysis, however, is that which occurred in the move from diachronic or historical views of language to synchronic linguistics. Thus I begin my brief account of a discourse theory by reference to the initial breakthrough of Saussurean linguistics, which enabled the emergence of poststructuralism. Ferdinand de Saussure answered two important questions: What is language? and How is it produced? His answers initiate the move away from representation and carry an implicit view of language that best fits the current assumptions of feminist theology. Review of these two questions leads to further questions about power and the relation of language to the social formation.[12]

The accomplishments of postmodern linguistic theories come from the radical possibilities set into motion by Saussurean linguistics. The importance of this trajectory of language theory is not that it was the

---

[12]I am not appropriating French feminists' approaches to gender and power. Although the work of Hélène Cixous, Luce Irigaray, and Julia Kristeva would be relevant, I find the work of Foucault and John Frow on discourse and institutionalities to be more accessible to the kind of criticisms I wish to mount.

only one. Others made inquiries into the constitutive nature of language and did so for similar reasons—for example, to avoid a transcendental consciousness, the Cartesian subject, or the subject-object dichotomy. Continental hermeneutical theory from Husserlian phenomenology through Martin Heidegger, Ludwig Wittgenstein, and Hans-Georg Gadamer took language seriously as a route away from the Cartesian subject. Edmund Husserl at least recognized the intersubjectivity of consciousness. The route from Ferdinand de Saussure, Swiss linguist of the early twentieth century, however, has led to theories that bring to prominence the codedness, the differential signifying or textual nature, of all of reality.

Saussure argued that the synchronic components that make meaning are more important for understanding language than are the diachronic, or the history of words. (His insights were not singular; Charles Peirce developed parallel views as the science of semiotics. Although they worked separately, Peirce and Saussure produced sign theories of language that corrected representational accounts of language.) Synchronic linguistics offered alternatives to the idea that language consists of labels or descriptions that match up with extralinguistic objects, that language or some form of language provides access to reality in a direct or incorrigible fashion. Sign theories determine that language consists of signs which make meaning in relation to other signs.

The move to sign systems redirects the trajectory of investigation. To say that a sign makes meaning by means of other signs affirms the conventional character of meaning processes. To understand a sign, one does not look for its empirical referent; nor does one reduce language to its simplest incorrigible components; nor do signs reflect or represent the inner self/consciousness. As Fredric Jameson says of Saussure, "The lines of flight of his system are lateral, from one sign to another, rather than frontal, from word to thing."[13] (For Peirce, the route through other signs is traced through the process of semiosis, where a sign is linked to its object by means of a third element, the interpretant. The interpretant can itself become a sign, so the process of meaning continues infinitely without ever reaching an incorrigible fact outside of the [social] signifying process.) For Saussure, the process occurs somewhat differently, for language is a system of differences. The creation of signs occurs by virtue of the inseparably connected signifier (acoustic image—/woman/) and signified (mental

---

[13]Fredric Jameson, "The Linguistic Model," in *Language and Politics*, ed. Michael J. Shapiro (New York: New York Univ. Press, 1984), 187.

image of a woman), which have meaning as a sign "woman" in its relation of differences from other signs, such as "man." Meaning happens in a process of opposition, a process that occurs at a variety of levels, semantic and phonetic: man from woman, cat from cap, the singular from the plural, and so on. For both theories, however, words as signs are only able to mean by virtue of their relationships to other signs.[14]

In the move from views of language as representation to signification, Saussure and Peirce refute the idea of a natural language. A number of theories (e.g., early Wittgenstein, Bertrand Russell, Gottlob Frege) held that language "pictures" the world. Sign theories are alternatives as well to the notion that language expresses human experience or consciousness. The subject itself, as Peirce says in refutation of Cartesian subjectivity, is a sign.[15] Saussure and Peirce tell us what language is *not*: it is not labels for reality as such, or a medium transparent to reality, a lens to bring consciousness and ideas together. It is not the reflection of an a priori experiencing consciousness. Language *is* a process of signifying. As signs, words are only able to mean in networks of signifying relationships. Words or descriptions, even what appear to be the most natural kinds of claims, are not defined by their correspondence to space-time entities, but to each other and their associations.

To see what is revolutionary about the notion of signifying, we need to understand how signs make meaning. Here Peirce is a helpful foil to help focus on Saussure's contribution and the trajectory of poststructuralism. For Peirce, the semiotic process occurs by means of infer-

---

[14]Ferdinand de Saussure's opponent was linguistics as a historical enterprise. He opposed the positivism of a purely diachronic interest in language with the synchronic model where the identity-difference polarity is the condition of meaning. The capacity to distinguish these differences is what makes identity possible; the meaning of any term is dependent upon it not-being something else. An important work was his (posthumously produced) *A Course in General Linguistics*, ed. C. Bally and A. Sechehaye in collaboration with A. Reidlinger, trans. Wade Baskin (New York: Philosophical Library, 1959). On Saussure, see Jonathan Culler, *Ferdinand de Saussure*, rev. ed. (Ithaca, N.Y.: Cornell Univ. Press, 1986). For a helpful explanation of the fundamental insights of Saussure's breakthrough, along with its inherent limitations, see Jameson, "The Linguistic Model," 168–92.

[15]Peirce replaced the Cartesian subject with the sign, arguing that we cannot have an immediate intuition of our self-consciousness; all knowledge or cognition depends on a prior cognition made possible by inferring a relation of signs. See his 1868 essays, "Questions Concerning Certain Faculties Claimed for Man" and "Some Consequences of Four Incapacities," in *Peirce on Signs: Writings on Semiotic by Charles Sanders Peirce*, ed. James Hoopes (Chapel Hill: Univ. of North Carolina Press, 1991), 34–53, 54–86. See also Walter Benn Michaels, "The Interpreter's Self: Peirce on the Cartesian 'Subject,' " *Georgia Review* 31:2 (Summer 1977): 383–402.

ences, the connections between signs. The potentially infinite nature of semiosis comes to a temporary halt because the making of meaning yields what Peirce calls a habit, a much-practiced series of associations between signs.[16] For Saussure there is an arbitrariness to the relation between signifier and signified and between signs that is not resolved by an appeal to a reality external to signs. In contrast to Peirce, the intersection with concrete practice is not the grounding of meaning in Saussure's account.[17] Actual meaning is grounded by viewing language as a system. Thus a sign is composed of an acoustic image — the signifier — and the concept with which it is paired — the signified; there is no natural relation between the two. The signifier /cat/ and the signified "cat," a furry mammal categorized as feline, constitute a sign that has no given meaning, no essential definition, except as produced in a system of differences. *Cat* is a sign that gets its meaning in oppositional phonetic relation to /bat/, /hat/, and so on; in oppositional semantic relation to *dog, tiger, leopard,* and so on. Moreover, it is only the North American English language as a system (*langue*) that grants these identities.

For difference to matter, of course, we need to say *how* "cat" differs, or, to put it another way, what differential systems are most important.[18] For a feminist interest in meaning, the point that difference is inherently a relational social judgment is best understood by reference to semantic oppositions. For North American communities the oppositions are more likely to be with breeds of animals found on that

---

[16]Saussure, *A Course in General Linguistics.* I depend here on a helpful analysis of Peirce on habit: Teresa de Lauretis, "Semiotics and Experience," in *Alice Doesn't: Feminism, Semiotics, Cinema* (Bloomington: Indiana Univ. Press, 1984), 158–88, esp. 168–86. Also see Thomas E. Lewis, "Reference and Dissemination: Althusser after Derrida," *Diacritics* 15:4 (Winter 1985): 37–56.

[17]Shapiro compares the two and suggests that the closest thing in Saussure to Peirce's "interpretant" is the notion of linguistic value. Michael Shapiro, *The Sense of Grammar: Language as Semeiotic* (Bloomington: Indiana Univ. Press, 1983), 7. Saussure is not totally consistent; on occasion he contradicts himself regarding the principle that language is only differences, or negativity, by positing some positive terms in language. See *Course (1916),* trans. Wade Baskin (London: Fontana, 1974), 120–21.

[18]For a helpful explanation, see Jane Tompkins's "A Short Course." She elaborates the more sophisticated version of "differences" that Derrida develops out of the succinct Saussurean version. For Derrida, the term *différance* is the nonword which stands for the differential process that makes us able to hear and understand oppositionally constructed meaning. If we refuse to concede that the practice of attributing the signifier /cat/ to a furry animal is a signifying process that depends on differences (that cat is an icon for /cat/), we have the problem that for another community this reference would not work; *gato* or *chat* in fact would coincide with that furry animal. A more fundamental difficulty is that the communities could just as easily have defined that physical thing as "dog." This problematizes even more the assumption that a clear extrarelational foundation exists for the reference.

continent; in the Tibetan highlands the conventions would be different. The point is clear, however: the meaning of a sign is its position in
a system of differences. When we move to systems of differences to
account for meanings, we imply that the world is a set of semiotic systems of differences, that one cannot get behind the signifying to some
reality in itself. We know what *cat* is, not because there is a third term,
a reality to which *cat* refers that founds us securely in a basis from
which to move on and make distinctions. *Cat* is rather a term whose
meaning is utterly dependent upon its relation to a host of words that
we already know that make *cat* appear (*rat, fat, sat*, and so on). The *c* is
something because it is not *r* or *f* or *s*. It is dependent upon an English-
speaking community that has, at one point in its history, put together
(figuratively speaking) a convention to use a set of letters to represent
sounds to do the work of indicating a certain set of animal characteristics. Thus an elaborate set of relations lies behind the assumption that
it is obvious what *cat* is and how it is different from *bat*.

If the rules about the relationships of components of a language determine the meaning of signs, differential relations are inextricable
with the meaning–making process. Differences constituted by these
rules seem to have no other positive source than the system, and the
system is a given without origins as well. This relatively unsatisfactory way to account for positive meaning is a source of Saussure's
structuralism. However, the valuable insight that it contains for our
feminist interests (and what makes his work important for poststructuralists and moves Saussure away from Peirce) is this notion of the
nonsubstantive, non–content-based nature of signs. The differential or
relational character of meaning is its synchronic and nondenominative
nature. As any learner of a foreign language knows, one must know
the language's system of relating terms and sounds—the differences—in order to understand it.

Saussure (and poststructuralists after him) gives an additional
answer, then, to the question, What is language? Language is a system
of oppositional differences. In this case the definition foregrounds in
another way the fundamental difference of sign theory from representational notions of language. Representational views assume that content is associated with language, that language (or some privileged
forms of language) names "real" objects, space-time entities or facts.
The former understands that what is peculiar about language is its
nonsubstantial character, or, put positively, that language is, like other
forms of intelligibility, differential relations. The implications of sign
theory are that signs are to be understood by their location, their work
or function in a system, or within the bounded process of signification
in which they occur. Although feminist use of this account will want

to talk about the particular meanings that come to be associated with signs, my point here is that a representational account of the language-content relation will not do this satisfactorily. Only this initial recognition of arbitrariness will support a later move to the site of production and the political critiques feminists require. Only the initial assumption that all meanings are conventional will allow us to maintain consistently that all discourse has the property of finitude.

key

Repositioning feminist inquiry

How is this move to signifying beneficial to feminist thinking? The replacement of the notion of *nomenclature* with *differences* in accounting for language, argues Catherine Belsey, created the revolutionary trajectory for linguistics after Saussure.[19] Feminist inquiry is repositioned by this theory with regard to gender meanings in significant ways. If language is a system of conventionally constructed, differential signs rather than labels for extradiscursive realities, we cannot turn to naturalized accounts of gender proposed by religious communities or academic disciplines, nor can we go to so-called natural bodies to discover the meanings associated with women's oppression and liberation. Signs for gender direct us to other signs, from "woman" to "man" and to other significations and the differences constituted by them, which are crucial to understanding what "woman" might mean. There are no given, natural entities, such as subjects, methods, or textual objects, once we recognize that these entities are constructed in discursive fields of difference. The analytical path of representation, which directs us from "woman" to the real thing—to the extralinguistic object named by the label—is a dead end.[20] "Woman" only has meaning in its relation to the system of discourse in which it is constructed, most typically in relation to "man." Thus, "woman/female/feminine" are what is "not man/not male/not masculine."

Judith Butler helps us see the force of this shift to the textuality of reality for feminist analysis.[21] In her work to subvert the hegemonies of heterosexuality, Butler discusses the problems of representation that

---

[19]Catherine Belsey, *Critical Practice* (London: Methuen, 1980), 38.

[20]Modleski, however, thinks that the poststructuralist concern with signifying is problematic because it takes women out of feminism, and that the shift to gender studies (over feminist studies) is detrimental as well, linked as it somehow is to poststructuralist anti-identity concerns. See Modleski, *Feminism without Women*, 14–15.

[21]Judith Butler, *Gender Trouble: Feminism and the Subversion of Identity* (New York: Routledge, 1990).

come with the appeal to woman, the appeal that has for so long defined feminist politics. Her voice is one of several criticizing
essentialism—the various ways of identifying something as basic to or
definitional of woman—an assumption clearly important to the forging of commonalities upon which to build a liberation movement.
Butler's antiessentialism, however, is distinctive from many other
challenges to "essentialist" feminisms (those that remain content with
challenging constructions of gender) because it explores the importance of the poststructuralist turn to signifying.[22]

Implicit in the criticism of the false universal subject is the idea that
the use of "women" as the identifying rubric for feminist politics
commits its most obvious error when it assumes that women have the
same needs insofar as it assumes that they share the same identity. The
more subtle problem, however, is that identity politics relies upon representational notions of language that would direct our attention to the
thing outside the sign. This engages us in a fruitless search—as if we
could define a "real woman" outside of a particular language and the
differential systems of meaning employed. What is worse, identity
politics reinforces the binary man-woman. The terrain of "real
woman" assumed as a natural or self-evident thing outside of language is precisely the site already filled in by oppressive definitions.
One has only to think of the cultural fill-ins for the phrase "real man"
to realize the oppositional features that already define "real woman."
Questions such as Who has the power to define male/female? and Who
has the power to define bodies? are ignored in the continually unchallenged assumption that signs re-present the thing. Representational assumptions fail to trace out the full map of signifying relations that
construct "woman," the differences that are hidden or erased, and the
implications of these meanings for the distribution of power. Butler
poses sharply, then, the importance of the shift to signification.

I have already moved beyond Saussure's formulation in this analysis. The Saussurean account is inadequate not only because differences
are articulated in it as if in a closed system of meaning, but also because
the signifier is a concept, a mental image. If we think of his initial
breakthrough as one that makes it possible to consider language as a

---

[22]Such feminisms as cultural or radical feminism are well known for their responses
to both patriarchal definitions of reality and to liberal feminism. In the former some
essential woman is given a divinely ordained or natural place and denigrated in the
myriad of ways available to a dominant discourse. In the latter, the appeal to equality,
the ostensible sameness of women and men, effectively denigrates women. Radical
feminism valorizes woman in response, yet courts the very biological essentialism that
characterized the worst of antiwoman theories. See Jaggar, *Feminist Politics and Human
Nature*, 27–50, 83–122, 173–206, 249–302.

game, its grammar analogous to rules, then we acknowledge that this makes available the theoretical insight that the signifer "woman" only has meaning according to the rules of the game—for instance, in relation to differences with such signs as "man." This insight is helpful because one can imagine the produced rather than natural meaning that is attached to signs for gender. The "rules," as it were, are suggestive of the social construction, and the potential social conflict, that lies behind the processes of rule-making. Saussure's account, however, does not allow access to the rule-making, the site of production. Its structural idealism prevents it from moving to an analysis of the deeply ingrained practices, codes, and social relations that constitute the "rules" and that alter and fill in these relations. Butler assumes these practices must be part of the analysis.

There are no closed grammars, no languages or sign systems that construct the meaning of gender, for there are always openings, fissures, and intersections with other signifying patterns. In a word, the crucial insight that meaning occurs in a differential system is only a condition of meaning; it is inadequate as a sole determiner of meaning. The inadequacy of the sign system is precisely the need for entry into the places where meaning is produced. The correlational constituents of meaning are not simply the signified as concept, but signifying processes embedded in social relations, which are not only embedded in but indistinguishable from social practices. We must take the principle of difference and move feminist analysis out of this structuralism.

Textuality and discourse analysis

One way out of the closed system is recognition of the textuality of reality, where "textuality" is a metaphor for the inescapability of signifying process. As process, textuality is not predetermined by deep structures that control meaning. A post-Saussurean formulation of the arbitrary nature of meaning retains the principle that the signifier precedes the signified, the wedge against natural language that characterized the radical potential of structuralism. This principle is disruptive of any attempt to seal off the signifying process permanently.[23] Every "inside" has an "outside," any identity an "other," a proposal for unity of meaning an excluded supplemental. However firmly fixed a

---

[23]Without being identical, deconstructionist approaches are poststructuralist, the most noted figure being Jacques Derrida. For the view that there is no distinction worth making between structuralism and poststructuralism, see Philip Lewis, "The Post-Structuralist Condition," *Diacritics* 12 (Spring 1982): 2–22.

language, a grammar, or a technical vocabulary may be, some alteration is inevitable as long as signifying processes come into contact with other languages. Even the most insular technical vocabulary is parasitic on signifying practices of its location, if only because the appearance of any pronouns, the enunciating subject, implicates that vocabulary in the transient, local meanings of its utterance—the "I," "you," the "here," "there." That dependence alters it, potentially in a long-term way.[24]

In taking the route away from Saussure's structuralism, however, the value of poststructuralism is not the loss of pattern or structure altogether, but its function to destabilize a *dominant* signifying pattern. A post-Saussurean analysis will respect the arbitrary or nonnatural character of meaning, then, by virtue of its recognition of gaps and openings in meanings. We need a new set of distinctions, however, to think about this. Saussure's notions of values and relationality as replacements of substances or entities are not enough to get at positive meaning. It is insufficient just to say that all of reality is coded by signifying, that all of reality is textual.

For a feminist theological analysis, meaning is in some crucial respects not arbitrary at all. The openness and indeterminacy of discourse needs to be identified so that the cracks and openings for slippage can be identified in a politically and theologically useful way. Thus feminist analysis, moving from the signifier "woman" to other signs, again raises the question of the production of meaning, the ordering of signification. Judgments about production, about patterns and the way in which different conventions are already in place are necessary to an analytic of discourse. One that can attend to existent conventions will lead inevitably to issues of power.

Primary issues in the production of signs have to do with the site and the unit of analysis. Actual communication, or the setting of conversation, is the place of entry into a specific game of signifying. In the break from the system as generative of signifying linguistic analysis after Saussure, what Saussure called the *parole* takes center stage as the site of the production of meaning. Thus, to take a self-consciously sit-

---

[24]Theological grammar—liturgical vocabulary, for example—is parasitic upon the value of "I" and "we" in a particular location. This is one of the obviously changing sets of signifiers in almost any discourse, not simply in the sense that different persons fill the spaces of the pronouns, but in that the meaning of the "I" as a space for anyone changes. Simply noting historical variance is not the point. There is an opening here for a more poststructuralist unraveling of the unity of the discourse.

uated approach to the analysis of signifying we must engage in discourse analysis—an analysis of communicative practice.

This change in the site where meaning is generated also dictates a
change in the significant unit of analysis. It is the statement, rather
than the sign and its binary, that better encompasses the meanings at
stake in differential networks.[25] The turn to discourse does not mean
we abandon the important ways in which binary signs, such as "man-
woman," do the work of constructing realities. However, it widens
the range of signifying we explore to domains of meanings that incorporate statements and their relational effects. Discourse encompasses
any signifying or meaning-making element and the discovery of the
different meanings that such binaries as "man-woman" may have in
different "statements."[26]

Discourse analysis gets us to a site of production: utterance or writing. We require more than the appeal to conversation, however, to
benefit from the radical shifts made possible by the notion that meaning is made via differential systems. If signs make meaning in differential relations, it is not the case that we should simply analyze the
dialogues women have, or the semantically oppositional statements
made by and about them. Rather, we must analyze situations of utterance as the intersections of differential systems of meaning and the
rules that order them. In the turn to discourse we do not lose the insights that generated the revolutionary trajectory of the sign, but we
must examine more complicated differential associations.

Let us take, for example, discourse about what it means to be a
"real woman." In a system of cultural rules for "real sexual identities," "woman" might be defined as "not-man," a binary that disval-
ues "woman." The binary is further specified by associations of
femininity with softness, gentleness, and passivity in opposition to associations of masculinity with hardness, brashness, roughness, and aggressiveness. This differential system of meaning never exists by itself,
however, but intersects with other systems of meaning that construct
actual "women." A differential system of meaning found in Christian
discourse about human beings, for example, constitutes being a person
out of notions of uniqueness, value, sacredness, and so forth, meanings
created differentially in opposition to the nonperson or to nature.

---

[25]Emile Benveniste, *Problems in General Linguistics* (Miami: Univ. of Miami Press,
1971); see esp. "Subjectivity in Language," 223–30. See also Diane McDonnell, *Theories
of Discourse Analysis: An Introduction* (Oxford: Basil Blackwell, 1986).
[26]McDonnell, *Theories of Discourse Analysis*, 1–23. See Wesley Kort's use of discourse
to refer to theologies in *Bound to Differ*.

Discourse about the goodness of persons does not mean anything, however, until it is used in a situation where it intersects with other meanings. In a situation where such meanings intersect with the discourse of binary gender identity, for example, signs about the value of persons may be taken to apply to both men and women — unless, of course, rules exist that specifically deny personhood to women. The point here is that the meanings (or "statements") that define a subject in one system of differences carry over for subjects when they are defined by other networks of meaning. The associations in any one system of meaning — in this case that of real sexual identities — will be evoked in the other systems with which it inevitably intersects.

These convergences of a variety of differential systems account for the instabilities of meaning that characterize communities, and the fact that what it means to be "woman" changes from one community to another. Christian communities formed by the discourses of liberalism and equality that shaped U.S. national self-understandings were able to live for at least two centuries with the contradiction between Christian discourses about the value of all persons and discourses about women's subordinate state. The potential egalitarian effects of associations between the liberal and religious discourses and gender remained dormant for the majority, and the dictum "all men are created equal" remained gender-specific. But it was an unstable convergence of meanings as the resistances of Elizabeth Cady Stanton and Matilda Joslyn Gage made clear. The associations with gender eventually exposed the conflicts and transformed gender discourses so that women became part of the theoretical class of "equal" subjects.

To capture the fact theoretically that situations of utterance or usage are the place where meanings come into being, we need another alteration in the terms of sign theory. As my example suggests, political liberalism, Christian anthropology, and gender discourses each have integrity as separate domains of meaning, but do not really make meaning as discrete domains or systems. Once we admit that meanings are generated out of convergences of signifying processes, the term *system* implies more cohesiveness than ever actually adheres to processes of meaning. *Differential networks* is a more accurate way to indicate the generation of meaning out of differences. By looking at the effects of multiple differential networks of meaning and their unpredicatable effects, we are better able to appreciate the openness of signifying processes and to focus discourse analysis on situations of utterances. We can take a position somewhere between the hypothetically closed system of structuralism and the undifferentiated field of discourse of deconstructionism.

This position works best for feminist theory, because we cannot understand the oppression of women without connecting processes of signification to multiple networks of meaning-production.[27] The need to get at the openings between networks and the hidden contradictions in the meanings around gender compels feminist theorists to refuse structuralist temptations to achieve order by closure. Judith Butler uses this process to unravel the binary definitions attributing maleness and femaleness and heterosexually defined desires to bodies. She finds gaps in constructions of bodies as only male or female. Feminist interests also mean that the poststructuralist look at difference must attend to the institutionalization of differential meaning. The existing convergences of meaning patterns are the transitional "real" with which we must work for change.

For a theological feminist analytic, we have interest in the transitional real of determinate situations where patterns are entrenched and instability—the openness for change—exists as well. Attention to the situational networks of meaning will identify particular forms of gender oppression and resident meanings that potentially unravel them. The gaps and contradictions that will attract our theological interest will be those at the intersections of discourses (or statements) that create space for signifying the goodness of historically identified women and refusal of gender domination. This is what a theo/acentric grammar of finitude and care for the stranger requires.

The multiply positioned subject: "woman" as opposition

Poststructuralist discourse analysis is significant at a final point, one that creates the most controversy for feminist adoption of poststructuralism. It is not simply the representational function of language that is displaced by the turn to discourse. The subject gets a negative review as well. With the omnipresence of textuality or signifying, it is not possible to conceive of the subjective consciousness as the origin of meaning. Both structuralist and poststructuralist accounts of signi-

---

[27]Rosalind Coward and Catherine Belsey employ poststructuralist strategies to find the oppositional meanings in standard literary interpretations of the classics, undermining the readings that ignore gender. The group of postmodernist feminists I have in mind here are French feminists, who use deconstruction, psychoanalysis, and poststructuralism and have been (not uncontroversially) viewed as apolitical: Julia Kristeva, Hélène Cixous, and Luce Irigaray. Janice Radway, Rosalind Coward, Catherine Belsey, Gayatri Chakravorty Spivak, and a host of other feminists use poststructuralist theories along with political accounts of discourse.

fying "kill" this subject, to paraphrase the now familiar reference to the "death of the subject." To put it less dramatically, these accounts discredit the Cartesian subject, whose unencumbered mental space provided a foundation for certainty in Enlightenment notions of reason. The Cartesian subject still qualifies in many accounts of literature as the site where meaning originates.[28]

Already subject to criticism in the earlier account of a liberation epistemology, this subject is problematic from a number of quarters. It has been called the glassy essence that allows philosophy to present itself as the transcendent, all-seeing, unsituated gaze; it allows for the notion that self-reflection affords direct access to one's own subjectivity.[29] The logic of the post-Saussurean attack on this subject adds to these critiques one generated by the omnipresence of signifying. Like prevenient grace, the sign is always already there, inescapable to the constructing of cognition. This priority in the construction of meaning is completely at odds with the notion that there is a consciousness, a knowing, that precedes language.

The notion of discourse itself foreshadows the decentered subject. Without language, there is no "I," as Emile Benveniste indicated: The subject comes to exist in language as an effect of language. Once implicated in language, the subject's definition occurs in the relational processes linking signs to signs, turning on its head the common wisdom that "I" am controlling what "I" mean. Language *subjects* the subject, and an inherent instability is thereby inscribed on discourse and subjects as foci of agency or meaning. As Foucault says, "Expressing their thoughts in words of which they are not the masters, enclosing them in verbal forms whose historical dimensions they are unaware of, men [*sic*] believe that their speech is their servant and do not realize that they are submitting themselves to its demands."[30] The

---

[28]This famous comment refers broadly to the end of modern humanism; Michel Foucault, *The Order of Things: An Archaeology of the Human Sciences* (New York: Vintage Books, 1973), 303–44, 386–87. Regarding the "death of the subject" as it connects to the "death of the author," see Michel Foucault, "What Is an Author?" *Screen* 20 (1979): 13–33. Also see Roland Barthes, "The Death of the Author," in *Image Music Text*, trans. Stephen Heath (London: Fontana, 1977), 143–48.

[29]Richard Rorty, *Philosophy and the Mirror of Nature* (Princeton, N.J.: Princeton Univ. Press, 1979). It is the culprit in the anxious search for objectivity that characterizes the Cartesian heritage of reason, as Richard J. Bernstein puts it in *Beyond Objectivism and Relativism: Science, Hermeneutics, Praxis* (Philadelphia: Univ. of Pennsylvania Press, 1983). The decentering which I do not take up is that of the "unconscious," or the re-reading of the construction of subjectivity by Lacanian Freudianism. Many feminists who use poststructuralism invoke Lacan's version of the relation of sign systems to the "subject."

[30]Foucault, *The Order of Things*, 297.

language that creates the "I" is part of networks of signifying with their own locations and meanings. The "freedom" that the controlling "I" has is an illusory freedom, as what can be spoken is only what is possible in the determinacies of a discourse, the demands of the cultural-political orders.

The "death of the subject" is not, however, the end of the individual. It is the reorienting of the way the individual is a part of the signifying process.[31] It is the discrediting of a view that participation in language happens by way of a mental space, a precultural, free, experiencing self able to bypass situation—what signifying processes represent—to generate its own "original" product. It is the death of this subject, the "single ordering point of will and consciousness" who postures as the all-seeing gaze, as Donna Haraway puts it. The death is inflicted by the priority of the signifier and its differential webs of other signs.[32]

What is controversial in such a move, not surprisingly, is its seeming removal of responsibility or intentional subjecthood. It would appear disadvantageous at best for marginalized groups such as women to applaud the devaluation of what they have yet to achieve.[33] The benefit, however, lies in the possibilities for tracing out the orderings that construct differences. An account of ordering or origin is *decentered* (rather than "killed") that is inadequate to the relationships of power in which different subjects come to be "women." For feminists it is, as Chris Weedon remarks, not the resisting, feeling, thinking subject that is decentered, but the rational, autonomous subject of liberal humanism and the essential female subject of some feminist theory.[34] We require some theorization that accounts for the fact that women have always been agents, have produced and have "originated" ideas and projects and strategies throughout history, and are still subjected

---

[31]For a feminist account of this new poststructuralist subjectivity, see Chris Weedon, *Feminist Practice and Poststructuralist Theory* (Oxford: Basil Blackwell, 1987), 74–106, 111–13. This death of the subject is also connected to a rejection of the modern concern with "man" as a field of Western knowledge. See Foucault's *The Order of Things.*

[32]Donna J. Haraway, "Situated Knowledges: The Science Question in Feminism and the Privilege of Partial Perspective," in *Simians, Cyborgs, and Women: The Reinvention of Nature* (New York: Routledge, 1991), 193.

[33]I have cited some criticisms of feminists' appropriations of poststructuralist work; this is a central piece of that argument. Modleski is a powerful critic of this loss of identity; she takes on Butler as one of the prime exponents of it. I think she may score against Butler in terms of the small-scale terms of Butler's alternative, parodic practices. Modleski avoids the issues, such as the problems with power, that have engendered such proposals, however; *Feminism without Women.* See Jana Sawicki regarding the correction of the possibilities of disabling women as subjects in Foucault, *Disciplining Foucault: Feminism, Power, and the Body* (New York: Routledge, 1991).

[34]Weedon, *Feminist Practice,* 125–26.

subjects. Location of the origination of meaning with subjects simply does not account for that. The decentered subject is crucial to a reappropriation of the production of meaning as it applies to women.

Constructively speaking, we have a new kind of subject with this move: the "opening of non-isomorphic subjects, agents, and territories of stories unimaginable from the vantage point of the cyclopian, self-satiated eye of the master subject," in the words of Donna Haraway.[35] The decentered subject is fragmented and multiple rather than unified and self-initiating. This claim is rather like the Saussurean discovery about language: The subject is not an entity, a substance, but a relation, or sets of relations. Its identity is always forged out of differences. The notion of differences is no longer confined to signs. It can now be read as the oppositional discourses that constrain women in their social location and, at the same time, create new significations that may figure escape.[36] "Woman" is a subject position with a variety of relations, some of which are positions that are connected to gender, some of which are oppositional in relation to "man." The non-isomorphic subject is implicitly connected to the conventions of social locations for her meaning(s).

Butler's critique of feminist identity politics is helpful in sharpening this point, for she rejects even the multiple subject position of Haraway and Weedon. The organization of a liberation movement around the identity "woman" implies a unified self-identical subject as well as a unified self-identical notion of gender. We saw that Butler refuses the kind of reference implied by this politics (the trajectory of reference from the signifier "woman" to the "real female" body), in order to direct us to the multiple significations that converge in the creation of what we call subjects. Rejecting this account of language brings with it the recognition that there is no mental space free of significations—no natural female subjectivity. Just as there are no natural woman bodies, there is no natural woman's experience and no experience that is identical to itself (for it has already become other than itself through language). In this way Butler makes the point that feminists should not ascribe commonality too quickly.[37] Her critique is more than the refusal of premature commonalities, however; she argues that retention of the notion of subject position, of multiple constructed identities, risks another naturalization.

---

[35]Haraway, "Situated Knowledges," 192. The related subject is a fundamentally *situated subject.*

[36]Weedon articulates this new account of freedom as the intersection of discursive processes in *Feminist Practice,* 107–35, 168–75.

[37]Butler, *Gender Trouble.*

Butler argues that the retention of "woman" even as a multiply constructed identity is problematic. She makes this case by identifying the discourses that construct the binary "man-woman," the statements, as it were, that fill in or inscribe Western notions of real women and real men. Discourses which create anatomical boundaries determine that certain genital configurations constitute "femaleness" and certain domains of other bodies constitute "maleness." It is not simply the case, she continues, that two rigid categories of sexual difference are created and maintained by the continued use of "woman" and its opposite. In addition, certain causal connections are rendered between the "naturally female" body and its desired object, and vice versa. The discourses that construct desire, then, are the meanings that determine correct pairings of the oppositionally defined bodies (so male desire is defined by its right object, the female body, and homosexual desire is defined as an inversion).

Here a binary is complicated not only because it defines two orders of bodies, but because it attributes their right relation as well. As discursive practices that define subjects, the heterosexist definitions, in effect, create them. In the bodies and subjects that purportedly fall outside the dominant discourse, we have striking testimony to the power of discourse when these significations are not treated as empirical descriptions. The bodies that resist this binary construction, the desires that resist heterosexual oppositional pairing, are not "real" or appropriate, but unnatural, mistaken, or deviant (like Aristotle's notion of woman as deficient). The hermaphrodite is Foucault's mesmerizing account of these bodies that disrupt the unifying energy of heterosexual discourse.[38]

Butler's point is that continuation of "identity" politics reconfirms this heterosexual discursive network. The politics of "women's experience" re-creates the oppressive ordering that gender criticism resists. The failure to see the connections between gender as discursive ordering and sex as discursive ordering leaves male and female divisions of bodies as "natural" realities. Appeals to an identity called "woman" ostensibly reinscribe these "natural" unities. Butler's alternative to identity calls for contestation of heterosexuality and its fixed sexed identities with the notion that gender is a performance. The parodying of binary sex and of the idea that persons have a "real sexed identity" is the only way she suggests to call into question the oppressive regime

---

[38]Ibid. See *Herculine Barbin: Being the Recently Discovered Memoirs of a Nineteenth Century Hermaphrodite*, ed. Michel Foucault, trans. Richard McDougall (New York: Pantheon Books, 1980).

of heterosexuality, the regime that feminists' continued appeals to gender identity support. The question is, why the continued hegemony of *this* construction of difference over others?[39]

Modleski is right to wonder, however, if the move completely out of gender identity is not a bit precipitous. She treats Butler's poststructuralism as one of the worst cases of the failure of feminist thought to take seriously the social formation. Abandonment of "women" as the subject of feminism lends itself too easily to a postfeminist era that is certainly utopian but has the likely outcome of providing support for the reactionary attitudes of a postfeminist backlash.[40] It is crucial to appreciate, however, the importance of Butler's analysis. Reinforcement of the heterosexual matrix is unquestionably a danger with the invoking of "woman," even if we multiply that identity. There is no way around the fact that any definition of "woman" assumes a host of characteristics that socially implicate the interpreter and invoke their opposites in other women (and in "man"). Naturalized assumptions about the sexed body go unrecognized in the feminist distinction between gender and sex, and no doubt this is more dangerous for some bodies than for others. "Heterosexual woman" is the privileged identity. Feminist theological analysis must bear this contradiction in mind.

I think the critics are right, however, in calling our attention back to what counts as historical women at present—to those who identify themselves as women and are identified by others as women. (This is not a totally unproblematic question: one wonders if transsexuals are counted as "women.") Women of color still invoke notions of identity and do not by that fact obliterate other grids of oppression.[41] There is much to be denaturalized in these subject positions "woman" before the move to gender as performance or sheer multiplicity might be the only alternative. There is also more to be displayed about the joys and pleasures and emancipatory practices of different subject positions that

---

[39]Butler, *Gender Trouble*. Jonathon Dollimore raises this question in a powerful way, charting some of the ways that homosexuality gets constructed as the "other," in *Sexual Dissidence: Augustine to Wilde, Freud to Foucault* (Oxford: Clarendon Press, 1991). Monique Wittig's proposal that lesbians are a third gender is a move to destabilize, although not one satisfactory to Butler. See "One Is Not Born a Woman," *Feminist Issues* 1 (1981): 47–54; "The Category of Sex," *Feminist Issues* 2 (1982): 63–68.

[40]Modleski, *Feminism without Women*. Bordo, "Feminism, Postmodernism."

[41]With the point I have just made, I must confess the false universalizing rhetoric of my "our," for I cannot assume that nonheterosexual women will go along with me at this point. Modleski and Bordo make this point about women of color. Modleski, *Feminism without Women*, 18–20; Bordo, "Feminism, Postmodernism," 149–50. Audre Lorde and Bell Hooks do wonderful work on the complexities of subject positions.

attach to gender, and a position that refuses even accounts of multiple subject positions cannot display this.

If we cannot assume an identity "woman" as the place to begin—and we certainly cannot—then the task of feminist analysis is not ended. It simply shifts to the multiple construction of subjects.[42] Feminist analysis must trace the many orderings that constitute this non-isomorphic subject, asking when "woman" is the most pressing, oppressing opposition, and what it means. These questions will be community-specific. Butler's critique is a reminder that "woman" is an oppressive gendered position in particular ways and (perhaps) only for a temporary time. It does not, in my view, suggest that "woman" is a discourse that may be dispensed with as yet. Thus I will retain the notion of gendered subject positions with an eye toward the oppressive possibilities of that notion. I do so out of commitment to a particular, if transient, "community": women in situations of oppression.

Thus far the issue of the production of meaning has been addressed with reference to two questions: whether processes of signification are closed and whether they can be understood to originate with subjects. I have proposed that feminists are best served by poststructuralist respect for the openness of semiosis along with recognition that meanings are produced in situations of utterance. The source of meaning, however, is to be found neither in some free-floating neutral consciousness, nor in an essential feminine subjectivity. To analyze "woman" as a subject position, we must attend to discourses that make statements as well as pose binary oppositions, discourses that define whole regions of reality such as gendered bodies and heterosexually desiring complementary subjects. By pursuing this analysis, I depart from reliance on women's experience as a natural warrant for claims. I challenge notions that any account of women's experience can re-present such realities; and I depart from liberal feminism, radical and cultural feminist theory, and standpoint feminist positions.

---

[42]In order to mark off the nonessential and yet located character of the position "woman," we need to think of the convergence of multiple discursive processes, connected to the apparati, as Louis Althusser would say, of the social formation of Western international capitalism and its structuring by patriarchal power. Subject position is not the determinist "causing" of preexisting subjects, but the conditions of possibility for subjects; therefore the best way to signal that convergence is with the term *overdetermination*. This term is associated with the Freudian process by which an image becomes the symbol of a multiply layered set of meanings condensing in the unconscious. Overdetermination suggests how the convergings of a variety of realities—mode of production, cultural meanings, religious meanings—constitute subject positions. For feminist analysis, it can indicate that gender discourse condenses a multiplicity of oppressive relations and oppositions.

Discourse and the problem of reality

The turn to discourse has led to a decentering of the concept "woman," but does not result in loss of a feminist analytic. I say that because the place from which gender oppression is to be judged will be concrete, historically defined women and the discourses that construct them. Before I can move to consider specific women's discourses in order to illustrate a change of subject for feminist theology, however, the long-deferred question of power in relation to discourses must be examined. That question has been sharpened somewhat by the post-structuralist analysis of the constitutive character of language. By offering an account of discourse that claims that anatomical sex and desire are "constructed" as well, poststructuralist theory has moved so far beyond the social construction of masculinity and femininity that one may doubt its adequacy to attend to the full realities of women's oppression. To insist that signifying is omnipresent, that one cannot get outside of it, might appear to make language a virtual prison. Such a confinement of feminist interest to language would bypass institutional and material realities that are fundamental to any feminist analysis of patriarchy. Does the analytical route I have taken end up reducing reality to language? This would certainly seem to rule out theological claims, a topic to which we must eventually return. More immediately, power would then appear to be reduced again to ideas, a problem reminiscent of my complaint against feminist theology.

No doubt it would be an error to identify discourse theory with linguistic reduction in the work of Marxist feminists who employ poststructuralism—Rosalind Coward, Belsey, and Weedon. These feminists move beyond the dichotomizing of reality into ideas and matter with their employment of discourse theory. Combining their Marxist commitments with discourse theory, they offer an alternative to that dichotomizing that will enable a move beyond similar problems in feminist theological work. In order to clarify that alternative, however, I will proceed by inquiring about the relation of discourse to language and the precise kind of reality claims that are involved.

One may misunderstand the reality-constitutive nature of discourse in feminist theory as a claim akin to a form of subjective idealism, the denial that there is reality outside of our minds/ideas. To take an earlier example, the insistence that discourses construct male and female bodies or that anatomical binary sex needs to be read as a discursive formation seems to invite such a suspicion. The charge of idealism, however, confuses the claim that *is* being made—namely, that discourse constitutes objects—with two that are not—that discourse is language and that reality is coincident with conceptuality. In order to understand that the appeal to discourse encompasses the full array of social relations and not simply ideas, it is helpful to clarify "discursive totality or practice" in relation to idealist/realist and idealist/materialist debates.[43]

I begin with the first misconception. It would clearly be contrary to feminists' interests to reduce all reality to language or to ideas. The terrain of women's oppression is never simply language or ideology; it is social structures, reproduction, the violation of bodies. It is the state and its politics and system of governance and military, the "civil order" or cultural institutions of church, education, and entertainment, and the economy as mode of production—the entire social formation—that construct women's lives and possibilities. The claim that discourse orders bodies (or any other reality) does not mean that bodies are reducible to language.

Language is only one of the many sign systems. Although Saussure worked with language, he envisioned that the subsequent science of semiotics (semiology for Peirce) would incorporate multiple sign systems. Peirce included music, movement, and nature in his vision of a science of signs. The sign system of fashion is a better known example of nonlinguistic inscriptions or codes.[44] The discursive ordering of bodies is a more recent realm of exploration by feminists. The anorexic female body is a set of social inscriptions.[45] Body decoration, the distribution of the erotic on the female body, the sign systems of Madison Avenue advertising that constitute bodies as beautiful and as objects of pleasure—these are only a few of the codes that order bodies as female and define their failure to be female as well. In short, my claim that realities are constituted by discourse acknowledges that gender signifying is much more complicated than language.[46]

---

[43]For what follows, I am greatly indebted to an argument offered by Ernest Laclau and Chantal Mouffe over these issues: "Post-Marxism without Apologies," *New Left Review* 166 (1987): 79–106. This is not what Foucault means by "discursive," which in *The Archaeology of Knowledge and the Discourse on Language*, trans. A. M. Sheridan Smith (New York: Pantheon Books, 1972) remains an analysis of linguistic discourses. I admit that the relation of "constituting" is more complicated than I am able to take up here. See Hubert L. Dreyfus and Paul Rabinow on this in *Michel Foucault: Beyond Structuralism and Hermeneutics*, 2d ed. (Chicago: Univ. of Chicago Press, 1983).

[44]Roland Barthes, *The Fashion System* (New York: Hill & Wang, 1983); also *Mythologies* (New York: Hill & Wang, 1972).

[45]Susan Bordo, "Anorexia Nervosa: Psychopathology as the Crystallization of Culture," in *Feminism and Foucault: Reflections on Resistance*, ed. Irene Diamond and Lee Quinby (Boston: Northeastern Univ. Press, 1988), 87–117. Rosalind Coward, *Female Desire* (London: Paladin, 1984).

[46]My position on discourse is broader than some, who still confine the term to linguistic signs even as they include other signifying processes in their analysis. Foucault,

It still may appear that the constitutive power of discourse reduces reality to ideas even when it is understood that discourse is not language. Feminists would be right to avoid such a view for reasons already suggested. The view that all that exists is ideas (which get expressed in language) is a subjective-idealist position. This is the brand of idealism that has realism as its opponent, realism being the conviction that there are existing entities outside of our ideas. If discourse is construction in this way, then Butler would be saying that whatever we think about bodies is real. Since her feminism takes seriously the entrenched character of the patriarchal order, it is not likely that her claim (or those like it) entails a denial of reality outside of feminist imagination.

Existence versus being

Something else is at stake in the claim that bodies are discursively ordered. To get at that "something else," I propose that the idealism-realism question be dispensed with. Instead we can observe a distinction between the *existence* of an entity, its "thatness," and its *being*, its "whatness."[47] Thus when we treat bodies as constructed, it is not their existence that is called into question, but the fixed character of their meaning. With this distinction a position such as Butler's can be read to mean that the givenness of something called bodies is not the same thing as the being, and that it is the latter that is constructed and negotiable. It is the place for the feminist struggle.

The usefulness of this position can be illustrated with an example that poses the question in terms of what constitutes a meaningful practice. Let us take the act of forced penile-vaginal intercourse performed by a male on his female spouse. This act consists of both physical (nonlinguistic) components and linguistic components. The physical aspects of the act in convergence with the pertinent judicial (linguistic) code that also defines it give even sharper definition to the event if we give it an outcome—for example, the woman's complaint and legal nonrecognition of that complaint. In addition, the event in-

---

for example, uses it in such a way and refers to "nondiscursive" for nonlinguistic entities and formations.

[47]Laclau and Mouffe point out this distinction as one between the entity (*ens*) and the being (*esse*) of an object. "Post-Marxism," 84–85.

cludes the fact that she lives in a state that does not recognize marital rape.[48]

Neither the physical nor the linguistic aspects can account for the event as a totality, however. In order to treat the event as a whole, to put together the physical and nonphysical elements that result in a legal procedure (or lack of one) against the man, we are interested in its meaning. Yet its meaning cannot be limited to either linguistic or physical aspects. The legal code by itself does not define the act; the coital bodily act does not offer forth its meaning. Insofar as there is a totality constructed by these aspects—marital rape or simply a bad night—it is unhelpful to think of that whole as linguistic or nonlinguistic. Although that whole includes both, it is, strictly speaking, neither. It is precisely the work of the category "discourse" to enable us to characterize these elements as a totality, a meaningful whole. That whole is a configuration of significations or discourses; it is a *discursive totality*.[49]

Understanding discursive constitution of reality in this way, we avoid the dichotomizing of reality as meaningful (linguistic/ideational) and nonmeaningful (everything else). Discursive ordering is what gives nonlinguistic entities and linguistic entities meaning as wholes or totalities. Discourse is no more a denial of the reality of the event in its physicality and existence than it is a reduction of that event to language.

My example shows that the discursive ordering of bodies can be a fundamental claim about the power of signifying without denying reality. *What* the act *is*—legitimate marital relations or brutal rape—has reality effects of enormous consequence for the subjects who are constructed by it, their roles and purposes. Think of the enormity of the difference between the construction of the "woman" here: as victim of a brutalizing act for whom the full recourse of the legal system and compassion of the state is available, or as a subject who is at best a nonperson, at worst an embarrassing disturber of the sanctity of the private realm. These are simply different realities, with different players, different rules and goals. They get their being from the entirety of the discourses.

---

[48]For example, in North Carolina: "Husbands cannot be charged for rape of wife unless parties living apart." See Diana E. H. Russell, *Rape in Marriage*, expanded and revised edition with a new Introduction (Bloomington: Indiana Univ. Press, 1990), 380. (As this book goes to press, North Carolina has just changed this law.)

[49]With this example I create one analogous to Laclau and Mouffe's of brick-laying. "Post-Marxism," 82–83.

Less contested orderings of the body make the same point. Under the ordering of the discursive totality of medicine or science, the body is an assemblage of cells, muscles, organ systems, a web of particles, neutrons, and molecules. Under the discursive totality of loving sexual intimacy, the body is unique and personal, an instrument of pleasure, beauty, and mystery. In the former case its being is constructed out of scientific discourse. The body has a different being in the latter, a different inscription of relational value, of organization, use, and purpose.

In addition to a way to think about unities, discursive totality enables us to think about the character of a whole in another way. As a totality that unifies an event, a discourse is also a game or *practice*. As such it constitutes different players, subjects, goals, and values along with the bodies. It is within this broader terrain of discourse that the feminist notion of multiple subject positions can be understood. There are multiple constructions of subjects—hence complex subject positions—because individuals are constituted as subjects out of a variety of games or practices. The pathologist is constructed as one kind of position in relation to bodies as specimens and as an altogether different subject position in relation to bodies as personal partners in erotic love.[50] The end or purpose (when there is one) of the unified subject is found in this convergence.

The discursive orderings that compete in my first example highlight the stakes in identifying any event as a totality. These stakes are simply less apparent in the second example. The more obvious ambiguity in the act of forced intercourse and the fact that it allows so easily for competing discursive totalizations also make the point that discursive construction is a refusal of idealism in the second way that concerns feminist analysis. Discourse theory refutes the notion that reason is adequate to the real. Here the debate is between idealism as the conviction that the essence of reality is conceptual, and the materialist position that change and contingency are fundamental to reality, thus frustrating the adequacy of the concept.[51]

---

[50]While I might want to say that the "same" body has a different meaning or subject position under the orderings of different discursive formations, that claim would need to be carefully clarified. It could not be understood to mean that the real meaning of the body—like the real subject—lurks behind (is prior to) its discursive manifestations. Then one would simply need to get access to it for the truth about the body to appear. However deeply one presses, it is discursive orderings "all the way down." I thank Terrence W. Tilley for the example. See his "Incommensurability, Intratextuality, and Fideism," *Modern Theology* 5:2 (January 1989): 87–111.

[51]Again I follow Laclau and Mouffe here. See, however, John Frow's questions about the risks of extending the textuality metaphor to social reality: "Intertextuality

The physical act of penile-vaginal intercourse can be construed as rape or as marital (legal) sexual relations, depending upon a host of other discursive constraints, such as the historical and geographical location of the judgment and the community making it. The legal community participates in one discursive ordering of the act; the feminist community in another. Prior to this century, the latter reality did not exist. Once one recognizes this plurality, no appeal to the "form" or concept of coitus is adequate to settle what the reality is. Discursive constitution undercuts such conceptual idealism, as Ernest Laclau and Chantal Mouffe insist. It does this because the *real* move away from that kind of idealism, typically termed "materialism," is not made by an appeal to matter or stuff outside of discourse, or to a determinist account of the forces of production, but by consistent attention to the particular and the changing relations that constitute reality.

Materialism as I use it here is one answer to the question of what kind of reality is "out there." Recognition that an act or object gets its being in multiple discursive orderings—the legal definition of the act as marital coitus versus the feminist reading of the act as rape—defines reality as not constituted by *form* (and thereby available to fixed concept) but by change, complexity, and flux. No matter of appeal to the bodies involved in the act will determine its meaning.[52] Radical and cultural feminist appeals to women's bodies and their reproductive and cyclical functions cannot be cited as materialist appeals to counter the idealist and dualist thought patterns of patriarchy on this definition. There are two reasons for this.

First, such appeals participate in the maintenance of dichotomies between material stuff external to meaning—bodies, economic processes, institutions—on the one hand, and ideas on the other. Second, when they grant priority or essential reality to bodies (to stuff), these feminist arguments make the error (which even materialists commit) of failing to move away from idealism.[53] They assume that whatever meaning they read on these bodies—their goodness, their natural-

---

and Ontology," in *Intertextuality: Theories and Practices*, ed. Michael Worton and Judith Still (Manchester and New York: Manchester Univ. Press: 1990), 45–55. For a harsher view see Terry Eagleton, *Ideology: An Introduction* (London: Verso, 1991), 215–20.

[52]The *use* of an appeal to the real meaning of the bodies in this act, of course, gets the meanings of dominant codes, as does any appeal to the "real."

[53]Laclau and Mouffe in "Post-Marxism" point out that Karl Marx's own formulation of the relationship was inadequate, because he invited determinist accounts of the relation between the economy and the other ideological components of social existence. These social processes are crucial to the discursive formation that orders bodies. They are discursive (meaningful), not outside of their relation to other processes of meaning, such as the state or cultural processes, but only in those unstable relationships.

ness—is coincident with the truth, a truth that holds for all female bodies. Contrary to this, women's bodies are differently constituted by class and other aspects of location. The turn to discourse requires that bodies be constituted by these relations. They no more "speak" the truth outside of these relations than do official legal or philosophical concepts. Haraway is right to warn us against the separation of our bodies, or any so-called natural objects, from the social relations that produce them.[54]

When Marxist feminists appropriate discourse theory, then, they move out of orthodox Marxist positions that separate ideas (or ideology) from the forces of production. Essences can no more be based on the forces of production than they can come from concepts. Refusing to give a fixed meaning to the material realities of social existence outside of discursive relations is necessary to this position, just as recognition that the process of reproduction extends to child care requires a nuanced view of changing forms of reproduction. All the processes of social reality need to be considered within discursive totalities and practices. What makes an analysis "materialist" and enables it to resist the reduction of reality to ideas is the widening of the relations that are understood to construct an entity. It entails the refusal to treat these social environs as natural, as nondiscursive.

To return to my example, the discursive relations judged to define the act of intercourse have to be widened to include the processes of the democratic state, the postindustrial capitalist economy, and the processes of culture as they co-constitute women into *discursive* subject positions.[55] The processes that create the middle-class woman as a marital partner and that construct her body as desirable, for instance, are practices that get their meaning from a culture articulated (linked) with commodification. The ordering of marital life in terms of what counts as a "right" and what counts as "private" is as much reality created by the democratic state and its patriarchal codes as it is by the

---

[54]Donna J. Haraway, "Animal Sociology and a Natural Economy of the Body Politic: A Political Physiology of Dominance," in *Simians, Cyborgs, and Women*, 10–11. The two positions to avoid are: (1) biological determinism of our social position; and (2) capitalist-inspired separation of culture against nature. For her more complex account of the contemporary social relations out of which women's bodies are constructed, see "A Cyborg Manifesto: Science, Technology, and Socialist-Feminism in the Late Twentieth Century," ibid., 149–82.

[55]Rosalind Coward charts the commodification and creation of the desires of the ideal middle-class woman in *Female Desire: How They Are Sought, Bought, and Packaged* (New York: Grove Press, 1985). The literature on the domestic/private versus public sphere is vast. See Jaggar, *Feminist Politics and Human Nature*, for a bibliography. See also Glenna Matthews, *Just a Housewife: The Rise and Fall of Domesticity in America* (Oxford: Oxford Univ. Press, 1987).

meanings contributed by other social relations. By widening discursive totalities to include the social formation, Marxist feminists remind us that it is impossible to pose essences without ignoring the specificity and instability of realities that are created in these social relations.

The move to discourse, to signification, from the view of language as representation is best summarized as the claim that relations constitute meaning. I have argued that relations for feminists' interest are necessarily broader than signifier-signified, binary signs, or intersubjective discourses. They must incorporate social relations in meaningful totalities in order to encompass the terrain upon which gender oppression and possibility occur. The turn to discourse is not idealist in the sense of denying the existence of reality outside of minds; it is, in fact, materialist. The differences that construct signification are widened to include the discourses of a mode of production, the processes of the democratic state and the "ideological" discursive processes of the culture.[56] Feminist discourse analysis is clearly not a reduction of reality to language; its question is whether the relations analyzed in a construction of subject position are defined widely enough so that these social processes are incorporated.

The power-discourse relation: hegemonic and local

The entanglement of discourse with power can no longer be ignored. Allusions to power in relation to the social formation have already threaded my argument. When discourses are contested, as over the meaning of a coital act or a "real woman," it is a reminder that some relations of power have more solidity than others; their reality effects do more harm. Some discursive totalities and the practices they constitute are "realer" than others. In the first place, then, an account of hegemony, or dominant discursive orderings, is necessary to a feminist account of power. That hegemony refers to the role of the processes of capitalist patriarchy in reproducing meanings and locations oppressive to women. Another form of power needs attention as well. The poststructuralist move to discourse opens to view a form of power that is everyday, local, and omnipresent with discourse, power that is epitomized in the procedures of modern normalizing and disci-

---

[56]Rosalind Coward and John Ellis, *Language and Materialism: Developments in Semiology and the Theory of the Subject* (London: Routledge and Kegan Paul, 1977).

plinary technologies. Without this second account of power, feminist
theology cannot break away from the notion of externally conceived,
negative oppression, problematic because it fails to connect to
women's daily lives and make sense of their practices. Following brief
consideration of the hegemonic character of patriarchal power, I will
outline the second form of power, which is specific to certain poststructuralist views.

Feminist analysis commonly appeals to some kind of dominant
force or forces to account for the continued oppression of women, to
indicate the entrenched character of gender asymmetries and the difficulties of moving to a society and a world where gender justice, mutuality, or relations beyond gender might exist. Without pretending to
be an adequate treatment of this topic, particularly with regard to the
impact of racism on gender, or sufficient yet for a theological description, my claim is that some such reference point is necessary. That reference point is capitalist patriarchy, which refers to the multifaceted
but clear hegemony of oppressive gender practices characteristic of
North American late twentieth-century social reality.[57] This definition
is not an account of the origins of patriarchy, but of its contemporary
Western face. It recognizes that the powerful influence of a mode of
production—postindustrial capitalism—effects and shapes the way in
which male dominance, a vestige of a variety of social arrangements
dominated by the patriarchal household, is supported and reproduced
in this late twentieth century. With the term I indicate that the current
form of patriarchal power is not the same as the oppression of women
in other periods.

A few features of capitalist patriarchy will be sufficient to aid in understanding the specifics of women's practices that I take up later in
the book. The distinctive character of contemporary patriarchy gets its
shape historically from the rise of industrial capitalism. Along with the
rise of science and demise of religion, this "event" fundamentally re-

---

[57]Zillah Eisenstein coined the phrase. See her "Some Notes on the Relations of Capitalist Patriarchy," in a book she edited, *Capitalist Patriarchy and the Case for Socialist Feminism* (New York: Monthly Review Press, 1979). There are a variety of versions of this
view, but all consider the specifics of patriarchy in the West to be inconceivable without
the forces of capitalism. In addition to the dialogue between Marxism and feminism,
which included attempts to put the two together, some feminists I have drawn upon use
accounts of discourse to think about the relation between mode of production and "ideologies." See Haraway, *Simians, Cyborgs, and Women*; Coward, *Female Desire*; Janice
Radway, *Reading the Romance: Women, Patriarchy and Popular Literature* (Chapel Hill:
Univ. of North Carolina Press, 1984). Haraway has gone the farthest to articulate the
new global situation where a "homework economy" has created a new form of work
and poverty for women. See her "A Cyborg Manifesto," in *Simians, Cyborgs, and
Women*.

ordered society and began the denaturalization of women's place in the natural/divine order; it did this by removing production from the home to the market, and by fundamentally altering the legitimation of male authority.[58] The specific impact of capitalism is such that the elements of the social formation, state, civil society, culture, and economy do not operate separately from each other, but are all hegemonized by processes ordered to produce surplus and profit. This is accomplished in part by the commodification of entities (labor, crafts, products, persons, information) by removing them from the social relations and context of use.

Much has been written about the effects of this process on the state, on culture, on information dissemination, and on the most obvious indication of that hegemony, the maldistribution of income and access to resources. In order to understand the impact of capitalism on the dissemination of information and the political processes, one would have to look, for example, at the problematic character of the public talk about democratic process and equal opportunity, which is continually opaque to the entrenched inequalities of impact and access.[59] My interest is in the impact of these processes on gender.

Insofar as natural and divine legitimations of women's inferiority are at least theoretically undermined by the hegemonies of industrial capitalism and science, the latter provide their own versions of the dependence of women. One feminist story of that dependence traces the "woman question" through nineteenth-century medical science and Freudian versions that legitimate the inferiority and dependence of women.[60] The contribution of capitalism adds another set of processes creating positions of subjection for women. The definition of a commodity is something that has been removed from the social relations and context of its use. The effect of such a process on gender has been the commodification of women's bodies, of beauty, of personal relations, of the women's movement itself. The removal of an entity from its context of use and social relations is an invitation for exploitation,

---

[58]The power of the pre-industrial patriarch was characterized by the naturalness of gender relations, a naturalness confirmed by religion, the organization of the family, and a struggle with the seasons. The move to a society organized around production in large factories wrested authority and power from the male and located it in the market. Accompanied by the rise of science and the undermining of religion, industrial capitalism spelled the end of the "naturalness" of patriarchy and the appearance of the "problem of women" for the first time. So argue Deirdre English and Barbara Ehrenreich, *For Her Own Good* (Garden City, N.Y.: Anchor Books, 1979).

[59]See C. B. MacPherson, *The Life and Times of Liberal Democracy* (Oxford: Oxford Univ. Press, 1977).

[60]English and Ehrenreich, *For Her Own Good*, 14–17.

the denial of ambiguity, of corporate relationships, of change, of death, of finitude, of tragedy, and of complexity. These various commodifications have a kind of unity in that the overall impact of processes which work to create profit also work to reproduce complementary binary genders. What is most debilitating about this binary is that the very being of one gender is dependence—a dependence that is characterized by the features of commodification. Dependence is idealized as female, whether it be a personality structure, a physical image, or an ordering of opportunity such that women continue to be economically dependent.

Dependence, however, is not a reality in the same way for women in different social locations. It gets "communicated" and dispersed differently and constructs different subject positions. Generally, dependence impacts the construction of access to the means of survival and well-being. By "construction of access" I stress again that we have to do with discursive practices that create access, not with simple access. We must look at the effect of signifying systems on women's reality: the definition of gender, the continued effects of public-private spheres, the continuation of discourses that reproduce heterosexuality and ideals for "real women," the force of gender constructions on job training and access, the commodification of dissent, and the manipulation of positive human traits.[61] These and a host of other constructions of access personalize or differentiate the discursive totality of patriarchal capitalism and create the varied subject positions to which we must connect women's practices of faith. Of the various ways patriarchal capitalism is personalized to social location, three discursively constructed "dependencies" will guide my analysis.

First, the move of production out of the home issued in the de-skilling of women's domestic productivity and the re-creation of the home in the twentieth century into a unit of consumption, producing new "skills." For nonpoor white women in particular, the processes of patriarchal capitalism worked to undermine women's craft tradition, create consumers out of women, and trivialize the home. This discursive process creates the distinctive kind of dependence and accompanying oppression characteristic of the subject position of the middle-to-upper-middle-class housewife, a subject position that tended to be largely white.

Poor women and working-class women are subjected to the discourses that construct the homemaker's dependence. The dependence

---

[61]They are oppressive to and for women and by implication for the gender relations of the entire social order—for everyone.

produced by capitalism at this location is utter and has to do with access to means of survival. These women are located on the bottom of the economic ladder, something epecially true for women of color. For lower-class women, capitalism reproduces dependence in the form of lower-paying service jobs or part-time employment. The processes of the entire social formation work to undermine access to goods and services for these women, from education, health care, public dignity, to political participation. This second development of the discursive processes of capitalist patriarchy constructs subject positions of non-personhood. It shapes oppression–liberation as survival issues for these women.

A third discursive process converges to constitute the positions of women with higher education and professional employment. The effects of capitalist patriarchy that are most pertinent here have to do with what characterizes the subject position of the professional, namely, the production of ideas. These women occupy positions in the social order that are still dominated by men, and their oppression has to do with the predominantly male ownership of the production of ideas that characterizes the professional managerial class. Thus the issues of this subject position have to do with display of resistance to that hegemony as opposed to unemployment, minimal sustenance, or economic dependence. The possibilities of the professional subject position and the constraints on resistance will not be totally other than those of the first two dependencies, but will clearly differ.

For all women, patriarchal capitalism reproduces desires for things it will never provide—bodies, faces, homes, possessions, and heterosexual intimacies. For all women, it reproduces subject positions of dissatisfaction, triviality, and vulnerability to abuse, which thread their lives with permanent and pernicious dependence.[62] The three discursive processes of dependence that suggest the differentiation of patriarchal capitalism as it is disseminated in the social order are not mutually exclusive; the poor woman can be affected by the idealiza-

---

[62]For example, dependence understood in terms of social relations and ambiguity would include an acceptance of aging, of changing bodies, of the potential priority of environment over human concerns. Commodified female dependence is not about finitude at all but eroticization of an idealized female size, body, and availability. It is a sexualization of powerlessness and refuses to explore all the other aspects of human dependence. For women whose dependence is literally on the state for survival, we should note that this discourse simply disqualifies them as "really feminine"; a host of other race-specific images are necessary to fill this subject position. With my negative judgments I assume that this is some kind of distortion or violation of a good. The discursive ordering out of which I make that judgment will be explicit later.

tion of the domestic just as the woman with means to redecorate her house. They are, however, all pieces in a binary gender system that supports the continuation of patriarchal hegemony. The possession of power is unequal, according to this account of hegemony, because the idealizing of this picture of reality keeps getting reproduced.

Patriarchal power as ordinary: incitements, production, and oppression

Patriarchal oppression is open to challenge, just as the instabilities in discursive practices would indicate. The three discursive practices or effects of gender dependence that I have identified, however, have roots in state and cultural apparatuses, in boardrooms and multinational corporate linkages—systems and processes that appear to have all the power. In line with my criticism thus far, we require a picture of patriarchal power as male dominance nuanced to the differences in the social location of women. My account of capitalist patriarchy mitigates this picture of power somewhat, because it is a model that suggests the differently disseminated character of patriarchal capitalism: it constructs problems of access differently for women by identifying different discursive effects for women in different social locations. Two kinds of effects result: (1) Women do not all suffer from patriarchal capitalism in the same way. (2) Although patriarchal capitalism is hegemonic in that the reproduction of subject positions of female dependence theoretically benefits the male gender, all men do not benefit from such a system in the same way.

We must also account for the gap between the power held by such forces and the acceptance of patriarchy by women. Furthermore, the hegemonic kind of power does not allow us to recognize women's distinctive ways of refusing oppression, the ways in which women are sites of the production of meaning. Power is not simply a negative or obliterating force possessed by some and imposed on have-nots. We need to think about power as a fluid, omnipresent phenomenon that works differently in different locations. An analytic of power aids in the exposing of gender oppression, the understanding of women's resistance, and in theorizing how it is that patriarchy is successful. For these purposes I propose a poststructuralist account of the local and omnipresent practices that effect and reproduce gender oppression in women.

Power works because "it traverses and produces things, it induces pleasure, forms knowledge, produces discourse" and operates throughout the social body.[63] This description of Michel Foucault's is of modern biopower, which he argues has largely replaced the models of power that still captivate the Western political imagination, the juridico-discursive repressive power of premodernity and its monarchical version as violent force. Foucault is a critic of notions of power for which the dominant images are the negative repressive power of the law and the power of sovereignty (the ruler as the image of absolute power), which gets its paradigmatic display in the excesses of public torture and executions. Monarchical power is at once more barbaric-seeming than modern power; it is designed to have public effects. It shares with the power of the law the assumption that power is a negative, that it says no. Foucault argues that repressive power, even the barbaric power of the spectacle exemplified in public torture, is actually less efficient and less comprehensive than modern power.

By contrast to the negative, repressive character of juridical power, modern power is normalizing and disciplinary. It is productive of docile bodies and subjected individuals. Its emergence in such practices as the reform of prisons in the late eighteenth century laid the conditions of possibility for capitalism.[64] The exemplar of this biopower is the panoptical design for the modern prison, an architectural design that created the maximum exposure of inmates to visibility in order to produce in them the sense of being constantly watched. With this eighteenth-century reform, Foucault is defining the essence of a disciplinary power that became "polyvalent in its applications"; it became the modern way to treat patients, workers, schoolchildren, the idle. Disciplinary power describes a virtual "political anatomy" that replaced the relations of sovereignty and the legal systems of repression by creating a society where the power of surveillance has replaced the power of force and violence. It is a power that centers around permanent exposure and visibility to authorities, being watched all the time—the condition of the inmate in the Panopticon. Surveillance is duplicated in the modern technologies of categoriza-

---

[63]Michel Foucault, "Truth and Power," in *Power/Knowledge: Selected Interviews and Other Writings, 1972–1977*, ed. Colin Gordon, trans. Colin Gordon et al. (New York: Pantheon Books, 1980), 119. Also see Foucault's numerous other articles on power in this same collection. For Foucault's critique of the repressive hypothesis in relation to sex, see his *History of Sexuality*, Vol.1: *An Introduction* (New York: Vintage Books, 1990). For a brief account of our transformation from a disciplinary society to a society of control, see Gilles Deleuze, "Postscript on the Societies of Control," *October* 359 (1992): 3–7. Biopower has not gone uncriticized. Haraway finds it "flaccid." See her *Simians, Cyborgs, and Women*, 149–50.

[64]Capitalism, Foucault says, required this kind of population to succeed. *Discipline and Punish: The Birth of the Prison*, trans. Alan Sheridan (New York: Pantheon Books, 1977), 220–21.

tion, which count, survey, place, and normalize. Its effect is a subject who is "free" from the tyranny of absolute power as force, more individualized than ever, but one who is docile, subjected as much by her/his own internalization of surveillance as by any forces of authority.[65]

Although Foucault's account of this modern political anatomy is complicated and assumes two poles—control of the body and of the species—it is helpful to review the outline of this idea of disciplinary power for the linking of women's practices in different locations with the hegemonic role of patriarchy. Strategies of discipline occupy the prisoner, categorize and locate him/her, and inscribe the authorization of this control within the subject him/herself. At the heart of disciplinary power is the assumption that being watched (and the internalization of the knowledge that one is watched) has become the most effective way to create subjected, docile subjects. Sooner or later, these subjects become their own disciplinarians, they police themselves.[66] Thus it is not simply the prison that disciplines; its technologies are paradigmatic for modern society's production of docile subjects— subjects who are rendered "countable," part of populations, made into "cases" and definable by discourses of normality and abnormality or perversion. The docile body is a combination of the analyzable and the manipulatable body. Such docile bodies are good candidates for the processes of advanced capitalism, with its own strategies of "individualization."

In this account of disciplinary power, feminists follow Foucault's insight that modern schools, hospitals, and social organizations all operate to create docile bodies in the form of subjects who internalize the gaze of the Watcher, the Guard, the Man. The process of subjugation works, as he indicates, because something is being produced—

---

[65]Ibid. The best summary I have read of the change in a whole political discourse represented by biopower is found in Dreyfus and Rabinow, *Michel Foucault: Beyond Structuralism*, 133–42. The Aristotelian-Thomist tradition of politics as concerned with the just and good life, and the Machiavellian notion of political rationality, where the power of the prince is the end of politics, are both superseded by a kind of statism where the state itself is the end. Policies are designed around the increasing discipline of citizens, not for the good or the just society, or even for the increase of a particular ruler's welfare, but for the institution itself and the increase of power for power's sake. It is this kind of political rationality that underlies the development of modern power, and in which "normalizing" techniques would be so vital.

[66]Foucault, *Discipline and Punish*, 195–228, esp. 205, 208. The exception here is schizophrenic subjects. See Gilles Deleuze and Felix Guattari, *Anti-Oedipus: Capitalism and Schizophrenia* (New York: Viking Press, 1977). Foucault's is not a conventional history of the prison, but an accounting of the present and its biopower that is prepared for by the past developments of punishment. A fascinating extension of Foucault's account of power to scientific experimentation is developed by Joseph Rouse, *Knowledge and Power: Toward a Political Philosophy of Science* (Ithaca, N.Y.: Cornell Univ. Press, 1987).

activities, rule-following, work for the prisoners, knowledge about sex for the medical scientists, inner truths about the self for the psychiatric patient, bodily rituals for the woman. "Individuals" are being produced: "Discipline 'makes' individuals; it is the specific technique of a power that regards individuals both as objects and as instruments of its exercise." These workings of modern biopower are "humble modalities" compared with that of "the majestic rituals of sovereignty or the great apparatuses of the state"; however, they are modalities as crucial for the lives of women as those more majestic patriarchal forces, such as the apparatus of the state, papal decrees, or the physical threat of rape.[67]

Disciplinary power works because pleasures are involved and desires are being constructed. As Sandra Lee Bartky points out, the compelling nature of this explanation of power is the fact that it allows us to see how women are bearers of their own oppression. There is no better example of what Foucault calls the "major effect of the Panopticon" than the internalization by women of the Male Gaze. It "induce(s) in the inmate (woman) a state of conscious and permanent visibility that assures the automatic functioning of power," namely, women's constant worry and dissatisfaction over their looks, judgment of their bodies by male standards of thinness, body shape, face, hair.[68] The productive nature of disciplinary power means that women respond by internalizing the judging Male Gaze and engage in endless bodily rituals and self-flagellations in an effort to attain standards of sexualized beauty that can never be met.

One support for such disciplinary power is the pleasure it produces. For women it can be the pleasure of being the object of the admiring gaze and the pleasure of exercising skills at being "feminine." For therapeuticized subjects it is the pleasure of the production of self-knowledge, of confession, and search for the "inner truth" of the self. The negative side of such discipline is the subjection and diversion of women's energies, the rendering docile of women. The connection of this discipline with the erotization of violence associated with the Male Gaze is as much an aspect of this productive power as is the pleasure. What this account of power adds to the analysis is the convergence of what feminists would call oppressive hegemonic power—the beauty business of patriarchal capitalism—and ordinary practices of everyday

---

[67]Foucault, *Discipline and Punish*, 201. See articles in *Feminism and Foucault*, ed. Diamond and Quinby. See also Sawicki, *Disciplining Foucault*.

[68]Sandra Lee Bartky, "Foucault, Femininity, and the Modernization of Patriarchal Power," in *Feminism and Foucault*, ed. Diamond and Quinby, 61–86. Foucault, *Discipline and Punish*, 170, paraphrase mine.

women's lives. These are capillary powers, as Foucault calls them, found in the microtechnologies and rituals and networks of everyday life. These forms of power are in some ways more illustrative of the ambiguities that constitute possibilities for further oppression than the forms that rely upon highly focused and centralized wielders of control.

In addition to identifying the everyday sites of power for a feminist analysis, the concept of biopower and its disciplinary strategies makes more of the constructed character of reality, for it is not simply Marxist constructionism or the sociology of knowledge. What is made, not natural, is coextensive with power and invested with interest. Power is not just in the hands of oppressors; power has an internal relation to knowledge. What this means is that one cannot step outside of discourse to make judgments about what ought to be, because one is always already in discourse. For Foucault, this means that truth and knowledge are relations of power.[69]

This is not to say that everyone's discourse is true (at least not true in the same way), or that a kind of ultimate relativizing and democratizing of truth and power occurs. It is to say that in any dominant discourse the terms of truth (that is, what counts as true) are defined by the discourse. Thus, in a sense those who have the power to create culture seem to shape the terms of the normal and the true . . . but not entirely.[70] The power/knowledge relation of the modern age opens to view a form of power that suggests that all subjects are subjected by discourses of normality, even those who appear most in power to effect it. Regimes of what counts as true apply to those in power as well.

It is clear from the three versions of women's dependence, however, that disciplinary processes are more problematic for some than for others. Discursive analysis is not accurately described as the search for the meaning of language, or even of sign systems, as Foucault says, but for the relations of power, conflict, and struggle that show forth in

---

[69]Foucault, "Truth and Power," 109–133.

[70]Criticisms abound of this account of power/knowledge. See, for example, a critical appropriation by Nancy Fraser, *Unruly Practices: Power, Discourse and Gender in Contemporary Social Theory* (Minneapolis: Univ. of Minnesota Press, 1989), 17–66; critiques in Sheldon S. Wolin, "On the Theory and Practice of Power," in *After Foucault: Humanistic Knowledge, Postmodern Challenges,* ed. Jonathan Arac (New Brunswick, N.J.: Rutgers Univ. Press, 1988), 179–201; and Alasdair MacIntyre, *Three Rival Versions of Moral Enquiry: Encyclopedia, Genealogy and Tradition: Being the Gifford Lectures Delivered in the University of Edinburgh in 1988* (Notre Dame, Ind.: Univ. of Notre Dame Press, 1990), 32–57, 196–215. For a theologian's overly brief criticism, see William C. Placher, *Unapologetic Theology: A Christian Voice in a Pluralistic Conversation* (Louisville: Westminster/John Knox Press, 1989), 92–104.

discursive relations.[71] Any position must recognize its own complicity with power relations and the degree to which any proposal of an emancipatory practice participates in webs that are effected by the dominant form of knowledge/power. Feminist discourses can no longer claim naiveté in this regard.[72] The implications of this connection for appeals to universals, to claims that attempt to transcend these webs of relations, are severe. As we will see, for a feminist position to take this seriously will require some way to distinguish between discursive practices in order to commend practices as liberatory, but it will not allow that practices can ever be purely liberatory.

At this point several tentative conclusions can be drawn for the constructing of a feminist theology of discourse. First, I note the obvious. If we cannot step outside of discourse, there is no place outside of the power that attends it, no realm free of the effects of the productive character of power. The practices we judge to be counter to an oppressive dominant are always already participant in the production of other potential hegemonies. The feminist discourses that enable the reading of the woman's body as wrongly violated, as raped, in the act of forced marital coitus are an example of a liberating discourse of the body—liberating, that is, in relation to the practice that creates the female body's nonintegrity in the public realm. Such feminist strategies—exemplified in the feminist theological principle that only that which supports the full humanity of women is revelatory—construct that body as deserving of value and justice.

These strategies will not deliver that body to the realm of unadulterated "truth," however, they cannot move the body outside of power and its production by other discourses that range from ambiguity to new forms of harm. Discourse and power, like discourse and reality, cannot be separated. The standard for "full humanity" is precisely what we do not have or know. Consequently we must attend to the deployment of discourse and to the many layers of social relations that can always be adduced to expose the noninnocence of any partic-

---

[71]Foucault, "Truth and Power," 114–15. This raises the interesting question of the benevolence or agonistic character of ultimate reality, one to be discussed at a later point. I do not think accepting this account of the struggle- or power-related character of discursive relations makes it impossible to argue for other kinds of relations than Foucault will allow.

[72]The debate over whether one can do ethics after or with Foucault is a long one (related to that of a post-Nietzschean ethics). I am not following Foucault here in my appeal to the notion of "our question" and implicit judgment that certain forms of oppression are wrong, intolerable, and need to be changed. I continue to turn this into a liberation discourse, which his is not, at least unproblematically. For one account of what Foucault's procedure was (interpretive analytics) after he abandoned archaeology, see Dreyfus and Rabinow, *Michel Foucault: Beyond Structuralism*, 104–125.

ular position. At the same time, recognition of the knowledge/power relation is not the end of work for liberation. Nor does it create a vicious relativism (i.e., one thing is as good as another). Rather, it allows us to follow out the possibilities for transgression of forms of discipline.

This notion of power helps display the complexity of patriarchal power, particularly with regard to the reason it "sticks" and the support it gets from its "victims." By contrast to the model of disciplinary power, the idea that patriarchal power is a unidirectional, negative force that obliterates women, appears less adequate and resonates more with Foucault's notion of absolute monarchy and the repressiveness of juridical power.[73] The work of the forces of capitalist patriarchy have to be brought into relation with the capillary everyday technologies of power that construct women. What are the technologies that construct the "homemaker" position? What are the pleasures and possibilities of its dependencies? These questions apply to the dependencies of the professional subject position as well, for no subject position is free of the reach of power. This overlapping of practices and formations also means that the marginalized are neither outside of nor totally lacking in power. If power is not the sole possession of "oppressors," then we must look to the marginalized, to each community subjected by capitalist patriarchy, for the ways in which power is productive in their bodies, both making them docile and opening up the possibilities of resistance.[74]

It is the discourses outside of a dominant discourse that have the potential to destabilize its power to function in an utterly determinist, monolithic way. Hegemonic discourse—such as heterosexuality, for example, which surely qualifies as a totality that shapes practices in a variety of sites—does not work to blot out the discourses that do not fit; noncompliant bodies are not (always) obliterated. The male gaze of patriarchy disseminated so widely by capitalist culture and its beauty

---

[73]The distinction between power and domination has yet to be made, and it is a difficult one to determine in Foucault, as Jana Sawicki points out. I will suggest one distinction characterized by Christian grammar in the next chapter. See Foucault, "Two Lectures: Lecture One: 7 January 1976; and 14 January 1976," in *Power/Knowledge*, 78–108. See Sawicki, *Disciplining Foucault*.

[74]In his now well-known account of modern sex discourse, Foucault argues that sex was not repressed in the nineteenth century; it was produced, created, managed, and organized as a discourse. Sex was manufactured as a scientific topic and as a diagnostic tool; it was used to create categories of subjects, such as the homosexual, the pervert, the masturbating child, and the hysterical woman. The hegemony effected by these discourses is problematic, but it is productive, not simply negative. The use of sexual identity as a source of discipline, the creation of a pathological identity, is also a discourse of resistance of the gay community, suggesting the multiple possibilities of discourses.

industry is not completely effective either. The creation of other aesthetic practices is one of the transgressions of that discipline; these can work as alternatives that parody what is available.[75]

I conclude that the possibilities for resistance reside in the complex subject positions in which women find themselves. The poststructuralist refusal of fixed meaning is a reminder that the convergences of multiple discourses are always their potential destabilization, a destabilization that disperses power and precludes essentialist views of oppression *and* of liberation. Other signifying networks always intersect with the dominant orders—with the discourses of dependence supported by patriarchal capitalism—and they are always capable of being organized as practices, which undermine, alter, and even contest these "official" definitions.[76]

In short, the articulation of discourse with power raises problems for some of the ways feminist theologians conceive of oppression. Feminist theories that treat power as the sole possession of a monolithic patriarchy are no longer viable on the terms of discourse theory. It is true that an important way to conceive of gender oppression is still in place. What it is possible to say in any situation is clearly dependent upon the "languages" in power, and the asymmetrical valuing of male over female is embedded in that language and reproduced by patriarchal capitalism. The three different positions of dependence are instances of that hegemony. Power is everywhere, however, not simply in the hands of the white male elite. Notions of oppression and liberation must be impacted by this fact. Not only is power everywhere in the sense of some shared capacity or potentiality to act or respond, but in the more insidious sense missed by monarchical, juridical accounts of oppression. This is where Foucault's work is useful. Recognition that power does not work simply as a negative, prohibitive force, either legal or military, helps us see the deployment of multiple networks and relations in contexts that control and divert desire.

Thus Foucault is right when he says that power works because "it traverses and produces things, it induces pleasure, forms knowledge,

---

[75]Butler develops the notion of gender as parodic practice. See *Gender Trouble*, 79–149.

[76]Work in cultural studies, especially the British traditions of Raymond Williams and Stuart Hall, has focused on the dispersal of power and the need to recognize resistance in popular culture. Antonio Gramsci was instrumental in the widespread concession that power is not the sole possession of those in command; his notion of hegemony includes that recognition. For a helpful summary of this work and bibliography, see Patrick Brantlinger, *Crusoe's Footprints: Cultural Studies in Britain and America* (New York: Routledge, 1990).

produces discourse" and operates throughout the social body.[77] To understand the work of patriarchal oppression, it may be necessary to
redo an account of misogyny analogous to the monarchy or all-powerful state and as centralized and unified. In place of the all-powerful
Man, we must pursue the networks and productive pleasures that patriarchal visions have induced, and pursue them in local contexts.

Theologically, this more complex view of power is important in
two ways. First, the ambiguity and omnipresence apparent in power
conceived in Foucaultian terms are suggestive of the view that I proposed as a theological grammar of social contradiction, identifying the
grounds for the possibility of sin in social manifestations. These social
manifestations are candidates for thinking about sin, because they are
not simply cognitive error or cultural lag, they involve social practices
that harm and deny the goodness of creation as potentially honoring
God. They manifest themselves and work as particular, located social
formations and practices, not as the formal structures of finitude and
threat that characterize the individual. These social discourses construct individuals, but they are never reducible to individual sin. Further, they show human bondage in that harm; the production of docile
bodies is always tied up with goods and pleasure. They show human
complicity in that harm by way of the production, containment, and
degradation of human pleasure and desire that it requires.

Second, the threat of this account to overrun a theological grammar
of liberation and redemption by virtue of its potential totalization of
the will-to-power may be real, but, in my view, it is not debilitating.
The liberation theological task is to discern the effects of discourses,

not to determine the nature of the real outside of historical practices,
which it already has gambled upon as gracious. We are not bound to
construe this power/knowledge relation as an ontological statement
that the reality outside of our practices is agonistic. While such an agonistic ontology is the typical way that Foucault is understood, even
he assumes that there is always resistance; disciplinary power is always
transgressed. A theo/acentric practice assumes that the conditions of
recognizing harm are some practices characterized by grace. It gam-
bles that such occurrences are worth a narration that points to and
evokes gracious practices in history, that this is part of what it means
to be ordered theo/acentrically. In my analyses, then, I will attempt to
discern and produce other possibilities for grace as the transgression of
inescapable webs of power.

---

[77]Foucault, "Truth and Power," 119.

Discourse versus representation: stifling difference

As a theory of power, language, and gender, the account of discourse I have proposed differs at a number of points from those earlier identified assumptions of feminist liberation theology on these topics. The view that reality is constituted by signifying shuts off access through language to the thing-in-itself. Discourse theory entails a realism of the sort that requires a look at convention and at the relations of power that inscribe or define what counts as real. It entails a materialism that avoids dichotomizing the mental and the physical by the incorporation of social processes in an analysis of discursive ordering. At every point terms of oppression and liberation require that the intelligibility of reality be understood in terms of its creative instability—an instability displayed in all discourse. Dominant discursive formations neither silence all dissent nor present themselves with no boundaries or seams for the defining of an entity.

In contrast, the appeal to women's experience in feminist theology can be taken to assume that there is a natural referent, "woman," the "we" who share oppression and common humanity. The natural is, according to discourse theory, not a given, a neutral meaning, that may be read off of bodies or actions, but an unarticulated realm already ordered by discursive processes. This problem is not resolved by pointing to feminist experience rather than prediscursive experience. It is not just a problem of experiential grounding, something George Lindbeck has identified in criticizing liberal theology. More than an infelicitous epistemic justification is at stake. The use of women's experience is connected to an account of power that is inadequate for the situation of all women, and may in fact disempower the "other" woman.

A feminist account of power is problematic when it attributes a virtually monarchical negative force to patriarchy. It is also incompatible with a theological grammar of the bondage of sin. The extreme case of that incompatibility occurs in the treatment of language as the conveyer of harmful information in the form of dominant male-valorizing content. In its simplest form, the inclusive-exclusive language discussion, language works as the conveying of ideas. Its force is cognitive, and the meaning conveyed is negative: language renders women invisible and invalidates them. The simplistic cognitive nature of the language-power relation—the suggestion that understanding is the realm of harm—is mitigated a bit by the notion that language works in the form of networks of symbols that shape experience. That view still relies upon the content of patriarchal traditions, however. Without recognition of conflict and desire, or of the systems of meaning that make every subject a coded subject, feminists suggest a one-

way understanding of the force of power and imply that it is
undifferentiated, that ideas have the same impact on everyone. In such
a configuration the appeal to women's experience supports a cogni-
tive-communicative view of power that operates with a representative
view of language (the view that language points to and can convey a
reality) and drastically narrows a feminist theological vision.

It may seem that I have caricatured the way feminists understand
power.[78] By focusing only on their identification of the harmful, antiwoman character of much of the content of the tradition, I deflect attention away from the fact that feminists always also recognize the *use*
of the tradition against women and structures of power. Continued
comparison with discourse theory, however, suggests the problem is
more profound. Not only power but a whole way of thinking about
power, gender, and language is implicated in the appeal to women's
experience. Insofar as feminist theology is based on the norm of
"women's experience," it risks perpetuating this configuration.
Review of the main points of feminist liberation theology *as method* in
light of discourse theory gets us closer to a more serious verdict on the
problematic account of language, and therefore of power, employed
by liberation feminist theology.

Feminist theologies answer the question What is language? with
various accounts of its representational character. They rely upon the
nominalizing work of language, the view rejected by the poststructuralist theory that language is relations or differences. This work is exemplified in the notion that the dominance of male pronouns and
images excludes women and that, conversely, to name the female effects their inclusion. This view treats language as a process of naming,
operative outside complex relations of difference. The impact of being
named could be utterly negligible if we factor in social relations of
class—a subject position of poverty, for example. The metaphorical
character of theological reflection in the work of Sallie McFague is
relief provided to pursuit of nominalizing accounts of language; however, all share the notion that theological claims, figurative or otherwise, "express human experience," a reinstating of the same problem
that bypasses the coded nature of any experience.[79]

---

[78]Feminists articulate other accounts of power, to be sure; the notion of co-creative
power is found in most feminist thinking to counter domination. This view is not connected with the operative view of language, however, so it does not get to the problems
I am criticizing. I thank Carol Robb for reminding me of this point.

[79]This has been discussed in terms of Rosemary Radford Ruether. Sallie McFague,
Models of God: Theology for an Ecological, Nuclear Age (Philadelphia: Fortress Press, 1987),
29–57.

To my second question, How is language *produced?*, feminist liberation theology points to at least three sites. First, when it does refer to a subjectivity prior to discourse, the privileging of "women's experience" locates the origin of meaning in subjects. It suggests the illusory notion that "our speech is our servant," as Foucault says.[80] This appeal is consistent with the view represented by Rosemary Radford Ruether, that even as meaning is social and gets mediated through communal traditions, it is after all an individual consciousness that is the origin of religious traditions and their renewals.[81] We must assume, the logic continues, that the experience which binds women together is just such a realm of consciousness from which new transformative traditions will be generated, or at least confirmed. As the destabilizing of the subject indicated, presenting the subject as the originating site of meaning production universalizes women's experience with an uncoded subject and perpetuates the very practice feminists sought to expose and undermine—the false universal, man.

The methodological pattern of feminist theology accounts for the production of language in its recovery of historical meanings, particularly from scripture.[82] Because the theological task requires more than simply the original contributions of contemporary women's consciousness, feminist theologians also appeal to the Christian tradition, where they show evidence of their assumptions about language. A prominent form of that appeal occurs in the search for the real meaning of a biblical passage, exemplified in feminist defenses of women's ministries, and in the references to the histories of patriarchal oppression of women.[83] Whether in the use of biblical-critical tools to get at what the text (usually Paul) meant then, or in the recovery of the women hidden by the texts of the official traditions, the recoverable, decipherable meanings about women in the Christian biblical and postbiblical tradition supply meaning for feminist theologians. This supply is dependent on the tools of historical-critical method. While such an approach is in line with the rules of the theological academy, it

---

[80]Foucault, *The Order of Things*, 297.

[81]"Since consciousness is ultimately individual, we postulate that revelation always starts with an individual." Rosemary Radford Ruether, *Sexism and God-Talk: Toward a Feminist Theology* (Boston: Beacon Press, 1983), 13.

[82]The focus on scripture is understandable, given the importance of its use in the Christian community to exclude, construct, and otherwise shape believers' lives. Occasionally we find a search for meanings generally—in Western culture, such as Catherine Keller's *From a Broken Web: Separation, Sexism, and Self* (Boston: Beacon Press, 1986). But my interest here is the methodological constants of liberation feminism, which focus on scripture. What scripture means with regard to gender is much more important, it would seem, than any other tradition, written or oral.

[83]I will discuss these issues in the next chapter.

is itself a social system of meaning. Subject to a critique of positivism in its reliance upon recovery of "facts" and "events," the historical "what really happened" is reminiscent of the appeal to the "natural," yet is *not* the system of meaning that orders the biblical text for all women.

The third source for positive meaning is in feminist theologians' recognition of the social structures that create and sustain the conditions of gender oppression. The appeal to the social is definitional to liberation feminist theology. What we do not see, as I have argued, is the connection of the stuff of social structures, actions, and practices, with the realm of signifying, of meaning (the connection of social systems of meaning with coded subjects). Instead we find the separation of language/ideas from external reality. Idealist dichotomies of the "material" and the ideational, the external realm and the internal realm, are perpetuated. The recognition of patriarchal structures is never correlated to the discourses of women in particular subject positions. Even if all women are constructed by the processes of capitalist patriarchy, there are multiple discursive games or totalities that create different subject positions and practices for them.

The gap between the hegemony of capitalist patriarchy, for example, and the discursive practices of the poor woman is not filled in. Her resistances are rendered invisible; the texts of Christian patriarchal scripture and their oppressive power are the only indication of local discourses that liberation feminist accounts leave us. (We must assume they would be the "same" for women in different social locations.) In short, meaning is produced by history, by the biblical text; it is affected by social structures, but there is no way to theorize its production at the site of utterance by different systems of meaning. There is, consequently, no way to theorize that the convergence of history, biblical text, and social structures might need to be conceived in very different terms for women in different subject positions.

Liberation commitments versus liberal modernist language theory

The separation of signifying process (in this case language) and the social (or everything else) is possible in liberation feminist theology because the view of language as a conveyer of fixed meaning is more problematic than first appeared. Two metaphors about language help portray what is problematic about that view and show it at odds with liberationist commitments of feminist liberation theology. The most straightforward indication of the view is in feminist theologies' claims that appear to be about the constitutive character of language: language conveys the realities outside of it—patriarchal intentions—in the sexist content of the tradition, and conveys affirmation of women in traditions that recover and name women. I say "appear," because in light of discourse theory, this no longer is an accurate statement. Rather than constituting reality in the way that patterns of signification do, leaving no unmeaningful "stuff" outside to be dealt with later, in feminist theologians' accounts, language carries or mediates a reality outside of it, whether that be the divine, women's experience, or patriarchal power.

The primary way the seriousness of gender oppression is articulated via the convergence of language, power, and gender in the sexist text—the pernicious tradition—is exemplary of this view of language as mediator. That formulation reduces power and attributes it inappropriately. It is based on a dichotomy between the stuff of social structures, of the external world of economy and state, and the realities of language. The metaphor best capturing the notion of language in this formulation is that language is a vehicle or container that passes information between subjects.[84] Ironically, the notion of the sexist text—the very attempt to indicate the impress of location on knowledge—is implemented with a view of language that leaves virtually invisible the differential processes of signifying which accompany it. This observation connects feminist theological method with a liberalism that is surely contradictory to its liberationist commitments.

What is problematically liberal in this treatment of language as a medium are the features it shares with the epistemic notion of language that Timothy Reiss terms "modernist." Herein is found a second metaphor. Modernist accounts of knowledge are characterized by their failure or incapacity to acknowledge the imprint of the enunciating subject on the enunciated.[85] In order to acknowledge complicity in discourse, it is necessary to give up the notion of a free space prior to its discursive ordering, whether that space be found in the imagination, in primal, prereflective experience, or in a carefully de-

---

[84]Interestingly, Brian Wren rejects this metaphor. Although he perpetuates essentialist notions of feminine and masculine, his work comes the closest to moving away from a communicative account of language. *What Language Shall I Borrow? God-Talk in Worship: A Male Response to Feminist Theology* (New York: Crossroad, 1990). For a discussion of the "container" metaphor, see George Lakoff, *Metaphors We Live By* (Chicago: Univ. of Chicago Press, 1980).

[85]I use quotes around "subject" to indicate some breadth of interpretation here. I do not want to confine the notion of the imprint of the enunciating subject to the individual, creative consciousness. Reiss, *The Discourse of Modernism,* chap. 1.

fended Cartesian notion of founding intuitive self-knowledge. It is this self-defining, autonomous subject that characterizes the liberal notion of the self, as I have already argued. In the light of the linguistic assumptions of modernism, the fact that feminist theologians are critical of liberalism does not extricate them from participating in its practice.

Modernity's dominant metaphor is the telescope and the controlling gaze, according to Reiss. While it is clear that this is an ordering that encompasses far more than liberalism's discourse, it is compatible with the notion under inspection. Within the space of this metaphor, language has the status of a lens that can alternately serve to mediate reality to the cognizing mind or to alter the shape of that reality—by focusing it more sharply or fuzzing its edges. The point is that language's claim to do the former is rendered suspect by the latter. As long as the roles of the lens and the knower on the product are acknowledged, we have a space for the discussion of production and accountability.[86] Once language is allowed to substitute for the reality, to stand in for it, or to re-present it, the role of the lens disappears in the discourse of knowledge.[87] What is more, the control exercised over the product of the technology is elided; one appears to be cognizing reality itself. The claim of neutral access and the option to claim the display of the world as it really is both become possibilities. Both ways of thinking about reflection characterize Enlightenment universalizing reason and obscure the embeddedness of discourse in power.

Recognition of the complicity or the position of the subject in reflection, as I argued in chapter 1, is one of the hallmarks of feminist theology. In it we find neither an assumption of neutral access nor a claim to display the world as it really is. Moreover, because feminist theology participates in the historical consciousness of modernity, it grants that its own voice is limited, partial, experimental, and historically relative.[88] Despite these good intentions, feminist theology does

---

[86]This premodern stance characterized Galileo's use of the telescope. With it he emphasized the distance between the object and the mind and was able to think about the impact the telescope/lens had on the object of knowledge: what is seen through it is different than that object seen with the naked eye. Reiss, ibid.

[87]This second move is initiated by Descartes, but finalized most clearly by Cartesianism. It is in Cartesianism that the collapse of the object and the language's capacity to represent it occurs. Reiss's example is the Port Royale Logic. See ibid., chap. 1.

[88]This concession fits Reiss's category of the shift to the process of knowledge and its finitude, a feature of nineteenth-century historicism. Thus we might compare this kind of acknowledgment to the recognition that theological reflection is a description of the human process, rather than of God-in-Godself, which is how he described historicism. Reiss, ibid., 21–37. Also see Reiss's description of Baconian experimental discourse, ibid., 34.

not escape the failings of the telescope metaphor when it relies upon this methodological pattern. That is seen more clearly with regard to its own status as a discourse. What feminist theology fails to do is articulate the webs of meaning/power that constitute even its own ostensibly "natural" claims. Without attention to the kind of discourse in which its reflection is constructed and its institutional location, feminist theology as a kind of liberatory reflection is implicated in some of the features of the modernist grid of intelligibility by virtue of its erasure or occlusion of the full dimensions of that location.

Simply to confess historicality and transitoriness is not enough. Nor are authorial confessions of social location sufficient, since the individual consciousness is not the (sole) source of oppressive formations.[89] This kind of relativity does not flesh out the multiple orderings that create differences in women's positions. Language—sexist language—as currently understood stands in for the realities, such as practices, subject formations, and the social relations and desires that construct them. Feminist theology has yet to foreground its linkages with power *as discourse*, and discourse *as power*.

To recount the problems with language: language is, at best, figurative in feminist accounts. There is no way to understand the significations of nonlinguistic reality and the social systems of meaning that construct the coded subject. The appeal to prediscursive experience is one example of this, where women's experience serves as a warrant. Another example is its inability to reflect upon the discursive ordering of bodies and the resulting occlusion of the heterosexist bias in feminist liberation theology. The heterosexist binary is the continually invoked content for oppression and liberation, a practice connected, according to Butler, with compulsory heterosexuality. The discursive ordering of male-female bodies and the formations of heterosexual desire that accompany it make feminist theology an unwitting reinforcer of compulsory heterosexuality with its appeal to women's experience and identity politics.[90]

---

[89]The logic of poststructuralism makes this problematic. If writing does not express the inner reality of the subject, neither does personal locating get at the discursive economy, for example, of the academic text. See Paul A. Bove on the problem of the humanism perpetuated rather than challenged by oppositional intellectuals who fail to distinguish their role as perpetuator of the status quo due to confusions about the subject. *Intellectuals in Power: A Genealogy of Critical Humanism* (New York: Columbia Univ. Press, 1986).

[90]Butler is not the only one making this kind of argument. Although her position is not the same, Eve Kosofsky Sedgwick argues for the ways in which gender and sexuality are best treated as distinct issues, but always with awareness of their co-implication. *Epistemology of the Closet* (Berkeley: Univ. of California Press, 1990), 27–37.

The linkage of language with power also implicitly silences voices of other women of faith: texts' meanings are fixed, power is monarchical. Those whose experience differs from the model of "women's experience" are not accounted for, or constitute a lobotomized casualty of patriarchy, one of Mary Daly's "fembots."[91] This is not to say that feminist theologians do not want to be challenged by other women's experience or that they do not invite it. It is to say that the methodological pieces are not challenged simply by contrasting experiences, for the epistemic grid is the problem that experience cannot touch. The purveyor of these blindnesses, the "telescope" or occluding and occluded instrument in feminist liberation theology, is found in the methodological discourse with its indebtedness to modernist liberal notions of subjects and texts.

Feminist method relies upon the warrants and sources of women's experience in convergence with the judgment that certain contents of the tradition are sexist and others liberating. This constellation prevents the kinds of questions that might open up the specific subject positions, desires, and technologies of power that construct women in different subject positions. Perhaps those texts are different for other women. Minimally those questions require respect for the complexity and variety of gender oppression and forms of its resistance. That respect requires a move out of the liberal grid of intelligibility regarding experiencing subjects, representational language, and oppressive/liberating texts.

A way out of these problems is offered by the very discourse theory that brings them into focus. As feminist theologians we will better display our commitment to the situated character of knowledge by finding a feminist way to articulate an opening for other women's practices, women who are not the "we" of the feminist account. To do this, feminist theology needs to understand itself as constructed in a discursive order—a system of meaning—and as contributing to dis-

---

[91]See Meaghan Morris's harsh criticism of this category in "Amazing Grace: Notes on Mary Daly's Poetics," in *The Pirate's Fiancee: Feminism, Reading, Postmodernism* (New York: Verso, 1988), 27–50. It is not the case that feminist theologians *develop* the implications of this, that women are passive and obliterated by patriarchal power. Elisabeth Schüssler Fiorenza, for example, argued for a recovery of her story, refusing the implication that patriarchal oppression blotted out women's agency; *In Memory of Her: A Feminist Theological Reconstruction of Christian Origins* (New York: Crossroad, 1983). The way oppressiveness is theorized and attributed in relation to language is still problematic, however. Even though there is recognition (especially by Daly) that women internalize patriarchy's sexist views, therefore becoming the vehicles of their own oppression—a more adequate image of power—the dominant model limits the way the overdetermination of oppression and multiplicity of resistance can be appreciated in feminist theological analysis.

cursive practices, particularly to women's emancipatory faith practices, not as a partially figurative and multivocal form of reflection and not as reflection on women's experience.

This alteration in definition entails viewing liberation feminist theology as a discursive practice located in a situation of utterance. Discourse, we remember, is a set of statements that get their meaning via networks of differences, intersections with other discursive formations. Discourse has its own stabilities and its own emancipatory thrusts. To admit that feminist theology's appeal to "women," then, is (as it sometimes acknowledges) to *certain* women's experience — those who work for women's liberation and against all injustices — is not to disqualify liberation feminist theology *as theology*. Rather, it means that this "experience" must be seen as constructed from converging discourses, their constitution by differential networks, and their production of certain pleasures and subjugations. While it may have practices and insights for women in other social locations, it is not representative of a natural realm of women's consciousness, religious or otherwise.

Feminist theological discourse can be identified and given shape as signifying processes that open up resistance *in a particular way*, as well as participate in forms of oppressive power. This alternative entails identifying feminist theologians as institutionalized academics as well as participants in other social practices, such as ecclesiastical organizations. "Feminist theologians" occupy subject positions that are constructed out of multiple discursive totalities — from the smaller totalities of the academy and local culture and church, to the larger totality of patriarchal capitalism.

I conclude that until the shift from women's experience to women's faith practices in discursive totalities is accomplished, feminist theology presents its own ruminations as a form of realist representation, not necessarily emancipatory discourse.[92] With realist representation, feminist theology appears to appeal to truth outside of power, to take a position outside the struggle, and thereby to perpetuate the hegemony of the liberal false universal. Feminist theology needs to understand itself as discursive *practice*, meaning in a rather trivial way that it incorporates more than linguistic (oral and written) significations, and in a more significant way that it is co-constituted by the games of the academic institutions that produce it — a discursive totality, by church, and by the social formation of patriarchal capitalism as well.

---

[92]Rebecca S. Chopp has argued for the shift to discourse in *The Power to Speak: Feminism, Language, God* (New York: Crossroad, 1989).

To proceed in the formation of feminist theology as emancipatory discursive practice, one must offer alternatives to its problematic aspects, the methodological features. In chapter 1 I argued that this account was problematic because it did not presume a coded subject who is constructed out of social systems of meaning. In this chapter, I have identified this methodological problem more specifically as the remnants in feminist theologies of a *liberal discursive order*. I have focused on the importance of the criteriological woman subject placed in relation to the fixed text or its recoverable meanings that harm by virtue of their contents and thus ignore the complexities of desire and conflict in power.

In the next chapter, I will take up the question of biblical texts and the possibilities in a theory of discourse for connecting women's practices of faith with texts so as to provide alternatives to this liberal discursive order. Alternatives will enable us to identify the systems of discourse that constitute women's faith practices relative to different locations in the social formation of patriarchal capitalism. When such differences can be seen, we can better read women's practices as emancipatory and constrained without resorting to a hegemonic notion of women's experience as their common denominator or to fixed texts that oppress or liberate simply by virtue of their contents.

With an alternative set of constants with which to read different women's practices of faith, the task of chapter 3, I will return again to feminist theology as a theological discourse. I will ask how a form of reflection that is called upon to respect different faith practices can be both theological and feminist. Feminist liberation theology is a discursive practice within a totality that includes institutional social location. Once its universalizing gestures are reined in, the powerful and distinctive effects of this practice can be seen—effects that contribute to an emancipatory speaking between women of different positions, rather than the enforcement of categories that discipline the "other"— the nonheterosexual or the nonliberal.

3
Chapter
From the One Text to the Many: Women Performing Scripture

> Writer and reader are not the fixed and isolated origin and conclusion of the textual process, nor is their relationship that of a constant fact to an uncontrolled variable (like Iser's oscillation between and conflation of implied reader as textual function and a real reader). Both "writer" and "reader" are categories of a particular literary system and of particular regimes within it and only as such are they amenable to theorization.
>
> —John Frow

I have determined that in some important ways we cannot "change the subject" using the categories of feminist theology because its assumptions about language, gender, and power rely on communicative, mediating notions of language, on particular contents and their cognitive appropriation to describe the negative (and positive) workings of the Christian tradition for women. Insofar as feminist theological method retains the liberal frame of an appeal to uncoded experience, we cannot use it to move away from a representative account of language and its accompanying juridical version of power. The desire to create analyses that enable all women to work on the oppressive structures that constitute a gender-biased social formation cannot be supported by this liberal, modernist grid of intelligibility.

From women's experience to an analytic of women's discourse

An alternative to the modernist categories is a feminist analytic of women's discourses. If we analyze women's discourses rather than ex-

117

perience, it will be possible to specify social locations and their respective construction of "woman" out of local economies of meaning. A discourse is incomplete without the discursive totality in which it has meaning. I am not replacing a feminist grid but, rather, the notion that there is an essential woman, an inner consciousness, or a natural body that transcends all particularities to which we can appeal in order to join women together in a shared dilemma/oppression and a shared vision of emancipation. Replacement of this false universal with an analytic of women's discourses will allow reconsideration of the specific productions of positions for women: What discourses construct the middle-class white churchwoman's position? the poor Pentecostal woman preacher's? the liberal-academic liberation feminist's?

More specifically, my focus is on the particular ways in which Christian traditions are constitutive of both oppressive gender constraints and emancipatory possibilities for different communities of women. The implications of poststructuralist analysis on the subject for a theological analytic support a look at how Christian traditions converge as specific women's practices of resistance to their oppression. This is because poststructuralism dissolves the credibility of a generically liberating or sexist Bible. In this sense, my analytic departs from work to recover women's practices as such.[1]

With this focus I recognize that, in the first place, Christian women do "make trouble" with their faith in ways that advance their gender emancipation. Thus a feminist analytic is interested in the places where gender issues *have become issues* through women's faith practices in a variety of social locations. The feminist theological task is to ask how women's faith traditions are constitutive of their emancipatory practices. In the second place, my proposal pays attention to the need to de-essentialize both judgments that Christianity (or any tradition) is always emancipatory or that it is always oppressive. It is thereby a correction of the strategy that lays the white, middle-class liberation agenda on all women.[2]

---

[1] The desire to alter the invisibility of women's presence in standard histories has been a necessary project of the past decades of women's studies and feminist theology alike. The recovery of women is one way to read the call to change the subject of feminist theology to women's discourses. A number of critical issues about retrievals and how literature is related to feminist interests in women have emerged after the initial stage of images of women in literature and locating women authors for the canon. It would be interesting to trace parallels for feminist theology. For some of the complications in literary theory, see Toril Moi, *Sexual/Textual Politics: Feminist Literary Theory* (London: Methuen, 1985).

[2] Thus my use of the category "discourses" is narrow in a particular way. It is not inclusive of all practices by women, such as the work of Rebecca Chopp, which iden-

This look at particular instances of Christian practice is an alternative to what can be dangerous in the view that anything women do is resistance or is exemplary subject matter for feminist theology. Were I to define women's discourses in such a general fashion, I would be resorting to another kind of essentialism. One's being counted a woman would then be the reason one's practice was privileged.[3] Such issues are sticky, to be sure. My point is not that feminism should become so antiessentialist that women get excluded. It is, rather, that we should look at places where resistance does occur in order to think about liberation theological projects, even when that resistance is not intended to be feminist.[4]

The lens of gender criticism has made it impossible to assume the liberating character of Christian tradition as such. The mirror image to that assessment, the judgment that Christianity is essentially patriarchal, is also a dead end. Both positions represent judgments that are essentialist; they are not credible because they make a judgment about all of Christianity. It is not just to avoid essentialism that I make the shift to discourse, however. My second reason for the development of a new position refers to the fact that Christian traditions have not been

---

tifies the spatial, temporal, and bodily practices of women, including adornment, cyclical modalities of existence, and benevolent corporality, which she argues resist the dominant ordering of the social order by virtue of their location on the margins. Nor does it refer to a population of women, such as the work of Sharon Welch on African American women's literature, whose ethical practices are mined to counter the dominant white middle-class ethics. It refers to the convergences of biblical Christian communities in the construction of women's faith practices. Therefore mine has more affinities with the work of Katie Cannon, Renita Weems, or Kwok Pui Lan. Rebecca S. Chopp, *The Power to Speak: Feminism, Language, God* (New York: Crossroad, 1989), 99–128. Katie Cannon, *Black Womanist Ethics* (Atlanta: Scholars Press, 1988); Sharon D. Welch, *A Feminist Ethic of Risk* (Minneapolis: Fortress Press, 1990).

[3]My position that subjects are constituted by converging discourses is enough to invalidate that route, were it not also pedagogically problematic, as Diana Fuss points out, when simply being a woman gets one exclusive privileges not only of the floor, but to speak about gender oppression. See Diana Fuss, *Essentially Speaking: Feminism, Nature and Difference* (New York: Routledge, 1989), 113–19.

[4]My proposal limits the ways in which "difference" can be articulated. Differences are axes of categorization that have typically been articulated in terms of gender, race, class, and sexual preference. None of these axes is adequate for the assessment of domination-resistance in the United States, nor are they adequate to the kinds of differences that obtain between subjects. The articulation between gender and constructions of desire and sexuality raised by Judith Butler is just one example of the multiple intersections of discourses that constrain and oppress yet do not fit neatly under any one axis. By choosing to look at particular women's discourses of faith, I will miss some of the differences that matter; the gain, however, will be the alteration of certain problematic ways of thinking about the convergence of Christian texts and gender discourses with the creation of a broader lens to look at more ways subjects resist and are constrained. See Eve Kosofsky Sedgwick's helpful discussion of axioms that review this topic in *Epistemology of the Closet* (Berkeley: Univ. of California Press, 1990), 1–63.

constructed by feminists with enough complexity to allow for all the ways in which resistance and oppression occur in Christian communities of women. Womanists have long argued that the oppressive biblical text read by Euro-American feminists is not the one African American women read.[5] Another "destabilization" is in order.

Not only do I want to look at the places where women are supported by the Christian tradition to resist, but to argue for a theoretical redefining of Christian tradition as well. Feminist reliance upon the false universal "women's experience" has moved us too quickly away from the ways that many Christianities serve women in different locations. Out of respect for the existence of many resisting Christian women and in the spirit of Michel Foucault, this attention to women's discourse is an inquiry into the conditions under which Christian tradition supports practices that resist particular oppressions. It is also concerned with the complicity of that tradition in oppression.[6]

In this chapter I argue for an alternative to a given of hermeneutical theory that supports the assumption that there *is* "one Christianity," namely, the notion of the one text of scripture upon which feminist theology has relied. If we grasp the fact that the position "woman" is differently constructed in different Christian communities, we recognize related differences in how texts are read and practiced, particularly the text of Christian scripture. We also see the way in which oppression and resistance work at the micro-level, at the level of everyday practice. The route through particular discursive practices is necessary to avoid the absolutizing and generalizing of a monolithic patriarchy and its accompanying sexist scripture. With ways to recognize the different kinds of resistances and constraints that Christian tradition constructs for women in different social locations, it will be possible to turn again to the question of common structures of patriarchal oppression.[7]

---

[5]Katie Geneva Cannon, "The Emergence of Black Feminist Consciousness," in *Feminist Interpretation of the Bible*, ed. Letty M. Russell (Philadelphia: Westminster Press, 1985), 30–40. Renita Weems, "Reading *Her Way* Through the Struggle: African-American Women and the Bible," in *Stony the Road We Trod: African American Biblical Interpretation*, ed. Cain Hope Felder (Minneapolis: Fortress Press, 1991), 57–77.

[6]This position is articulated with great elegance by Sharon D. Welch in *Communities of Resistance and Solidarity: A Feminist Theology of Liberation* (Maryknoll, N.Y.: Orbis Books, 1985). I assume that versions of this assumption operate in the work of Welch, who commends African American women's texts because survival is resistance.

[7]See Michel Foucault, *Power/Knowledge: Selected Interviews and Other Writings, 1972–1977*, ed. Colin Gordon, trans. Colin Gordon et al. (New York: Pantheon Books, 1980), 98–103. For a feminist version of Foucault's account of the work of networks of power and those of the more central apparatuses, see Biddy Martin, "Feminism, Criticism, and Foucault," in *Feminism and Foucault: Reflections on Resistance*, ed. Irene Diamond and Lee Quinby (Boston: Northeastern Univ. Press, 1988), 3–19.

The question of women's faith practices requires new ways to think about texts, other elements in a discursive totality, and the resistance and oppression therein. When I call into question the notion of the experiencing subject in relation to sexist or liberating text, I raise the issue of the need for alternative categories for hermeneutics as well. Because scripture is a prominent feature of women's faith practices, I will first review the effects of poststructuralist literary and cultural theory on the hermeneutical frame, interpreting subject in relation to biblical text as these are retained in prominent feminist strategies. The discourses of academic feminist theology, which I analyze in chapter 6, are not biblical practices, strictly speaking. As practices that make meaning in relation to other texts, however, they are subject to the same terms. My thesis is that the homogenizing of differences found in the false universal, woman, has its correlate in the framework of interpreter-text. In what follows I review the needs of a theory for women's biblical practices in light of the nature of discourse. A review of the options in prominent feminist strategies about texts will lead me to an alternative proposal.

Framing women's relationship to scripture

The move to discursively produced women's social locations has implications for how I frame women's relationship to scripture or any defining text. It rules out some approaches. This relationship cannot be articulated with the notion of subjects as centers of consciousness, because I have argued that subjects are coded and need to be thought of as texts of a sort themselves; they are constituted out of the discourses that construct women's subject positions. Another inadequate approach would assume that there is a biblical text which must be placed in relation to this subject and to her context. This second false option remains to be discussed, and I will argue that it disappears along with the notion of the substantial identity of the subject. In short, two alternative hegemonies—either of the text as such, or the subject as such—must be avoided.

It is important to understand the embeddedness of all discourse in power, and thus in the fallibilities that attend particular social formations. Therefore, a theory of women's relationship to the scriptures and other religious traditions must be constructed that does not posit women's discourses as somehow "innocent." This would mean that any reading of scripture women offer is somehow liberating. At the same time, we must also avoid perpetuating an account of women as victims, either by virtue of the force of a unilaterally functioning tra-

dition or from the failure to recognize a kind of resistance that does not
register as liberation feminism.

What I seek is a theory of texts and women's relationship to them
that accounts for the oppressive working of the Christian tradition,
yet is able to recognize the practices of women who do refuse particular patriarchal arrangements. To develop this account of women's resistance and its biblical construction, I need a theory that portrays the
instability of the biblical text, on the one hand, and its stabilizing by
way of a community of reading that is constrained by its own setting
and history, on the other.

The logic of my move is contained in the elements of poststructuralism and the turn to the site of utterance via discourse theory. These
theories require that the often hidden connections between discourses
be respected. These theories suggest that what we miss with the frame
of interpreter-text are precisely the cultural codes that construct and
connect each of the terms. To put it another way, textuality, the manifesting of reality in signifying processes, encompasses more than a
particular text called scripture; it encompasses readers, practitioners of
scripture, as well. We must appreciate the embeddedness of the interpretive relationship in textuality—in an undifferentiated field of
discourse—before we allow for the differentiations that we typically
call "readers" and "interpreters" or "practitioners."

The example cited in chapter 2 of the discursive totality of the act of
forced marital intercourse blurred the "natural" boundaries of bodies
and their meaning, and acts and their meanings. Similarly, boundaries
between interpreting subjects and the interpreted object need to be
blurred as we think about the differences in women's faith practices.
As I pursue the constitutive connections between subject positions for
women in relation to Christian texts, I will argue that they undermine
notions of the objective text and the kinds of closure that come with
several critical methods used by feminists. This is because they participate in some of the modernisms that Stephen Moore identifies with
biblical criticism. While feminists have made good use of these modernisms in strategies, their continued unproblematized use will not aid
the project of respecting difference.

Holding feminists back: modernisms in biblical scholarship

Two shifts occurring in biblical studies have relevance to feminist
questions. The first shift is from diachronic to synchronic interests, indicated in the critical attitude toward historical method and the impor-

tance of narrative studies. The other, not yet fully accomplished in theological circles, is the response to the epistemic shift of poststructuralism, the outlines of which were the subject of chapter 2.[8] This second shift is most important for feminist work in biblical scholarship. Based on my characterization of poststructuralism as not only the turn to signifying and the problematization of representation, but a change in the way power is conceived as well, I agree with Stephen Moore in his judgment that the efforts to take poststructuralist literary criticism seriously appear incomplete. The criticism in biblical studies is an intensified modernism, he argues, that follows a Kantian trajectory. Such a trajectory acknowledges that the structures of the subject do have a role in constituting what is known, but such a subject is still a constant and able to ward off the implications of poststructuralism. These implications make it impossible to grant an inherent closure to the meaning in the biblical text, a closure that biblical criticism continues to find according to Moore.[9]

The not-yet character of this second shift in biblical criticism is also related to the fact that criticism and interpretation, which converge in the world of the readers, have yet to be related to the larger social forces and discursive orderings of power that create readers. Even when squabbles over meaning and texts are put aside and scholars pay careful attention to the priority of interpretive interest, they construe the character of that interest relatively narrowly. A poststructuralist discursive economy would recognize that social relations and political elements such as postindustrial capitalism and modern disciplinary technologies are implicated in the construction of readers and texts. With the exception of liberationist thinkers, those who raise questions of "interest" rarely make it this complex.[10]

---

[8]Stephen Moore, *Literary Criticism and the Gospels: The Theoretical Change* (New Haven: Yale Univ. Press, 1989), 130. Moore is not the only one pressing the implications of poststructuralist and other literary theory for biblical scholarship. He is, however, one of the most articulate and specific. See also Mark C. Taylor, *Erring: A Postmodern A/Theology* (Chicago: Univ. of Chicago Press, 1984), 74–93; Carl Raschke, "From Textuality to Scripture: The End of Theology as Writing," *Semeia* 40 (1987): 39–52 (edited by Charles E. Winquist). Edgar V. McKnight does not define poststructuralism (he calls it "postmodernism") as these do. *Postmodern Use of the Bible: The Emergence of Reader-Oriented Criticism* (Nashville: Abingdon Press, 1988), 13–65.

[9]As I have already indicated, Elisabeth Schüssler Fiorenza is moving in this direction. Other notable exceptions include Elizabeth A. Castelli, *Imitating Paul: A Discourse of Power* (Louisville: Westminster/John Knox Press, 1991). See Stephen Moore's excellent article, "The 'Post-'Age Stamp: Does It Stick? Biblical Studies and the Postmodernism Debate," *Journal of the American Academy of Religion* 57:3 (Fall 1989): 543–57. He grants the power of feminist liberationist concern to resist certain modernist problematics.

[10]See Stephen Fowl, "The Ethics of Interpretation or What's Left Over after the Elimination of Meaning," in *The Bible in Three Dimensions: Essays in Celebration of Forty*

Moore is fairly harsh on the failure of biblical scholarship to enter fully into this poststructuralism: "Today, it is biblical criticism itself that cries out for demythologizing." This diagnosis stems from Moore's attempt to demonstrate that New Testament literary criticism has been content to combine criticism of traditional historical methods with "safe" New Critical methods.

In the judgment of New Testament scholar Gary Phillips, biblical criticism has failed to pursue the paradigm shift that should have accompanied its appropriation of some literary theory. Were literary criticism applied with consistency, it would put biblical interpretation face to face with the endless chains of signifying. With the decidedly un-Kantian reader who was not a formal cipher, the text would be endlessly re-created. To provide a synopsis of the sins of modernism, Moore offers three "hypostasizations," which are ways of treating texts that contribute to the premature closure of meaning (and enable New Testament literary criticism to avoid the threat of poststructuralist versions of literary theory). Those hypostasizations are: (1) a "transcendentalized textual content"—the assumption that there is an idea to be got from the text that endures independently of its inscription (outside of its written form); (2) an original situation with a self-contained meaning independent of its renderings; and (3) a similarly positivist notion of authorial intention that, it is assumed, will sooner or later yield up the secret of a text.[11]

I take up this diagnosis, not to render judgment upon the entire field of biblical studies, but because it captures succinctly the implications of my account of discourse for a feminist analytic of women's

---

Years of Biblical Studies in the University of Sheffield, ed. David J. A. Clines, Stephen E. Fowl, and Stanley E. Porter, *Journal for the Study of the OT Supplement Series* 87 (Sheffield, England: Sheffield Academic Press, 1990), 379–98. See also Mark G. Brett, "Four or Five Things to Do with Texts: A Taxonomy of Interpretive Interests," in the same volume, 357–77. The exceptions to this are the liberationists who have worked with semiotics, poststructuralism, and forms of materialist readings: Ched Myers, *Binding the Strong Man: A Political Reading of Mark's Story of Jesus* (New York: Orbis Books, 1988); J. Severino Croatto, *Biblical Hermeneutics: Toward a Theory of Reading as the Production of Meaning* (Maryknoll, N.Y.: Orbis Books, 1976). The liberationist hermeneutics are broader than this, of course. Cain Hope Felder, ed., *Stony the Road We Trod*; David Jobling, Peggy L. Day, Gerald T. Sheppard, eds., *The Bible and the Politics of Exegesis: Essays in Honor of Norman K. Gottward on His 65th Birthday* (Cleveland: Pilgrim Press, 1991). See also *Poststructural Criticism and the Bible: Text/History/Discourse*, ed. Gary A. Phillips, *Semeia* 51 (Atlanta: Scholars Press, 1990).

[11]Moore, *Literary Criticism and the Gospels*, 172. These are conclusions drawn from his arguments in chapters 3, 5, 7, and 8. For Phillips's account see Gary A. Phillips in Heinrich F. Plett, ed., "Sign/Text/Differance: The Contribution of Intertextual Theory to Biblical Criticism," in *Intertextuality*, and ed. János S. Petöfi, ed., *Macerata, Research in Text Theory* (New York: Walter de Gruyter, 1991), 78–100.

biblical practices. Any notion of a meaning in itself, whether a principle with an eternal meaning or some version of an original meaning, abstracts signification from other practices that give it meaning. Its closure is always a function of interest, a repressing of some lines of meaning and power. As always in feminist analysis, interest needs to be acknowledged. This closure is the other side of the coin of recognizing the instability of the text and the way a feminist theological analytic might want to locate readers as the site of (temporary) stabilization.

As I look critically at feminist uses of these hypostasizations, I should point out that they may also be seen as strategies. The use of a "real" historical meaning ("what Paul intended") can contribute to located strategic resistance for women. It is worth our while to review the implications of these features so that we see their limitations as well. On the one hand, when feminist liberation hermeneutics insists upon the political and interested nature of all interpretation, it pushes at the edge of the "transcendental contents," the positivist "site of origin," and the "intention" of the author—the three modernist features that plague biblical criticism. The implicit challenge of feminism to this modernist discourse is epitomized in Elisabeth Schüssler Fiorenza's insistence that the practice of biblical criticism is a political-ethical rhetorical practice.[12] On the other hand, the appearance of these hypostasizations in feminist biblical scholarship may not destabilize texts and reading communities adequately so as to support a move beyond modernist assumptions to an analytic of women's discourses.[13] It is not that feminist accounts of scripture are not inevitably working toward the destabilization of the unity of the biblical text. It is that, as separate strategies, these unravelings never quite complete the task.

---

[12]Elisabeth Schüssler Fiorenza, "The Ethics of Interpretation: De-Centering Biblical Scholarship," *Journal of Biblical Literature* 107 (1, 1988): 3–17. Her most recent commentary is exemplary in moving to the different rhetorical practices of different women's communities. See *Revelation: Vision of a Just World*, Proclamation Commentaries, ed. Gerhard Krodel (Minneapolis: Fortress Press, 1991), 1–31.

[13]My article "Contesting Feminist Canons: Discourse and the Problem of Sexist Texts," *Journal of Feminist Studies in Religion* 7:2 (1991): 53–74, does not cover the varieties of practices and their work as strategies with great nuance. For a much longer account of ten strategies, see Elisabeth Schüssler Fiorenza, *But She Said: Feminist Practices of Biblical Interpretation* (Boston: Beacon Press, 1992), 21–39. An extremely helpful taxonomy is offered in "Feminist and Womanist Readings," in *The Bible, Literary Theory, and Cultural Critique: A Roadmap to Contemporary Biblical Exegesis*, coauthored by George Aichele, Fred Burnett, Elizabeth Castelli, Robert Fowler, David Jobling, Stephen Moore, Gary Phillips, Tina Pippin, Regina Schwartz, and Wilhelm Wuellner (New Haven: Yale Univ. Press, forthcoming).

Jesus was a feminist, and other problems with historical appeals

One of the strategies in feminist work has been the use of historical-critical methods, as I said in chapter 2. From the perspective of the question in this chapter (elided closure of meaning), historical-critical retrieval bears consideration for its implications with regard to the relation of different subject positions of women to the text. To be sure, search for the historical meaning of the biblical texts on gender, as well as broader forays into the hidden histories of women in church history, have been major topics of academic feminist work with texts. Such work focuses on retrievals that range from inquiry into the actual situation of the church at Corinth to explain Paul's strictures on its women, to the reconstruction by Schüssler Fiorenza of women who are obscured or only obliquely indicated in the biblical canon. The former characterizes justificatory use of historical criticism; the latter, the more sophisticated recovery of women's agency by means of a hermeneutic that has moved beyond a history of women's oppression.

This search for historical meaning can be identified in a number of ways, ways that reflect disagreements not simply between biblical scholars but with theologians as well. A concern with historical meaning can characterize different positions with regard to the location of meaning and what it has to do with a contemporary understanding. The desire to find the original meaning of a text is not always matched with the conviction that a recovered sense of a text *is* its contemporary meaning. There are far more "things to do with a text," as one critic puts it, than simply figure out how to bridge Krister Stendahl's famous and inadequate distinction between original and present meaning.[14] What the researches for the historical meaning may imply, however, is that such a thing *can* be located and is somehow necessary to understanding the contemporary meaning of a text. Thus even if one refuses to identify the contemporary meaning of a Pauline epistle with the original intent of its author(s), one is always concerned that the latter be part of the inquiry.[15]

---

[14]Krister Stendahl, "Biblical Theology, Contemporary," in George Arthur Buttrick et al., eds., *The Interpreter's Dictionary of the Bible*, vol. 1 (Nashville: Abingdon Press, 1962), 418–32. Drawing on social scientific disciplines that now contribute to biblical scholarship, Brett notes that "emic" approaches, concerned with the "native's" point of view, and "etic," the "scientific explanation" using concepts foreign to the community, can be combined with diachronic and synchronic interpretations applicable to texts. The fifth possibility is the treatment of "texts as such." Brett, "Four or Five Things."

[15]The goal of historical-critical work is not simply to identify the author's intention, although it may include that, and much feminist and antifeminist ink has been spilled

In some respects this search, whatever site it prioritizes—the author, community of origin, or some stage of a tradition's history—is part of every feminist theologian's practice. For evangelical feminists, the historical origin is often of paramount import (what Paul "really meant"). At the same time that Schüssler Fiorenza denounces positivist historical work and identifies every practice as participating in rhetoric, she can distinguish the practice of a feminist reading from what the text meant—a use invoking its historical effects. Her more recent strategy is to distinguish the rhetorical use then from the rhetorical use now. Even a proponent of literary criticism such as Phyllis Trible makes the appeal to historical meaning.[16] It is difficult to conceive of an academic feminist position within Christian theological circles that does not invoke historical meaning—whether that entails the belief that some practice in the church's past must directly authorize women's practices today, or whether it is unclear about the role the past fills.

To criticize this approach is to tread a minefield, for it is nearly impossible to conceive of Christian faith without historical reference and knowledge, not to mention the great mileage that feminist theology has gotten out of critical usages of the past. My point, however, is the way in which a historical appeal is understood, the work that it does. When historical reference serves to rescue claims from their embeddedness in discourse and interest—to protect some kinds of information from the situated, valuational nature of knowledge and its inseparable connection to power—then historical reference is presented as "natural," unshaped data, characteristic of a modernist desire for incorrigible facts. The resulting gap between the grid of the historian and the givenness of an event effaces the subject position of the historian.[17]

---

over the intentions of the apostle Paul. This is because biblical studies always runs up against the diffusion of that elusive figure, the author. See William K. Wimsatt, Jr., and Monroe C. Beardley, "The Intentional Fallacy," in *The Verbal Icon: Studies in the Meaning of Poetry* (Lexington: Univ. of Kentucky Press, 1954), 3–18. The inaccessibility of many of the communities out of which much of its traditions come make that inquiry a virtually endless one. The poststructuralist criticism, however, is not reducible to that problem.

[16]Schüssler Fiorenza, *But She Said*, 40. Her clearest articulation of the implications of the discursive constitution of reality for the use of history is found in her description of a "feminist rhetorical paradigm of historiography," see 88–92. Phyllis Trible, *Texts of Terror: Literary-Feminist Readings of Biblical Narratives*, Overtures to Biblical Theology, ed. Walter Brueggemann and John R. Donahue, S.J. (Philadelphia: Fortress Press, 1984).

[17]Although more historians admit to the interested nature of historical recovery by allowing that all history is interpretation, a kind of sleight of hand occurs with the reinstatement of the event as something prior to the narrative or grid the historian brings.

Historical retrieval as the recovery of "what a text originally meant" is under attack by poststructuralist critics for precisely such evasions. Moreover, it transgresses the commitment of feminist liberation theory to resist the naturalization of interest.[18] A blind spot in the charting of interest is perpetuated when feminists rely on historical recovery to account for the meaning of biblical or other texts, or of a reconstructed history of misogyny that is separable in theory from a discursively displayed interest.

To put it another way, when feminists "discover" that Jesus was actually a supporter of egalitarian relationships, or a feminist, or unusually supportive of women for his age, they posit foundational facts. While we can and must make such claims about Jesus, as I will argue later, it cannot be done as if these are givens to be rescued by the clear-eyed historical investigator. When we say that the text (the past) tells or shows us that Jesus was like this, we elide the process in which our interests provide the grid that makes these features of the text (past) outstanding—the grid that grants them their being.[19] We suggest with our historical "find" that the discursive material interests which construct us are irrelevant to the search. Thus anyone with the proper tools should/would "find" the same thing.[20]

It is important to remember that the distinction does not entail the denial of the existence of reality. It is the claim that this resistance which we call the event is always and only available as being, as its "whatness," that is discursively constructed. Historical representation is always the latter, so it cannot avoid the ethical-rhetorical mode of what it would naturalize as its "finds."

[18]For examples of criticisms of history as representation, see Didier Coste, who discusses the problems with the distinction of chronology and narrative, event and fact, and the notion of "past actuality" in *Narrative as Communication*, vol. 64 in *Theory and History of Literature* (Minneapolis: Univ. of Minnesota Press, 1989), 16–25. Also see his section on the truth discourse of nineteenth-century historians in the same volume, 269–75. See also Michel de Certeau, "History: Science and Fiction," in *Heterologies: Discourse of the Other* (Minneapolis: Univ. of Minnesota Press, 1986), 199–221.

[19]Stanley Fish is good on this. See *Is There a Text in This Class? The Authority of Interpretive Communities* (Cambridge, Mass.: Harvard Univ. Press, 1980), esp. "Interpreting the 'Variorum' " (147–73), "Interpreting 'Interpreting the "Variorum" ' " (174–80), and "How to Recognize a Poem When You See One" (322–37). See also Fish's *Doing What Comes Naturally: Change Rhetoric and the Practice of Theory* (Durham, N.C.: Duke Univ. Press, 1992).

[20]It is impossible to conceive of Christian faith as being disinterested in the past—in exploring the past, reconceiving it, criticizing it, celebrating it, being in some sense accountable to it. Nor is it possible to talk about the past without a rhetoric of finding, of subject-object distinctions. I am not denying this. These claims will look different, however, when theological work takes account of the poststructuralist recognition of the inextricable relationship of the "interpreter" with the constructing of the past.

Liberation feminists avoid the most egregious versions of historical appeal—egregious because of the ostensible reliance upon interest-free, historical-critical recovery. These depend upon an original historical meaning as a privileged site that is granted the power to justify women's contemporary practices. This kind of warranting is more characteristic of evangelical feminist work. Most liberation feminism must avoid treating the conclusions of the past as authorizing practices simply because these conclusions regarding women are judged too restricting.

Even the indirect use of the past is problematic, however, if that past is understood to be the discovery of a fact, an incorrigible datum that is available to the objective, noninterested investigator. When feminists "discover" that Jesus was a feminist, as did Leonard Swidler (or as was implied in Schüssler Fiorenza's notion of Jesus' egalitarian practice), regardless of what is done with that observation, it is a candidate for presentation as a natural, prediscursive reality that any clear-thinking observer extricated from "false consciousness" could have seen.[21] This discovery is a candidate for such presentation, that is, within an epistemic setting that treats signifying practices as outside of interested and political orders.

Reliance upon recovery of historical meaning risks the production of at least two of the three hypostases Moore insists need demythologizing: the transcendentalized *Sitz im Leben* and the similarly privileged authorial intention. When we develop Schüssler Fiorenza's claim that historical inquiry itself is rhetorical, we can acknowledge that strategies of historical-critical tools belong in a discursive economy tied to class and other social relations. The fact that the use of historical-critical method is not available to all women is not incidental to the stakes of acknowledging this rhetorical character. At best we can say that failure to acknowledge the fully constructed character of the inquiry means that feminist use of history can be inconsistent in breaking away from modernist assumptions.

Schüssler Fiorenza rightly calls feminist historiography a "rhetorical communicative practice"; *But She Said*, 92.

[21] I think Schüssler Fiorenza's position has modulated on this; she thinks not. As long as she has been against Rankean positivist history, she has only recently been straightforward about the constitutive rhetorical nature of historiography and has helpful things to say about the discursive construction of history. She posits this practice in the frame of traditional distinctions between rhetorical historical-critical work, literary criticism, and other kinds of criticisms, and this seems odd to me. I would think the move to discourse would at least shake those distinctions up. See *But She Said*.

The text does the work: literary critical strategies and their problems

We can see the modernist assumptions of mainstream biblical scholarship also reflected with a move to the text itself in feminist use of
literary criticism. Literary critical analyses appeal to an "intrinsic
meaning," which is to say their design is to let the text control the
meaning, according to Phyllis Trible.[22] Its background is the U.S.
New Criticism of the 1930s to 1950s, a literary movement arguing the
nonrelevance of author's intention and historical context for a text's
meaning. In their place, New Criticism advocated the work of form
in the text itself. Although form criticism has paid attention to such
questions in biblical criticism, historical reconstruction (if Moore is
right) was incapable of respecting the organic integrity of form and
content and the way in which a text generated its own meaning.
Biblical studies' appropriation of literary critical approaches, particularly narrative study, has contributed to the current disdain in some
scholarly biblical circles for the historical-critical paradigm and its inability to respect the way textual strategies are inseparable from meaning.[23]

The rewards of this approach are a greatly enhanced display of the
complexity of gender discourse.[24] Once the effects of such key com-
municative-shaping forms as genre or enunciative position are consid-

---

[22]Trible, *Texts of Terror*, 1–7. It is a growing industry in current feminist publishing
on scripture, from Trible (one of the pioneers in Christian feminist literary treatments of
this text) to the more recent work of Mieke Bal, Esther Fuchs, Mary Ann Tolbert, and
Dana Fewell. More than one volume of *Semeia* devoted to literary critical methods contains a feminist piece: "Text and Textuality," no. 40 (1987); "Speech Act Theory and
Biblical Criticism," no. 41 (1988); "Narrative Search on the Hebrew Bible," no. 46
(1989), and "Poststructuralist Criticism and the Bible," no. 51 (1990).

[23]For critics of the historical-critical paradigm, see Hans Frei, *The Eclipse of Biblical
Narrative: A Study in Eighteenth and Nineteenth Century Hermeneutics* (New Haven: Yale
Univ. Press, 1974), and "The 'Literal Reading' of Biblical Narrative in the Christian
Tradition: Does It Stretch or Will It Break?" in *The Bible and the Narrative Tradition*, ed.
Frank McConnell (New York: Oxford Univ. Press, 1986). See also McKnight, *Postmodern Use of the Bible*. Frei's work has been pivotal in rescuing the priority of a biblical
discourse (narrative as literal sense or reading) over against the contemporary community in normative frameworks. This is a result of his recovery of the work of narrative
from the breaking up of the text effected by historical-critical method. This strategy
reifies *that* inscription, however, as I will argue.

[24]With the extraction of a content, "the feminine," significant differences are missed;
between, for example, an appeal to the feminine embedded in a nineteenth-century domestic novel, and the feminine occurring as a subversive register in a contemporary
feminist satire or as part of a modern medical discourse. For more recent examples, see
Mary Ann Tolbert, *Sowing the Gospel: Mark's World in Literary-Historical Perspective* (Minneapolis: Fortress Press, 1989); and Mieke Bal, *Lethal Love: Literary Feminist Readings of
Biblical Love-Stories* (Bloomington: Indiana Univ. Press, 1987).

ered, it makes little sense to ignore the form of inscription as vital to the meaning of a text. Phyllis Trible has done a masterful job of showing the effects of textual strategy on the terrible tales of murder, dismemberment, and rape of women in the Hebrew Bible. Narrative strategies that depersonalize the woman in Judges 19:1–30 add intensity to the excess character of the violence in the story. Literary analysis is able to communicate the force of "the unnamed woman" in a way that content summaries are utterly unable to represent.[25] Imagery that may appear either straightforwardly neutral (or sexist) is uniquely determined by its placement and working in a text. Such elements as its relation to the narrator and the kinds of authority communicated by strategies of enunciation enter into meaning and prohibit the extraction of "ideas." Even in cases where the analyses go on to invoke other meanings "outside the text," literary analysis focuses feminists' attention in new and inventive ways on the inseparability of form and content in terms of the work of the text itself.

Literary critical strategies not only support many feminist analyses of how biblical texts work, they also offer an important corrective to another of the trespasses of historical searches for meaning. This approach places a check on thematic unifications of biblical books, or of scripture as a whole. It is a check that can be extended to a similar practice of feminist theologians, which separates form and content in the appropriations of past meanings. Feminist use of historical recovery has allowed presentation of a history of oppression to be capsulized in certain contents or principles. Once detached from their textual display, these meanings become concepts that come to possess fixed meaning.

Examples such as the retrieval of early Christian egalitarian discipleship or of the liberating prophetic trajectory of the scripture can become ideas separated from their mode of utterance or practice.[26] The judgment that male imagery of the divine means the valorization of men, for example, occurs as the proposal that a certain idea is always patriarchal, is always sexist, or, conversely, is always liberating. This separation of form and content represents the third hypostasis of the modernist approach to language, the transcendentalized textual content. The very notion of a formless content is one that as-

---

[25]Trible, *Texts of Terror*, 65–91.

[26]The feminist criticism of Archimedean principles, a debate waged mainly between Schüssler Fiorenza and Rosemary Radford Ruether, is only a swipe in the direction of this issue. See the pointed criticisms of feminist biblical scholarship on this kind of separation in thematic analysis, as well as on the limits of literary criticism, in Mieke Bal, "Tricky Thematics," *Semeia* 42 "Reasoning with the Foxes" (1988): 133–55.

sumes "immaterial signifieds which somehow exist in the writer's mind even before signifiers are found for them," as one literary critic puts it so well.[27] Like the search for the author's intention, the positing of these kinds of signifieds can work to facilitate escape from the constraints of situatedness.

The work of literary criticism itself is problematic, however, if it serves to provide closure to meaning by locating it intratextually—in this case, intrabiblically. This would appear as the claim that a meaning is provided by the text and can simply reinscribe the authority of that canon. A hermeneutical position that relied purely on the text's own self-contained meaning is actually a hypothetical one, a "heuristic fiction," according to one New Testament critic.[28] For feminist criticism to rely on internal evidence alone is largely a theoretical possibility; any avowed feminist interest is generated and identified external to the text. Nevertheless, attribution of a misogynist agency to the text itself is the most likely example of such an approach.[29] The practice of literary critical analysis inevitably invokes and relies on the contexts of reading, an invocation that inevitably will undermine tendencies toward New Criticism, with the mining of inscriptions from a self-sufficient text.[30]

The practice of formal literary criticism relies on an unstated set of inferences that comes from co-texts and contexts, a point conceded by some feminist biblical critics who use it.[31] The view that the text creates, signifies, refers, and successfully produces meaning without the aid of readers is contradicted by any acknowledgment of the readers' role in providing proper inference or otherwise contributing to the sense of the text. Their contribution is sometimes attributed to the secondary influence of context; this is simply a stop-gap procedure. Its more problematic implications, as shown by Mieke Bal, have to do with the hegemonic understandings of meaning that can occur with

---

[27]John Sturrock's comments explicating Roland Barthes are quoted in Stephen D. Moore, *Literary Criticism and the Gospels*, 64–68.

[28]Richard Hays, *Echoes of Scripture in the Letters of Paul* (New Haven: Yale Univ. Press, 1990), 26–27. Hays is referring to the event of intertextual fusion. I think the same holds for any notion that the readers are not counted in the theory of meaning.

[29]By this I mean judgments such as that of Patricia Milne, "The Patriarchal Stamp of Scripture: The Implications of Structuralist Analyses for Feminist Hermeneutics," *Journal of Feminist Studies in Religion* 5:1 (Spring 1989): 17–34. Schüssler Fiorenza identifies what she calls "positivist textualism" in literary critics' refusal to relate the strategies of the text to historical events. See *But She Said*, 85–86.

[30]One ploy to stop this slippage is the implied author/implied reader that are encoded in the text. Susan Lanser, "(Feminist) Criticism in the Garden: Inferring Genesis 2–3," *Semeia* 41 (1988).

[31]Lanser, "(Feminist) Criticism."

this strategy. Bal criticizes feminist Christian scholars for finding authorization for their views in proposals for theoretical accounts of meaning in texts with literary analyses. She challenges the notion that any meaning is other than produced.[32] In the terms of Moore's hypostasizations, this criticism hits the target of the guaranteed unity of meaning provided by the frame of the text.

My concern does not stop with Bal's decentering of hegemonies of meaning, however. The pertinent question is how different woman subject positions might be connected to the biblical text, given this feminist strategy. The hypostasizations of literary aspects (or themes, for that matter) in the biblical text have disastrous implications for a feminist theory of discourse that respects difference. Attributing all the meaning to a text renders women captive to what is virtually the hegemony of black marks on a page. For example, the readings of scripture narrated by Pentecostal women ministers of the early part of the twentieth century are readings fairly innocent of both historical-critical discovery and of academic theory of figure and form. Nevertheless, as I will argue, they are productions with resisting emancipatory implications for these women. Were we to rely upon the text as such, whether as a text deeply structured by patriarchy or providing relief in its rhetorical strategies, we would miss the creative dissonant and grace-giving meanings that women have wrested out of the bleakest of religious prescriptions. Reliance on the text and its inscriptions as sole agent in the meaning process has the advantage of putting back together the many variables that idealist feminist history separates; however, it is accompanied by the disadvantage of cutting off the site where production really matters.

Models of text-interpreter: the reader shares the load

Inevitably, then, feminist criticism relies on the context for analyzing textual meaning. Within that context, two broadly related feminist strategies appear to take on the very problem of the modernist subject of my critique. The first is reader–response criticism, the interest in readers' experience as part of the production of textual meaning. The second is the appropriation of Gadamerian hermeneutics. Taken up increasingly by feminist biblical scholars, reader–response criticism does

---

[32]Bal, "Tricky Thematics." Getting back to an original meaning is like "unscrambling the omelette," as Edmund Leach said, quoted in Bal, *Lethal Love*, 1–8.

not represent a theoretically unified position. Its literary versions range from the work on implied readers (Wayne Booth) to real readers, from existentialist analysis to empirical ethnographic research (Janice Radway).[33]

Both speech–act and reader–response theories as used by feminist critics, however, move feminist theological thinking away from the closure of the fixed text in fundamentally important ways. Susan Lanser acknowledges that the conventions and codes of communicative discourse which are necessary to make sense out of texts require us to see that reading is open–ended. The text is *reproduced* by new readings. Because the contexts are always changing, so are the reproductions. There can be no "ideal, objective reading; there are only readings."[34] With this claim, Lanser takes the plunge toward decentering both the universal subject as interpreter and the fixed character of scripture. Such a move invites (or is at least an opening toward) consideration of the productive practice of women constructed in different subject positions, and of the material social realities that support any reading.

While not always dependent on reader response, the positing of resisting readers is an important move by feminists toward the productivity of women. For example, women are said to read generic language differently as they are constructed out of the discourses of liberal democracy. Womanists, Asian American women, and *mujeristas* offer practices that cannot be subsumed under the theories of contemporary criticism, but do acknowledge that the production of liberating meaning requires signifying processes *brought to* the text.[35]

Two modernist tendencies in much of reader–response criticism, however, blunt the critical edge of whatever destabilizing dynamics it contains. The contribution of the text remains—a text that is never placed entirely in a constructionist economy in the work of feminist biblical critics. With the exception of a work like Radway's where actual ethnographic account of a reading community is brought into

---

[33]For a helpful account of at least six kinds of reader-oriented criticism, see Susan R. Suleiman and Inge Crosman, eds., *The Reader in the Text: Essays on Audience and Interpretation* (Princeton: Princeton Univ. Press, 1980). See also Jane P. Tompkins, ed., *Reader-Response Criticism: From Formalism to Post-Structuralism* (Baltimore: Johns Hopkins Univ. Press, 1980); and Elizabeth A. Flynn and Patrocinio P. Schweickart, eds., *Gender and Reading: Essays on Readers, Texts, and Contexts* (Baltimore: Johns Hopkins Univ. Press, 1986).

[34]Lanser, "(Feminist) Criticism," 77.

[35]See Judith Fetterly, *The Resisting Reader: A Feminist Approach to American Fiction* (Bloomington: Indiana Univ. Press, 1978); also Flynn and Schweickart, eds., *Gender and Reading.*

relation with Romance texts, the problematic risk of reader-response work is the subject position of readers. Readers are identified in terms of gaps, elisions, blanks in texts that create work for them to do. Despite the "generic" reader of nonfeminist reader-response critics such as Wolfgang Iser, feminists specifically account for the readers of these gaps as women; for example, in invitations to identify with gendered "generic" language and the immasculization of women readers by that process. We are still speaking of a "universal reader," however, whose task is thereby set up, a task that relies on the text's provision of meaning.[36]

The risk in reader-response criticism is one I connect to those strategies that locate the meaning either in the original situation (pre-text) or in the text itself. The bedrock is still a reliable, objectively obtainable meaning-fact, even if the readers are given a part in its formation. While the logic of reader-response criticism will ultimately dissolve any concept of an objective text, many of its proponents still rely upon that objective text to control meaning — or so Jane Tompkins warns in her review of these forms of criticism that rely on the text's objective contribution.[37]

Modified reader-response work simply divides up the sites where meaning is ordered, refusing to take the risk of recognizing the relational ongoing process of signification opened up by the text it has only partially destabilized. A second point noted by Stephen Moore is the reliance on highly cognitive notions of readers, whose affective or aural modes of reception remain generally unexplored.[38] While oral delivery and literacy issues are certainly pertinent to questions of the original audience for scripture, issues of class and social location of a contemporary audience make them doubly pertinent. Feminist reader-response criticism that duplicates these biblical critical habits may be identifying readers who are made in their own image in terms of class and education. It is not clear how such theory could respect the unlettered Pentecostal woman's performance of the Word.

---

[36]Janice Radway, *Reading the Romance: Women, Patriarchy and Popular Literature* (Chapel Hill: Univ. of North Carolina Press, 1984). See Wolfgang Iser for an example of the reader-response strategy that provides the universal reader; "Interaction between Text and Reader," in *The Reader in the Text*, 106–119.

[37]Tompkins's list includes Stanley Fish's work through 1970. See Tompkins, ed., *Reader-Response Criticism*, ix–xxvi.

[38]Robert Fowler is the sole exception recognized by Moore in gospel criticism. Moore argues for the dominance of the academic guild's ideal reader in the reader-response work in biblical studies. Moore, *Literary Criticism*, 84–107. One of those dealing with the issue is Walter J. Ong, *Orality and Literacy: The Technologizing of the Word* (New York: Methuen, 1982). See also *Semeia* no. 39, "Orality, Aurality and Biblical Narrative," ed. Lou Silberman (1987).

A related model of biblical use bears mention, not only because it represents the philosophical agenda that informed some reader-response theory, but because in many respects it represents the best way to describe the refusal of a modernist notion of objectivity that characterizes feminist biblical work. Hermeneutics as a philosophy of interpretation represents the clearest defense of the interpreter-text frame in feminist work. This frame is the last element in the set of liberal assumptions in feminist theological method from which I wish to depart.[39]

Refusing classification as a method, Gadamerian hermeneutics is a grid that resonates with feminist accounts of biblical texts. This hermeneutics posits the fundamental relationality of understanding and points resolutely away from the positivism of fixed meanings. It could be argued that my portrayal of feminist choices as reliance on historical real meaning or the text in itself is a distortion in light of hermeneutical theory. Generally feminists link their attention to the past and the text as an historical trace to an interested subject — posing an inseparability that belies a search for incorrigible data. Liberation treatment of the issue of interpretation might better be compared, then, to philosophical hermeneutics, which is distinguished by its own criticism of a modernist grid of intelligibility.

The trajectory of hermeneutics from Martin Heidegger to Rudolf Bultmann takes the linguisticality of human being with utmost seriousness in order to transcend Kantian subject-object dualism.[40] These attentions to language are highly criticial of the modern subject and modern notions of language as representation, and are congruent with my insistence on the inevitable differences in meaning when discursively constructed readers engage a text. Philosophical hermeneutics implies the subjection of the subject and text to the currents of linguis-

---

[39]Wolfgang Iser's work is concerned to identify the work of meaning with neither text nor the reader (subject), but in a transaction. This displays the influence of Hans-Georg Gadamer and the desire to leave behind the pernicious subject-object split. See Iser, "Interaction Between Text and Reader." I thank Ray Person for pointing this connection out to me.

[40]Hermeneutical theory is useful in anthropology (Clifford Geertz) and other social sciences. For biblical scholars and theologians, however, it is human texts and practice conceivable as a text that are the primary focus of hermeneutics. Paul Ricoeur and Hans-Georg Gadamer, as well as their forerunners, Rudolf Bultmann and Martin Heidegger, are the main philosophical resources. Gadamer's major work is *Truth and Method*, 2d ed. (New York: Seabury Press, 1975). Paul Ricoeur, "The Model of the Text: Meaningful Action Considered as a Text," in *Hermeneutics and the Human Sciences: Essays on Language, Action and Interpretation*, ed. and trans. John B. Thompson (Cambridge: Cambridge Univ. Press, 1981), 197–221.

ticality, or effective-historicality, as Gadamer calls it.[41] Gadamer's gesture away from the subject as locus and origin of meaning is carried
out by means of a focus on the historicality of human being and the
inevitability of prejudice, or shaped interests—an embeddedness that
is constituted by the linguisticality of human being. Prejudice not only
locates an interpreter in history, but makes engagement with another
"text" possible, whether written document or dialogue partner. As a
consequence, any encounter between interpreter and text has as its
outcome something different from the meaning that could be ascribed
to either one alone. Insofar as one understands a text, one always understands differently.

Despite the attractiveness and malleability of philosophical hermeneutics, feminists themselves identify serious problems with the Gadamerian version. Schüssler Fiorenza criticizes this hermeneutics for
the way it affirms the past, affording a hermeneutics of "consent" to
the tradition that constructs women by vilifying or erasing them. In a
highly sophisticated recent theoretical program for feminist theology,
Mark Kline Taylor agrees with Jürgen Habermas's well-known critique of Gadamer's traditionalism and takes it further. Taylor insists
that an account of the process of interpretation must be tied to the
well-being and respect for the "otherness" of the marginalized, a subject that brings us to the deeper criticism of Gadamer.[42]

Feminist criticism of the character of the hermeneutical subject
comes close to poststructuralist liberation criticism of the humanism
involved. It is not enough to see that the power granted to effective-
historicity to construct the contemporary situation is an altogether too
sanguine affirmation of the past. Sheila Briggs makes the more damn-

---

[41]Gadamer, *Truth and Method*. Paul Ricoeur's turn to language involves similar criticisms of modernist assumptions. Polly Ashton Smith, however, has shown the problematic effects of his work in the hands of biblical critics. Ricoeur's is a "sophisticated
example of a philosophy of language which emphasizes the priority of a unified experience, a 'reference' or 'presence,' over against the 'exteriorization' or 'mediation' of language." His hermeneutics is "a process of moving from the understanding and
explanation of an original meaning (the text) to the appropriation of this meaning in a
second understanding, an understanding that is meaningful to readers in their present
context (as Ricoeur phrases it, 'to make one's own what was previously foreign.')."
Polly Ashton Smith, "Contrasts in Language Theory and Feminist Interpretation,"
Union Seminary Quarterly Review 35:1–2 (Fall/Winter 1979–80): 90.

[42]Elisabeth Schüssler Fiorenza, *Bread Not Stone: The Challenge of Feminist Biblical In-
terpretation* (Boston: Beacon Press, 1984), 128–36. Jürgen Habermas, "A Review of
Truth and Method," in *Understanding and Social Inquiry*, ed. Fred Dallmayr and Thomas
McCarthy (Notre Dame, Ind.: Univ. of Notre Dame Press, 1977), 358–60. Mark Kline
Taylor, *Remembering Esperanza: A Cultural-Political Theology for North-American Praxis*
(Maryknoll, N.Y.: Orbis Books, 1990), 67ff.

ing case that consensual hermeneutics relies on an essential, shared human nature, the reappearance of the universal, ostensibly nongendered subject that refuses Otherness even as it presents its tolerant face. Gadamer's use of the universal of linguisticality undermines his intent to move beyond subjectivity.[43] As another feminist critic puts it, Gadamer "not only abstracts from differences between interpreters in a given culture, but he imports assumptions about universality which derives from an unacknowledged history of relations between subjects."[44]

What is problematic in this hermeneutical model is not even solved by Taylor's attempts to thicken the interpreting subject by linking it to the marginalized.[45] The feminist insistence on the biased nature of all interpretation does not completely escape the failings of such a hermeneutical approach. These are failings that have to do with the reliance on the unitary *understanding subject* as the locus for an interaction with a text. Despite the fact that feminists do important work by challenging the view that "subjectivity" is a negative in interpretation, it is not enough to define bias as a feature of an interpreter. The subject-object frame that creates the conditions under which this conversation occurs fundamentally limits its possibilities. When Taylor reproduces this frame, even with a correction of Gadamer, those limits go unchallenged.

Those limits are reminiscent of the concern with the false universal subject, woman. Notions of interest as abstract or formal features of interpreters—being for meaning, being for/against women—entail the theoretical incapacity to thematize the discursive orderings that are not within the horizon of the intending subject. Even the gain made by recognizing that the interested subject is a necessary part of the hermeneutical spiral (as Gadamer puts it, without prejudice there is no

---

[43]Sheila Briggs, "The Politics of Identity and the Politics of Interpretation," *Union Seminary Quarterly Review* 43:1–4 (1989): 163–80.

[44]Robin Schott, "Whose Home Is It Anyway? A Feminist Response to Gadamer's Hermeneutics," in *Gadamer and Hermeneutics*, ed. Hugh J. Silverman, vol. 4 of *Continental Philosophy* (New York: Routledge, 1991), 208.

[45]Taylor, *Remembering Esperanza*. Taylor defends appropriation of Gadamerian hermeneutics and offers a serious attempt to rectify the problem of this universal subject. Borrowing from "explanatory" theories of sexism and gender, he expands the interpreter-text model to include a cultural-political approach that takes on sexism, racism, classism, and heterosexism. He defends the subject-object frame by expanding the matrix of understanding, highlighting Gadamer's image of understanding as conversation. Taking the post-positivist features of Gadamer's account of understanding, Taylor prises out its synchronic and liberation-oriented features or possibilities. His aim is to transform the dualist, diachronic frame of hermeneutics and to infuse some critical emancipatory energy into Gadamer's overly respectful stance toward tradition.

investment) is not enough to address the question of the boundary of interest. Is interest the conscious intent of the interpreter, her/his will to find something for women or to get the larger questions of meaning answered? If interest has its origin in subjects, then we are left with the search for intention and motive. We move into the realm of the mental space reminiscent of the unitary liberal subject. If we add the term "context" to indicate the shaping or influencing of the subject, we simply beg the question by delaying the problem of boundaries: What counts as context? How can it be limited in a meaningful way? What context creates the feminist reader's interests?

Horizon, Gadamer's term for situatedness, is not a helpful answer. It is, at best, a trope for being situated, since one cannot have a horizon except from a particular place. It is an image of unlimitedness, however; it invokes the boundlessness of being situated, the open-ended way in which the interpreter (and the text) are part of larger realities. Little methodological good is served by the frame of interpreter-with-horizon in relation to a text-with-horizon. Horizon, like interest, in this model is a formal attribute of a subject and/or a text. An attribute is a secondary appendage to a unitary subject who is then, in a secondary way, somewhere and interested.

Insofar as horizon is a trope for bias, it would seem to substitute for the configuration of discursive processes that constitute subject positions and their instability. Thus, although we have gestures at thickening out the matrix of oppression and liberation, the frame of interpreter-text reinstates the solidity of the unitary subject as a priori to situatedness—the uncoded subject. Discursive networks that construct a more complex phenomenon cannot appear.

When one adds the "other," the marginalized as participant in the conversation, more thickness may seem to appear. Interest is even specified as commitment against sexism, racism, classism, and heterosexism. Because it is based on a unitary subject, however, it is an interest characterizing processes of understanding, not the orderings that construct these processes themselves. The very subjects with the power to commit to the oppressed remain implicit origins of benevolence even as they articulate well-meaning self-critical desires to hear the other. With its reliance on unitary subjects in relation to texts, this hermeneutical model supports a notion of the task of feminist theology that begins with an account of understanding abstracted, as noetic categories always are, from material practices and their locations and supporting institutions. It is no accident that Briggs, the sharpest critic of hermeneutics, points us to practices as an alternative to hermeneutics. Why not, as Briggs proposes, begin with practices, or reinvent "understanding," and move away from a kind of tolerant reflection that is not materially identified to a practice that is?[46]

Limits of feminist terms for texts

The problem with much of feminist work on scripture reflects the problems of biblical interpretive methods that still operate with modernist assumptions about language, found in the closure of meaning that occurs in Moore's three examples of transcendentalized meaning. The dominant feminist approaches to Christian texts, biblical and extrabiblical, press on the edges of these assumptions with their own commitment to the situated, interested nature of all knowing. They do not go far enough, however, because of their failure to press the very notion that texts have fixed meanings. Fixed meaning assumes a unitary subject; and the complexity of interest, its webs of social power, can be developed no further than as attributes of a unitary subject and the fixed text. The failure to complete the shift to the constitutive character of language—or rather, to discourse—short-circuits the capacity to explore all positions as part of discursive orderings complicit with power. This incapacity stands in the way of an approach to women's practices that could acknowledge differences in women's subject positions, and therefore in their reading practices and the discursive totalities that construct them.

That theoretical claim can be illustrated. On the one hand, reliance on historical recovery assumes that a meaning exists external to the networks of signification/power that surround it, and occludes the role of the interests that bring it forward. As central as historical criticism is to the work of the academy, as I will show, the readings of women who live in Christian communities without access to historical-critical tools cannot be respected if we assume there is a real meaning for a text. On the other hand, reliance on the tools of literary criticism might appear to open up appreciation for literal readings—validating "the way my grandmother used to read her Bible," as one scholar has commented. However, the readings of literary critics are

---

[46]Taylor's account of theology as understanding/explanatory theories/Christian address is materially based and needs unpacking as such. Even reading feminist hermeneutics through Gadamerian lenses with a transcendence of meaning over subjects and objects fails to figure the configurations and economies that "subject" the subject. The fact that Taylor tries to thicken the description of his conversation partners by adding the oppressed as its privileged participant is a sign that he sees the problems with the model. However, there seems to be no reason to tinker with a model that begins with and relies on understanding developed by explanatory theories.

notoriously intellectual and do not automatically connect to matrices of power.[47] Literary criticism, too, can fail to get at the inextricable connection of interest and knowledge.

The turn to the world of the interpreter in conversation with the world of the text, or modified reader-response criticism, does not deal successfully with the issue of women's different locations. Despite the broadening of meaning—the plurivocal possibilities of any text—that occurs with these dialogical models, a Gadamerian proposal still relies on a subject for whom horizons are the inadequate social locator, a subject who invites the universalizing I have already found unusable. The modified reader-response approach continues to assume there are fixed features in the biblical text that, properly approached, are constitutive of its real meaning. There is, still, an "objective" guide in the form of these features that constrain what can be considered adequate. The danger here is that class differences and the role of education in the construction of women's ways of "reading" (a term that must be broadly construed) will have an impact on determining which women's reading practices fall outside the circle of "good reading." This is particularly acute when women's practices include illiteracy or partial illiteracy.

Because of the incompleteness of our moves to decenter texts and subjects, there is an implicit privileged site for fixing the meaning of the Christian tradition in various feminist strategies: in history, in the text itself, or in some relation between the text and interpreter. Although a case could be made that each of these strategies is important in particular locations, I draw attention to the assumption we leave intact about texts, one that still partakes of modernist assumptions similar to those found in the use of the false universal "women's experience." The acknowledgment that feminists are more frequently making—namely, that the epistemic realities of understanding biblical texts are socially located—needs to have an account of the discursive-political construction of texts as well as "subjects" (subject positions) to support it. The linkage between a temporary unity called "the text" and the subject position must enable us to avoid the privatizing (because it is an ultimately unsituated modifier) notion of a "context."[48]

---

[47]Andrew K. M. Adam, *New Testament Theology and the Problem of Modernity*, Ph.D. diss., Duke Univ., 1991, pp. 1–7. One exception might be Kathryn E. Tanner, who has tried to correct some of the problems in George Lindbeck's and Hans Frei's model of the literal reading by tying it to an account of communal practices. See Tanner, "Theology and the Plain Sense," in *Scriptural Authority and Narrative Interpretation*, ed. Garrett Green (Philadelphia: Fortress Press, 1987), 59–78.

[48]There are moves in this direction when Schüssler Fiorenza identifies the ethical

Modern biblical scholarship is a function of a temporal and class situatedness that assumes certain things about education, progress, and preferred kinds of knowledge and expertise, those tools afforded by the modern university. In addition, the bypassing of this situatedness is a feature of liberal understandings of reason that rely on its universality and are warranted by objective evidences. Thus my complaint is not simply an anti-intellectual plea for the nonexpert reader; it refers to the occluding of the "expert's" embeddedness in social matrices of power.

Untying the text: women's performances of scripture

How can feminist theology think about women as reader-practitioners of the Christian tradition with respect for their different forms of oppression and resistance? The interpretive model errs by (1) locating the meaning of readings of scripture within the parameters of a subject-object relation, (2) tying that meaning to certain modes of access to texts (or their pre-texts), and (3) by identifying the text's relation to power by attributing properties of perniciousness or liberation to it. As an alternative I propose that we reconceive the feminist task in relation to the text. Just as poststructuralist feminist theory requires that we replace a universal woman with multiple subject positions, we must recognize the existence of many texts as they appear from multiple subject positions.

The turn to discourse makes the intuitively obvious distinctions of subjects and texts problematic. If we cannot get behind discourse to experience (or meaning), then the very positing and arrangement of such "objects" as subjects, texts, and contexts is itself a construction. It is true that such distinctions appear natural, the basis for other agendas and interests. (What else do we have if not an interpreter and a text and an ostensible first meaning that must be negotiated in relation to a context that the interpreter must come to terms with?) What we have in the positing of these three entities, however, is a particular kind of discursive game. This complex is no more bedrock reality than the rearranging of the discourse in another game—a game, for example, that creates a practitioner for whom the ostensible "text" has no orig-

---

rhetorical character of her guild. She attributes it as a feminist strategy to marginalized accounts of interpretations. *But She Said*, 35–36. It is implicit in liberation feminists' reliance on the context of woman-church, the struggle for liberation as the hermeneutical center for biblical interpretation.

inal historical meaning, but a spiritual meaning that blurs distinctions between past and present, having force (or not) in its facilitation of ecstatic displays. In this kind of game the "context" is not a third piece of a hermeneutical problematic, but the theater of God's glory, if one grants it an existence at all. It is not a separate problem but inseparable from the eschatological linkage that smooths away any distance between past and present, or cultural locations.

In short, the construct of interpreter-text-context may have a use, but it must be seen as part of a totality or game if we are to avoid the risk of occluding the situated character of biblical practices that do not fit our own. Some options, then, can simply be ruled out from the beginning in order to propose an account that makes room for different "games" that constitute women in relation to scripture (or any other defining text). The opposition posed as text or subject in control is a false one, as is the compromise that allows both to contribute. I say this not only to respect the field of discourse that flattens natural distinctions, but also to suggest that something else organizes women and their resistances than is accounted for by parsing up meaning between texts and interpreters (and contexts).

The first move toward an alternative to the interpreter-text grid is multiplication of the text. Such multiplication means reconceiving the task as one feminist biblical critic poses it when she speaks of understanding "the same bible as enslaver and liberator."[49] *Pace* this formulation, it is not "the same Bible" that "we" read. The destabilized text is a necessary coimplicate of the multiple-subject position. Women's subject positions and their distinctive dependencies (problems of access) differ. The position occupied by the Pentecostal hillbilly woman differs from that of the middle-class Presbyterian churchwoman. The Pentecostal woman is related to a different scripture than that of the middle-class Presbyterian. If this recognition is not inscribed in method, then a notion of the "right readings" is maintained and the specific "scripture" that the differently constructed woman has access to, finds meaningful, and is constrained by is missed. Feminists must continue to relate biblical texts to enslavement and liberation, but continuing to assume that it is "the same Bible" that "we" read and failing to explore the multiple constructions of the "we" are two errors that can no longer be afforded. These errors are connected to interpretive methods that simply cannot do justice to the varieties of Christian women's practices.

---

[49] Mary Ann Tolbert, "Protestant Feminists and the Bible: On the Horns of a Dilemma," *Union Seminary Quarterly Review* 43 (1989): 1–17.

This shift does not erase subjects or biblical texts that shape them. Nor does it signal that a text can mean anything that one wishes or means nothing at all. Again, the boundaries are simply being redrawn to allow us to think of the possibilities for women in situations very different from those of middle-class, educated subject positions. This redrawing means that I relocate the weight for stabilizing this unstable text (scripture), not to remove text or interpreter, but to see how larger domains of discourse and of social location bring them into being. To put it in terms that will break the false alternatives of sub-ject-object-context, I commend Stanley Fish's proposal that the interpretation and the text come into being together. If interpreters are themselves embedded in institutions and the larger social formation, then, we are not simply attributing control to the community, but broadening the discursive field that must be taken into account.[50]

To pursue this idea of relocating the stability of a text, I return to the notion of discursive totalities. The conditions of productive energy, so to speak, do not come from isolated objects, but from a social totality, an organizing practice, that grants them meaning. Just as a leather-covered spherical object is constructed as a useful object, along with subjects and movements constructed as players and playing out of a discursive totality called "baseball," a text is constructed as a whole, as useful, authoritative, as scripture out of a particular discursive totality: living a Christian life. To say that use of a text as scripture is part of faith practices that are defined by a game of sorts is to say, as David Kelsey does, that the game of Christian faith practice entails reading scripture as part of its overall faithful enactment.[51] The practice creating the text includes a variety of elements, such as the way a community construes the text as having a meaning in relation to itself. What to read, how to read, the critical use of the text against the community—all of these are discursively produced, part of the social practice of Christian faith.

---

[50]Presenting the choices in this way, either there is real objective meaning anchored in the text or subjects can have a field day making anarchy and projecting their fantasies on texts. This is a possibility only if one thinks of subjects as prior to discourse and communities of discourse. The operative issue when subjects and objects are conceived this way, as Fish points out, is *control*. See Stanley Fish, "How to Recognize a Poem," and *Doing What Comes Naturally*.

[51]David Kelsey would add that this totality also entails construing that scripture as some kind of whole, a precursor category for canon. He uses the analogy of baseball, too, to illustrate how using scripture for theologizing is analytic in "playing the game." He does not develop this idea as discursive constitution, however, and writes of monolithic communities, but I think he points in that direction. *The Uses of Scripture in Recent Theology* (Philadelphia: Fortress Press, 1975).

To understand what the text is, why these construals are made, we must conceive of the subject or community from the beginning in terms of the ends of the practice and the social relations that are constructive of the activity "reading scripture." We discover that for one community that reading is for edification or moral uplift of the individual believer; for another it shapes a political practice; for another it teaches a doctrine. Thus we do not discover something about the text itself; we discover something about the ends or the purposes of the community which has brought that scriptural use into being. Scriptural meaning is not a nugget wrested from the text and then applied to women and their context, or to any other participant in the game. It is produced by the discursive totality, the game, in which they are players.

The example of the game of baseball offers some parallels that help develop the notion of women's productive practices. Playing baseball is a discursive totality that constructs certain practices out of movements. It creates a variety of players out of subjects, constitutes a baseball out of a spherical object, and assigns certain goals to the whole activity. "Reading scripture" is like baseball in that it is a discursive practice that is part of the larger discursive totality of faithful Christian discipleship. Totalities construct practices, text, and subjects, and are presided over by certain ends. Thus one cannot begin with the force of the text without understanding the social practice that literally brings that text into being, just as one cannot begin with the round leather-covered object without understanding the practice of baseball.

Because the discursive totality constitutes the entity or practice, as I argued in chapter 2, we can see that the practice which orders it is responsible for granting a certain kind of stability to a fundamentally open text. Although a baseball may seem an extremely stable object, this is not necessarily the case. It is not difficult to imagine that a leather-covered sphere could be meaningful in a variety of practices. A subject totally unfamiliar with baseball, for example, could construe it as a weapon or a holy object. No one is bound by nature to employ the round object within the discourse of the game as a baseball. To move to another level, even a person who knows what baseball is and is unable to think of the sphere in any other way does not necessarily construct it in the same way as does a participant of the game. A pitcher, for example, knows the baseball's uses and limits and possibilities within a set of habitual practices that the game itself creates. Likewise, someone outside the game or practice of Christian faith does not construct the biblical text as "scripture." Participation, broadly conceived, is an element in the construction of its realities. Thus even though the "outsider" may be able to identify the object as a Bible that is authoritative for believers, she or he does not have participatory knowledge of it.

The baseball analogy suggests the constitutive nature of a social practice on the production of entities, on granting objects their meaning. It is a reminder that the stability of entities is relative to how widespread the agreement about their use. The analogy, however, is less useful in suggesting the open-ended possibilities for playing under the rubric "baseball," that is, its openings for contested and conflicting accounts. The instability of any entity and, consequently, of the possibility of multiple readings of it is better illustrated by my example in chapter 2 of different accounts of the act of forced marital intercourse, the instability of which is seen in the debate about rape versus right. The text of the Bible is similarly unstable and evokes an infinitely open number of readings, even when the social practice—faithful Christian living—is, formally speaking, construed as the same.

The act of reading scripture has involved different texts and practices in different times and social locations, just as social practices concerning gender, private-public realms, and other state and cultural apparatuses define the act of forced marital intercourse differently, depending on the time, geographical location, whether one reads the act from a feminist or nonfeminist position, and so on. Not only is multiplicity inherent to the biblical text as a performed entity, but its practice in any one instance is constructed out of both the religious and the other cultural-political discourses that create a social location.

In short, what might appear to be a single activity—reading scripture—is actually comprised of varying and often conflicting constructions. This variety holds synchronically as well as diachronically, and not only with regard to different communities. One can be a participant in several practices that entail different constructions of scripture that are conflictual or mutually undermining; thus multiple readings can refer to a subject as well as to differently located communities. We may accept that the text is always a function of the social practice that creates it, but this is not explained by reference to "the text itself." Thus it is not helpful for a feminist analytic to begin with some "text as such," liberating or oppressive, if we are to theorize the way women in different social locations practice scripture. We must begin with the assumption that there are many texts, and that these texts are inextricably connected to the uses made of them.

When we connect the constitution of texts with a social practice and its use of texts, we do something else. We respect the fact that the very being of texts precludes our defining them simply in terms of academic use, the use characteristic of feminist strategies. For some non-academic communities, a primary academic use of texts (exegetical) is inherent in the rules of the game of reading scripture. Thus what I have reviewed as academic strategies can be appropriated by their practices, even if in less sophisticated forms. (We will see that in the Presbyterian women's community of reading.) Communities constructed out of other practices, however, do not use the text this way. For some, ecstatic oral practices constitute faithful "reading"; for an illiterate community, the text may have more meaning recited from memory or even sung than deciphered with scholarly tools.

Thus we must qualify "reading" scripture as an entailed practice of Christian communities. To the point that a fundamentally different scripture is produced by different social practices, I add another. The inseparability of use and meaning requires that we speak of the "practice" of scripture or, to borrow a phrase of Nicholas Lash, "performing" the scriptures. This alternative to "reading" or "interpreting" indicates that many more features of a discursive ordering go into the constituting of scripture than simply a cognitive response to a written text.[52]

My first move, the untying of the biblical text, allows us to open up the possible construals of the relation of women to Christian scripture. It does so by recognizing that there is no "real Bible" but that it is discursive orderings "all the way down." Any attempt to get at "the real meaning of scripture" is an avoidance of the networks of meaning that form the search and the game(s) that one is playing. This avoidance is part of the problem in the closure that Moore's criticism finds in modernist biblical criticism. For a feminist analytic, whose agenda is to get at these networks, determining the constitutive game or social practice that orders scripture for women is the first step in finding whatever stability the text might have.

The text untied: community-based performances?

The multiplicity of the biblical "text," and the relation of the many scriptures to the many "games" faith communities play, seem to invite a move to a communal hermeneutics as the next step in the analysis.

---

[52]"For different kinds of text, different kinds of activity count as what we might call the primary or fundamental form of their interpretation." Nicholas Lash, *Theology on the Road to Emmaus* (London: SCM Press, 1986): 37, 37–46, also see chap. 3. Lash uses this image to contrast reading scripture to reading/uses of kinds of texts other than religious. I will contest the notion of a homogenizing scriptural performance.

Christian theologians interested in correcting the work of objective historical-critical studies are increasingly emphasizing the corporate, ecclesial faith context out of which the Bible is construed as scripture. A focus on the faith community and the corresponding theological patterns that order scripture has served as a way to identify the significance of Christian scripture as scripture (the sacred text of a community), as opposed to a text that gets broken apart (in historical criticism) or is simply read and appreciated as literature.[53]

Traditional approaches such as Lash's or Kelsey's are examples of attempts to construe the text as the sacred/authoritative text of a community in order to privilege a Christian reading of the text. Kelsey's often-cited work analyzes different ways that theologians have construed scripture out of ecclesial contexts. He insists that patterns and uses of scripture are relative to particular community-formed images of divine presence that entail some version of appropriate use of scripture in relation to the goal or end of the community.[54] These communally oriented proposals might be taken to suggest something like my

---

[53]See Kelsey's *Uses of Scripture*. The point has often been made that Christian community has a different posture toward the text than a university religious studies department. See Gerhard Ebeling, "The Bible as a Document of the University," and James Barr, "The Bible as a Document of Believing Communities," in *The Bible as a Document of the University?*, ed. Hans Dieter Betz (Chico, Calif.: Scholars Press, 1981), 5–24, 25–48. Even this fails to put the question in all its complexity, however. As modified reader-response criticism or any other interpretive frame confined to the subject-object scheme of hermeneutics misses full attention to the discursive practices that matter in the differences (and convergences) of the subject positions "woman," so the postliberal theological attempt to place the Christian reading of the text over against non-Christian construals of scripture puts forth another false set of alternatives, one that ignores the multiplicity in "Christian community." Stanley Hauerwas takes Fish seriously and recognizes the impact of the state on interpretive communities. However, he still fails to identify the multiplicity. See his *Unleashing the Scripture: Freeing the Bible from Captivity to America* (Nashville: Abingdon Press, 1993). Stephen Moore presses this point in "Negative Hermeneutics, Insubstantial Texts: Stanley Fish and the Biblical Interpreter," *Journal of the American Academy of Religion* 54:4 (Winter 1986): 707–720.

[54]Kelsey, *Uses of Scripture*. Kelsey's work is an older piece in a line of work by theologians and biblical scholars that focuses on the ecclesiological meaning of scripture. More recently see his "The Bible and Christian Theology," *Journal of the American Academy of Religion* 48:3 (September 1980): 385–402. See also Gregory Jones and Stephen Fowl, *Reading in Communion: Scripture and Ethics in Christian Life* (Grand Rapids, Mich.: Eerdmans, 1991). Richard Hays speaks eloquently of "scripture-shaped communities" in "Scripture-Shaped Community: The Problem of Method in New Testament Ethics," *Interpretation* 44 (January 1990): 42–55. While these accounts often recognize the liberal state as constitutive of the contemporary church community and its reading of scripture, they do not meet the feminist questions head on about conflicting and subordinated voices that comprise "Christian communities." These latter remain unified abstractions in their work, which concern themselves with what are to my mind dominant discourses even though they aim at making Christian communities counter-communities.

point that discursive games of faithful discipleship construct objects and practices such as scripture and the terms of its faithful performance.[55]

Some initial similarities exist between these communally oriented proposals about scripture and my interest in an account of scripture that attends to the constructing social practice. Feminist interests, however, lead my analysis in another direction because of the importance to feminist concerns of contradictions and multiplicities within communities. A feminist analytic exposes these communal-shaped hermeneutics as inadequate for three reasons. In order to read women's practices as gender resistance within the orderings generated by "the Christian community," we require distinctions for divergent textual use within what is a fairly abstract theological unit—"community"—as it is used by Lash or Kelsey.

The first problem with a position that relies upon "the Christian community" is that it gives us only the dominant discourse. Regardless of how specifically this notion is spelled out in terms of different imaginative construals of God's presence (as in Kelsey's case), it offers only the religious communities' official theological self-understandings, when it is the resisting discursive practices of women in which a feminist analytic is interested. Although we cannot look outside of the official self-understanding and practices of a religious community, since this is the discourse out of which resistance is constructed, the dominant theological definitions will never be sufficient to provide the creative practices of subordinated subjects.

A second problem with a formal communal hermeneutic is its failure to include the effects of the larger discursive workings of the social formation that intersect with ecclesial communities. A feminist interpretive apparatus must be able to articulate this relation, and the appeal to Christian community rarely does. If social practices such as ecclesial discipleship are embedded and constituted in other social relations, for instance the mode of production, civil, and cultural processes (as are the conditions for defining an act of marital rape), then it is highly problematic to conceive of a purely theological (or philosophical) construal of textual or biblical meanings. One can no more conceive of purely religious communities as the origination of meaning than one can treat

---

[55]Lash says that "what counts as an appropriate strategy of use or interpretation will depend upon the kind of text with which we are dealing," suggesting that texts dictate their own meanings. Yet he supports my proposal when he says that what really counts are the performances behind and in front of the texts, not the texts themselves. Without further definition of what is in front, this undercuts the first claim. Lash, *Theology on the Road*, 40.

isolated interpreting subjects that way. Communities as well as subjects are part of discursive totalities such as patriarchal capitalism. This
is not to say that communities may not resist the social formation, but
that the discourse of that encompassing totality is inescapably part of
their constitution.

To avoid the homogenizing effects of communal hermeneutics, a
feminist analytic requires more than analogous notions like practices,
objects, ends, players, or practitioners that are constituted by the discursive totality of faithful Christian discipleship. It requires distinctions between dominant and subordinated voices. Our analytic must
be able to place discursive orderings of the text in several intersecting
"games." Given that any performance of scripture is a practice embedded in social relations, a feminist analytic is in need of something
more. A third problem with the communal hermeneutic is the temptation it presents to replace the "interpreter-text" frame with a "com-
munity-text" frame and thereby return to a representational way of
thinking. This temptation occurs because the shift to the communal
matrix of interpretation continues to work with a stable term, "community."[56] Effective as a signifier that assumes a unity to the notion of
what it means to be Christian and what is held corporately by Christians, this term implies that Christianity is an uncontested notion that
occurs as a singular form rather than as multiple forms of corporate-
ness.

In this move to the communal site of the production of biblical
practices, I have avoided the false options of the dominance of the interpreter or text. Now I want to avoid the alternative of a hegemonic
community as well. From the position of a feminist analytic, "community" is a false unity and needs to be contested as such, lest it be
allowed to replace the universal subject in relation to the text. In place
of such a naturalized signifier as "community," which controls what
might count as a faithful performance of scripture and limits what
might count as women's resistance, a feminist liberation analysis must
articulate a relation between scripture and Christian communities that
does not begin with a closure of meaning on either end. We need an
account that allows for the multiple practices that construct women/
communities. This account must also allow for the constitutive character of social-material relations in that aspect of discourse that
inevitably gets left out—its channeling of desire/power.

---

[56]The move to "community" in the work of those theologians I have used as examples is always formal and defined by a minimalist set of beliefs or practices.

The graf(ph)t of social location

To ensure that my analytic is not constructed out of a formal sign—an empty conceptual space, "community"—I wish to indicate the mark of social location in my grid for a social practice. Part of thinking about the differences that construct women's subject positions has to do with the effects of social location on faith practices. In addition to the stabilizing that comes with the complicating of "community," the social location needs a place in this analytic as an element in the discursive totality. If women are truly constituted as subjects by such things as their place in capitalist patriarchy, then we expect that their faith practice will be marked by that reality. The kind of marking I have in mind is not the judgment that nonexegetical or ahistorical practices of scripture are marks of poor or lower-class, uneducated communities. This view is precisely what I am refusing, because it implicitly privileges the academic and bourgeois class positions as the site of preferred biblical practices.

The marking I seek is more difficult to articulate, because the complex relations between something like class and literature (the scripture that is produced in relation to that class) are easily rendered in a reductive manner. One of the likeliest missteps in marking social location is to duplicate the notion that inner experience is somehow expressed in writing or literature. A parallel error here would have it that class, race, or gender as features of a subject are expressed in some straightforward way in texts (in this case biblical texts). This error posits homologous understandings that view a (written) text as a reflection of a social location; it is reminiscent of the modernist notion that interests, like messages, are conveyed outside of the complications of discourse and power.[57] Clearly the fragmenting of subject position suggests that no one feature—gender, race, class—of location provides an adequate definition of any particular subject, and thereby cannot be found mirrored in a textual reading or performance.

For purposes here, I cannot take up the nuances of theory but will signal the irreducible nature of the relation of location and performance (when we have left liberal expressivism behind). Just as the interpretation and the text come into being together, we need to indicate how subject position is a constructing element in a social totality as

---

[57]These issues are much discussed by Marxist and literary theorists, because early proposals tended to propose a homology between class and certain forms of literature. See Raymond Williams, *Marxism and Literature* (Oxford: Oxford Univ. Press, 1977); Fredric Jameson, *The Political Unconscious: Narrative as a Socially Symbolic Act* (Ithaca, N.Y.: Cornell Univ. Press, 1985).

well, rather than a remainder. To do otherwise is to leave context outside as an extra element to be factored in, inevitably too little too late. The social location of its participants is no less a constitutive ingredient of the community's practice than its telos. The best we can do is mark that relation as one fundamental to the lifeblood of a community or a subject position within it.

The inseparability of the social constraints on women performers and their readings of texts is elegantly articulated by Laura Donaldson when she argues that the stabilizing of feminist readings of texts needs to respect women's role in the production of meaning.[58] Donaldson indicates the relation of locatedness and its effects on texts with the use of a Derridean trope, "engraf(ph)ting." A solution to the inadequacy of the endless textuality of poststructuralism and the alternative strategy of simply investigating the social situation of women behind a text, graf(ph)ting poses the linkage of subject position to text as itself a "writing" of the text. A work is socioculturally produced by a reading, a process captured neither by a fascination with text or context. In contrast to the pursuit of endless textuality, the graf(ph)t of this production is a writing that evokes the living, material social realities at stake.

The Derridean play on the term *graf(ph)t* (combining *graphion*, Greek for stylus, and *graft*, a horticultural practice) evokes the materiality of writing by means of the horticultural practice that joins a cutting of a plant with another rooted one.[59] A graft is other than the plant, even as it redirects the flow of sap, and depends for its life on the host; it creates a new plant. Similarly a reading is an engraf(ph)ting on a text; it is not a mirror of a text, a repetition or imitation. A reading writes a text anew, stimulates its flow of meaning in new directions.

I have already established a similar notion by saying that a community produces a text. What is gained with the horticultural trope is the inseparable—indeed, the constitutive—effect of social relations on the writing (the production) of reader-practitioners, and the effect of reader-practitioners on the "text" produced. A graf(ph)t is dependent on the host for its life/meaning, but it redirects the flow of sap/meaning. At the point where the new cutting joins the sapling, a fracture occurs. A reading is like a cutting; when graf(ph)ted on the text, it rewrites the text, redirects the flow of meaning. A reading is a graf-(ph)ted subject position, a textual position constructed out of the

---

[58] Laura E. Donaldson, "The Con of the Text," in *Decolonializing Feminisms: Race, Gender and Empire-Building* (Chapel Hill: Univ. of North Carolina Press, 1992), 52–65.

[59] See Jacques Derrida, "The Double Session," in *Dissemination*, trans. Barbara Johnson (Chicago: Univ. of Chicago Press, 1981), 173–286.

codes of the social formation. In the rewriting of the text, the redirected flow of that text is a splicing that directs our attention to the material relations that bring it into being. The graf(ph)t creates breaks, fractures, and joints that mark off the needs, desires, pleasures, and fears of a subject position and elicit previously nonexistent possibilities in the text.

Such tropes are not causal explanations, of course; they suggest that production and closures of meaning are like the splicings of plants. Subject positions are texts, codes of dependency that construct women's practices; these practices are engraf(ph)tings on scripture as well. When we look at women's productions of scripture, we see the flow of desire, the distribution of power/pleasure, and the directing of sustenance that come with social location. Women are themselves inscribed by desires and the limitations of sustenance, yet they produce new graf(ph)ts of meaning out of biblical texts, even in settings that are poverty-stricken and minimally sustaining. A graf(ph)t will seek the places where nourishment (the flow of sap) can be found, even when that flow is choked and minimal.

With the trope of graf(ph)ting, Donaldson suggests how to think about the production of nourishing textual lines by women and about the oppressive occluding effects of these productions as well— graf(ph)t as corruption. The breaks at the point of splicing signify the redirections, the avoidances, the shut-offs of flow that accompany any gra(f)pht. For a theological analytic, these breaks and the avoidances that come with them signal the denials that accompany the diminishing, pernicious effects of social sin and its ideologies.

By positing the relationship between text and context as graf(ph)t, we locate the stability of women's performances of texts. That stability is achieved not simply by the ends or purposes of a social practice and its construal of a text, but with the effects of desire and the distribution of power and pleasure. The grammar of sin will expect to find these effects as denials, social fractures, and brokenness. The unending possibilities for these denials are helpfully imaged by the layers of textuality that the indeterminacy of poststructuralism has helped us see. The "brakes" on an endless multiplication of these layers come from the convergences that Donaldson helps identify as graf(ph)ts.

To ask about gender oppression in relation to a text, we do not ask about the meanings in the text and how they represent women, nor do we simply ask about the historical context to be studied. When women "read" a text, we may find that their production is constrained and limited. This will signal the mark of the social graf(ph)t, however, its lines of flow and blockages between readers and texts, and the ideologies of both. It avoids a diagnosis of women's utter passivity and

oppression by an obliterating sexist text. We look for the generation
of meaning in biblical performances precisely at the places where
women's subject positions help us see what they have wrested out of a
religious tradition and what about it is sustaining.

Posing the relation of social location to the text as one of engraf-
(ph)ting does not specify the precise relation of various features of a
subject (race, class, gender) to the biblical text. It does something
more valuable, however: it indicates that the alternative to some
notion of real meaning, found in either text or context, is not just an
infinity of possible readings. The alternative is rather the tracing of
(temporary) stability by way of conflicts and desires and the meanings
these trigger. This is a stabilization that helps us think more complexly
about what is involved when woman is an oppressed subject position
in a community that construes a text out of its vision and purpose.

I propose that an alternative to the "real" meaning of a biblical text
for a feminist analytic must display women's production of well-
being, a production that will activate textual constraints, ideologies,
and possibilities for a refusal of their patriarchal oppressions. This
meaning is only available when the discursive totality — the faith community that constructs women as performers and the social formation
of patriarchal capitalism — help us locate the graf(ph)ting of their particular subject position onto the possibilities in biblical and traditional
faith, a tradition they produce.

In search of a theo/alogical economy

I have created an opening to think about how women produce and are
produced by processes with very different effects depending on how
they are situated. As engraf(ph)tings, these productions can be viewed
in relation to the constrictions and openings made possible by social
location. This relation is not a simplified account whereby we know in
advance what gender or other oppression will look like in relation to a
biblical text.

Another question needs to be taken up, however, that of the place
of normative theological construction of women's practices in this analytic. To address it, I need to show how this account can respect both
the grammatical character of feminist theological practice and the instability that comes with my theo/acentric grammar of discourse,
which prevents a proposal of a normative grid that is simply imposed.
From my perspective, to impose such a grid would require that a
norm or standard have force that works outside of semiotic process.

As a liberation theological analytic, the question of a normative rubric for the assessment of women's scriptural performances is not about whether they instantiate an entire theological system of rules. This is a violation of the production of meaning—no one can use (or needs) all the rules of grammar when speaking in a particular situation. Moreover, a liberation analytic begins with the question of the particular meanings that converge around gender, its oppressive practice and its liberation, and the issues of difference.

What I have argued thus far is not antithetical to the prioritization of some ends for a community. The influence of poststructuralist criticism on my proposal does not mean that any or all construals of the text are to be valued the same. A feminist account must assume that Christians do not hold to all their convictions in the same way, however, that different convictions may be employed or challenged at different times. It must also assume that our convictions—those a theologian might articulate as the closest thing to grammatical rules of faith—orient us toward different stipulations of relevance. It is stipulations of relevance, as Fish calls them, that issue in the varieties of our responses to challenge.[60] Feminist stipulations of relevance have to do with the prioritizing of certain grammatical convictions—Christian faith as resistance to sin and right relation to God as inextricably related to social justice—that lead it to develop a politics of resistance to the social sin that is dispersed as patriarchal capitalism.

With this situational account of the pertinence of theological grammar, it is virtually analytic in Christian communities that scriptural meanings will be ordered around the figure of Jesus of Nazareth in some way; but questions about the adequacy of a Christology only get raised in feminist theological inquiries based on stipulations of relevance. One does not simply begin with a complete theological grammar and require its full enactment. Normativity for feminist theology is negotiated as a response to particulars: how, out of infinite possibilities, emancipatory meanings get produced; what the points of stress and brokenness are in a practice; what exigencies of sinful oppression are operative in a community to support blindness and refusals; and how certain reinventings of tradition support openings for pleasures and redemptive spaces for women.

My account differs from two other notions of the way the elements of a grammar might be brought into prioritizing relationships. This difference is a result of my theological appropriation of discourse theory for my feminist analytic. A review of the implications clarifies

---

[60]See Stanley Fish, "Change," *South Atlantic Quarterly* 86:4 (Fall 1987): 423–44.

the theological issues at stake. I propose an *intertextual* economy in the place of either the ostensible *extratextualism* of liberal theology or the *intratextualism* of so-called postliberalism, two current theological options.

An economy is the "reciprocal exchange between two instances that have no existence outside of that exchange," says Michael Ryan.[61] Attention to the relation rather than to the preexisting entities simply continues the principle that meaning is produced out of differences. It allows us to extend Moore's poststructuralist criticism of biblical hermeneutics to "normative" theological models. Asking the normative question in terms of an economy of elements in a discourse allows us to grant priority to particular domains of discourse, without refusing to acknowledge the fluidity of discursive practices in different social formations and the meaning effects of these arrangements.

We may ask about the economy of grammatical elements pertinent to the production of meaning by women in different faith communities. This is to ask how the relation of these elements opens up women's resistance. The important question is not whether there is any determinate or preferred meaning, for there always is. The important questions are: (1) how well a theological analytic is able to inspect the effects of the discourse (a Christological grammar, for example); (2) what work is done by the reliance of a preferred meaning upon an "other" (how a fixed Christological norm might continue to produce "others" in unacknowledged ways); and (3), given the inevitability of occluded discourses, what they are and how women are affected.

The model of intertextuality

Implicit in my presentation of the discursive constitution of reality is an understanding of the relations between elements in the practice of Christian faith as a relation between texts or signifying processes. Intertextuality, a term coined by Julia Kristeva, allows us to understand that the distinctions we need are not those of preexisting subjects (centers of consciousness) and the fixed biblical text and context. In this model we are required to think of the process of interpretation as the "static hewing out of texts," as Kristeva puts it. Intertextuality thematizes the fact that a structure of meaning does not simply "exist but

---

[61] Michael Ryan, "Poststructuralism and Radical Teaching," *Yale French Studies* 63 (1982): 57.

is generated in relation to *another* structure."[62] Even more, it finishes off my entire argument that we should theorize women's resisting faith practices and the different "texts" involved by recognizing how these meanings (even as systems of meaning) are never contained in texts, be they biblical or other. They are generated by other discourses. Thus there is a dynamism to signification that is inimical to permanent closures, but does not prevent specific practices.

The issue of theological normativity arises in two ways when the practices of faith are taken up as intertextuality. An intertextual economy can help us ask what is affected by various orderings of discourses. For example, does the notion of the critical function of scripture work to enable women to produce spaces where they can care for the neighbor (and themselves) in relations of mutuality? Does the prioritizing of christological rules over those that require resistance to relations of domination shut off the possibility of asking about the effects of certain languages on women's well-being? The point is to see how texts are always ordered in some way and are never available prior to that ordering.

The question of the relation or ordering of elements of discourse is the sense of "normative" that I will take up here. On the basis of that kind of normativity, one of the assumptions that my criticism is designed to undermine is the assumption that a fixed biblical text (or subject) is required for theological norms. An internal economy forbids precluding a text from a relation. This is different, however, from the second and larger question of how a theological practice can be regulative. The regulatory force of a theological position asks how an intratextual (or other) position works as an institutionally embedded practice. How does the theologian reproduce the priority of the scriptural narrative, the biblical world as that which shapes the interpreting community? This second question, also necessary to judgments about the effects of discourse on women, I will take up in chapter 7.

Thus I propose that the interests of a feminist theological analytic are best served by an intertextual economy, which is preferable to extra- and intratextualism as a way to weight theological norms. If we understand everything as discourse (the textual field of reality), the logic has already been set up for understanding the relations of various entities, the distinctions in the field as intertexts, as relations between signifying processes. The term does not turn everything into a written

---

[62] Kristeva uses the term *intertextuality* to introduce the work of Mikhail M. Bakhtin, particularly his account of the dialogical character of signifying. Julia Kristeva, "Word, Dialogue and Novel," in *The Kristeva Reader*, ed. Toril Moi (New York: Columbia Univ. Press, 1986), 34–61.

inscription, or even into language. I have shown why this is not so. I employ the term because it is a continual reminder of the constitutive character of signifying and the semiotic character of every piece of the social.[63] It is the latter that both extra- and intratextual positions cannot protect.

The limits of extratextual and intratextual positions

I have already argued that the extratextual position of liberation feminist theology is not sufficient to answer these questions. Following a brief review of those as grammatically inadequate, I will show the intratextual as an equally problematic way to create an economy of grammatical elements.

An extratextual proposal is found in the textual discourse of liberalism, some of whose features plague feminist liberation theology. Extratextualism, the position outlined by George Lindbeck to characterize (and possibly caricature) liberal theology, is distinctive for positing a site, a subject position, where there is access to "real meanings" outside of signification. This site is common human (religious) experience. External to any culture's language, this extratextual site is used to translate differences in meaning between cultures into meanings that are virtually the same. The ultimate meaning of the deities of different religions, for example, are amenable to translation into virtually the same God. For liberal theology the topic of commensuration, or what is translatable into the same, is human religious experience. The parallel in feminist theology is the universalizing prediscursive grid of women's experience, a sometimes prediscursive norm that I have argued is found in some forms of the feminist appeal.

An extratextual economy is problematic, Lindbeck says, because it sells the distinctiveness of a religious tradition for a mess of universalizing pottage. The extratextual experience that makes possible the translations between different cultures of meaning is not itself without meaning. The problem is that its source is unacknowledged. In the case of feminist complicity in it, extratextualism erases the distinctiveness of different subject positions "woman." The occluding effects of discourse have to do with the failure to acknowledge that closure is a

---

[63]See John Frow, "Intertextuality and Ontology," in *Intertextuality: Theories and Practices*, ed. Michael Worton and Judith Still (Manchester and New York: Manchester Univ. Press, 1990).

temporary and fallible procedure in a theological position, which always represses something.

Extratextualism closes off certain elements from scrutiny by naturalizing realities that are themselves inscribed with signification—"experience" and "social structures," a term typically invoked for everything external to the text. The appeal to such extradiscursive norms obscures real but unarticulated power arrangements, those that privilege the interpreter of the "common" experience. When this model is applied by one faith community in relation to another, it is patronizing of other religions; in feminist hands, it is patronizing of women of other social locations. By relying upon what is external to textuality as the norm for the text, the theorist of extratextualism obscures her or his own power in important ways. She posits what I have called a text outside of a relation.

The postliberal alternative to extratextualism is an *intratextual* proposal, designed to honor the distinctiveness of communal (faith) knowledge by refusing the so-called generic, prediscursive realms of experience. In other words, not only is there no prelinguistic meaning, but the normative generation of meaning will be provided for by a grammar that specifies how communal rules (the *regula fidei*) order the practices of different Christian communities.

In order to regulate all religious claims with the specificity of Christian communal grammar without disallowing for changing vocabularies, the intratextualist relies on a set of meanings identified as the core lexicon found within the text, "the biblical world."[64] In addition to the core text, this position accords normative status to faithful grammatical practice in two respects. First, intratextualism relies on grammatical practice to allow change in vocabulary; different Christian communities with different world views will practice (and speak) their faith differently. Second, faithful practices are prioritized over the meaning of texts as such as the telos of Christian practice.

What distinguishes this position from an intertextual view is that it does not recognize that signifying practices cannot be completely controlled. The desire to ensure that the grammatical rules are dominant allows their virtual removal from the processes of ordinary semiosis. The power of a core biblical lexicon, the "world of the bible," to signify in one direction shows that certain textual unities have such force

---

[64]This position is given its exemplary form by George Lindbeck, but relies on Hans Frei's work privileging the literal reading of biblical texts. See Frei, *The Eclipse of Biblical Narrative*; *The Identity of Jesus Christ: The Hermeneutical Bases of Dogmatic Theology* (Philadelphia: Fortress Press, 1975); and "The 'Literal Reading.'"

that they are not subject to the constraints of ordinary signifying processes. They do not participate in the instability of signification.[65] Practitioners of the faith as readers are not, in the end, signifiers with any power. How that happens is important to consider.

Practices of faith that look different, such as the Christologies that have appeared between early biblical Christianity, fourth-century orthodoxies, and later departures from orthodoxy, actually mean the same thing when they are judged according to the grammatical rules. Grammatical rules of doctrine are the constants that can be used to assess the changing formulations of communities over the ages. These rules appear to "operate beneath language, directing its configurations the way a magnet determines the configurations of iron filings on a surface," as Wesley Kort puts it.[66] As such, we must assume they, too, escape the ordinary process of semiosis. Grammar, and the scriptural lexical core that escapes the processes of reciprocity, thereby create another problematic realm of commensuration.

The problems with intratextuality come from several distortions of the process of signification that it produces in its attempts to protect the integrity of Christian communal meaning. Let me focus on Lindbeck to display these problems. Lindbeck uses intratextuality for the workings of the dominant normative discourse, the "biblical world." The lexical core of scripture, a narrative that renders the character of God through the story of Israel and the actions of Jesus, functions in such a way that its terms create meaning only in relation to one another. The webs of signs that constitute this core are powerful enough to alter the meaning of the world outside the text. The various semiotic systems that construct the worlds outside of the text, however, do not have the normal force of signifying processes, which would be to signify terms of the biblical lexicon as signifieds and thereby create new signs in an ongoing process.

What this analysis seems to imply is that it is possible to define the status of the biblical code so that the significations of the biblical text simply do not translate into the significations of other discourses. Intratextuality does not, then, function to deny the potential compre-

[65]George Lindbeck, *The Nature of Doctrine: Religion and Theology in a Postliberal Age* (Philadelphia: Westminster Press, 1984), 116.

[66]Wesley A. Kort, *Bound to Differ: The Dynamics of Theological Discourses* (University Park: Pennsylvania State Univ. Press, 1992), 38. There are numerous critical assessments of Lindbeck's position. One of the best is Terrence W. Tilley's article, "Incommensurability, Intratextuality and Fideism," *Modern Theology* 5:2 (January 1989): 87–111. See also a special issue on The Nature of Doctrine in *Modern Theology* 4:2 (January 1988); *The Thomist* 49 (July 1985); and William C. Placher's more benign assessment in *Unapologetic Theology* (Louisville: Westminster/John Knox Press, 1989).

hensibility of the biblical text in different settings. Rather it functions to deny the co-constitutive role of other semiotic processes, those that construct subjects in different locations, in the very process of understanding the biblical text. With such a situation, which seems implied by Lindbeck's version, it appears that we have a "universal discourse" in the core biblical text. Differences in women's readings of scripture, particularly departures from the grammar, are not comprehensible in this intratextual world, except to say they are simply wrong.

To criticize intratextuality is not to rule out a construal of the biblical text as a set of codes that are granted the status of an ordering discourse for the signs of one's contemporary situations. This is part of the economy of a discursive totality. I have argued that the positing of a critical function of the biblical text in relation to a community is itself a creation of the social practice as a whole. A critical economy is not the same thing, however, as the denial of the reciprocal workings of signifying processes. The intratextual position simply denies the role of its proponents in construing the biblical code, and the possibility that pernicious effects of meaning might cause one to change the reading of the text.[67]

Consequently, even though the intratextual position attempts to acknowledge the place of the practitioners' culture in the community's faithfulness, the process of semiosis is simply contradicted at two points. First, the signifiers of place and location disappear from the commensurating grammar. The idea that Christologies of Chalcedon and of the earliest Christians at Ephesus really mean the same thing may be slightly suspect. It is certainly easier to swallow, however, than the idea that post-"Godspell" Christologies or the Christology of woman-church might conceivably be the same as Chalcedon (or need to be). Second, the very different functioning of the biblical textual lexicon from that of changing cultures does not allow a role for the signifying practices of a community. The condensing of power in the hands of those who decide about the grammar and what qualifies as "the same" is the result of what, like extratextuality, is not a real economy. Unlike the feminist extratextual position, however, the intratextualist makes no attempt to ascribe interest or positionality to his/her position.

Intratextualism contradicts the process of signification. In this process, a sign cannot make meaning without other signs. However

---

[67]Intratextuality as it is used to prevent readers from having any impact on the text often seems to work to create an inner and an outer world of semiosis, a world of the text and a world of the "corrupting culture." This ignores the fact that the former does not exist without the latter.

stable and productive that set of differences may be in the meaning that emerges with signifying, it can always be placed in new relationships with other practices. In some important but unacknowledged way, the use of intratextuality in postliberal theology is akin to the positing of texts over against blank or at least passive reader/performers. To this I demur; there simply cannot be such a thing as a text that only signifies one way.

Such a view brings us back to the problematic implication that communities which do not read correctly are somehow at fault. While this is certainly conceivable with an account of ideology (which is not provided by intratextualists), it is quite problematic coming from a theological position (postliberalism) that is trying to move to morally shaped accounts of faithful practice rather than rationalist ones. By contradicting the nature of semiosis, it also proves antithetical to interests in the way power is inscribed in all discourse. An economy that relies on grammatical rules in order to respect the changing vocabularies that have inevitably come with thousands of years of Christian living needs to show what the difference in social location will make on its practice. If it has no impact, a real economy is not being offered.

Although Lindbeck has turned to a cultural-linguistic model in order to respect changes in faithful practice, he has implicitly allowed structuralist closure of signification to operate at the level of grammar. Oddly enough, when viewed in terms of signification rather than in terms of representational views of language, intratextualism has remarkable similarities to a liberal economy. *Somebody* has the power to determine what faithful practice is, just as somebody has the power to name women's experience. Lindbeck identifies these judges as the saints. Somebody also has the power to define the extradiscursive biblical core. Because this core is not reciprocal with its readers' signifying practices, this is not a "somebody" subject to inspection. Lindbeck's position may allow that middle-class women's faithful practice of scripture will differ from poor women's at one level, but the grammar requires a commensuration. At the level of doctrine they must mean the same, and someone will have the power to define "the same."

The use of cultural linguistic practice to think about the integrity of Christian faith on the analogy of the integrity of a semiotic system is important. It suggests a grammatical economy that constructs communities in relation to the biblical text. Its failure to pursue the relational character of signification consistently, however, is fatal to feminist purposes. Recent attempts to flesh out Lindbeck's model by allowing for different construals of the "plain sense" of scripture mitigate its structuralism. Kathryn Tanner defines the "plain sense" of scripture as a communal consensus that works critically over against its practices, offering a gesture that recognizes that scriptural performance is based on constructions. This is no longer an intratextual position, however.[68] Consistent intratextuality commends a commensurable set of rules that is ultimately free of history; its instantiation into different communities is in the form of a fixed narrative textual core. It again violates my principle that an economy cannot propose a "text" outside of a relation. Intratextuality represents a failed solution to the issues that raise the need for a constructionist position. As I develop an alternative to the subject–object frame of interpretation, it will be important to distinguish it from the problems of intratextuality.

Both extratextuality and intratextuality fail as real economies by virtue of the central role they give to domains of meaning—"texts" outside of a relation—that violate the processes of semiosis: women's experience conceived as external to discourse in the first instance, and an unchanging grammar linked to a text with fixed meaning in the second. These fail as economies because they rely on commensurating realms that are either prior to meaning or unacknowledged sites of meaning production. By doing this, both in their own way call into radical question the integrity of communities of readers that are differently located. Extra- and intratextual models do not render intelligible the possibility of alternative readings of Christian texts—a possibility that requires signification be reciprocal between entities. Although I find both intra- and extra-textualities problematic for different reasons, it is important to develop an alternative that respects the integrity, the patternedness, of Christian communities' practices of scripture as well as the instability that comes from the turn to signification. This must be done, however, without locating all the power to read rightly or define what right reading would be in places that fail to admit their situated character—the mark of "gra(f)phting" on any reading.

---

[68]Tanner, "Theology and the Plain Sense." Tanner defends and develops Frei's account of the "plain sense" of scripture, arguing that it is a precondition of the distinction between "expository" and "applied" senses. As the communal way of reading becomes identified with "what the text itself says," that is set in tension with the further use of it. She defends the narrative plain sense as the most open to difference in social situation and "unperturbed by change" (p. 75). This is a helpful set of distinctions. It fails to recognize the power-laden character of the decisions made, however, and returns to the "text itself" as a critical convention of the community. The extent to which "critical" has any force is totally unthematized. Tanner's account cannot legitimately be called "intertextual" because any assessment of "critical" requires the signifying practices of the culture/community.

I am sympathetic with Lindbeck's attempt to create levels of discursive constitution (to show that some discourses are more important than others). I maintain, however, that a feminist theological analytic must resist granting agency to a core biblical text as satisfactory to this end. How, then, can we think of the regulation of theological meaning in the face of such an outrageously open account of the Bible as that which I imply? We can think of it as the critical attention paid to living practices of particular communities and their willingness to attend to (or to occlude) the political horizons of their practices. The feminist theological economy privileges the grammatical rules that require "right worship" to be displayed as resistance and transformation of the sinful distortions of the lives of certain historical subjects "women." This is not the only set of rules that might be privileged, but that does not disqualify its pertinence. Feminist theologians judge that these pieces of a theological grammar are pertinent now, in Western patriarchal capitalist society. This is not to claim that an entire grammar is necessary and in place always and everywhere.

My proposal for an intertextual reading of women's performances of scripture relies on the irruption of women's resistance as its constant, not the adherence to a realm of commensurating grammar. The conditions of regulating Christian practice for feminist theology do not require that Christians do or believe the same thing. The processes of making meaning show these to be impossible ideals. A project that defines theological normativity as semiosis disrupted in the interest of positing identity between a contemporary position and what Christians have always believed or done undermines the more radical and living kind of stability. That living stability is discerned when we focus on Christian practices that create emancipatory space and widen the realm of God's kingdom.

For the conclusion of this account, I will draw together the elements of my feminist analytic in terms of the intertextuality of women performers of scripture, their discursive communities of faith, and the way they are graf(ph)ted on the social formation of patriarchal capitalism.

An intertextual economy for women's performances of scripture

I have defined discourse in a way that encompasses social relations, language, bodies, and objects in order to resist the affinities to idealism that plague theological proposals. I use discourse to bypass the dichotomy frequently posed between ideas and stuff. As reducible to neither language nor mind, discourse incorporates what are usually termed economic structures, social and political realities. In order to maintain this connectedness, a way of taking up texts as part of a discursive social practice must display an all-encompassing approach as well. To this end the notion of textuality serves as a metaphor for cultural and social realities as well as written texts. When everything is textualized, so to speak, we can explain the relation of the community and social formation encompassing the reading of a text as an *intertextual* relation. An intertextual economy allows that the production of meaning is "inter" (between) rather than "intra" (within) or "extra" (outside of) written texts and subject positions.

A word about the other resonances of intertextuality is in order. The origin of the term was in part an attempt to articulate the multiple levels of signifying that are folded into any text—the dialogical character of signifying. Texts do not simply contain influences; we might say that texts criss-cross one another. They are networks of referentiation.[69] Intertextuality in its simplest sense has been used to indicate that the only way readers can make sense of texts is by virtue of the other texts they have read. It is used by theologians to indicate the codes and references to other texts that are embedded in a (typically biblical) text.[70] Thus, intertextuality can be narrowly conceived so as to refer to specific quotations or allusions to other texts. It can also be broadly conceived so as to invoke the intersignifying of any literary whole with the world as social text, as I am using it here. We might, then, think of intertextuality as a way of indicating that any one text is a virtual Rorschach test of potential intertextual meanings.

My use is not intended to continue the habit of doing more source critical work, of finding texts embedded within the biblical text. My purpose is to broaden the idea that one can only understand written texts because of other written texts one has read in order to indicate that practitioners of scripture and of Christian faith are themselves coded. Thus I add that the community in relation to a text will set up certain kinds of networks, because a community is a complex of signifying processes itself. When a community "reads" (or practices) scripture, the codes that constitute the community are necessary ele-

---

[69]Frow, "Intertextuality and Ontology."

[70]John McClure has a useful analysis of preaching that is developed from semiotics. McClure uses Robert Scholes's definition, "a text lurking inside another, shaping meanings, whether the author is conscious of this or not," quoted in McClure, *The Four Codes of Preaching: Rhetorical Strategies* (Minneapolis: Fortress, 1991), 9, from Scholes, *Structuralism in Literature: An Introduction* (New Haven: Yale Univ. Press, 1978), 150. Richard Hays develops intertextuality in his investigation of Paul's writing with the image of echoes; see *Echoes of Scripture*.

ments in its coding/reading of that holy text. To the image of a text as
a Rorschach test of potential meaning, we must add that its possible
layers of signifying processes are triggered by the convergence of elements involved when communities practice their faith—the discursive
game and its graf(ph)t with the social formation. Any economy, in
other words, that truly recognizes the processes of semiosis is intertextual. Thus, a community's own codedness is fundamental to scripture's having any meaning. This is what I have been arguing all along.

Intertextuality is not confined, then, to a literary exchange occurring between texts (texts as written or oral linguistic units), although
it has been taken that way. Instead, we come back to my earlier notion
that scriptural reading or performance is constituted by discursive totalities. Intertextual relations are the production of meaning through
reciprocal processes of signification, processes that encompass the entirety of the practice under consideration, namely, faithful Christian
discipleship. Trading on the notion that other texts one has read give
one the capacity to understand, discursive intertextuality is how we
theorize that the "texts" of one's social location—the subject position
of housewife for the middle-class Christian woman, for example—are
as much a part of one's reading practices as the contents of one's book-
case.

A provocative proposal of intertextuality by John Frow furthers
this analysis. Frow conceives of intertextuality as a spectrum of inter-
significations that highlight not only the fluidity of the meaning of a
text, but the specific power relations attached to different readings.[71]
An account of women's performances of scripture inspired by his version of the intertextual relation not only moves us out of textual es-
sentialisms, it opens the way to theorize nondeterminist accounts of
patriarchal power.[72]

Four categories are necessary to construct the intertextual relation
for a feminist analytic. These categories will break down the idea "discursive totality" and place it in some analytical relation to the social

---

[71]Frow's aim is to avoid the vagueness of a textualized world, on the one hand, and
the narrow interreferencing of books quoting books and the attendant reduction of signification to language, on the other. For a poststructuralist position, the potential in the
term lies in its use by literary theorists as an alternative to "consciousness," "horizon,"
or other vague invocations of the world outside the text, uses found in Kristeva and
Barthes. John Frow, *Marxism and Literary History* (Oxford: Basil Blackwell, 1986), 125–
69. For a review of different takes on intertextuality, see *Intertextuality: New Perspectives
in Criticism*, vol. 2, ed. Jeanine Pausier Plottel and Hanna Charney (New York: New
York Library Forum, 1978).

[72]Frow's account develops the work of the Russian formalist Jurij Tynjanov in particular to connect intertextuality with notions of literary systems. *Marxist Literary History*, 83–102, 178–80.

formation, thus concluding my proposal of an alternative to the biblical canon and the fixed subjects or communities. The categories needed are: (1) a way to map the patterns of determinate meaning for Christian faith in a particular community; (2) a way to determine practices that are subordinated and potentially resisting to that dominant pattern; (3) a way to identify both resistance and compliance with the dominant patterns; (4) a way to articulate the graf(ph)ted relation of the patterns of faith with the orderings of the social formation, patriarchal capitalism in its hegemonic and localized displays of power.

Frow's comments are instructive in establishing categories to indicate the stabilization of a Christian community's faith and the meaning of its scripture, as well as for texts of literature:

> Writer and reader are not the fixed and isolated origin and conclusion of the textual process, nor is their relationship that of a constant fact to an uncontrolled variable (like Iser's oscillation between and conflation of implied reader as textual function and a real reader). Both "writer" and "reader" are categories of a *particular literary system* and of *particular regimes within it* and only as such are they amenable to theorization. (Emphasis added)[73]

Two analytical elements are offered in these remarks: a literary system and particular regimes within it. Together these elements can display the social practice I have called the faith community's discursive totality and the differing, even conflictual, practices within it. Analogous to the literary system in a theological analytic will be the rules or canon of a religious tradition. The notion of reading regimes will refer analogously to the ways a particular faith community practices scripture. These categories will prove far more useful than those of the author (historical meaning) or individual interpreter. Tradition as a system and the corporate reading practices it produces will serve, then, to replace the subject–object poles of the liberal frame of hermeneutics.

If the system is something like a grammar, regimes are somewhat analogous to the situation of utterance that specifies the possibilities of a language system. The regimes, the actual ways scripture is practiced, in other words, are defined by (in some ways limited by) the possibilities in the general notions of what good reading is, the system as "grammatical rules for reading."[74] The canonical system to which

---

[73]Ibid., 185–86.

[74]Frow's interest is in countering the Saussurean polarities, *langue* and *parole*, by thinking in terms of utterances and their situations of utterance in relation to a universe

Frow would have us attend, however, is much more complex than a grammar. The social practice that organizes a community contains rules for reading or performing the scriptural text; further, as a system of a religious tradition, it supports a "regime of reading" in more implicit and institutionalized ways than simply the publicly acknowledged hermeneutical regulations. In its defining limiting function, this system provides the possibility of stable patterns of meaning and prevents us from thinking of an individual interpreter with a primary relation to an objective text, scripture. It also will allow us to ask about constraints and possibilities that are not part of explicit rules.

Canonical system in literature

It is instructive to review the notion of canonical system as it applies to literature. This approach will help suggest how a canon is a set of norms, or a stabilization of meaning, that is not identical with explicit doctrine or belief but must be viewed as inseparable from social practices. The canon or literary system is not an official list or literary dogmatics, although it may have that yield; rather it is the partially explicit, partially implicit set of rules and codes that enable a piece of writing to be received as literature. As Jane Tompkins puts it, a text becomes a classic not from its intrinsic merit "but rather from the complex of circumstances that make texts visible initially and then maintains them in their pre-eminent positions"; classics are "the bearers of a set of national, social, economic, institutional, and professional interests."[75]

A literary text does not have meaning in the first place simply by referring directly to the "world"; it does not act directly on the world, either to name, change, disrupt, or confirm it. A text's meaning is first of all a matter of its being recognizable as a kind of writing. This means that the writing of a literary text occurs in relation to the codes, conventions, and rhetorics of the going institution of "literature" in a

---

of discourse, or what he calls a "discursive formation." Examples would be legal, religious, scientific, literary, and even everyday discourse. I find parallels here with the system of a particular religious tradition—Christian denominations in the cases I choose—and the regimes of reading within those systems that emerge in women's scriptural practices around gender. Obviously, many reading regimes could exist in a particular religious tradition. See Frow, *Marxism and Literary History*, 67–69.

[75]Jane Tompkins, *Sensational Designs: The Cultural Work of American Fiction, 1790–1860* (New York: Oxford Univ. Press, 1985), xii. This, of course, does not mean that a "classic" text has no merit, but that achievement of public recognition is related to who is culturally influential in any particular period.

particular age. For that matter, any writing (or cultural practice) is dependent on the familiar, even when it is devised to break with convention. The familiar is institutionalized in some form. Writing relies on the codes and conventions of a culture and the accompanying expectations about literary forms and genre. The familiar "once upon a time" is a convention which clues hearers that what follows is a story and not a laundry list, a political speech, or a geography lesson.

From simple conventions of reading comprehension to the more complex components of the conditions of a particular discursive practice—the definition of who can speak and on the basis of what qualifications—the canonical system is a crucial piece of the intertext. In the example of a literary text, this relation is easy to see. In order to be received as a novel, a text must employ the codes and conventions of the novel. Likewise, the detective story has its own conventions. The audience is guided by having its expectations of character, plot, and plot device confirmed in some way. It is equally true, however, that a text's ability to do this is relative to a particular setting. It is precisely these external conventions, in Tompkins's words, that make one see the "intrinsic merit" of a work. What is more, if this point is accepted, the longevity of a text's reputation has to do with its creation as a different text by virtue of the changing assumptions that make it intelligible. A story by Nathaniel Hawthorne, for example, is not the same text when its different aspects are appreciated in different times. The work admired by critics of the 1830s is rendered intelligible as a different text by critics of the twentieth century, for whom post-Freudian psychological categories have replaced notions of the moral self.[76]

Such rules and definitions do not simply exist in people's minds. They are embedded in conditions that support the reception of the genre and are part of the definition of canonical system. The definition and fate of the novel or mystery story are not the result of individual preference, or even of a public preference comprised of thousands of like-minded subjects. Even less are they internal truths of the text that do the same, situation-transcending work in different times and situations. Institutional supports and profit-making agendas are necessary to the canonical system that conditions successful texts in the U.S. popular press. "Culture" and "taste" are integral to the reception and choice of books; these are not matters of private whim but are shaped

---

[76]Ibid., 8. In her survey of a century of reviews of Hawthorne's *Provincial Tales,* Tompkins observes, "The practice of psychiatry in the twentieth century organizes the space the text can occupy much as the existence of the Unitarian Church does in the nineteenth." Ibid., 15.

and driven by apparatuses of production with not incidental relations to profit-making. The norms for what counts as "classic" or "real literature," similarly, are institutionalized norms, which are counted here as part of the canonical system. As Tompkins shows with American classics such as Nathaniel Hawthorne's work, the achievement of status is connected to the processes that brought his work (similar to other writings of his day) to public attention and reproduced it. These norms or conditions are manifestations of the distribution of power, the power to authorize and legitimate a text. Such power is tied up with the possession of expertise and its support of procedures of credentialing.[77]

The notion of canonical system has to do, in other words, with the authorities that generate and support the reception of a text. This is clearly a matter that is larger than the power of individual persons. It is helpful to speak of the conditions, both explicit and implicit, of a text's reception. In the case of a contemporary university English department, these orderings are the system that says what literature is and how it works, who is authorized to say so, and what the institutional and wider social supports are for that set of definitions. Current protests against this system by historically marginalized groups is testimony to its reality and its power.

In the case of communities that honor Christian scripture, these orderings have the specificity of a denominational or local religious community's tradition, its canons of reading and practice, and the institutional-social supports for it. The canonical system can be viewed as a broad and institutionally entrenched set of practices that define experts in the field and legitimate translations and interpretations. The institutions involved include presses, denominations, seminaries, and universities.

It is possible, if more complicated, to develop the intertextual relation in a similar fashion for scripture and tradition. The canonical system is the primary organizer of the "text"—its intertextual relations are the norms against which the original production of the text is designed. The complication with the intertextual relation of scripture is that scripture is multiple literatures. This claim makes some sense even without poststructuralism, because the scriptural text, whether

---

[77]Ibid. Tompkins's book illustrates this set of apparatuses in her account of the publishing history of American nineteenth-century canonical fiction writers and their contemporary writers (often women) who wrote as well but did not flourish. Frow offers a theory for this. His version develops a three-level system he finds in the Russian formalist, Tynjanov, which includes a text's relation to a synchronic system, its "autofunction" and its "syn-function." *Marxism and Literary History*, 83–102, 178–79.

the Protestant or Roman Catholic canon, has many institutionalized readings.

This can be illustrated diachronically. Like a literary text, the Christian Bible was generated out of meanings and meaning-making conventions available to its original "authors," a canonical system of sorts. Unlike a literary text, however, it was generated in a many-staged process of production by a number of systems. Systems of religious or sacred texts existed that had some engendering relation to the texts that are now considered the Bible; the number of systems is vastly increased by virtue of the years of existence of Torah and of a two-testament canon in oral and precanonical collections.[78] Like the literary canonical system, such a discursive system includes the semantic aspects of a text, its rhetorical forms and conventions, and strategies such as genre. It also includes the rules that order reading, interpretation, the institutional supports for its existence and dispersion, and rules of access and authorization for its readers.[79]

Admittedly, conceiving of specific intertextual relations in the full sense for the Christian canon is difficult, because that "text" has more productions, reproductions, and intertextual relations than could possibly be outlined. Given its complex composition, an attempt to take the Bible as text in terms of its "first" production over against some version of that first authoritative literary system(s) as intertext is unwieldy at best, at least in comparison to the same analysis for a nineteenth-century novel or other literary text.[80] (One can more easily imagine such an analysis on a section of biblical writings, although the issue of canon as an intertextual genre is a possible way to take the whole.) The organizing rubric of canonical system, however, is not the same thing as the searches of source and form criticism.

Intertextuality is not reducible to source criticism because the system of ordering requires that the actual features of an intertext must be conceived more broadly than quotations, allusions, or formulas. A community and its religious tradition create a canonical system for scripture. If we take a fundamentalist theological tradition as an example of the discursive totality, the intertext would include such elements as the rules for reading for a fundamentalist reading of passages on

---

[78]The terms *religious* and *sacred* are awkward here. Either term carries an entirely different connotation in the modern world, suggesting a separate realm or aspect of a secular and divided world. This would not have been the case in the ancient world.

[79]We also bypass the issue of the "author" of a text, because the process of making meaning occurs over the head, so to speak, of any particular author.

[80]Richard Hays works with the idea of intertextual relations in Paul, but not with as broad a conception as Frow's. Hays focuses on Paul's "actual citations of and allusions to specific texts." *Echoes of Scripture*, 15.

women in this canonical system. This notion is some distance from a notion of the original sources for a text. It encompasses the production of fundamentalist reading habits, as well as the educational and cultural conventions of the communities that support and reproduce these habits.

A second departure from source criticism is found in the way a relationship is constructed — the way a text as a whole is understood to rely on its canonical system and the particular connections that come into view. The production of the intertext is itself a practice and as such is always generated by an interest. We might even say that the interest that constructs an intertext is a nascent element in the creation of a regime of reading, whereby some consensus allows a relatively stable construal of that text as a certain kind of thing.

The fact that interest is the generator of intertextuality is important for my analysis of an intertextual relation for women's practices. My analysis is designed to trace certain kinds of interrelations around women's oppression and liberation. Thus we have a category for interest that avoids its inadequate formation as an attribute of a subject, a mental disposition. Interest now has discursive shape. It is found in the category of a reading, taking the text as a certain kind of thing — in this case, a feminist search for the readings that resist the dominant rules of the system. Recognition of the interest at work in this analytic process is what keeps intertextuality from being a search for origins, or source criticism.[81]

Interest is not, then, a feature of biased, privatized subjects or unobjective scholars, but actual patterns of defining, using, and construing texts forged in relation to existent codes. Frow's point here, not to be missed in light of my critique of feminist treatments of scripture, is that power and interest are displayed not by individuals with attributes, or by texts with permanent features, but with patterned interrelations — *regimes* that order the reading of a text. Clearly, reading regimes get practiced by individuals, but they are socially created grids, not subjective or private whims. Not all intertextual readings generated by interests get reproduced by communities, but for my purposes I will look at some that have been. I will look at reading re-

---

[81]The notion of a regime of reading is akin to Stanley Fish's notion of interpretive communities, whose agreements and conventions determine the meanings of texts. However, regime is located more specifically in the institutional-social productions of literature intertextuality as defined by Frow in *Marxism and Literary History*. One might argue that a search for origins can be placed in an interest regime, but the point here is that change-oriented interests dictate an intertext. On Frow's terms the search for origins as an objective search does not qualify.

gimes as the places where the situation of utterance for the system is located, and where idealized and contesting utterances may be identified.

An ideal regime of reading

Two intertextual relations must be examined in a feminist model for assessing women's practices of faith. The first comes from the canonical system that creates the religious community engendering women as practitioners of faith. That system includes the goal of the community's practice—anything from the saving of souls to the creation of justice in history. It also includes rules for reading scripture, rules concerning what scripture is about (its "plain sense"), rules about who is qualified to speak and interpret, about orderings of faithful practice and of gender distinctions, bodily display, and so forth. Thus the canonical system engenders an ideal regime of reading—an ideal performance, as Lash might say.

To indicate that any reading of scripture is part of a reading-for something, part of a practice of being faithful, I will speak of a regime of reading-performance. It would be a mistake (one this notion of regime prevents us from making) to locate canonical system simply in creeds, doctrine, or authoritative denominational discourse. Although what constitutes this complex does encompass these official discourses, it includes other inexplicit meanings that are not encompassed in notions like Lash's performance. These include forms of bodily practice and rules about expertises and justifications that a feminist analytic will highlight.[82]

The second site of production I will examine is the regime of reading found in the subordinated discourses, those nonofficial practices of scripture that I identify as women's performances. By calling women's practices of scripture "reading-performance regimes," I ask how they depend on (or are intertextual with) the canonical system and its ideal regimes of reading in women's religious communities. This analysis will suggest what canonically authorized meanings are invoked by women's practices that identify who they are and provide the field where support of the status quo occurs. These canonical meanings also

---

[82]My sense is that when theologians are interested in practice as a category for scripture, their main agenda is to emphasize that it is faithful living rather than belief that is essential to Christian faith. This seems to be Lash's point and Lindbeck's as well. They do not include in their categories ways to recognize the complex intersection of discourses nor the existence of dissenting practices in a community.

provide the field on which resistance to the gender status quo is played
out. Although the canonical system limits the possibilities in a community, it also provides clues to the strategies that displace the rules.
When women's regimes of reading performance are resisting regimes,
they are still intertextual with that ideal regime and the canonical
system it represents.

Obviously there can be an open-ended number of treatments of
a reading regime, either subversive or official. I will attend to ideal
regimes of reading and practice as displays of interest that support
particular gender constructions. Women's regimes of reading are, likewise, interested and multiple. They issue in resistance when they effect
a departure from the canon around issues of gender oppression; that is,
when the graf(ph)t is gender-related. These practices are resistance
when we can see significant convergences of desire, need, and fear signified as graf(ph)ting of social location onto readings. The lines of
splicing, of avoidance and constraint, will direct our attention to the
sites of conflict. This means that a feminist theology errs when it attempts to determine the sexist or liberating status of scripture, or to
essentialize one of the countless regimes. More productively, it should
ask about women's performances of scripture around gender issues in
different regimes and explore the full range of intertextual connections.

My feminist theological analytic locates patterns of determinacy in
the (temporary) stability possessed by scripture and Christian patterns
of meaning. This stability is discerned by attending to intertextual relations, which are defined by reading regimes interacting with canonical systems. In the place of individual subjects, whose subjectivism is
neither controlled by objective meanings nor left unfettered by this
definition, I posit socially coded interactive readings. In the place of
objective texts, I posit relationships to these readings that are forged
out of reactions to normative systems. The site of production, however, is identified by the resisting practices of women, which graf(ph)t
the discourses that produce them into resistance of sin.

A complication of these two contributors to production, the canonical system and the regime of reading practice, is the interstructuring
of any religious tradition with nonreligious meanings of its social
location—the discursive processes of the social formation. These processes are basic to an intertextual economy, which must assume that
theological systems are not impervious to the discursive formations in
which they are embedded. It is the feature of signifying processes
denied most blatantly by intratextual models of doing theology.

The canonical system of any religious tradition, its ideal reading
regime, and the potentially resistant reading regime are all textured by

the resident notions of gender in a location. These meanings are constitutive of the graf(ph)t I identify for different communities of
women. Prime examples are the three kinds of gender dependencies
produced by patriarchal capitalism that were identified earlier. None
of the intertexts that produce scripture and the tradition can be conceived as somehow absolutely distinct from these processes, ordinarily
lumped together as "culture." To conceive of a religious tradition in
absolute distinction from this culture of gender, which not only op-
poses and surrounds its community but is part of its lifeblood, is to
participate in another form of the essentialism that feminist analysis
must resist. Thus we will consider such discourse as it pervades the
system and reading regime and not as something separate from them.

Women's resisting regimes

The next three categories of a feminist analytic follow quickly from
my account thus far. As the canon is a system that orders the definition
of a particular form of literature and conditions for its maintenance
(and, by analogy, for a particular reading and practice of scripture), the
system does more than determine what gets received in the proper
way. It is a necessary ingredient in the possibility of challenge, as well.
In order to mount a challenge, a literary text depends on intertextual
devices that orient the reader adequately to an authoritative form.
Only by creating or invoking conventional expectations can there be
something to disrupt, challenge, or transform. The possibility for a
text to challenge a practice, to transform the world, is thus dependent
on its use of the rules of the system out of which that challenge comes.
This is equally true of a text's potential to support the status quo.[83]

Implicit in this account of intertextuality is the inaccuracy of notions that texts shape the world, that they act directly on readers or
situations in order to liberate or oppress. A text—the Bible, in my
analyses—does not refer directly to the world at all; it signifies by

---

[83]Reading regimes will have cogency for thinking about women whose determinacy
is a convergence of practices that may in effect create a new religious tradition. Appalachian religion, most agree, is peculiarly distinct from any denominational norm. The
point of the regime is to identify women's practice of scripture as carved out of some
religious tradition and its accompanying system. This intertextual relation provides
them with the terms and the regulative habits that construct their position as "women of
faith." This regime is what may be identified as the discursive practices that potentially
repeat but inevitably alter a religious canonical system. Other discourses, not necessarily
religious or in the tradition, may be as constitutive of the regime as any denominational
system.

means of the systematic domain that defines it. (Conversely, it is not accommodated to the world in some direct referential interchange.) The question of how a text might challenge this system—as in, for example, the current challenges to the Western canon in universities—is precisely what the notion of intertextuality is about, and it allows feminist questions about women's resistance to be answered without the imposition of liberal feminist notions on all women.

Categories for identifying nondominant scriptural practices are found in the notion of resisting regimes. If a reading regime is defined as what a particular community of readers forges out of a system of rules for reading and practice, it is possible to imagine both an ideal regime and a departure from it. One would expect that the way in which women practice resistance with their Christian faith will appear in this category and will have intelligibility in its intertextual relation to the terms of a canonical system. If, for example, the canonical system of a religious tradition (1) dictates that scripture is to be read in certain kinds of units, (2) limits the authorization of the clarifying of scripture to certain kinds of readers, and (3) construes those textual units as ostensibly plain directives about marital hierarchies, then regimes of reading in its communities will embody these assumptions. One would expect that not only compliance but the resistance as well of the women in such a community would take its shape from these rules of the regime. Resistance not formed in relation to that system would simply not be heard and could not have the system as a target.

A judgment about resistance is, then, a relational one. It asks how women's regimes of practice forge alternatives out of the constructions of gender in their Christian traditions and the way in which they continue to support and reiterate the gender-oppressive practices of their tradition. The movement out of gender oppression will always be contained in the terms of its concrete situation. A feminist analysis begins, then, not with a preconceived set of sexist texts or contents (the formalistic proposal of feminist liberation theology), but by attending to the changes that occur within the limits of a discursive field.

The creation of an academic text of women's stories to form another feminist canon and liturgies, to take another example, is a kind of resistance with little or no intelligibility in a nonliturgical community without access to documents from other religions. To appreciate women's performances of scripture in varieties of communities, we must read them intertextually. Because a discursive totality, a systemic ordering of meaning, is not "merely" linguistic but includes forms of authorization, bodily and institutional practices, we will not expect that all practices of scripture are written texts, nor are all forms of resistance or oppression written. Content and form are rejoined in this proposal for resistance and oppression and freed from their ideational prison.

We need a bit more flesh on this theory of regimes of resistance. For there to be a distinguishable resisting regime, one must assume a corporate practice by women. An obvious example would be women's groups or organizations in religious communities, or some practices that are distinctive to the women in a community. Clearly, not all such groups are feminist, so the question of resistance raises the need for an alternative category other than the litmus test of liberation feminist theology, and for a theological rationale for calling practices resistance. I propose that contradictions in the discourses are signs of tension or strain in a community. Around the contested terrain of gender, these contradictions will not necessarily be named as resistance. In fact, in some conservative communities the women refuse feminism as they understand it. Their practices nonetheless will appear as bids for the expansion of women's terrain that are produced by transgression of the canonical system.

Women's practices can be characterized as resistance and as liberationist when they are rejections of the kinds of dependencies generated by patriarchal capitalism and when they mount refusals through their sources of Christian faith. Only a narrowly liberal feminism can fail to appreciate the multiple convergences of oppression that constrain women and can be seen to create more pain at some points than others. Only a doctrinaire rationalist approach to the tradition can fail to appreciate how certain appropriations of Christian tradition in these locations work *for* these women rather than totally against them. The point is not to retrieve for all women what in other sites of utterances are patriarchal signifying processes. The point is to perceive the linkages between social location and discourse and to respect how what is liberating for *us* may not be immediately applicable for others or vice versa.

The concept of register

The relation of social location to these practices, which are most frequently centered around appropriation of scripture, is of crucial importance to my argument. This relation is signified by speaking of the graf(ph)t of subject position on a reading. In order to distinguish practices at the level of women's biblical performances, another analytic category is needed. What I have referred to as social expectations — codes and rhetorical practices that connect systems to readers — are not helpful without a unit of analysis with which to identify a reading-performance regime. The term that will provide such connecting points between regime and canonical system is *register*, a term Frow uses interchangeably with discursive *genre*. More specific than context or style and more general than specific utterance, register is a constellation of meaning, a type of sorts around which social expectations have collected. Used by sociolinguists and literary theorists to differentiate language uses, register serves to indicate that *what* is said and *how* it is said are inseparable in discourse analysis.[84]

Recognizable patterns that qualify as registers are sometimes tied to a social situation (as liturgy is tied to religious service) and sometimes not (face-to-face conversation is a discursive genre not tied to a particular situation). A register or discursive genre can be as contained an utterance as prayer, or as broad a unit as a technical language like legal discourse. A type of literature can be identified as a genre containing within it a number of subgenres or registers. What connects these examples is their susceptibility to analysis by three variables that create unity out of a situation of utterance (i.e., make it a register): (1) field or subject matter; (2) tenor or quality of social relations; and (3) mode, the linguistic symbolic organization or channel of communication. Correlating to semiotic functions, the variables suggest how the content function of language, its interpersonal or social function, and its rhetorical or textual function are all constitutive of situational meaning and must be looked at together to suggest what meaning potential is generated.

The genius of the concept is its fluidity. Examples of register cut across every conceivable social domain. One example is the register of a mother's game-playing with her small child. The subject matter is the ideas in the interaction; the tenor is a dominant-subordinate helping (cooperative) relation; and the mode is spoken dialogue, or pragmatic speech—"language in action."[85] By organizing analytically the situation of utterance, register allows us to conceive its meaning with some transcendence of its "author's" intentions and to incorporate such signifying elements as the bodied meanings when they are part of a situation of utterance.

In short, the first accomplishment of register is access to a unit that

---

[84]Michael A. K. Halliday, *Language as Social Semiotic: The Social Interpretation of Language and Meaning* (Baltimore: University Park Press, 1978), 31–35.

[85]Ibid., 35, 60–62, 108–126. Halliday distinguishes the function of register from the function of dialect, which refers to "variety 'according to the user,' " as opposed to register's analysis of "variety 'according to the use' " (p. 35). (Dialect would be a helpful addition in a thorough account of women's discourses. I am simply not competent to take it up.)

rejoins form and content, as we see that tenor or mode can alter the force of the subject matter, as field can alter the others. The tenor of the mother-child interaction will be key to its distinctive register. Second, register opens to analysis the way a pattern of utterance gains new meaning when irregularities are introduced into one or more of its conventional elements. For example, in a register where one variable is characteristically dominant—tenor in military commands, for example—expectations about that register will be clustered around its relational aspects. One expects certain tone and affect to a military command; if that command is delivered in a soft, quizzical style, one wonders "what is up" (sarcasm? parody?). In a register where certain subject positions are equated with its use, its appropriation by an "unauthorized" person will effect some challenge to its conventional effect, as well.

Register provides a unit of analysis that moves beyond the notion that there are contents or subject matter which always have the same signifying effects. We must ask about the tenor of a discursive practice and about its mode, both of which will have significant effects on the meaning. As an element in a feminist analytic, register can correct the idealism linked to the practice of attributing fixed properties to texts.[86] It offers the possibility of identifying the patterns of meaning employed by women in a particular situation, both in terms of the continued use of registers that make up the canonical system that forms them, and in their alterations according to the social associations that attend them. Register offers access to the way women "make" their own gender possibilities ("liberation") as well as the way women are "made" by the restrictions of the social discourse available to them ("oppression").

A register is feminist when it is a resistance or alteration of its canonical system in a way that challenges the restrictions on women, and any dependencies exacerbated by their subject position.[87] Such a judgment is made on the basis of the kinds of registers that women

---

[86]Frow uses the category "register" for a form of intertextuality that is less explicit than the direct reference, arguing again that the connections between semiotic systems are more complex than simple duplication of thematics. Redefining the category "genre" to accommodate orderings of meaning that go beyond categories like "novel" or "sonnet," Frow uses "discourse genre" interchangeably with "register." He offers a way to identify these complex reactions and challenges in women's practice of scripture and tradition. Frow, *Marxism and Literary History*.

[87]This does not entail the claim that the women who practice their faith in these registers are feminists. Many would refuse that label. My primary interest here is in the work of discourse, not in individuals and their intentions or self-interpretations. My analysis is of how discursive practices circulate—i.e., have effects not intended by their practitioners.

employ in their reading regimes, on the expectations attached to those registers, and the ways in which these expectations are altered. In my look at the practices of middle-class churchwomen, poor and working-class Pentecostal women, and academic feminist theologians as practices of resistance, I will focus on the variables of field, tenor, and mode. These variables are cues to the changes in process in relation to the setting and target of their practices. Changes include the space these women are able to create for themselves with their practices, and their chances at sustaining changes at the second level of feminist concern, the systems with which these practices intersect.

When new forms of women's stories are posed by Ruether, for example, as a counter to the closed canon of scripture, we have a field-dominant form of resistance. This constitutes a fairly significant challenge to the grammatical system of theology pertinent to certain institutional conditions. A register that creates more space for women in the interpersonal realm will be dominated by tenor, to give another example. An interpersonal transgression of a convention may have as its target a less entrenched form of power than that against which Ruether's open canon takes aim; it will be assessed accordingly. The point is that one must locate the site of contestation for each different kind. A feminist theological analytic of women's discourses moves inevitably to the question of how Christian or scriptural performances occur in a larger setting that reproduces poverty and patriarchal relations. The fate of women's practices in light of that social formation is part of this inquiry, as well as the reach of a register in relation to the religious canonical tradition.

The final category, the impact of the social formation on an intertextual economy, is a necessary part of the analysis because of our shift away from cognitive notions of oppression. If language does not represent or reflect reality or individual experience, neither is it a reflection of group experience. The poor do not have their common reality expressed in language; neither do women. Only the particular relations of discourses in a setting produce the truth. This means that the processes which reproduce the social formation and its support for patriarchal capitalism will impact communities in different ways. Gendered subjectivities disable women relative to other discursive practices and will have different effects in a poor community than in an affluent one. The three different discursive constructions of dependence identified in chapter 2 constitute the points of entry for exploring this question, which I signify with the trope of graf(ph)t for the relation of women's subject position to their production of the text. The problems of resistance will be shaped by the kinds of dependence that characterize working-class and poor women's subject positions, and the differently shaped problems of access for nonpoor and professional women as well. Registers and their reach must be looked at in light of context-specific dependencies.

Paying attention to the most disabling subject position for women and recognizing that it will not be the same for the different communities of women does not preclude analysis of how the social formation as a whole supports patriarchal relations. Although I cannot do that further work in this project, I begin it by insisting that feminist analysis must attend to the different sites where meaning is produced. An issue might well be: Did a regime of reading transgress the rule of who can read? instead of: Did the women get it right about what Paul "really meant"? For women who do not find the dominance of male language for deity problematic, who do not agree with liberation feminists' judgments of the sexist texts of scripture, it is now possible to pose a variety of ways to attend to their rereadings or performances as resistance. Such variety is possible because we have moved from reflection theories of language to those that incorporate the social conditions of existence in their understanding of signification.[88]

Thus I propose to look at a greater number of things than simply a practice's "feminist" content. Changes in the canonical rules around gender will provide the opportunities for feminist analysis: alterations in ways of reading, in the subject of the discourse, in strategies of authorization, and in the supporting institutional forms, all important discursive realities where women either take on gender oppression or are complicit in its continuation. For this broader analysis I propose to investigate the registers that constitute the intertextual for my samples of women's discursive practices. From analyzing the reading regime as it is made up of registers, we will find that resistance ranges from direct or explicit—as in a women's reading regime that counters the explicit teaching of her religious canon regarding women's ordination—to the more subtle challenges that only appear when the entire canonical apparatus is brought into view.[89]

Further judgments about identifying the relative feminist character of women's scriptural performances await my final chapter. The anal-

---

[88]Maria Black and Rosalind Coward, "Linguistic, Social and Sexual Relations: A Review of Dale Spender's Man-Made Language," *Screen Education* 39 (Summer 1981): 69–85.

[89]The move out of gender-specific content as the limiting or definitional boundary for what counts as oppressive/liberating discourse for the subject positions "woman" brings with it a fuzzing of the subject matter. As feminist analysis consistently discovers, oppression or liberation does not confine itself to gender-specific subjects. This is an old observation when it comes to content or composition analysis.

ysis of these performances and their resisting registers must return to the question of difference and why my position moves away from simply the celebration of inclusion. For the next three chapters, I move to an intertextual feminist analysis of three resisting regimes found in the practices of women whose faith performances are as diverse as they are graciously productive.

4 Decently and in Order: Discourses of Self- and World- Transformation

Chapter

Reflections on Judges 4-5:
Deborah loved her home, but she loved her people, too. She was a homemaker, but she was a responsible citizen. She was gentle and womanly, but she hated injustice. . . . May God grant that Christian women of this day be like Deborah of old and march with the people of the Lord against the destructive forces of hate and prejudice and injustice.

— *Presbyterian Women*, 1957

Only a housewife — but with power to change the world!
— *Outreach*, 1952

What does resistance look like in a community of women on record more than once as denying that it wants independence from the male half of the church? What possible feminist registers can be found in a group that has to be implored by male leaders to make its opinions known when women's ordination is up for consideration by the ecclesiastical body? That community is Presbyterian Women (PW), the group of predominantly white, middle-class churchwomen of the Presbyterian Church (USA).[1]

---

[1]The term *Presbyterian Women* refers to a predominantly white women's organization in the PC(USA), the denomination that brought together two previously unified Presbyterian bodies, the UPC(USA) and the PCUS in 1983. This group had pre-reunion forms; the northern group called itself United Presbyterian Women (UPW), and the southern group was known as Women of the Church (WOC). The initials UPW or WOC will be used to refer to the (former) northern or southern group. PW now has a technical meaning: the reunited communities of UPW and WOC officially called Pres-

Developing out of the women's mission work of late nineteenth-century Protestantism, progressivism, and the educated womanhood of the early twentieth century, Presbyterian Women is a community that has traditionally disavowed interest in feminist labels.[2] Yet not only is there resistance in their discourse, these women have much to teach a feminist theology about gendered constraints and possibilities as these are produced by capitalist patriarchy for middle- and upper-middle-class white women. Presbyterian Women have done much with the subject positions offered by their own tradition as they have widened women's domains and aimed to change the world.

Presbyterian Women is an organization comprised of mainstream Protestant churchwomen, mostly white, middle-to-upper-middle class. One of the three liberal Protestant denominations that founded the nation, the Presbyterian church split into northern (United Presbyterian Church in the United States of America) and southern (Presbyterian Church in the United States) branches during the Civil War, reuniting in 1983 as the Presbyterian Church in the United States of America.[3] The Presbyterian church continues to be disproportionately represented (along with the Episcopal, United Churches of Christ, and Jewish communities) in the upper echelon of civic and corporate America, even though its numbers and outright power have waned in this century. The incomes and education level of Presbyterians are in the highest cluster of U.S. religious groups, in contrast to the lesser status of moderate Protestants (Methodists, Disciples, Northern Bap-

---

byterian Women. (Thus there are women in the Presbyterian church who are not included in this group.) The journal of that "new" body is *Horizons* (1988–).

[2] The work of women in their own mission organizations has been well documented. For a fine study of women in missions that includes Presbyterian women, see Patricia R. Hill, *The World Their Household: The American Woman's Foreign Mission Movement and Cultural Transformation, 1870–1920* (Ann Arbor: Univ. of Michigan Press, 1985). Specifically on Presbyterian women in missions, see Frederick J. Heuser, Jr.'s dissertation, "Culture, Feminism, and the Gospel: American Presbyterian Women and Foreign Missions, 1870–1923" (Ann Arbor, UMI Press, 1991). On women's volunteerism, including the role of churchwomen in the period from the benevolent societies of the eighteenth century through the 1930s and movements for social justice, see Anne Firor Scott, *Natural Allies: Women's Associations in American History Women in American History Series* (Urbana and Chicago: Univ. of Illinois Press, 1991). For some of the class constraints of women's activism, see Nancy A. Hewitt, *Women's Activism and Social Change: Rochester, New York, 1822–1872* (Ithaca, N.Y.: Cornell Univ. Press, 1984).

[3] Wade Clark Roof and William McKinney, *American Mainline Religion: Its Changing Shape and Future* (New Brunswick, N.J., and London: Rutgers Univ. Press, 1987), 85–87. Among that elite group, Presbyterians are ranked behind Espiscopalians and UCC. Status is judged according to "education, family income, occupational prestige, and perceived social class." Of the five denominations classified as "top rank" in the status hierarchy, in 1945–46 and currently, Presbyterians remain the fourth highest. Changes in status have occurred mostly in the bottom and middle ranks. Ibid., 107–117.

tists, Lutherans) and lower-class or working-class Protestants, including Pentecostals. The women of the PW community are justifiably identified as middle or upper-middle class, at least by virtue of their spouses' status.[4]

This class position—typified by mid-level management as opposed to laborers, on the one hand, or owners of the means of production, on the other—directs my analysis to the subject positions constructed by capitalist patriarchy for these women. Consideration of the kinds of dependence visited on the American middle-class homemaker will yield one set of discourses pertinent to the Presbyterian woman and her constraints and possibilities. Her position in the social formation is key to understanding the ambiguities attached to the practices of world-transformation in which Presbyterian Women engage. It will be important to perceive the distinct character of their biblical practices in light of this, because of the great difference between PW and working-class and poor Pentecostal women's discourses.

In addition to being shaped by their class-related subject position, Presbyterian Women practice a faith inherited from John Calvin's Reformed tradition of Protestantism. The American Presbyterian version of that tradition is most relevant for the discourse of PW literature of the 1940s to 1970s. During the period under consideration, American Presbyterianism is a tradition in the process of leaving behind a conservative Princeton theology and deeply entrenched views on the authority of scripture that exclude women from the ecclesiastical public sphere. This tradition provides the second set of discourses that construct PW's subject position.

Given the primacy of scripture in the Reformed tradition, the logical place to look for a reading-performing regime of resistance might appear to be debates over the passages in scripture that are traditionally used to prevent women from taking positions of leadership in the

---

[4]They are likely to be in the group (or more likely married to members of the group) recently identified as a third class arising between 1890 and 1920. This new class, added to working class (wage laborers) and capitalists (owners of the means of production), is the professional managerial class. This group is defined not by its ownership of the means of production, but by its role in the support of the capitalist class (it produces the means to reproduce capitalism) and its nonaligned, sometimes antagonistic relationship to the working class. Barbara and John Ehrenreich distinguish this third class from the petty bourgeoisie, the only possible Marxist category that would be a candidate for nonproletariet noncapitalists. The professional managerial class is defined as "salaried mental workers who do not own the means of production and whose major function in the social division of labor may be described broadly as the reproduction of capitalist culture and capitalist class relations." See Barbara and John Ehrenreich, "The Professional-Managerial Class," in *Between Labor and Capital*, ed. Pat Walker (Montreal: Black Rose Books, 1978), 5–45.

church. One would expect that women's interpretations of scripture that countered these negative readings would qualify as the central elements of resisting regimes. PW does not rally around the issue of ordination, however. We must assume that either these women are utterly passive, or that resistance is going on somewhere other than around the issues of leadership valued most by men. In fact, the intertextual relation forged out of the discourses that construct PW's options is created elsewhere than in such debates. The logic of their alternative form of resistance requires a look at the discourses of class and religious tradition, particularly those of turn-of-the-century American Presbyterianism and the constraints, pleasures, and dependencies of the middle-class housewife.

Word of God and reforming performance: a reading regime for scripture alone

The Reformed theological vision and the American Presbyterian form of it make up the discursive field on which Presbyterian Women must perform. It is a field dominated by the view that the Protestant Bible is foundational for faith, doctrine, and life. This text-centeredness makes the category transfer possible from theory developed for literary texts to religious discourse. The two theories are not, after all, the same kinds of discourses. Canonical systems for Christians are much more explicitly developed than their analogues in literature, as are the communities of reading and performance in which Christians are constructed as believers. With some minor adjustments, however, the categorical scheme of discourse analysis can be applied to Presbyterian practices beneficially.

Differences in the way Protestant communities read scripture first need to be indicated, and the category *canonical system* allows for this distinction. The canonical system of Presbyterian communities includes both the explicit theological norms, creeds, and doctrines, and the implicit institutional supports for that discourse as a way of life. Theological orthodoxies or systems of beliefs, however, are genres with no exact analogues in the study of literature. To place in the foreground possible similarities, it is necessary to identify what would count as the reading regimes idealized by Presbyterian theological norms so that we can then focus on the question of women's resistance. With an outline of this ideal and its supports, the practices of Presbyterian Women can be seen intertextually with the canon, both in terms of how they conform to it, as well as how they alter or transgress its gender restrictions. In a model that assumes theological dis-

course is not impervious to the social formation, we look also for the
registers of resistance and status quo maintenance in relation to patriarchal capitalism.

A complete account of the canonical system ordering a Presbyterian
reading regime would entail the many layers of tradition that constitute the Reformed tradition, of which the U.S. Presbyterian community is only one. From that thicker tradition and its origins in the
Protestant Reformation, one persisting element is the claim that scripture is the defining text for the community's faithful life. Thus the
reading/performance regime is defined by the question, How does one
faithfully read scripture? Throughout the inevitable changes in hermeneutical rules, the telos of the regime is to enable a life faithful to God.
To find specific guidelines for that requires specification of the authority of scripture. We find this in Reformed confessions, theological
texts, and the constitution of the PC(USA). There we are offered an
even more specific set of rules to direct faithful reading.[5]

The presiding rule in faithful reading, the basic Protestant theological ordering of this text, comes from the soteriological issue in
Luther's initiation of the Reformation. "Scripture alone"—shorthand
for this rule—specifies justification by grace through faith, designed
originally to refuse the authority of the Catholic Magisterium. This
theological rationale for the persisting element of the regime is taken
up by John Calvin, the closer ancestor of the Reformed tradition.
Continuing to insist upon salvation by faith through grace alone as a
hermeneutic for scripture, Calvin developed the authority of scripture
with more specificity than Luther in order to sustain ecclesial reformation in the congregation and community—to reform the entire social
order, as it were.[6]

These defining moments contribute explicitly to the rules by pro-

---

[5]A full account would include consideration of the marks of the church. In addition
to being the one, holy, Catholic apostolic church, the Reformed tradition articulates
those marks as the word preached, the sacraments rightly celebrated, and (with a defining but unofficial status) the disciplined community. We are interested here in the impact
of these moments on rules that order the reading and use of the text scripture. The texts
include John Calvin's *Institutes of the Christian Religion* and specifically Reformed confessions, such as the Scots (1560), Heidelberg Catechism (1536), Second Helvetic
(1566), Westminster (1647), Barmen Declaration (1934), and Confession of 1967. The
constitution consists of the Book of Church Order, Directory of Worship, and Book of
Confessions.

[6]A third defining moment in the creation of a Presbyterian canonical system was the
appropriation of these traditions to develop an ordering of ministry and congregations
in a representative form of government. This is a part of the canon that is drawn upon
in the argument for ordination. It will receive less attention here because PW did not
feature that battle in their discourse.

viding an iconoclastic and evangelical end for the Reformed reading regime. In more conventional terms, this defining period for Protestantism generates a theological grammar: the doctrinal insistence on salvation by grace through faith alone. That doctrine orders faithful reading in the Presbyterian tradition as articulated in the motto *ecclesia secundum verbum dei semper reformans et reformanda*, the church reformed and always reforming. A kind of soteriological iconoclasm—namely, the refusal to let anything save but God's grace through Jesus Christ—is seen in the various ways the tradition has insisted that the Word is Christ, including the gospel proclaimed as well as the written text scripture. Incorporating justification by faith rather than merit becomes not only a protest against bibliolatry (the making absolute of texts or readings of texts) but is also found in the canonical system's approach toward its confessions. When this community calls itself a confessional church, it means not just that its confessions aid in the interpreting of scripture. It means that there can be no final confession in light of the evangelical sense of God's Word as living and new.[7]

The principle that scripture alone norms the community is interpreted as an evangelical as well as iconoclastic purpose for the reading regime. This interpretation represents the idea that the purpose of scripture is to bring God's saving presence to the community, to reform sin. The Holy Spirit, as Calvin says and the tradition continues to assert, must make the word come alive in the believer's heart for it to be God's Word. When we look for more specificity about that transformation, this canon points to the church and to the principle of love.[8] The trajectory of the Word as evangel is ecclesial and, ultimately, social. The work of Christ, the Word rightly proclaimed and lived, is the demonstration of God's love that entails the reformation of the social order, as Calvin's attempted reformation of the city of Geneva indicated. In the ordering of church life and ministry, this principle eventuated in a system of representative government, whereby the graded courts and the refusal to allocate power in the hands of a bishop guarded against the sinfulness of "man."[9] In a different fashion than the Lutheran, the Reformed community under-

---

[7]See David Willis, "Authority in a Confessing Church," *Journal of Presbyterian History* 59:2 (Summer 1981): 97–111. A disclaimer for the finality of any Reformed creed is attributed to the First Helvetic Confession.

[8]A rule for exegeting this claim, Luther insisted on the priority of the living Christ to the written text of scripture. In Calvin the objective revealed character of the entire text was asserted along with this appeal to the living Christ—the evangelical meaning of the Word. These rules are expanded in the formula that norms scripture as the *written* word of God by the proclaimed Word of God, as well as the living Christ as the Word of God.

[9]Much of the history of this was Scottish Presbyterianism.

stood the purpose of faithful reading to extend beyond the reformation of the individual into the worldly kingdom of Christ. The obedient reformed life has varied from the proscribing of dancing in sixteenth century Geneva to contemporary definitions of justice in a social order corrupted by transnational capitalism.

In light of the peculiarly Calvinist twist to Luther's justification by faith alone, faithfulness is life lived in active obedience to God's call in the whole of society. There is some expectation that society itself will be reformed, not simply left intact as the realm of the lost that Christians must endure. The insistence on the corporate-public nature of salvation is the definitive and often repeated hedge against private or individualistic faith. This insistence is integral to the ecclesial and societal trajectory of the system. As one Reformed theologian characterizes it, this is a world-*formative* religious piety rather than a world-*avertive* piety.[10]

The implication for a reading regime is that scripture is authoritative for "faith and life" (as the constitution puts it). Faithful reading is faithful practice. We may speak of faithful performance of scripture and understand that the stage of that performance is the life of the individual and the society (even if there is no explicitly political hermeneutic for the text and that performance).[11] God's love is its motivation. Although love is the least developed aspect of the canonical system, in the last analysis, love is to texture that performance.

These rules imply that a text cannot be faithfully understood outside of such rubrics—namely, iconoclasm for the purpose of a telos of transformed community and social order. There are as well other less explicitly theological Reformed views of the text. One is the specific hermeneutical rule of the Reformers that what is unclear in scripture is to be interpreted by what is clear. A second is Calvin's belief, in contrast to Luther's, that the entire text of scripture is revelation, God's Word. Calvin held this sense of the entirety of the written word as Word in tandem with the conviction that the living Christ is the paramount Word. It is fair to say, therefore, that a faithful reading outside of the work of the Holy Spirit in the believer is a violation of the rules

---

[10]Nicholas Wolterstorff, *Until Peace and Justice Embrace: The Kuyper Lectures for 1981 Delivered at Free University of Amsterdam* (Grand Rapids, Mich.: Eerdmans, 1983), 3–22.

[11]Despite this extension of Christian faithfulness into the social order, one taken in liberation theological directions by contemporary theologians, the iconoclasm of the canonical norms is reasserted in the refusal to allow the identification of the gospel with any social system or arrangement. Until liberation theologians, there were no social-political hermeneutics for scripture.

for Calvin. In other words, these textual practices are only maintained
with his overarching "rule of reading": that scripture is properly read
when the gospel or good news of God's saving grace is effected by a
reforming performance.

This description is confirmed by a more contemporary account
of seven rules for interpreting scripture gleaned specifically from the
Reformed confessions: (1) Jesus Christ as Redeemer as the central
hermeneutic and subject of scripture; (2) the plain text and its grammatical, historical meaning; (3) the inward work of the Holy Spirit in
confirming scripture; (4) doctrinal guidance; (5) the "rule of love" of
God and neighbor as hermeneutic; (6) the importance of study and
scholarship; (7) interpreting scripture in light of scripture.[12]

Two possible trajectories can be identified in these rules, trajectories
that have different openings for a Bible-based position on women's
place in this tradition. It might be argued that when Calvin and the
long-standing inclusion of the spirit-guided reading of the text are
taken seriously, they mitigate a flexibility in the treatment of the
"plain sense" of the text, even if the entire text is constructed as revelation. What is striking about the rules is that they do not account for
women's lack of access to leadership and the privilege of public
speech.[13] They imply that reforming performance is the primary rule,
thereby giving priority to the hermeneutic of christological redemption as the operative rule for reading. Considerable leeway exists for
judging that performance, inasmuch as a performance assumes that its
stage is the social order. We can conclude that despite considerable ambiguity for the ideal reading regime around the terms of a perfor-

---

[12]H. Jackson Forstman, *Word and Spirit: Calvin's Doctrine of Biblical Authority* (Stanford, Calif.: Stanford Univ. Press, 1962). These principles, as they are called, were
drawn up by the northern streams of the now PC(USA) in 1978 and reaffirmed in 1983
by the reunited church. Each has confessional grounding as follows: (1) Scots 3.18;
Barmen 8.05; Confession '67 9.27. (2) Scots 3.18; Westminster 6.007, 6.009. (3) Scots
3.18; Westminster 6.005, 6.010; Confession '67 9.30. (4) Scots 3.18; Heidelberg 4.022.
(5) Scots 3.18; 2d Helvetic 5.010. (6) 2d Helvetic 5.010; Westminster 6.008; Confession
of '67 9.29. (7) Scots 3.18; 2d Helvetic 5.010; Westminster 6.009; Confession of '67 9.28,
9.29. See Jack Rogers, *Presbyterian Creeds: A Guide to the Book of Confessions* (Philadelphia: Westminster Press, 1985), 167–71.

[13]It could be argued that the conviction that scripture should be read in terms of its
plain or literal meaning (the Reformers' move away from the Medieval quadriga with
its multilevel interpretative possibilities) made certain stances toward women inevitable
and part of the original explicit canonical system. However, the "plain meaning" or literal sense of scripture, while important in facilitating the move toward historical criticism, in my view is not a profound theological insight defining the Reformed or
Presbyterian tradition. This view puts me at some odds with the preceding list of seven
principles, but aligns me with it insofar as the first principle is understood to refuse a
narrow literalism. See Rogers, *Presbyterian Creeds*.

mance, it does not seem that the rules are inherently gendered. One is called to enact gospel in the world—nothing in the rules specifies the identity of the faithful.

It is, of course, possible to find gender restrictions in the biblical text. The rules, however, provide options for overriding such restrictions on faithful practice—iconoclasm against bibliolatry and the transcendence of the purpose of faithful reading over the letter of the text, to name a few. The plain sense might be centered in non-gender-specific texts, which are then used to clarify or correct gender prohibitions. When the rule requiring reformed performance is broken (by being ignored), however, and the transformative end of the good news is not included, the claim that the entire text of scripture is revelation can have a different impact on women. The "plain sense" of the scriptural text is open to a reading that shuts off the possibility that iconoclastic sensibilities might be brought to bear on ecclesiastical support for subordinated positions of women. Only the norms that are *not* part of the official canonical system, the practices stemming from the gender conventions of an age, then account for the position of women. (They account for it, that is, for the feminist reader; they are not recognized as operative in the canonical system.) Clearly, it is the operative rule about the "plain sense" that will either support or obscure that cultural accommodation.

No speaking allowed: divine prohibitions and subject positions for Presbyterian women

The Presbyterians did not have an explicitly gendered reading regime until the early nineteenth century. This point does not imply a golden period when women were not excluded by virtue of gender conventions. Specificity on gender in the canonical system is found in the rules of reading employed when the subject of "women" was first raised in the public (ecclesiastical) domain, in 1832. In that year the judicatory body of the church, the General Assembly, spoke officially for the first time on women, denying them the right to speak "in public and promiscuous assemblies."[14]

---

[14]Historians R. Douglas Brackenridge and Lois A. Boyd note that the belief of the church fathers from Calvin through the formative period of American Presbyterianism that woman's place excluded her from positions of authority was clearly stated in scripture. So supported were their beliefs by their culture that a stance on women never needed to be articulated in the constitution. R. Douglas Breckenridge and Lois A. Boyd, "United Presbyterian Policy on Women and the Church—an Historical Overview," *Journal*

The basis for this gender pronouncement was a view of scripture identifiable with the Calvinist assumption of objective textual revelation employed outside of the iconoclastic evangelical telos of the Reformed regime of reading. From the 1770s through the late 1920s, a view of scripture prevailed in the Presbyterian church that was designed to resist the rise of modern scientific knowledge. This view of scripture as plenarily inspired quieted any doubts about women's place by appeal to scriptures read as plain directives on these matters. Until key battles in what was called the Modernist-Fundamentalist controversy were won officially—decisively in the North when the church disavowed literalism, less officially in the South—a reading regime from the view of biblical inerrancy developed by Princeton theologians Benjamin Warfield and Charles Hodge was hegemonic in the Presbyterian church.

In a view not identical with Calvin or the Westminster Confession, Princeton theology held that the current biblical text was infallible in its science and history, not simply in its religion—this despite the fact that only the original autographs of scripture were judged to be inerrant. According to Princeton theologians, the intelligibility and accessibility of scripture's plain meaning was due to the Holy Spirit's role in its writing *and* to the conviction (buttressed by Scottish realism) that guaranteed an identity between the ideas of the ancient world and the understanding of contemporary believers.[15]

The Princeton theological vision of divine presence that founds this approach to scripture is an ideational image. In other words, God's presence as revelation is available as content or ideas. The advantage of the content mode is that it is most easily appropriated in the form of concepts, precepts, and ethical directives, all of which can be gotten directly from scripture, often with little debate over meaning. The implicit assumption in this image is that an identity exists between a content or idea in the Divine Mind and that content as found in the written text. This assumption virtually assures that such passages which provide directives or injunctions pertaining to women will be enduring candidates for exemplary cases of the "will" of God.[16] This

---

of Presbyterian History 59:3 (Fall 1981): 384. Jane Dempsey Douglas argues that even though Calvin maintained the exclusion of women, such views for him were inessential to the church; *Women, Freedom, and Calvin* (Philadelphia: Westminster Press, 1985).

[15]Jack B. Rogers, "Biblical Authority and Confessional Change," *Journal of Presbyterian History* 59:2 (Summer 1981): 131–58. Jack B. Rogers and Donald K. McKim, *The Authority and Interpretation of the Bible: An Historical Approach* (New York: Harper & Row, 1979), 200–379.

[16]David Kelsey identifies Princeton theology as exemplary of the theological construals of scripture that assume intellectual content is the way in which God is present.

is particularly so when no strong images exist to counter the image of will = textual content; sure enough, none arise.

In short, two things were indisputable. 1 Corinthians 14:34 and 1 Tim. 2:12 forbade women from having authority over men, from teaching or preaching. In light of Princeton rules for reading, there could be no doubt that these texts are God's will written because they are the inspired word. In addition, the notion of universal understanding guaranteed that historical distance made no difference in the meaning of the injunctions. There is no doubt about their plain sense. The injunctions are, therefore, still in force. It is clear that rules about access to public reading and interpretation have been added to the canonical system of the founding insights. Who can read and who can speak are defined in gender-specific terms; women are barred access to positions and registers of authority. The hermeneutical principles of the original canon, Holy Spirit–enlivened reading, an evangelical telos for reading—all the flexible possibilities in the canonical system for assessment of reformed performance are bypassed in this set of rules that now specify gendered authority for reading.

John Frow's account of a canonical system as more than the official discourse of a community about itself is a reminder to include the material conditions, the institutional supports for the further shaping of its rules and unwritten notion of access to authority. Such discursive conditions are integral to the explicit norms, as women's position in the community shows, and not simply cultural accretions that do not count in the identity of the community. In addition to the gendering of this reading regime, the institutional support for these rules is crucial to the canonical system. That support was considerable. On the basis of these rules and supports, the registers of preaching and sacramental liturgy were off-limits to women until the winning of ordination in northern and southern denominations in 1956 and 1964, respectively.

The ability to negotiate new answers to old restrictions depended in no small part on which of the stock of rules had status. Even the "plain" texts against women could be countered by others that appear contradictory. That would require historical criticism, which by calling the absoluteness of the texts into question, could undermine

---

Kelsey, *The Uses of Scripture in Recent Theology* (Philadelphia: Fortress Press, 1975), 14–31, 161. Edward Farley has explored the implication of the use of the literalized myth that I am attributing to this notion of God's will and scriptural text. I think the illogical endurance of these women passages is related to the fact that the image of "God's will" is so fixed in the religious imagination, and it does not get challenged directly by historical-critical method. Farley, *Ecclesial Reflections: An Anatomy of Theological Method* (Philadelphia: Fortress Press, 1982), 157–65.

Princeton theology's identification of the text with God's will. In a context of competing accounts, it matters quite a bit which ones have the official blessing of ecclesiastical judicatories and what gets disseminated in seminaries that reproduce the "reading experts."[17] Until the 1930s, Jack Rogers tells us, most Presbyterians operated with this Princeton doctrine of inspiration. Although alternative arguments appear, they have no force as long as the official support for Princeton theology remains unchallenged. This approach to scripture was disseminated in the seminaries of northern and southern churches until the 1930s.[18] The implication for the canonical system is that its theological rationales for excluding women were reinforced as long as the teachers who taught the preachers remained uninfluenced by historical-critical method.

By the 1930s the dominant approach to scripture that gave the "women passages" such unquestionable force was breaking apart. The delegitimation of the plenarily inspired account of scripture, a fundamental post of the canonical system that refused any overt change in the status quo, was well under way. With the rise of historical criticism, support arose for a different reading of those verses most frequently employed to deny women access to official ecclesial authority.

With a shift in the canonical system, the necessary shift in the rules for reading occurs—namely, the development of a variety of ways to unify and reorganize the contents of scripture. This enables distinctions between such passages as 1 Cor. 14:34 and 1 Tim. 2:12 so as to allow women to participate in the modern world. Various writers and committees put forth such alternatives as the "principle of equality" as arguments for women's leadership. These more flexible hermeneutics provide alternatives to the grip of the ideational image of revelation and its literalism. They get institutional support when neoorthodoxy and biblical theology begin to be taught in seminaries in the 1940s and '50s.[19] Scripture can be unified according to its broad themes, its prin-

---

[17]In the northern church, the General Assembly decided against biblical literalism in 1927 by disallowing that a judicatory could bind the conscience. In the South no decision was made officially. Historical-critical method was vindicated, however, in cases brought against a minister and two seminary professors for their use of critical methods in the 1920s and '30s in the South. For the entire story, see Lefferts A. Loetscher, *The Broadening Church: A Study of Theological Issues in the Presbyterian Church since 1869* (Philadelphia: Univ. of Pennsylvania Press, 1957). See also Bradley J. Longfield, *The Presbyterian Controversy: Fundamentalists, Modernists, and Moderates* (New York: Oxford Univ. Press, 1991).

[18]See Rogers, "Biblical Authority." See also W. Eugene March, " 'Biblical Theology,' Authority and the Presbyterians," *Journal of Presbyterian History* 59:2 (Summer 1981): 113–29.

[19]March, " 'Biblical Theology.' " (These don't always fit together nicely. The articulation of alternative ways such as neoorthodoxy allowed a bypassing of the historical-critical method and an emphasis on the evangelical meanings of the canonical system.)

ciples, and its function to proclaim Christ. Thus the institutionally supported version of the canon moves away from literalism—a crucial development. It also moves toward constructive alternatives to the hegemony of the "antiwoman" verses.[20]

The possibility of countering biblical arguments with arguments from the text and from the rise of historical-critical method and contextual readings of the offending texts, however, existed from the mid-nineteenth century. The former was always possible; the latter had official sanction at least from the mid-1920s. In the arguments over women's speaking and women's ordination, one finds evidence of the powerful force of scriptural verses read as prescriptions for the modern world, even with the dissemination of historical criticism and the influx of alternative constructive approaches to scripture. One simply had to deal with God's word written—at least on this matter.[21] Other ways to take those verses existed: appeal to contradictory scriptures, such as Gal. 3:28, the evidences of women speaking.[22] As early as 1889 a PCUSA moderator wrote a paper validating the rights of women to speak, preach, and be ordained in light of scriptural evi-

---

On the changes in theological perspective as they occurred in Presbyterian seminaries in this period, see John M. Mulder and Lee A. Wyatt, "The Predicament of Pluralism: The Study of Theology in Presbyterian Seminaries since the 1920s," in *The Pluralistic Vision: Presbyterians and Mainstream Protestant Education and Leadership*, ed. Milton J. Coalter, John M. Mulder, and Louis B. Weeks (Louisville: Westminster/John Knox Press, 1992), 37–70.

[20]This is an abbreviated account, to be sure, of shifts in rules for reading. The change in ordination questions, for example, is pertinent to shifts in construals of the text. Prior to 1977 in the PCUS (and in 1967 in the UPC) the ordination question was posed: "Do you believe the Scriptures of the Old and New Testaments to be the Word of God, the only infallible rule of faith and practice?" Presently the question is posed, "Will you be a minister of the Word in obedience to Jesus Christ, under the authority of Scripture, and continually guided by our confessions?"

[21]The continued need to explain the offending passages is displayed all the way through the 1960s in the arguments about ordination for women. In the 1962 GA report "Woman's Place in the Church" (PCUS), the authors argue that they are hamstrung in reaching the conclusion that ordination should be made available to women unless it can be demonstrated that 1 Timothy and 1 Corinthians are not rules that are "permanent and without exception." The report's conclusions must be in line with the confession of faith that scripture interprets scripture. Thus new rules about access to the authoritative registers of the community require exceptions to the contrary passages in scripture. Although the weight of evidence leading to their conclusion is attributed to the influence of women's work in the church, the theological argument is clearly the text-dependent one. It is justified by the textually warranted claim that God does new things. *Minutes of the 1962 General Assembly*, PCUS.

[22]See Mary Faith Carson and James J. H. Price, "The Ordination of Women and the Function of the Bible," *Journal of Presbyterian History* 59:2 (Summer 1981): 245–65. This article is an excellent summary of the case in both streams of the church. See Brackenridge and Boyd, "United Presbyterian Policy," 383–407. Also see Lois A. Boyd and R. Douglas Brackenridge, *Presbyterian Women in America: Two Centuries of a Quest for Status* (Westport, Conn.: Greenwood Press, 1983).

dence. A GA-appointed committee in 1920 reported that there was no scriptural evidence to prevent women's ordination, according to biblical scholars.[23] These arguments accord with other aspects in the reading regimes of the Presbyterian canonical system; they simply failed to count as "true" until 1956 and 1964.

Despite the number of arguments that challenged the gendered rules of reading, the conditions for truth that prevailed into the mid-twentieth century gave credence only to the significance of the offending verses. Little power was afforded the other elements of the theological canonical system, and no direct challenge was mounted against the literalized myth of God's will in the form of a text. Thus the canonical system of the Presbyterian community by the early twentieth century had a founding theological grammar, one that ordered the authority of God's Word as a written, christological, and transforming presence of God through the Holy Spirit, by its doctrine of justification by grace through faith. These were elements that hypothetically would allow for change and self-criticism. Its less explicit rules for reading, however—namely, how the biblical text is properly read, who has the power to define its meaning, and who may speak/read publicly—were heavily stacked against change that might affect gender relations, at least change that would appeal to the central norms of the community.

Gender discourses that construct Presbyterian women

The ineffectiveness of the rules about iconoclastic reforming performance is striking. The identity of the community is never officially linked to gendered notions; thus the perpetuation of views that exclude women from positions of authority in the community is due not only to the rules about plain meaning and ideational notions of God's

---

[23]George P. Hays, *May Women Speak?* (Chicago, 1889), cited in Boyd and Brackenridge, *Presbyterian Women*, 108. In a 1930 article a woman argued that neither precedent nor contemporary practice was the issue, but "the mind of Christ" in the present building of the kingdom and the situational character of Paul's counsel made his prohibitions no longer pertinent. Mary Herron Wallace, "A Woman's Reaction: A Woman Speaks Her Mind," *The Presbyterian Banner* (March 20, 1930), 11–12. She wrote in response to the Overtures sent in 1929 to the northern church allowing women a choice between full ordination, elders orders, and licensing as evangelists. Only eldership passed in the 1930 vote. For an account of this attempt, see R. Douglas Brackenridge, "Equality for Women? A Case Study in Presbyterian Polity, 1926–1930," *Journal of Presbyterian History* 58:2 (Summer 1980): 142–65.

will and their long-standing institutional reproduction, but to other unacknowledged aspects of the canonical system. In addition to the issue of widespread institutional support for historical-critical method, the second implicit aspect of the canonical system is gender discourses. These are necessary to account for the failure of the resources of official norms to dislodge the gendered rules for a reading that dominated for so long. These beliefs represent the cultural views about gender which define the community, yet which the community has no categories to acknowledge in its official accounts of authority.[24] Thus we do not fully account for the canonical system that will be relevant for women's practices until we note the gender discourses that construct Presbyterian women and the larger church as well.

It was not disbelief in the equality of the sexes that stood in the way of women's opportunities in the church, observed a powerful male cleric in 1928. However premature the view of the council for which he spoke, that most church people believed in the equality of women and men, this man was surely onto something when he insisted that the "mental attitude" about gender function was the real barrier.[25] The discourse of gender dominating the arguments against women's access to the register of authoritative reading and speaking is *gender complementarity*. Gender complementarity is the belief that woman's special nature is God-created and justifies her location in the domestic domain. This was a prominent cultural view in the nineteenth century and early twentieth century.

What won the ecclesiastical day in the Presbyterian church was the

---

[24]Only with the influx of the kinds of theologies that emerge from the 1960s on (liberation, feminist, and theologies of social criticism) is it possible to see the construction of Reformed theology as complicit with so-called cultural perspectives. See Mulder and Wyatt, "The Predicament of Pluralism," on the shift to such theologies in Presbyterian seminaries. These were not arguments that won access to ordination for women, however.

[25]As the vice-chairman of the General Council of the GA (PCUSA) meeting with "Fifteen Representative Women" over the unrest among churchwomen in 1928 comments, the issue of women's participation is not equality: it is highly unlikely that many disagree that men and women are equal. The issue is different functions. This historic meeting was precipitated by the distress communicated by women's groups when the church disassembled their mission board. It was an official meeting of fourteen influential male clergy and elders, with women to discuss women's dissatisfaction with the church. Rev. Dr. Henry C. Swearingen stated, "I think manifestly, the practice of the Christian Church has been based upon a conception of the definition of function." *Conference of the General Council with Fifteen Representative Women at the Fourth Presbyterian Church, Chicago, Ill., November 22, 1928*, Archives of the Presbyterian Historical Society, Philadelphia, Record Group #105, MS GAgc9w, p. 30.

belief in the positive advantages of women's special gifts. One might argue therefore that complementary gender has been a crucial unwritten rule of reading of the system—a rule that can work for or against women.[26] With a convergence of other factors, these gender convictions have simply been employed to support biblical reasons to alter the restrictive regime of reading rather than the prohibitions. The "Order of Creation," as the World Alliance of Reformed Churches puts it, expresses this conviction forthrightly: "men are men, and women women," a gendered order that cannot be disturbed.[27] Only with the assurance that this order would not be disturbed did many arguments for full access to church leadership succeed.

There is a more interesting point to what may seem to be an obvious argument that views about gender (or "prejudices about women") were crucial to the delay in access to the official registers of authority in the church. We find this point in the discourses of resistance for those who share the view of gender complementarity. In a tradition that centers its authority discourse on scripture and identifies its content with God's will, this reading regime seems to be the clear enemy for women. It contained explicit theological principles that assessed faithful reading in terms of reforming performance; however, its supports and implicit constraints included literalization of texts combined with complementary views of gender. These together granted the status of divine prohibitions to certain texts for much longer a period than seems intellectually defensible. The biblical literalism on gender issues that characterized the community at the turn of the century had force against women's full participation in the church until the mid-twentieth century.

---

[26]I make this judgment based on the presence in most arguments for and against women's ordination from the late nineteenth century on of some reference to the special gifts and nature of women. Those that appeal only to equality and an ostensible move beyond gender are rare; most appeals to equality mention women's special gifts as well. The centrality of this gender complementarity to Presbyterian Women is the subject of the rest of this chapter. The most sophisticated argument of the Princeton school includes this gender complementarity; R. L. Dabney, "The Public Preaching of Women," *Southern Presbyterian Review* (October 1879): 689–713. Dabney was a prominent systematic theologian in the southern church who operated with Princeton theological assumptions about scripture. This article contains an argument that takes on with great care each pro argument (Gal. 3:28, gifts and graces) and demolishes it.

[27]The World Alliance is for women's ordination, but indicates that such a change does not affect the order of creation. "While it is true that the Order of Redemption does not contradict the Order of Creation, and men are men, and women women, redemption removes all the disabilities in fellowship with God and in his service." Quoted in "No Theological Obstacle," *Presbyterian Outlook* 145:32 (September 16, 1963): 9.

In light of the canonical system of twentieth-century Presbyterianism, I propose that even the liberalizing of biblical literalism did not offer women much ground on the playing field. There had been counters to the arguments from historical criticism for their inclusion by theologians as early as 1879. Biblical criticism never challenged the image of God's will as a content, thus the powerful grip of its association with the plain meaning of texts on the community was barely loosened. The greatest problem, according to some, is the lack of an image to replace it that takes texts seriously and at the same time refuses "divine prohibitions."[28] Not only is the role of cultural constructions of gender in its reading regime invisible—for there is no way to acknowledge the community's role in constructing texts—but there seems to be more to be gained by pursuing the possibilities of gender complementarity than by appeal to the other rules of the regime. As a consequence, by positioning themselves in the discourse of gender complementarity, which they do, women are at odds with neither group in the time of transition.

In light of the minimum "give" in the hermeneutical principles of a Presbyterian reading regime, it is not surprising that PW's practice is not focused on the scriptural battle over women. Presbyterian Women did and do perform the Bible that was read to exclude them from leadership. They performed it without taking on the official registers of preaching, liturgy, and official interpretation—at least directly. Until the late 1960s and '70s, PW did not challenge the domain of the register denied them in the Presbyterian regime of reading, that of official interpreters of scripture. Given the dominance of the divinized text and the long-standing preference for certain parts of it that gendered the official reading regime, it makes sense that women in their class position would likely have been wasting their time to concert their energies resisting the Presbyterian reading regime of the first half of the twentieth century.

The difficulty of mounting a frontal attack on this reading of scripture may help us understand why women in the subject position of married housewives might need to resist gender oppression in some other fashion. They resisted by developing a part of the canonical system that was least developed: by performing scripture as faithful care for the stranger. In doing so they reinforced gender stereotypes,

---

[28]Carson and Price point out that the reliance on biblical principles, such as Gal. 3:28, was a strategy that bypassed dealing with the meaning of prohibitions and the issue of the canonicity of scripture. "The Ordination of Women," 257–62.

even as they stretched them in important ways. Presbyterian Women created new registers in the face of that authoritative register denied them—the register of a literature and community of self- and world-transformation.

I have argued that the gender convictions of the late nineteenth and early twentieth centuries combined with the dominance of a myth of literalism were not easily altered by the rise of historical criticism. The canonical system was made to seem airtight on support for the gender status quo. Even though the community had in its canonical system such rules as the enlightenment by the Holy Spirit (one employed by women in other communities), the rules for reading were institutionally entrenched and had long-term effects for what could be heard and taken as evidence.

Social subject positions: domesticity undermined

If it is no surprise that Presbyterian Women do not take on the register of authoritative reading and speaking, what other positions are available to them? How are they subjected by the social formation which is intricately embedded in the Presbyterian version of the Reformed canonical system even as it transcends that system? The specifics of oppression and possibilities for resistance for middle- and upper-middle-class women are found in the ideology of gender complementarity and its supports in the social formation. A primary yet increasingly devalued identity is offered women in the position of Presbyterian Women by the processes of industrial and postindustrial capitalism. That identity is the housewife, whose moral, spiritual, and emotional influence is understood in religious and popular ideologies to locate her in the home.[29] The home as the Christian base of faithful practice is a constant for Presbyterian Women, thus its fate in the modern Western world has an important impact on their possibilities in addition to that of the church's refusal of their public voices.

During much of PW's life, both in its preorganizational mission-society incarnation and through its work in the 1950s, a glorified

---

[29]Much scholarship has been devoted to the subject of domesticity—its religious supports, its use and expansion by women, and its refusal by feminists at the turn of the century. See Barbara Leslie Epstein, *The Politics of Domesticity: Women, Evangelism, and Temperance in Nineteenth-Century America* (Middletown, Conn.: Wesleyan Univ. Press, 1981); Dolores Hayden, *The Grand Domestic Revolution* (Cambridge: MIT Press, 1981); Sheila Rothman, *Woman's Proper Place* (New York: Basic, 1978); Amanda Porterfield, *Feminine Spirituality in America: From Sarah Edwards to Martha Graham* (Philadelphia: Temple Univ. Press, 1980).

image of domesticity circulated in the discourse of all Presbyterians. This included some form of the belief that woman has a natural and highly valued place which complements that of man. The social relations that supported this discourse were being undermined, however, by changes that were fully accomplished by the time PW literature was written. These changes were brought about by the development of industrial and postindustrial capitalism, as well as the burgeoning importance of science in replacing religious authority. Simply put, the industrialization of the American nonpoor home by the 1920s robbed it of most of its traditional functions and provided it with a new function.

The modern home became a key unit of consumption for the burgeoning capitalist economy. In the eighteenth and nineteenth centuries, although she was not equal to the man, there was no doubt that the white woman had an essential and productive place in society. Whether it involved producing soap, food, cloth, and reproducing the population of the republic as women did in the eighteenth century, or displaying their prowess in the creation of handiwork, more elaborate menus, and overseeing the moral development of the future citizens of the society, as women did in the nineteenth century, women's "place" was crucial to the social order. Historian Glenna Matthews judges that by the 1920s three of the four meaningful functions of the home of the mid-nineteenth-century "golden age" of domesticity were gone: (1) its political function and meaningful linkage of the housewife to the public sphere; (2) the function of the home to display and honor women's prowess; and (3) the sanctity and religious role of the home.[30] What was left (in addition to its new function of consuming) was the home's role as the locus of the affective.

Radical loss of status accompanied the reduction in function for the nonpoor white American woman and her home by the early twentieth century. This loss of status focused around de-skilling. The process occurred along with a change in the purpose of the home, and was accompanied by a change in its linkage to the social order as well. By the period of the PW literature of the 1940s, where I begin my reading, the

---

[30]Glenna Matthews, *Just a Housewife: The Rise and Fall of Domesticity in America* (Oxford: Oxford Univ. Press, 1987), chaps. 1 and 2, p. 93. In no other period was the status of the domestic higher and the appreciation of women's contribution to the public order greater than in the mid-nineteenth century, argues Matthews. Although women's productive labor may have been even more arduous in the eighteenth century, no discourse tying women's work to the social order was available until the late Revolutionary period. The phrase "domestic feminism" was used by historian Daniel Scott Smith to refer to the function of these skills to increase women's stature. Of course, being valued and being equal are not the same things.

shift from farm life and home-centered production to industrialization had completed the process by which the home was divested of its role as producer of goods necessary to society. Women had not been equal to men in preindustrial society, but their function in the social economy had never been in doubt.[31] The temporary rise in the status of the home in the nineteenth century, which contributed to the modern religious discourse of women's place, was over as well.[32]

Some scholars argue that by the mid-nineteenth century, public esteem for domesticity was at its peak. Men as well as women voiced high praise of (white, nonpoor) women and the home, motherhood, nurturance, domestic arts, and the family as key to the health and virtue of the body politic. This golden age of domesticity enhanced women's standing and, presumably, their self-esteem.[33] The status of women was signaled by public recognition of their prowess at cooking, sewing, management, and associated domestic arts; their moral-spiritual influence was at its peak in the mid-nineteenth century. This ideology of womanhood and domesticity supported the late-eighteenth-century image of the "Republican Mother," whose role was

---

[31]Conditions for social status (not equality) for the white homemaker—the ideology of domesticity and women's influence through the family—*were* present in a preindustrial society when the possibility of the individual citizen's agency in the social sphere granted credibility to the clout of the home in the larger society. Such conditions emerged in the American Revolution when connections were made between women's activities (cloth production, food production) and politics, with wartime boycotts. An ideology of "Republican Motherhood" expressed the key role of women in the new nation. So argue historians such as Matthews and Linda Kerber, who first described "Republican Motherhood." See Linda Kerber, "The Republican Mother: Women and the Enlightenment—An American Perspective," *American Quarterly* (Summer 1976): 187–205.

[32]It is fair to say that the view that de-skilling came with industrial capitalism is uncontroversial. There are more complex ways to discuss and define the benefits and make-up of domesticity in relation to the social order, however. The relationship of PW to these different nineteenth-century ideologies would be a fascinating study, but it is one that is too large for my purposes. See Epstein, *The Politics of Domesticity*. A number of studies have been done of the women's culture developed in the nineteenth century. See, for example, Ann Douglas, *The Feminization of American Culture* (New York: Knopf, 1977); Nancy Cott, *Bonds of Womanhood: 'Woman's Sphere' in New England, 1780–1835* (New Haven: Yale Univ. Press, 1977).

[33]By the mid-nineteenth century, an additional set of meanings were placed on women (white and non–lower-class) and the home that had not been present in the eighteenth century. This ideology required some shifts in domestic labor, too, argues Matthews; see *Just a Housewife*. Throughout the eighteenth and well into the nineteenth century, the home was central to the economy because it produced goods and services vital to the nation. A valuing of the woman did not necessarily accompany the central place of the home. The latter only happened well into the nineteenth century, when certain technologies (production of soap and cloth outside the home, and the invention of the stove, among other things) altered women's work enough to allow some of the more creative craft possibilities to flourish.

defined by the idea that women's sphere was crucial to the public and political welfare of the nation, to the social order.

This ideal was not to last, however. The industrializing and secularization of the home occurred as corporate America took over the production of food and clothing. Occurring gradually over the second half of the nineteenth century and speeding up dramatically with the change of centuries, it was a process that reduced the productive function of the housewife to the role of the private citizen in charge of family consumption. An insidious process of de-skilling was under way in this reduction. In order to take up the new "job" of consuming, women had to become willing subjects. By the 1920s corporate America had taken over not just the drudgery of housekeeping, the washing and cleaning, but had indiscriminately appropriated the production of food and clothing, the real arts of homemaking, as well. Its technologies were intended ostensibly to reduce the burden of housekeeping. As Matthews points out, this process could have served the housewife, simplifying the backbreaking work of keeping a family fed, sheltered, and clothed. Instead, the marketplace de-skilled her by appropriating the features of homemaking that constituted a craft tradition. The marketplace was unable to distinguish types of labor in the home. As a consequence, fine handcrafts and cookery were never to be the same after the rise of substituted processed and packaged forms of the 1940s.[34]

The rise of science and its incursion into the place formerly held by religion were also crucial to the creation of a consumer out of a woman whose home was the stage for the display of her prowess. The incursion of science was found even within religious communities. It greatly impacted the woman of whom PW is typical by contributing to the process of her de-skilling, even as its promise to make her life better proved ambiguous at best.[35] Not only did technology and science serve to undermine the housekeeper and her skills, but the promise of a reduction of her work proved false. When work was not

---

[34]Matthews, *Just a Housewife*, chap. 4. Matthews writes eloquently about the changes in cooking and the American palate that resulted from this de-skilling process. The criticism of the other ways women's practices were appropriated is developed in even more directions in Barbara Ehrenreich and Deirdre English, *For Her Own Good: 150 Years of the Experts' Advice to Women* (Garden City, N.Y.: Anchor Press/Doubleday, 1978).

[35]See Gabriella Turnaturi, "Between Public and Private: The Birth of the Professional Housewife and the Female Consumer," in *Women and the State: The Shifting Boundaries of Public and Private*, ed. Anne Showstack Sassoon (London: Hutchinson, 1987), 255–78. Matthews, *Just a Housewife*, chap. 5 and 6. Betty Friedan's *The Feminine Mystique* (1963) broke this story open. Ehrenreich and English, *For Her Own Good*, 127–64.

simply increased by "higher" standards of cleanliness, whatever time was saved from some of the drudgery was more than made up by the changing demographics of the middle-class nuclear family. The move to the suburbs created a new task for the housewife—chauffeuring. She gained a second home—her car.[36]

Even the home economics movement, representing attempts of educated women to move into the academy and broaden women's sphere, undermined the very things that had given many white women stature in the previous century. It did so by contributing to the cadre of experts whose "scientific" knowledge was to provide the sure route to progress no longer entrusted to religion. Employing these new domestic scientists to help create a market for their products, corporations set about convincing women to distrust their own judgment about how to cook, how to clean, how to sew. Thus the rise of "efficiency experts" and the factory-developed techniques of Taylorism were sold to the homemaker.[37] The simultaneous emergence of the expert in the professionalization of guilds and craft traditions in other fields besides domestic science (such as psychology, medicine, and child development) were well under way by the 1920s and worked to convince woman of her lack of knowledge and need of help. The expert became the new dominator to intervene in "her" domain as the middle-to-upper-middle-class woman aspired to do the best by her family.

A final contributer to the fate of women in this new order was the development of the notion of "true womanhood" in the nineteenth century, a relatively class- and race-specific ideology. It attained new functions after the period when women's nature served to connect the home to the social order. After industrial capitalism diminished the impact of the individual on society, assumption of the finer moral qualities of womanhood, a kind of romantic view lodged in the ideology of domesticity (one that permeates Presbyterian descriptions of women) could serve to support the increased split of the public and

---

[36]The appearance of *The Feminine Mystique* in 1963 is absolutely no surprise given the dependencies constructed for the middle-to-upper-middle-class woman's subject position.

[37]Taylorism reorganized the factory in order to increase efficiency and therefore production. In doing so it separated mental and manual labor and greatly fragmented and dehumanized the work of labor. Although there is disagreement about this, the application of Frederick W. Taylor's efficiency model not only did not produce anything of value for the housewife, but in some respects took the "mental labor" away from her and placed it in the hands of experts who told her what to do. For this discussion, see Matthews, *Just a Housewife*; Ehrenreich and English, *For Her Own Good*; and Turnaturi, "Between Public and Private."

private spheres and the consumer culture as well. Contrasting with what Barbara Ehrenreich calls "rationalist feminism," a liberal view of woman as person/citizen with natural rights, the romantic view constructed "woman" as innately nurturing, emotional, and of finer sensibility than man. Such a subject was not only best qualified to accept the restriction of domestic functions to the expressive, providing a haven in a heartless world, but also to be a consumer and to be a part-time, temporary, low-paid worker if the market ever did need her services. Instead of following the logic of liberal democracy and science, which would have entailed the inevitable freedom of woman from home and child-rearing responsibilities, this romantic ideology of womanhood helped create a woman who was the ideal subject for the new role of the home ensconced in America by the twentieth century.[38]

In view of the changes in the white nonpoor woman's place, centered around but not confined to her de-skilling, it is no surprise that by the twentieth century her link to the public sphere is altered in relation to the idealization of mid-nineteenth-century domesticity. No longer producing, she is "produced" as a consumer, and the crafts for which she was once admired are no longer valued, at least as the fruit of her labor.[39] What remains of the traditional functions of the home—the expressive—is hers, and the ideology of her "special nature" supports her adoption of this task, even as experts must tell her how to do it.

However long-lived the ideology of domesticity is in American thinking, the moral and political status of woman's link to the public is radically altered in credibility. Not only is this true because of secularization, but the possibility of individual influence in industrial society is radically undermined. Even more crucial to the diminished linkage

---

[38]See Ehrenreich and English, *For Her Own Good*, 13–26. Other conversations would distinguish variations in what Ehrenreich and English and lump together as "romantic feminism." These include the women's club movement activities, the suffrage movement, labor movement, and settlement house movement, which can be distinguished from women who were self-identified as feminists. Such distinctions would nuance the claim being made here, since some of the romantic views of womanhood contributed to moral reform (municipal housekeeping) while some were more class-constrained. The characterization is useful as a general one, however. This leaves another question to pursue: What discourses intersected with idealized woman's nature to create a sense of accountability for the social order? See Nancy Cott, "What's in a Name? The Limits of Social Feminism; or, Expanding the Vocabulary of Women's History," *Journal of American History* (December 1989): 809–828, 829.

[39]This analysis requires further tracing of the fate of the labors of the domestic sphere in late twentieth-century capitalism. For instance, the story includes the adoption by advertising and other discourses of public culture of these "crafts" and their commodification, including the appropriation of values of the "natural" and the "homemade" ("Just like Grandma used to make") to create new markets of consumption.

of home to the public sphere—the political influence of the good home/mother that characterized the golden age of domesticity—is the development of capitalism beyond the stage of industrialization. The hegemony of international corporations in global capitalism creates a market long past individual influence, and the possibilities of shaping the social order by nurturing a good citizen are thought by many to be illusory.

While the story of the home is surely more complicated than can be indicated here, a feminist narrative of the subject position for the homemaker must see it as an undermining process well under way by the twentieth century. The industrialization of the home undermines women's belief in their capabilities, their prowess with food, children, and the other crafts of homemaking. Many women have been recruited willingly into these processes and have experienced some benefit from them; therefore, we must speak of pleasures in the process of becoming a modern housewife—being up-to-date, progressive, doing the best for her family. However, there is no doubt that the effects of industrial capitalism on the home and woman have been destructive. They have de-skilled woman, induced her to distrust her own judgment, and conferred upon her the dubious honor of overseeing the new function of the nuclear family, consumption.

Home-based regime of resistance: a global domain

At least until very recently, Presbyterians' high incomes in relation to those of the other religious traditions in the United States have allowed most of the members of Presbyterian Women to be housewives. They have filled the subject position of idealized domesticity articulated with the Christian tradition, which also has defined them. The idealized version of domesticity is easily spotted in the gendered regime of reading in the Presbyterian canonical system. As I argued earlier, that tradition assumes the legitimacy of a "natural place" to honor woman, a place that simultaneously keeps her from the sphere and register of public authority. The religious canonical system has no categories for recognizing its co-construction by discourses of the social formation, so it is no surprise that woman's fall from status in the social developments of the world outside the church is not reflected in its rules for reading. The shift to historical criticism in biblical studies, which I am taking as the major intellectual inroad of this culture into theological consciousness, is slow to carry with it a recognition that gender constructions were as much a part of its norms as a theory of inspiration.

However much church spokesmen and churchwomen valued this subject position, it is a contradictory one at best at the time we pick up PW's discourse. The status of the typical Presbyterian woman as nurturer, homemaker, and provider of emotional succor is barely supported by the social formation. Secure by virtue of the class of her spouse, but truly dependent, an unskilled person with no expertise to carry out her primary expressive function and questionable status for her function as consumer, the housewife is in a contradictory subject position: privileged and precarious.[40]

Nevertheless, with the register of official interpreter of scripture closed off to them, Presbyterian Women create a more acceptable form of utterance. With their organization, or the distinctive unifying genres that constitute it, these women take up the practice of Christian faith in a way that at least appears to afford the least possible offense to the male-dominated ecclesiastical and secular world. To see their activities as a practice that also resists, however, we must see their literature as inseparable from the forms of community it organizes. Taking PW practice in its intertextual relations will display the creativity and the constraints that come with the contradictions in the position of middle-class housewife, as well as the constructive expansion of the canonical system with regard to scripture.

The literature that centers Presbyterian Women's regime of reading has its immediate heritage in the work of churchwomen of the turn of the century. That literature, *Presbyterian Women* (1946–1988) for the southern stream, and *Outreach* (1947–1958) and *Concern* (1959–1988) for the northern, is the offspring of late nineteenth-century women's missionary societies. Although the latter had a narrower focus than their modern counterparts, they epitomize the importance of domesticity as definer of place that will continue to construct Presbyterian Women. In the tradition of that unique sphere, the predecessors of PW did "Women's Work for Women."[41] One of the early convictions behind this tradition was that only women could reach heathen

---

[40]The women of PW are middle-/upper-middle class on the basis of their spouses' status and have been among the dwindling numbers of women who have not had to be employed outside the home. They are likely to be married to the group recently identified as the professional managerial class (see note 4 above). Their situation as producers of mental labor qualifies them for this distinction and allows us to better understand the privileged yet constrained character of women in this community.

[41]See Hill, *The World Their Household.* Earlier periodicals included those named *Woman's Work for Woman* (1871–1885) and *Home Mission Monthly.* See Lois A. Boyd and R. Douglas Brackenridge, " 'Woman's Work for Woman' and 'Home Mission Monthly,' " in "American Presbyterians: Writings That Have Shaped Our Past," *Journal of Presbyterian History* 66:4 (Winter 1988): 273–76. Boyd and Brackenridge, *Presbyterian Women in America,* 3–87.

women. Suggested by a cleric, the title indicated the focus of their work and how specially suited they were for it.

Officially organized in 1878 and lasting into the early 1920s, the women's societies generated enormous revenues from their practices of sacrificial "double giving," extra pocket money saved for their missions over and above their regular church contributions. Between 1873 and 1923, for example, the northern women raised $45 million, and the southern women were similarly successful. They were only briefly successful in gaining control over the money they raised. The seriousness of their power, however, is indicated by several official declarations (1913, 1916) of the national church judicatories that the women should be sure not to fail in giving the church its due portion.[42] To such insecure bombasts, always accompanied by fears that the women were plotting separatists, the women always respectfully demurred.

Foreshadowing the conversations of later generations, the women were at great pains to articulate their needs with modesty and gentility, denying any intent of separation or association with the secular demand for "rights." A wonderful expression of this relation of deference to male authorities is evidenced in the first request of the southern women for an executive secretary. The position was needed to expedite the organizing of their many local groups. Articulated as "The Nots," this document states a list of demands the women were *not* making:

> We are NOT asking more authority.
> We are NOT asking the handling of funds.
> We are NOT asking the creation of any new agency.
> We ARE asking more efficiency through better organization and closer union of our forces.[43]

The request was granted, but not without the standard fears expressed of the "ecclesiastical suffragettes."

Although the northern women had more autonomy in relation to

---

[42]Joan LaFollete, "Money and Power: Presbyterian Laywomen's Organizations in the 20th Century," unpublished paper (Johnson City, N.Y.: August 1989). See Margaret L. Bendroth, "Women and Missions: Conflict and Changing Roles in the Presbyterian Church in the USA, 1870–1935," A Presbyterian 65:1 (Spring 1987): 49–59.

[43]See Hallie Paxson Winsborough, Yesteryears, as told to Rosa Gibbins, PCUS (Atlanta: Assembly's Committee on Woman's Work, 1937), 28. Mrs. Winsborough was the secretary of Woman's Work. Her marvelous account of these early years is exemplary of the tone of gracious gentility and relentlessness that characterized the leaders.

the ecclesiastical hierarchy for a while, they too were reminded of their dependence when a reorganization in 1923 effectively took their independence away. The women's organization was consolidated under the Foreign and National Mission Board without their being consulted. The women's reaction was only slightly less genteel than the appeal of the southern women; they wrote of "unrest among the Women of the Church."[44] The nonconfrontational style of both northern and southern women was never a sign of their lack of courage or dedication. Their impressive financial success was only one indication of their persistence and commitment to their communities. Deference to the gentlemen shaped their practice, to be sure, but it never prevented creation of woman-identified practices, a number of which still survive. One of their early calls to arms captures this unique ladylike oppositional stance well: "Now don't be afraid! Keep your hair curled! And remember, the Lord God Omnipotent reigneth!"[45]

With the broadening of purpose beyond missions in the early 1940s, the identity of Presbyterian Women crystallizes as a women's community explicitly devoted to the practice of biblical faith in all areas of life. Certain features continue—discourse of gender complementarity, regular meetings and literature, collections of funds, a churchwide organization, mission activities, and the burgeoning interest in social conditions of the "stranger." New features appear as well. Small groups called circles provide the regular occasion for Bible study, mutual support, and other planned activities at the level of the local church. The monthly magazine, with some differences between northern and southern groups, organizes the use of other elements, such as Bible studies, special programmatic material, and leadership guides used in circles.

Presbyterian Women's discourse is complex. It is not simply one

---

[44]Boyd and Brackenridge, *Presbyterian Women in America*, chap. 4, 59–87. Other reactions were a bit stronger. The reorganization was called a takeover, and one woman is on record as pushing for the end to all restrictions on women. She was thought too pushy, however, and the tone remained true to the conviction of complementary functions for the sexes. Reassurances to the men that the women wanted neither conflict nor friction came with the steady push for lessening of restrictions. "We have no power of self-determination in the church," as one woman put it. See the GA-requested study written by Katherine Bennett, president of Women's Board of Home Missions, "Causes of Unrest Among Women" in 1926. An unprecedented meeting of church officials with fifteen prominent women to discuss women's issues took place in Chicago in 1928; see note 5 above. Brackenridge, "Equality for Women?"

[45]This call to arms is said to be a frequent remark of southern leader Jennie Hanna to other women organizers in the face of opposition to their organization in the 1910s. Quoted in Winsborough, *Yesteryears*, 29–30.

(written) text, nor is it simply the organizational activities. Our task is to discern patterns or subgenres within the written and organizational totality that is the Presbyterian Women's discourse—the connections, the cohesive pieces that offer regularities comprising an overarching register (field, tenor, and mode). What we seek are utterances that are regular enough to allow us to perceive the expectations that accompany them and, then, the alterations of those expectations. With a unifying register, a characteristic set of practices comes into being, and we can display PW discourse as a performance or reading regime. We are not simply looking for something distinct, however; our final interest is to see the regime in its intertextual relation with the canonical system of the dominant discourse. At that level, the registers of PW connect with as well as alter the male-defined canonical system.

It is important to reiterate the expanded sense of discursive genre being used here. Genre (the term is interchangeable with register) is not simply a literary unit or form; it encompasses the variables of an utterance. To take a discursive unit of male advice in the literature by itself, for example, might lead to the judgment of a sexist content. However, that would miss the (possible) alteration of this field variable by the tenor of the discourse. Another shift in meaning occurs when we treat such a unit as part of a larger discursive activity. With reference to its ordering function, Paul Ricoeur is right to say that genres are "to discourse what generative grammar is to the grammaticality of individual sentences."[46] The judgment on content alone would miss the effects of the other organizing registers. An overarching or dominant regime operative in Presbyterian Women's discourse brings some order to a multiplicity of subgenres and will help us sort out a variety of complex meaning effects.

I begin my analysis with the literature that constitutes these women as communities, *Concern* (formerly *Outreach*) and *Presbyterian Women*.[47] I will first review the variables of field, tenor, and mode of the complex, then examine how the subgenres are affected by the whole.

---

[46]A genre can be systems of rules as well as one of several utterances that are ordered by that system. Frow, *Marxism and Literary History* (Oxford: Basil Blackwell, 1986), 65–67. Paul Ricoeur, *Interpretation Theory: Discourse and the Surplus of Meaning* (Fort Worth: Texas Christian Univ. Press, 1976), 32–34.

[47]These documents are found in collections at the Department of History, PC(USA) in Montreat, N.C. (*Presbyterian Women*), and the Presbyterian Historical Society, Philadelphia (*Outreach, Concern, Horizons*).

Field: discourse of the global family

The category of *field* refers to the ideas of Presbyterian Women's discourse. Field in its simplest sense is the variable in register that performs the content function—content in both the written and performed aspects of the discourse.[48] Full discussion of this content will overlap with the other two variables, tenor and mode. Its separate consideration, however, allows us to identify the distinctive registers appropriated by Presbyterian Women and the degree to which they transgress the discourses of their religious tradition and the social formation.

First, we may define what ideas do *not* characterize Presbyterian Women's practice. The field of this discourse is not characterized by feminist ideas, at least in the first few decades. If anything, feminist and women's rights agendas are disavowed. These demurrals reproduce the genteel tradition of the Presbyterian Women of the 1910s and '20s. Although the issue of feminist theology appears in a few articles in the more liberal northern literature in the mid-1960s, the primary subject of the publications and circle material is the identity of the Presbyterian woman as the faithful Christian woman, who is first and foremost a mother and homemaker.[49] Focus on gender as a topic begins in the late 1960s and the '70s, in a literature uniformly affirming of the gifts of women by its reiteration of gender complementarity.[50]

In addition to missions, the most prominent subject in the literature is Presbyterian Women's responsibilities as Christians around the

---

[48]Halliday's definition is more complicated, and difficult to unravel. Field is about the content, but it occurs on a continuum, from activity with minimum language to a completely linguistic discourse. See Michael A. K. Halliday, *Language as Social Semiotic: The Social Interpretation of Language and Meaning* (Baltimore: University Park Press, 1978), 62–64, 115–17, 143–44, 221–25.

[49]In this period, articles in *Concern* introduced feminist topics, such as one about Betty Friedan, and articles by Valerie Saiving Goldstein and Letty Russell. This inclusion fits the progressive, intellectual character of the overall register, particularly the northern. It remains true that the *identity* of feminists is not appropriated by Presbyterian Women. In the issue that contains Goldstein's pathbreaking article (*Concern*, November 1964), the editors note that a survey indicates that older women are still mostly happy with roles of wife and mother. The number of demurrals is striking: the insistence that women have "no chip on the shoulder" like feminists (*Outreach*, February 1954), and the reassurance that Mrs. Bennett was not a feminist (*Outreach*, December 1952). Every time a movement toward opening church leadership to women occurs, in the 1920s, '30s, '50s, and '60s, the inevitable is: few women will want it, there will be no rush of women if ordination passes.

[50]These articles, including ones by Letty Russell and Arelia Fuhle, draw on liberation theology as well. Not only the discourse of inequality, but one of justice, is associated with gender.

themes of home and family. This domestic Christian vision simply cannot be missed. Homemaker is woman's identity. Although it has some resonance with the idealized domesticity of the larger culture, the PW idea of the homemaker is distinct. The PW notion qualifies that cultural phenomenon as specifically a Christian home, Christian motherhood, and Christian womanhood. "Where Does Your World Begin?" asks a 1947 article. The answer: "At Home!" where there is no higher calling than motherhood. This answer is repeated again and again. Focus on the home and the needs of children and husbands dominates the period following World War II. "Homemaker's Pledge," "Peace and Good Will Begin at Home," "A Creed for the Christian Home" are typical essay titles, and the studies of the period relate frequently to the duties of the Christian home in society.

The distinctive Christian calling of PW resonates with the new status of affectivity in the twentieth-century home; they are called "to create a calm center" and to fill "emotional needs" in the home. Numerous Bible studies inscribe this homemaker role in biblical women. Characteristics of the ideal homemaker are found in Mary, Deborah, and Esther, and epitomized by the householder of Proverbs 31.[51] The northern version of this identity is more progressive. In *Horizons*, it is the environmentally just home that is woman's base. This calling is still initiated in the home, however. As a typical 1953 article puts it, "Homemaking is my Vocation," and this is a "holy calling."

The PW literature of the 1940s and 1950s is saturated with the theme of domesticity. The typical member in the later '60s is still "a married housewife in her early 50's."[52] Even though the topic is less direct in the next two decades, the home continues to be the base for her identity. Articles cite the ideal home and its importance. "No one can do more to set and maintain a good climate for mental health in the home than a Christian wife and mother," says the author of "Just a Housewife," a 1969 article (*Concern*, October 1969). She is the "thermostat for the mental health of her household . . . in a position to control the emotional temperature of the family" (*Concern*, March 1963). That "washing dishes and cleaning house and tending babies can itself be a high calling from God" is confirmed by a look at biblical women (*PW*, May 1957 study of Prov. 31:10–31).

---

[51]These quotes come from 1947–49 issues of *Presbyterian Women*, but the theme is found everywhere in PW literature. In the later decades the surrounding issues simply change.

[52]This portrait was of the northern organization. In a survey of UPW membership, one-quarter were found to be employed and one-third had some college education. *Concern* (October 1969), 11.

All this may sound like the privatized domesticity of American capitalist culture in the themes of home and the expressive function of the housewife. In fact, it is not, at least when the full terrain of the discourse is considered. In numerous examples beginning in the late 1940s, the materialism of consumer culture and the cold, heartless world of success are criticized. The themes are distinct from the idea of the housewife as protector of a haven in the heartless world, even when the potential for privatization is there. The most striking theme of the discourse that marks it off from the invitation to support the status quo is the responsibility laid at women's door. PW are called to an overwhelming responsibility for change—an expectation of enormous proportions, considering that gender complementarity requires a social order where women's influence could hardly succeed.[53] Domesticity in PW discourse is an inherently expanding domain.[54] The identity of the Christian woman and her responsibilities are never discussed in terms of the home only; the home is the base for a domain of influence that includes the church, the community, and the world.

One way to account for this broad geographical vision in a literal way is the other of the two prominent subjects in the literature: missions. This expanded domain is developed in the topic of home and foreign missions in PW discourse. Home mission links PW to worlds outside the home. Examples include mission to Native American women and children; support of "Negro Work" in schools for girls (Stillman College) and helping "Negro presbyterial groups" in the first few decades; civil rights activism; the plight of migrant workers; the pluses and minuses of civil disobedience in the '60s and '70s. Overseas missions are regular topics, as well, articles and projects on foreign women and children, education, hospitals, and a variety of social problems. At one time or another, every nation on the globe is featured. The practice of special offerings for a selected mission, long-term relationships with educational projects for girls in Third World areas, and other undertakings indicate the expanded "home" responsibilities that characterize the dominant ideas of Presbyterian Women.[55]

---

[53]See, for instance, examples of male discourse that urge on woman the task of moralizing the ruthless domain of her husband. See the Moderator's address to Presbyterian Women in *PW*, November 1964.

[54]There is some parallel here with the theme of "municipal housekeeping" for women social reformers at the turn of the century. See this term in the introduction to Mary Ritter Beard's *Women's Work in Municipalities* (New York: D. Appletone and Co., 1915), x. It has its clearest roots, however, in the missionary women of PW's past. Patricia Hill identifies this in her wonderfully titled book, *The World Their Household*.

[55]It would be useful to sort out the changing accounts of domesticity in relation to

Universalizing the horizons of woman's hoped-for influence is a virtually inseparable aspect of PW's Christian domestic identity. It appears as one of the common organizing rubrics in the literature: "Home, Church, Community, World." Sometimes this universalizing logic is articulated as world evangelism. More frequently, however, as a 1959 issue of *Concern* puts it, this logic devises the notion of responsibility in much broader ways: "We exist in order to make a difference in the world." Making a difference means the responsibility "to go a 'second mile' in caring for . . . the sick, the illiterate, the homeless, the scholar, the child, and to seek for constructive solutions to great questions of poverty, of human degradation, of false religions."[56] The abbreviated version of this distinctive PW twist on domesticity is expressed in a constantly repeated refrain: "Who is my neighbor?" The ritualized PW response: "Anyone in need."

What appears to be merely a social concern, however, is not, as the complete look at this discourse as a biblical practice will show. The self-consciously religious versions of "making a difference" are not a primary aspect of the field variable. Although one can find meditations and religious reflection, these are mostly centered around the questions, What shall I do? and How shall I live? Rarely does the discourse reflect at length on the theological or spiritual nature of responding to the neighbor's need. Two examples of explicit reflection represent what I read to be the dominant field of the discourse. In the 1959 *Concern* issue quoted above, the formal statement of purpose happens to include both explicit religious belief and care for the neighbor. These practices are the expression of the "driving force" of the community: proclaiming, demonstrating the love of Jesus Christ, and acting it out.

A second example of explicit theological reflection on the convergence of the spiritual with loving response to the neighbor's need

---

moral reform that are behind the PW literature of these decades. Much has been written about the class vision of the home that was visited on American immigrants, the poor, and others subjected to moral reformers. Much of this idealistic reform included the imposition of middle-class ideas of home and family. While such reform efforts are undoubtedly part of the first couple of decades of PW mission, my interest is in the idea of expansion and its logic over the entire period. By the 1970s the self-critical posture is part of the discourse. See Nancy F. Cott, *The Bonds of Womanhood: Women's Sphere in New England, 1780–1835* (New Haven: Yale Univ. Press, 1975), and Scott, *Natural Allies.*

[56]This definition is found in "This Is Our Concern," by Margaret Shannon, *Concern* (January 1959). The identification of spirituality with winning persons for Christ is more apparent in the southern literature. That emphasis tapers off in the late 1960s, however, when the concern to put spirituality and social change together begins to emerge.

comes in a discussion of a program of prison relationships: "One Sister Outside for Every Sister Inside." The claim is made that a project to create sustained, ongoing relationships of care with women in prison *is* "preaching Jesus." Scripture is cited of Jesus' practice and the centrality of love to the conditions for change.[57] Sometimes "making a difference" in PW discourse means making sure the world has heard the gospel. The regularized practices that define the organization, however, include many non–soul-saving, neighbor-oriented practices that speak loudly of the dominant theology: a regular birthday gift to support a project addressing some social problem; a "friendship circle" where educational needs abroad are supported; dozens of regularly changing human need projects.

The politics of the PW theme of home, church, community, and world-transformation undergoes definite change. In the 1950s, concern with making good citizens dominates the southern discourse. Frequent topics for reforming attention include alcoholism, prejudice in the home, threats to democracy, displaced persons, and the importance of responsible citizenship to world peace. In the 1960s and '70s, "making a difference" is defined in more complex ways, moving beyond the linkage with good citizenship. Invoking more critical stances toward the United States, the domain of reforming practice includes such problems as civil rights, poverty, world hunger, and the prison system. The logic of the religious vision seems to press the political posture beyond the more privatized morality and benevolent paternalism of the early years. In the 1950s, "Negro Work" is discussed in terms of what "we" can do for "them"; "their" need for "our" education. In PW discourse of the '70s, we find scores of articles where Presbyterians are noted as a class and race that is complicit in the social oppressions of the globe.

This development of ideas is not simply a progressive liberalization. Even in the early years, the focus on need alters the vision and its middle-class politics. The needs of her children and husband and of her church never create boundaries for the Presbyterian woman. They provide the ordinary signifiers through which the needs of every other "neighbor" are brought to her attention. A 1947 article offers reflections on the church's responsibility to address the straits of all classes and the injustice of the concentration of economic power. The themes of saving masses for Christ, and the family as the basic unit of democracy are found alongside the claim that there is no peace without jus-

---

[57]"Presbyterian Women Go to Prison: One Sister Outside for Every Sister Inside," *Concern* (August 1977).

tice in the world (*PW*, November 1954), discussion of rooting out prejudice in the home in the 1950s, class issues, and coffee-klatch discussions of hate groups. Suggestions for things to do in the home to promote family togetherness appear along with articles on the devastation of Europe and lists of needs of the hungry and homeless. Concern for the unjust treatment of Native Americans appears in the late 1940s in *Outreach*, and discussions of racism are going full blast in the '50s.

Other subjects in the literature include the women's organization and its regular activities—conferences, speakers, projects, and discussions of church teaching, doctrine, and the Bible. Regular Bible studies at circle meetings address themes ranging from the new role of women to Christian citizenship and racism. A strong focus on being well-informed as one becomes accountable to every kind of human need echoes the contemporary cultural emphasis on science and education. Increasingly informative articles appear on the realities of the countries of mission. In contrast to brief facts in one-inch announcements in the '40s and '50s, we find long articles about "The Status of Women" in the '60s and '70s.

To sum up the field variable, in critical relation with traditional cultural ideas about the ideal homemaker as the supporter of a haven from a heartless world, a distinctive interpretation of domesticity dominates the ideas constructing PW's discourse. The globally understood neighbor's need is the Christian housewife's responsibility, as her *family*. Other subject matters cluster around three topics: the organization of PW itself, missions and world knowledge, and Bible and theology. The home as the housewife's base of operations still dominates the field variable. It remains the base from which to meet the needs of a suffering, sometimes unbelieving, unjust world. Domesticity dominates simply because it is *identity* or "who you are" discourse. The wide range of this domain stems from the ideas of mission. Thus we might say that domesticity organizes the other subjects of the discourse. What these other topics add to the discourse is that woman is to be an educated and organized responder to human need. How we might unify this content as a discursive practice, one with the shape of a reading regime, awaits review of the variables that construct registers out of these ideas.

Tenor: a subjected subject

The variable of content is not enough to display the full meaning effects of Presbyterian Women's discourse. The setting of utterance, of practice, is also crucial to our understanding of the process. The second element of that setting is tenor, the variable that has to do with the relational aspects of discourse, or, in Frow's words, the "relations of power and solidarity between speakers." In addition, tenor has to do with the participation function of language. It prompts us to ask, What kind of relation does the utterance assume and evoke between speaker and hearer, message and addressee?[58]

Tenor has to do with address and the relationship it evokes. Its significance relies upon the social expectations associated with that address and relationship. To the earlier example of the unequal pedagogical tenor characteristic of the mother-child interaction, we can add others with clear conventional expectations. Registers where tenor may be the dominant variable (the element around which the most regularized social expectations are clustered) include greetings, military commands, and amatory discourse. Tenor is clearly a variable with great significance for women precisely because of the centrality of its issues to the thing that PW typically do not have: authority. The kind of relations that are assumed and evoked by PW literature will have an important impact on its production of women as subjects.

A number of genres characterize PW's literature. As a monthly magazine it contains regular features, a variety of essay-articles with changing subject matters, announcements, lists, sermonettes, poetry, and moral inventories. Each of these is characterized by a different tenor. Out of this variety, four kinds of tenor are important for analyzing gender issues: (1) a tenor of personalized mutuality, found in genres of face-to-face conversation; (2) a tenor of objective, egalitarian didacticism, found in field-dominant genres; (3) a tenor of authoritarian or benevolent patriarchy, found in genres of expert address; and (4) a closely related tenor of interrogation found in several genres.

Personalized mutuality.   The tenor of interpersonal conversation is distinctive to PW discourse. Although face-to-face conversation is a situation of utterance in itself, I want to focus on dialogue as a feature that functions in this literature to create a tone of mutuality. The balance of power evoked by this dialogical tenor does not mean that conversation excludes disagreement or conflict from conversation. What is distinctive about the dialogical tenor of PW discourse is the egalitarian nature of the addressees' participation in the discourse. Although

---

[58]Frow, *Marxism and Literary History*, 68–72. See Halliday, *Language as Social Semiotic*, 62–64, 115–17, 122, 143–46. Mode also influences the variable of tenor. Several genres (for example, prayer, sermon, jokes) could be identified as either tenor-dominant or mode-dominant.

the mode is written, and therefore its genre is not literally face-to-face, the overall relation consistently evoked is a truly interpersonal one.[59]

An everday tone and informal directness characterize the address of PW literature to its readers, creating the effect of repectful conversation. This tenor is friendly, even chatty and warm at times. Its most frequent effect is utterly egalitarian. The rubrics of early articles announce the informality: "Let's Talk About . . . " is a regular heading in the 1950s, to be followed by "Let's Learn About . . . " into the 1960s. Although this chattiness may seem a bit juvenile to contemporary ears, the tone of address is invitational, comradely, and inclusive. The later, more direct and adult "we" of address evokes a relationship that solicits the reader seriously and respectfully as a co-partner in the journey of faith.

Another feature of PW literature that contributes to an interpersonal tenor is the personalization of the main subject matters. Distinct from the tenor of address, this form of personalization renders social problems in personal terms. A typical ritual in the literature, magazine and study resources alike, is the inscription of the self in social problems. Problems are personalized as the readers are invited to take on the task of faithfulness: "What can I do about . . . ?" This personalized response theorizes solutions in personal terms as well. In answer to the question, "What can I do on race issues?" for example, the proposed solution is to address race relations with changed personal relationships. This example from the 1950s is characteristic; even when the need for larger social changes is acknowledged, PW are never without proposals for individual, local response.[60]

Proposals of individual response to world problems are paralleled by the personalization of world geography and women's global accountability in a number of other ways. Missions projects are given personal narratives that invite the reader to identify with the subjects

---

[59]The shift to written discourse removes (or, as Ricoeur says, "shatters") the grounding of reference in the dialogical situation so that singular identifications can refer to "the here and now determined by the interlocutionary situation." A shared world is the grounding of the dialogical situation. Writing creates a gap for the ostensive reference; but some kinds of texts re-create for readers the situation of actual reference. PW's direct address does this, so its writing is able to re-create the personal. Ricoeur, *Interpretation Theory*, 34–37.

[60]The practice of merely personalizing responses to problems like race is more true of the 1950s in the South. *Outreach* and the later *PW* and *Concern* raise more complex aspects of change regarding racism issues. But it is always a practice in the PW literature to suggest things women can do, however large and intractable the problem. *PW*, August 1949. More recent examples include writing an open letter to Russian women, and the discussion of war from women's perspective.

and the projects. The Friendship Circle program, to cite an example, is a straightforward attempt to personalize missions by featuring individuals who are educated through the program. Readers hear about them and hear from them as well. One never gives money simply to a program; one gives to the communities that are personally represented in the narratives of individuals.[61]

Another regular feature of the literature advances the ethos of personalization: columns dedicated to ordinary, everyday topics. These short articles serve as opportunities for reflection on scripture and faith and as communications of women's practical wisdoms. Columns in the early years offer practical suggestions for circle activities and things to make for a variety of service projects. The columns in the 1970s are a bit more adventurous without dispensing with the ordinary. "The Thread," one such column, mixes ordinary homespun reflections with topics such as the nuclear threat. The "Button Box" is a melange of news, humorous anecdotes, announcements, and suggested resources for craft and volunteer projects. This column is reminiscent of early formats, where helpful hints took up more space in the magazine than almost anything else. From the early tips on what to serve at a circle meeting, to lists of environmentally just practices for the home and how-to's for a justice-related fast in the late '70s, PW literature personalizes politics by locating its origins in women's ordinary knowledges.

Still another way subjects are personalized is through the focus on the experiential dimension of matters. This practice is not unique to women, but PW make it their own as they apply it to their global family.[62] Bible study is personalized with the use of a frame of self-involving questions and identification with biblical women. Political issues are discussed in terms of what a social problem might be like as an experience. Topics such as war (the Vietnam, the Korean) are recounted as experiences of broken bodies and horror, not as facts and data or political news. The social problems of Third World countries are given a human face by featuring relationships with individuals. The life of a woman in the Congo is described, for example, and PW

---

[61]The Friendship Circle project affords Christian education to international students brought to the United States, who then go back to their native countries to teach in Bible and mission schools. The students are regular guests and speakers at the Montreat Conference, where PW regularly gather.

[62]Different modes of personal application characterize Sunday school programs designed for the whole church. See David C. Hester, "The Use of the Bible in Presbyterian Curricula, 1923–1985," in *The Pluralistic Vision*, 205–234.

are invited to think about what it would be like to live with the hardships of her daily routine.[63] The effect is a vicarious discourse whose
tenor, if not directly egalitarian, avoids the disruption of that relation.
It asks PW to identify with women whose social locations are radically
other to her own. Most significantly, it works to enhance the self-involving effects of the literature.

Objective didacticism.   Not eveything in PW discourse is personal and
vicariously experiential. A second characteristic tenor is found in the
field-dominant genre. PW literature shows an increasing concern with
education, idealizing the reader who is well-informed and up-to-date
on such topics as the foreign countries of mission, women's lives in
the Third World, and contemporary social problems. The literature
expands in size and carries an increasing number of lengthy, informative articles (a far cry from the foldout newsletter with which at least
the southern community began). The identity of PW as well-informed
housewives is supported by the presence in the literature of regular
columns with popularized scholarly presentations of "Presbyterian
Beliefs" and "Our Doctrinal Heritage." In these information-oriented
genres, the tenor is respectfully didactic. Readers are addressed more
or less as equals in the objective, uncondescending tone of a newspa-
per report or a textbook. The ideology of romantic womanhood that
contributes to PW discourse is shaped by educated womanhood as
well.[64]

Authoritarian or benevolent patriarchy.   A different relational effect is
created by other didactic registers. This tenor sets a tone of particular
importance for gender-related subjects of enunciation. Of the various
didactic registers found in the literature, pieces written by male authorities were regular features for a number of years. These authors
included seminary professors (male until the 1970s), male clergy, and
other male experts. To appreciate the tenor of this form, we must pay

---

[63]The reports are from women who have visited the countries and their mission con-
tacts there. These articles have become more respectful and less paternalistic over the
years. The early discussions of "Negro Work," for example, are full of references to
what "we" can do for "them." This is true of overseas missions as well; a self-critical
attitude is present about that colonialist posture in later literature.

[64]The image of educated womanhood identified in Cott's analysis of the turn-of-the-
century shift away from the ideology of "true womanhood" certainly is applicable to
Presbyterian Women. The comparatively high educational status of Presbyterians ap-
plies only with slightly less consistency to the women. See Sheila M. Rothman, *Woman's
Proper Place: A History of Changing Ideals and Practices, 1870 to the Present* (New York:
Basic Books, 1978), 97–132.

attention to the variable of mode as well. Didactic address of the women by these male figures could be interpreted to create the effect of a respectful tenor in its imparting of information. In part that tenor is shaped by its content, which is formulaically admiring and complimentary. A look at layout, presentation, and images of these male appearances in the literature is instructive.

Although not the only form, the exemplary instance of the male address is a more-or-less annual feature on *PW*'s cover, "The Moderator Addresses the Women." In these pieces the tenor is altered from respectful address of equals to one that evokes gendered and unequal relations. The alteration has to do with its mode of presentation. Usually on the front page, this printed speech features a large, imposing formal picture of the moderator's face along with a text that addresses the women as a whole. The speech is typically a welcome, but it usually includes reference to the special qualities of the women of the church and sometimes to their special calling.

The benevolent and admiring quality of the address does not transform what is authoritarian about the tenor. We see this in the effect of the mode, which intensifies the authoritative ethos of the addresses simply by virtue of who is communicating (the official head of the denomination) and what is going on (his annual address to the women). The authority attached to the position is heightened by the implication that once a year this man says something of great import for all Presbyterian Women—he speaks a universal discourse of sorts. The medium gives these observations additional meaning. The layout exacerbates the tenor of benevolent male authority: a male face stares out at a listening mass identified as "the women." For many years, such authoritative head-neck photographs were reserved for men. Women appeared only in action pictures—portrayed in crowds, talking in small groups, helping in mission settings, or in formal groups. Since head-neck shots are typically the pictures of professionals, of experts—the ones who instruct—the contrast in pictorial display heightens the difference between gendered bodies.

In contrast to these authoritative addressing faces, the surfaces of women's bodies appear ordinary and trivial, because we see them only in groups, or from the side, or from the back. They are often mixed with the "other," the native, the foreigner, the object of mission. In a context by themselves, these action shots might appear more interesting, more lively, more significant. To intersperse them with official formal heads, however, signals the maleness of authority, insofar as authority is evoked by a fixed gazing face that speaks at, teaches, and sets straight the female reader.

The authoritative tenor of the moderator's address is heightened considerably by the message as well. The discourse contributes to the benevolent control claimed by the moderator's talking, instructing head. In the admonition of the moderator to "the better half of the body of Christ" (1946), the address urges woman to use her native gifts to "bathe with your love the wounds of our world." He understands that woman's work to create "happy, harmonious homes where God's name is honored" may not be the most glamorous work, but it is absolutely essential (1958). In another issue, which came out immediately after the approval of women's ordination, one moderator admonishes women to take their special gifts of perceptivity and sensitivity to the religious realm and help save the church from its materialism and success obsession (1964). Women receive their vocation, their call to service, from this benevolent male face.

Another version of the authoritative tenor that comes with didactic address is found in the number of articles written by men that appear with an authoritative formal picture at the beginning and sometimes at the end of the article. The only authoritative addressing faces are male, and so the tenor is gendered once again, signaling, "Now we will hear what the experts (men) say about the subject." Even without the content—the reaffirming of women's special nature and importance of their place—these displays evoke a tenor of authoritative pronouncer/subordinate hearer.[65] The impact of the images (the mode variable) on the tenor, particularly in the annual moderator address, is to reinforce the notion that the woman's identity as special is being authorized, legitimated, and even granted her by the expert male gaze.

The tenor of subordination is paralleled in another subregister of the discourse by a second kind of didacticism, one that is best termed the moral imperative. The Presbyterian woman is taught, exhorted, talked at, and morally comandeered. An imperative discourse pervades the literature, the imperative discourse of faithfulness, which states the tasks of PW as they go about their calling of home, church, community, and world-transformation. It creates an effect of highly charged involvement and responsibility. "Know about the total program of the Church . . . " "Help to keep Circle members informed . . ." "Participate in community activities . . . concerned with the ministry of rec-

---

[65]These expert articles were written by male seminary professors and church executives as long as there were no women in these positions. In the late '60s we begin to get female experts.

onciliation . . ." These are three of a typical long list of imperatives (October 1963).

The marked intensity of the tenor of the imperative is not surprising in view of the incredible range of the Christian woman's accountability. In a typical workbook of circle service projects, she can choose between creating a baby-sitting service in her church, distributing Christian literature in bus and railway stations, starting a ministry to migrants, and creating a ministry in community to older people (*PW Workbook*, 1954). She is solicited by commandments that commit her to everyday practices against racism and nationalism.[66] If there is a dominant tenor in all this discourse, it is that of the invitation, the moral command, the imperative, the tenor of exhortation and imploring. She is addressed as one who *should know* and *can help*.

This tenor is not authoritarian, because it invokes an accountability that assumes the subjects' fitness for the task. The subject addressed is implicitly a very powerful person. The responsibility implied by the tenor of the imperative is enormous: "If your church should close tomorrow," queries one such address, "would your community suffer from this loss?" (*Outreach*, December 1953). She *is* to engage the needs of the world!

Interrogation. Presbyterian Women are also interrogated, a tenor with a related but decidedly different effect. Interrogation occurs in registers that also evoke the tenors of imperative, command, and moral-invocation. In the genres that call them to action and invoke their accountability, Presbyterian Women are sometimes invited to participate in a kind of self-interrogation. This form of address is similar to the needs lists and announcement genres that implicitly implore, enjoin, and exhort. Its questioning is on the order of "What Is God Calling Me to Do?"—a persistent heading whose self-involving force is familiar to PW from the many other ways they are personally addressed. The register of interrogation typically comes in the form of questions that exhort the reader to an additional task—not simply to care about an issue, to feel responsible for it and to do something

---

[66]"Ten Commandments of Goodwill," *PW*, July 1946. This tenor comes with the many announcements and calls for aid that fill the discourse. Their genres, according to Frow's categories, would be tenor-dominant. These are the regular short pieces in the late 1940s and '50s that announce, for example, the numbers of bandages, sheets, and first-aid kits that the displaced persons camps desperately need, or the longer articles that describe a need and tell of the means to attend the meeting, join the group, get the literature.

about it, but also to take on the responsibility of the caring and the doing and to feel remiss if she has not. It is a tenor that dominates the early literature. It alters a bit in the late 1960s and '70s but never disappears completely.

The discourse of interrogation is found in direct address about advice given: "Why not use churches for day nurseries? What does your church do to care for . . . deserted children, orphans, or children with one disabled parent?" (*PW*, June 1950). It ranges from general questioning about deeds done and left undone to checklists of questions to apply to the self: Am I a consistent Christian in my home? If I saw myself through my yardman's eyes, or my cook's eyes, what would I think? Do I stand for all that is pure and good and wholesome? Do I stand up for what I believe? Rubrics of the magazine typically follow some version of the categories home, church, community, and world; thus a woman is sometimes led through an exercise in self-interrogation regarding each of the widening spheres of her life. Such questioning ranges from a focus on sincerity and commitment to the devising of checklists that assess the sexism of a congregation: from "Is my life a true witness?" and "Have we really meant it when we . . . ?" to "How many women are trustees in the church?" and "Is your church secretary's salary just?" "How do I act, what does my face register, when a person of another race takes a seat near me on the bus?"[67] This address invites a self-scrutiny that undermines, in contrast to the imperative that grants the gift by assuming the fitness to the task.

The tenor of PW discourse is complex; it invokes the reader collegially, respectfully and warmly. It offers a sympathetic ear, speaking to and about the places of her everyday life. Through it she is implored and commanded in a corporate endeavor. The address of PW discourse hallows and honors the places of her everyday life and links them to the biggest and most complex issues of her sociopolitical contemporary world. As such it calls her to subjecthood; as a Christian housewife, she has the "power to change the world!" PW discourse also speaks patronizingly to her as a woman whose place is special, but *is* a place and therefore appropriately subjected to male authorities. It also interrogates her and invites her to undergo a process of constant self-criticism — criticism of her intention, motive, behavior, and the outcome. Whatever subjecthood is supported by the former two tenors would appear to be undermined or at least contradicted by the latter

---

[67]These examples are my paraphrases of actual questions from both northern and southern literatures of the 1950s to the 1970s.

two. Such assessments are premature, however, without attention to the effect of the third of the variables of register: mode.

Mode: literature of self-production

Of two primary modes or mediums that constitute PW discourse, I begin with the literature itself as it alters tenor and content. Mode is the variable of a register having to do with the encoding of meaning in a medium.[68] One of the mediums of PW discourse has already been discussed in my analysis: the effect of photography as an encoder of meanings not conveyed by the written text. The mode that encompasses these pictures is a written discourse; more particularly, its literary form is a monthly magazine with a distinctive format consisting of a variety of modes and genres. As a magazine, *PW* is a particular kind of utterance comprised of a number of forms of signifying that can only work in such a polyglot medium.

Communication occurs in a magazine via the medium of written discourse, essays, and information straightforwardly proposed, and also through drawings and photographs. The medium signifies through spacing and highlighting of titles and written forms of address, and location on the page as well as within the whole. All these signifying elements are peculiar to this form of utterance. These effects differ considerably from the oral mode or, within the written mode, from a single-theme text. Consider, for example, the difference the mode makes when we compare a magazine and a sermon on women's place.

A simple but important effect of written discourse is the fact that comprehension/reading can occur in private. Individual women are addressed in the act of reading, but it is an act they can control. A Presbyterian woman can shut off the moderator's subjecting address—or any of the discourse—by simply skipping the page, as she cannot shut off the preacher. In addition, a magazine offers a cacophany of voices interpolating PW into a subject position. There is no necessarily "straight line" communicated on any subject. The possibilities for contradiction and multiple messages, for complications of oppressive ideological effects that are present in any mode, are multiplied with the polyglot signifying of a magazine format. Any trajectory of

---

[68]Halliday, *Language as Social Semiotic*, 123, 144. He identifies the mode as the "textual component, representing the 'relevance' function of language, without which the other two do not become actualized." See also pp. 64–65, 115–17, 143–45, 222–25.

meaning planned by the editors is only hypothetical—a possible reading of the whole; wholes made by actual readers are not always pre-
dictable.

A second aspect of the modes of magazine and study materials is the
communicative power of pictures and layout. Not only is this important in featuring and highlighting the authoritative address, but the
content of particular themes in the field variable is affected as well.
Pictures can heighten the importance of a text not only with the more
interesting and lively character granted a topic by varied layout and
page appeal, but also because they communicate in ways that a quick
skim of dense informational articles cannot.

My earlier discussion of the message of the authoritarian male gaze
is complicated when we factor in the multiple voices of the mode of
the magazine. With a broader look at the mode, the photographic
messages about authority may actually support an advance in the
stature of women. Appearing along with men's pictures, women's
pictures support complementarity of gender. Male dominance is communicated by the positioning of men's authoritative faces; it is countered by a tendency over the years for increasing numbers of layouts in
the magazines that foreground formal head shots of women. Even as
early as the 1950s, female staff photos appear as counterimages to the
authoritative Man. By the '60s and '70s, *Concern* is heavily populated
with women's faces. Women appear on the cover and are shown in
teaching and addressing postures.

At the same time, the magazine never excludes male authors
or pictures. White men are rarely if ever shown in nonauthori-
tative positions (being taught, informally chatting, being helped) as
women of all colors and men of color are. We might take the increase of female head shots as a steady ascendance of signifiers that
authority's name is woman (mostly white, but not completely),
that women's faces are trustworthy, their knowledge expert, their
gaze sufficient to confer a blessing. All these possibilities, of course,
are complicated by the continued appearance of male gazes. The ideology of the original PW movement, we remember, refused a separatist organization. That commitment is reproduced in the pictorial
mode of the discourse, even as the cumulative impact of an overview
of the late 1940s through the 1970s reflects increasing stature for
women.[69]

---

[69]*PW* from 1945 to 1949 contains very few pictures; in the 1950s it features some
drawings and a few more photographs of formal male faces or men at General Assembly
and a few photos of women staff. There are more pictures of women in groups and of

Another effect on content of this mode is the power of pictures. Pictorial signifying is important and powerful because the other most prominent field topic to be imaged (besides the head shots of authorities) is the neighbor in need. Although it would be possible and important to analyze in depth the pictorial semiotics of the "needy" who are displayed as PW's objects of mission, I can only make some general points here. A heartrending picture of a hungry child is the not-infrequent magazine cover spread. Brown and black (and sometimes white) faces of despair stare at the reader. The homeless and the poor are captured in poses of need. The power of PW's message about accountability to the world neighbor is intensified by such pictures. The needy stranger is pictured almost from the beginning of the magazine's publication, and such pictures increase in clarity, number, and richness over the years. The imaginal mode does not simply inscribe despair in the shape and color of the non-Caucasian "other," although there is a danger of that message. The needy stranger is also pictured as agent and engaged in activities of change and hope and mutuality with the white Western helper.

The effects of these images are intensified because they are primary vehicles for scripture appropriation in PW discourse. Along with the self-conscious Bible study, where PW gather to share and personalize lessons aided by the exegetical tools of denominational studies, the inscribing of scripture in their own themes effects a mode-dominant register. One of the most effective patterns of imaging human need in the magazines is the use of scripture passages with pictures of the neighbor. Biblical images of love for the neighbor (The Good Samaritan), of serving Jesus in the neighbor (Matthew 25), of reconciliation (Eph. 2:13–22) are placed effectively across pictures of world community, communicating again and again the convergence of faithfulness to God with love for the stranger.

The prominence of pictures of the human face of need intensifies the content messages of the field variable. Most of the pictures are of children, old people, and women; they figure the calling of PW from its inception: women's work for women. This could easily be read as women's work for the helpless and victimized. I judge this conver-

---

people involved in mission. *Concern* in the 1960s is characterized by many more pictures, and more of them of women in postures of authority, but there are still enough photos of males in authoritative positions to prevent a totally female image. *Concern* in the 1970s presents the most strikingly womanized display, and it tends to feature more interesting pictures than head shots. What needs to be looked at more carefully is the display of non-Caucasian and non-Euro-Americans. They populate the magazines from the beginning as pictures of the "objects" of mission.

gence of idea and mode variables to create a communicative effect of such power that these signifying practices are stronger than any of the other subject matters of the discourse. They are distinctive and powerful scriptural practices as well.

The final aspect of the variable of mode brings us to the site of PW practice and to the task of assessing the discourse as unified and constitutive of a reading regime. The place where PW discourse actually happens as a discourse, other than in the private reading of the magazine, is in the circle meetings where PW come together and experience their identity as Presbyterian Women. Circles are ongoing groups of women who meet regularly as subunits of the larger organization. Ideally constituted of around twelve women, they are called circles to represent the unending nature of love.

The care evidenced in the literature concerning the purpose of the circle is reiterated through the years as discussions occur and measures are taken to see that its organization suits its purpose. The circle is to be a place where Bible study is done and projects organized, but primarily where all women feel cared for and heard. Despite variations, this community can be characterized by mutual commitment, support in crises, care through sickness and death, and mutual pleasures celebrated. At its best the circle is the enfleshment of the community that is idealized and analyzed by theologians and preachers for the wider church. It is the circle where women are "subjected" and upbuilt as subjects by the discourse of PW. It is in the circle where the intersection of PW's biblical practice and organizational practice can be described.

In the convergence of the three variables of field, tenor, and mode, there is a unity to PW discourse: it is a literature and practice of world- and self-transformation. Its narrative, insofar as there is one, might be the expansion of the home where all are loved to include the stranger—not just the making of a global family, but a family whose suffering members have priority. To be sure, it is an insecure unity always offering other possibilities. One need not accept but a part of the subject position offered. The mode rules out a process of control. The unity constructed by the discourse is a convergence of the call to expanding the domains of domestic accountability. The tenor is one of respect for PW and a climate honoring the domestic and the ordinary in an unresolved tension with subjection to·the domination of an authority and the interrogation of self-scrutiny. It is not just the identity of the Christian homemaker as responsible for the world neighbor that accounts for the discourse; the woman herself is being produced.

Resistance and repetition

My model assumes that texts do not transform the world but are constructed out of the traditions of religious communities and therefore operate in multireferential networks of meaning. To map out those networks I have used the canonical system of reading, the reading regimes that are intertextual with that system, and the intersections of both with the social formations in which they are forged. With the regime of reading we can see what Kenneth Surin means when he writes:

> The reception of a text is coterminous with its specific "inscriptions" in a social material process, and [it] generates its political consequences at the . . . specific points of its reproduction. . . . At these points . . . a text repudiates or reflects a particular social order depending upon whether or not readings given to the text resist or permit its integration in a system of discursive authority.[70]

The possibilities for support of the status quo in PW discourse will be found in the semantic connection they forge (understood as an intertextual relation) with the canonical system. That relationship is what makes PW's practice intelligible in their community. Thus the possibility of resistance requires that canonical system and its intertextual relation, just as conservative reproductions do, and depends on the dominant register of that relation and its capacity to activate new, unexpected, even transgressive meanings. Our next questions, then, are How is scripture produced by Presbyterian Women? How is that inscribed in material practices? How does their practice activate meanings pertinent to gender out of the possibilities of social location and canonical system? How does their reading regime resist as well as reflect the gendered canonial system it intersects? What networks of semantic options are activated by it?[71]

If we simply looked at content, the feminist eye would find what appears to be accommodating acceptance of patriarchal notions of submission, of women's place in the home, a refusal to protest the continued patronizing denial of their leadership. Why did a moderator have to implore the southern women to speak up when women's ordination was being discussed by the ecclesial authorities? Other rea-

---

[70]Kenneth Surin, " 'The Sign That Something Else Is Always Possible': Hearing and Saying 'Jesus Is Risen' and Hearing the Voices of Those Who Suffer: Some Textual/Political Reflections," *Journal of Literature and Theology* 4:3 (November 1990): 273.

[71]Halliday, *Language as Social Semiotic*, 123.

sons for feminist skepticism come from arguments that feminism does not encompass activities where women bond together to help others (or themselves) out of a shared consciousness of their nurturing qualities. Some feminists prefer to save the label "feminist" for consciousness that is "clearly oppositional, reformist or revolutionary" in relation to patriarchy.[72]

It is true that PW practices are not overtly oppositional against patriarchy. The question at issue, however, concerns social registers, for which the intent of the agents is not an adequate litmus test. Before we can identify a Christian practice as a feminist register, it is crucial to see what effects of patriarchy PW's practices do engage. To look for feminist content at this juncture would be to fail to recognize the contradictory subject position that constructs PW.

The crucial site for analysis of these discourses as inscriptions in material relations is that of PW's subject position and the dependence that characterizes it in the social formation of capitalist patriarchy. Recall that by mid-twentieth century, the status of these women's role as nurturer, homemaker, and emotional support was seriously weakened. To take this subject position as a coded one, as constructed out of discourses of the social formation of patriarchal capitalism, is to ask about the possible lines of nourishment and constraint that create this social location. Although privileged by class and race—they do not have to "work," after all—these women are not owners of capital, nor are they professionals or even wage earners. The irony that they may have other women (likely, of color and of less than middle class) working for them cannot be lost on us. Presbyterian women are dependent, however, in a way peculiar to this location: persons with no expertise to carry out their primary expressive function and questionable status for their other function, consumption. The housewife is in a position fractured with instability, privileged and precarious. The possible lines of nourishment and constraint that come from this social location will map the pleasures and fears that constitute this privileged dependence and help us understand the limits and possibilities of PW's resistance. Out of the religious and secular discourses about homemaker, Presbyterian Women forge a new domain.

The regime that graf(ph)ts new practices out of the religious and secular discourses about homemaker is built of several elements. The first is the operative intertextual relation of PW, which helps us under-

---

[72]Nancy Cott, "What's in a Name?," 821–27. She calls these other postures "female consciousness" and "communal consciousness." See Epstein, *The Politics of Domesticity*, for the limits of moral domesticity in religious consciousness.

stand what it means to say that PW discourse is a Christian *biblical* practice intertextual with its religious tradition. I propose that the genre of the discourse—self- and world-transformation—is the key to understanding PW's practice as a biblical one. By saying this I am simply following the implication of my view that it is more helpful to look at the convergence of variables and subgenres together than to extricate a single theme or subgenre by itself. Let us see what difference that makes.

What does it mean to say that PW discourse is a Christian biblical practice intertextual with its religious tradition? PW's practice is not straightforward scholarly exegesis of scripture. It would be a mistake to interpret PW scriptural performance as laypersons' attempts at scholarly exegesis, even though they do hear experts on the subject. PW scripture reading is neither characterized by commentary-dependent exegesis of passages for particular problems, nor is it the spirit-dependent interpretation of a Pentecostal practice. It never includes the kind of attention to the hermeneutical rules that characterizes its Reformed canonical system. That should not be surprising, because the register of authoritative reading was cut off to women during most of the formative years of Presbyterian Women. This does not mean that their discourse is not a biblical practice, however. According to Frow, the intertext includes the register that organizes the presence of references. Thus the question is, How does the discourse of self- and world-transformation *as a register* intersect with the Reformed-Presbyterian canonical system? What does this system enable them to *do* with scripture and, finally, their own situation of gender oppression?

PW have bypassed problems that identify scriptural dilemmas connected with specific "divine prohibitions." It is not that individual biblical texts do not come up at times in their literature, but the genre of their discourse redirects attention to other ways of practicing scripture. PW's practice of scripture is constituted by the subgenres of their literature, which focus on love for the suffering neighbor and involve Presbyterian Women in the activity of transforming that dilemma. Such genres present the neighbor as the Presbyterian woman's link with her personhood as homemaker. The neighbor is part of her family before God. Her vocation is inscribed in the faces of need. Scripture is rightly read as the hungry child's face is rightly read and responded to. To be sure, she finds a number of scriptures that model her own identity, as well, as a woman whose calling is domestic and unique. However, an identity defined by mission and need creates a hermeneutic of scripture that could never be restricted to woman-centered passages.

To make sense of the PW project, we must remember the conditions of their utterance, its canonical system. PW's dominant register is only intelligible as an intertextual relation with underdeveloped hermeneutical practices of Reformed faithful reading, those of the notion of lived faithfulness as reform not only of the home and church but of the social order. The register that activates this intertextual relation is Reformed by virtue of the distinctive vision of world-formative faith. PW's continuity with the Reformed canonical system is seen in the centralizing of faithful reforming performance as the sign of right reading. The evidence of good hermeneutical work in PW practice is world-formative practice that takes the principle of love as its evidence. Indeed, PW's discourse treads the territory the Reformed theological canon dared not, as the latter's fear of absolutizing social orders prevented development of these signs of right reading. Plunging nonexpertly ahead, PW discourse declares who the neighbor is and what God's love would require, and it supports the practice of that love.

I propose, then, that a judgment about a PW regime of reading requires consideration of the entire discourse as a production of self and world neighbor. This is how it creates an intertext with the canonical system, and, through that, we can see how it is a performance of scripture. Having refused to take on the official register of the Presbyterian canonical system, PW have forged a relation with that system on other terms. That relation is notable for the extent to which it expands their proscribed role, women's work for women. (So developed is the idea of accountability to the neighbor that their latest literature describes social injustices of such magnitude that their own class position is undermined by the changes imagined.)[73] The fact that this practice evokes its canonical system means that the self- and world-making of PW is something distinct from municipal housekeeping, as some accounts of women's use of domestic imagery for reform are called.

If faithful performance as practice of reforming love is the intertextual relation that PW activates with the Reformed canon, what, then, is the resistance? As we have seen, the register of self- and world-transformation is hardly a frontal attack on the restrictions of PW, who were denied access to the authoritative registers of preaching, public interpretation, and sacramental liturgy. There are constraints and sup-

---

[73]I have not included the history of PW in the 1970s, '80s, and early '90s, or the work of women's advocacy groups, which have joined efforts increasingly with PW since reunion in 1983. See *Concern* (February 1977) for a good overview, also *Horizons* (July/August 1988). Louise H. Farrior, *Journey toward the Future: A History of the Women of the Church, Presbyterian Church, U.S. for a Quarter of a Century* (1958–1983).

port of the status quo in PW performance of globalizing domestic relations, because it does not openly contest the question, Who can speak and interpret? Insofar as a regime implies rules for reading, even unspoken, the unspoken rules of PW's regime for most of the period considered were avoidance of a full-front separatist-threatening attack.

The register itself, however, is the appropriate place to look for resistance. It is misleading to imply that resistance would occur only as refusal of explicit male repressions. An implicit transgression of the rules occurs with the discourse of self-production. Not to see this transgression is to judge that the registers of expert interpretation and ordained ministry are the only legitimate and powerful registers. In a fashion of gentility and nonconfrontation similar to that of the ladies of the 1910s and '20s, PW bypass the restrictions of the system and create their own community and public space. They transgress by taking up registers of authority by speaking, teaching, exhorting, and preaching in their own literature. They transgress the limits of their canonical system with the sheer productive work of running a woman's organization for almost a century. By creating a literature and a distinctive biblical practice, PW take up the subject position denied them by the church. They enter the public realm on their own terms of value.

As gender resistance this practice also has targets particular to white middle-class American homemakers, the construction of their subject position by the combined religious tradition and social formation. The target hit or resisted by PW discourse is the undermining process visited on the homemaker by patriarchal capitalism. PW discourse contests the devaluing of the domestic; it contradicts the devaluing of the nurturing and other expressive functions of the mother and home, both its privatization and loss of meaning. PW discourse refutes the damning verdicts upon these places and functions that construct the social realities of woman's location. What is even more interesting is how, shaped by a Christian grammar of expanding care for the neighbor, PW's practice refuses to come out the way Barbara Ehrenreich and Deirdre English say romantic feminism *must*; that is, supporting capitalism and private escapist middle-class homes. The practice of self- and world-transformation refuses each of these diminutions of woman's place. It may sound like support of those at home, but it has included the suffering world neighbor in the definition of that home.

The distinctive register of self-production is a resistance of patriarchal capitalism as well. That production creates a subject position of worth out of the discourses of the religious tradition and the local culture, even in the ambiguity of its subjection of women to male author-

ity. The possibility for this upbuilding and its resistance effect is
located in the site where PW's practice is sustained. Not simply ideas
about woman's worth, or an institution that stands officially for that,
the small circle of regular support between women is the literal encoding of the best of the tenors of mutuality and respect that the written
discourse has to offer. It is the encoding of that register in bodies
present to one another, present in concern, in the affairs of the ordinary, the trivial, the griefs and pleasures.

Why sexist language and separatism are not issues

These resistances grant some intelligibility to the failure to take up
standard feminist theological accounts of sexist language. A look at
register shows more effectively how such language works. It is clear
that male imagery can signify negatively in this discourse. We saw that
in the way PW discourse is threaded with registers that construct positions of subordination for women, even as it offers alternative positions of female authority. We also see counter registers and registers
that work together to allow a different meaning effect to dominate.
Given the constancy of heterosexual gender complementarity in the
discourse, it is not surprising that the question of male-dominant language does not arise for PW—although it will arise in the later decades
from highly educated women experts. It is not, strictly speaking,
what immediately "oppresses" PW.

I do not mean that male imagery may not function at some level to
reaffirm the associations of maleness with authority; I do mean that
what is important for a feminist reading of any discourse is the question of what meanings are activated by woman's subject position
among the possibilities in the networks available. The codes of PW's
subject position prevent such terms as *father*, for example, from
simply registering as woman's negation. In part this is because of the
constraints of woman's dependence; some meanings have to be
avoided. In addition, other meanings activated by such terms as *father*
fit the trajectory of PW's emancipatory practice. Male language for
deity frequently has the semantic effect of a reminder of the universality of the family to whom one owes love. PW's theological grammar
for domesticity reads the fatherhood of God as the warrant to expand
the circle of care—not, at least for a number of years, as a signifying of
woman's oppressive dependence. PW's lack of interest in taking on the
battle for access to male subject positions of authority is mirrored in
the failure to take up patriarchy, the patriarchal family, or a male God
as a target.

There is also contradiction in this register of self- and world-transformation and its regime. Because it is a graf(ph)t, lines of flow and nourishment inscribed in the regime from the biblical and Reformed traditions of agape for the neighbor and the production of pleasurably autonomous selves are lines of avoidance and occlusion as well as the place for productive resistance. These lines shut off other possibilities, other constructions of biblical resistance with gender codes of emancipation. That is how these practices can restrict and constrain. As housewives, Presbyterian Women's existence is characterized by dependence in a social order that does not support them. PW are dependent on their spouses, and we see that their registers never challenge the way that gender complementarity diminishes their options.

Contradiction and impending fracture in their practice come from the very class positions they occupy. Their commitment to world-transformation leads to implicit challenge of their privilege, seen especially in the social changes investigated in the later issues of PW literature. As attention to the conditions necessary to a just world order gets more serious in the most recent decades of the publications, the contradiction in the privilege of their position becomes more pronounced. The women of color who provided domestic help for some and were the targets of mission, will be speaking to them more forcefully in later issues about racism. The very extension of their criticism of unjust treatment of the world neighbor threatens the life of their own fragile graf(ph)t.

Without their own means of support, PW are not good candidates for separatist women's communities. They invoke and desire a world of social subjectivity, of personalized accountability that is not supported by patriarchal capitalism. The dominant tenor of interpersonal conversation, which included personalization of social problems, has the disadvantage that all such volunteer practices for change do. It is still not a social order that responds to their influence. This contradiction is the particular form of patriarchal oppression that limits their subject positions. They are not oppressed by a patriarchal capitalism that denies them the means to survive, but by one that constrains their potential for rebellion.

The ambiguity of oppression-liberation

Still another instability in the discourse is the technology of their production as transformers of self and world. The dependence initiated and reproduced by capitalist patriarchy is not simply imposed on the middle-class housewife. The ideology of gender complementarity is a constraint upon her possibilities, but it is not forced on her. For oppression to stick, subjects must accept and internalize it. In that acceptance the ambiguity of oppression-liberation appears, and the possibility of the continued reproduction of sinful arrangements can be seen. The question is how domesticity in its constraining and dangerous form comes to be accepted by women. How, in Michel Foucault's terms, does the prisoner become her own warden?

One answer to that is the compensatory pleasures that are received in return for this constraint. These include the pleasures of heterosexuality and of all aspects of the home, church, and family. These pleasures provide the nourishment for the graf(ph)t of woman's work for women on biblical and traditional possibilities. The particular way in which middle-class Christian housewives are constructed in positions of dangerous dependence also needs to be analyzed as disciplinary power. Disciplinary power is the way in which modern technologies attached to capitalism subject subjects. It is a productive power, with effects of pleasure as well as docility.

This kind of power highlights the ambiguity in the production of Christians. This ambiguity is well-illustrated by the production of PW as accountable to the world neighbor. The earlier example of disciplinary power as it intersected with women's lives was that of the production of woman's body as a certain size, shape, and as a "feminine" display. These are disciplines that women have internalized as the panoptical Male Gaze, inscribing a permanent self-hatred for their bodies and faces. This power applies as an effect of the production of the self-critical subject, too, whose vocation is love of the neighbor and the global definition of family for whom God's love is intended. The positive register of command that inscribed accountability and assumed the fitness of the subject to the task is contradicted by the registers of interrogation which internalized the endless suspicion that woman will never be fit. These registers of interrogation produce her as a paralyzed subject.

The production of Presbyterian Women by the processes that inscribe them with moral accountability is not unfairly compared to the panoptical image for discipline.[74] When discipline is divinely administered, the internalized warden is a Divine Gaze. Interrogational genres internalize the voice of self-criticism in a fashion that is similar

---

[74]The distinctive aspect of Michel Foucault's notion of the subject is not the criticism of liberal power, but this production. See Alessandro Pizzorno, "Foucault and the Liberal View of the Individual," in *Michel Foucault Philosopher*, trans. Timothy J. Armstrong (New York: Routledge, 1989), 204–214.

to the Male Gaze. It is always ready with interrogational queries: Are my thighs too fat? Is my hair messed up? Did I really mean that? Is my attitude toward the poor sincere? The effects of this contradiction are significant. Their ambiguity is perhaps one of the most "oppressive" gendered versions of the sinful constraints that construct the subject position of the Christian middle-class homemaker and have made feminists critical of the idealization of servanthood for women.

Foucault reminds us of the incitements that come with any productive discipline. Like the pleasures associated with bodily disciplining, moral self-production creates compensatory skills that are not easy to relinquish. Skills of "goodness" are produced in this subject position, which may not be simply identifiable with the doctrinal error of works-righteousness. The intersections of pleasure and subjection that come with the shaping of moral individuals are the virtual conditions for that irritating effect of works-righteousness, self-righteousness.

Yet even in this fracture, the production of subjects accountable to an endless horizon of need, we see the possibilities for both transgression and subjection. For some, responsibility to care for the neighbor — a call to endless volunteer work — is subjection. For other women it creates the well-being of accomplishment. For some the pleasure of self-production may be short-lived. For others, the Divine Gaze is not so harsh, making possible the production of competent selves, nourished even in the anemic soil of a gendered discipline. The very transgression of the limits of woman's subject position coexists with the possibilities for her continued support of the status quo. For some it may be the creating of docile "souls" to match docile bodies; for others "goodness" is the creation of an escape route.

Presbyterian Women transgress the constraints that construct their subject positions. In these positions multiple discourses converge — gender, class, race, consumer, nurturer, homemaker, Christian — that are undermined by the contemporary social formation. Presbyterian Women "remake" their subject positions for global accountability. Their indirect targets, in the social formation, are the discursive processes of patriarchal capitalism that trivialize the home and de-skill and undermine women. More specifically, even while participating in both, they counter the discourses of romantic feminism/"true womanhood" and the rationalist feminism. Their transgressions are not those of liberation feminists. But they are significant productions of pleasurable, agapic, as well as ambiguous places. The places they produce mark off refusals of the patriarchal capitalist negation of the skills of homemaking and world-making.

There is no closure to the practices of faith. No ultimate judgment is needed about these discourses. However, we will take up their future for a feminist theology in chapter 7. My reading highlights their escape from the judgment of the social order upon them. Even as they are produced, Presbyterian Women are producers of wisdom from whom we have much to gain. Even in the colonializing tendencies of their embrace of the world neighbor, and even though their resistance to patriarchal capitalism is deployed as a discourse of interpersonal, face-to-face relations of well-being, PW signal judgments on our culture's failure to create or commit to world-neighborhood.

5 Joyful Speaking for God: Pentecostal Women's Performances

We give God all the glory
When we kneel to pray
We give God all the glory
Every step of the way

Chorus
Praise you, Lord, Praise you, Jesus
Praise you, Father, every day
Without your love, Holy Father
There is no other way.

God loves us when we're happy
God loves us when we're sad
God loves us when we're good
and God loves us when we're bad.

For God lives inside our bodies
And we praise God every day
So friends when you're in trouble
God is just a prayer away.

God never leaves us or forsakes us
God is merciful and cares
If there's doubt 'bout what we're sayin'
Spend some time with God in prayer

God has never let us down
God has dried our teary eyes
So we'll love the day we'll see him
When we're together in the sky

—Clady Johnson

The verses that open this chapter are from a song written by a Pentecostal mountain woman. Sung to the haunting melody of a mountain
ballad, they represent a performance outside the ordinary setting of
Pentecostal women's practice. But they display many of the same
convictions—radical dependence on God, the joy of a spirit-filled relationship with God, expectation of a future with God, and the maleness of this God. Pentecostal women like Clady Johnson occupy
subject positions that distinguish them from Presbyterian Women.
Pentecostal women of Appalachian communities, and many others
who are members of lower- and working-class communities, have
suffered the devastating economic crises of the century that have left
women in the ranks of the underemployed. With their radically reduced access to economic resources, Pentecostal women have been the
object of outreach efforts by more well-to-do, mainline denominations. Concern for the women of whom I speak in this chapter might
well be found in the literature of Presbyterian Women, targeted as objects of a mission to the "backward," "uncultured," and "primitive"
mountain folk, as they were perceived at the turn of the century. The
Pentecostal women and their families in regions such as Appalachia
are likely to be pictured on the cover of a PW publication focusing on
mission.[1]

    This chapter looks at the biblical practices of women who have in
common Pentecostalism and economic marginalization. It draws
from the call narratives of twelve women from southern and mid-
American rural and mountain communities who began their ministries in the 1930s and '40s and from distinctive worship practices of
women in Pentecostal folk communities.[2] This discourse comes from
women in the Church of God, Assemblies of God, and independent
holiness denominations. Linkages can be made between these and
other Pentecostal women in marginalized economic communities
such as Clady Johnson's, because they share the social location and re-

---

[1]See Deborah Vansau McCauley, "Appalachian Mountain Religion: A Study in
American Religious History," Ph.D. diss. (Columbia Univ., 1990). I read this intertextual relation of Pentecostal women with their middle-class Protestant sisters as an ambiguous one, a practice of care for the neighbor and yet a patronizing construction of a
victim.
    [2]The call narratives come from videotaped interviews conducted with twelve
Church of God women ministers by David Roebuck. These tapes are stored in the Hal
Bernard Dixon, Jr., Pentecostal Research Center, Cleveland, Tenn. I quote from ten of
these. Transcriptions I made of the videotaped interviews are in my possession. The
worship practices are documented by folklorist Elaine Lawless, who has done extensive
interviews with Oneness Pentecostal women in rural Indiana and Missouri communities. The similarities with the Church of God women ministers' stories are striking.

ligious practices characteristic of folk religious traditions.[3] One of the prominent features of these folk religious communities is their reliance on oral tradition, both as a way to pass on community belief and ritual as sacred memory and to produce a vital, ecstatic experience of God through oral performance. These practices are typically understood to be part of extremely conservative sect-communities of the Pentecostal wing of holiness and evangelical religious traditions in this country. In the hands of these women, however, that tradition is turned into practices that claim some rather powerful spaces.[4]

With an intertextual analysis of the call stories and worship practices of Pentecostal women ministers, I wish to trace the constraints as well as the transgressive nature of their practices. My readings agree with the women's self-descriptions that these practices are performances of joy and exhilaration. These practices create subject positions of great worth for the women, worth that counteracts a social formation that qualifies them as objects for special programs at best, disdains them at worst. My readings diverge from their own, however, in other respects. I do not share their interpretation of their practices as ideal or as God's will. Judgment regarding their patriarchal constraints is a product of my feminist grid, in light of which their

---

[3]For characteristics of folk religions, see Jeff Todd Titon, *Powerhouse for God: Speech, Chant, and Song in an Appalachian Baptist Church* (Austin: Univ. of Texas Press, 1988), 5–14, 141–49. Elaine Lawless, the preeminent writer on Pentecostal women, has focused on women in impoverished rural Indiana and Missouri. She comments that the dependence of these communities on limestone quarrying for their economic livelihood is similar to the dependence of Appalachian communities on mining. See Elaine J. Lawless, *Handmaidens of the Lord: Pentecostal Women Preachers and Traditional Religion* (Philadelphia: Univ. of Pennsylvania Press, 1988); *Women's Speech in the Pentecostal Religious Service: An Ethnography* (Ann Arbor, Mich.: Univ. Microfilms International, 1982); *God's Peculiar People: Women's Voices and Folk Tradition in a Pentecostal Church* (Lexington: Univ. Press of Kentucky, 1988). McCauley comments that Lawless's description of the worship practices of a Oneness Pentecostal church in Indiana is "particularly characteristic of independent Jesus Only churches in coal mining communities, as well as other independent holiness churches, in central Appalachia." McCauley, "Appalachian Mountain Religion," p. 174, note 77. Most of the Pentecostal preachers I quote come from a similar rural background.

[4]Scholars who wish to respect the integrity of these folk religions are increasingly able to recognize the distinctive force of this display while resisting its romanticization. Several have recognized the influence of regions on what are otherwise viewed as religious bodies or denominations abstracted from their settings. Thus treatments of Appalachian religiosity attend to the convergences of camp-meeting traditions, the Great Awakenings, and holiness traditions in independent Baptist churches, holiness churches, and Churches of God of numerous titles. These share many similarities in worship practice as well as the feature of being independent from the established denomination that may bear their name. I will not be making these finer distinctions, but see Catherine L. Albanese, *America, Religions, and Religion*, 2d ed. (Belmont, Calif.: Wadsworth, 1992), 324–49.

discourses have a transgressive but predominantly status quo relationship to the rules of their canonical systems.[5] There is some indication,
however, that interesting and more radical effects can result from their
discourses for women in situations of desperation when these women
have other options than the patriarchal communities of their religion.

Canonical system: the (in)stability of the spirit

Any idea of one canonical system for Pentecostal communities is a bit
of a contradiction. These churches are descended from movements
sometimes identified as sects, the form of religious association characterized by a rejection of the dominant culture in contrast with the
mainline denominations such as Presbyterians. Thus, the notion of
fixed system is in some sense counter to the original spirit of these
communities. Such criticism itself is part of an identifiable Pentecostal
essence. Thus we might begin a definition of the system by pointing
out that the Pentecostal movement was (and in some respects still is) a
refusal of certain forms of religiosity in North American society.

The classic Pentecostal churches—Church of God, Assemblies of
God, and Church of God in Christ—have begun to move into the
middle class in the past few decades. This kind of stabilizing institutionalization into class respectability emerged from a very different situation, which featured a variety of discourses that existed in lieu of
formal systems.[6] The formative days of Pentecostalism included the

---

[5]Instead of increasing percentages of women in ministry, Pentecostal denominational churches show a disturbing decline in numbers of women wishing to be "lady
evangelists." I suspect the rise in socioeconomic means may have effected a muting of
women's performances as well. Rather than claiming to find some hidden revolutionary
spirit in Pentecostal rural women, I wish to examine their biblical practices. The powerful effect of spoken, sung, chanted, shouted, and kinetic discourse in its immediacy
and exhilaration—the palpable joy that is truly shared—needs to be respected by a feminist account of gender, power, and language.

[6]"Sect" is Ernest Troeltsch's label to distinguish small antiestablishment movements
of Christianity from the church type. One of the preeminent historians of Pentecostal-
ism is Grant Wacker. I draw on his portrait here. See his "Primitive Pentecostalism in
America: A Cultural Profile," paper presented to the 13th Annual Conference of the
Society for Pentecostal Studies, 1983, p. 3, and the shorter version, "The Function of
Faith in Primitive Pentecostalism," Harvard Theological Review 77:3–4 (1984): 353–75.
See Richard Quebedeaux, "Conservative and Charismatic Developments of the Later
Twentieth Century," in Encyclopedia of the American Religious Experience: Studies of Tra-
ditions and Movements, vol. 2, ed. Charles H. Lippy and Peter W. Williams (New York:
Charles Scribner's Sons, 1988), 963–76. See also his The New Charismatics: The Origins,
Developments, and Significance of Neo-Pentecostalism (Garden City, N.Y.: Doubleday &
Co., 1976). See Roof on the perception of a move to the middle class. I am assuming
that an adequate account of the canonical intertext for contemporary middle-class Pen-

conviction that formal theology and denominational institutionalism worked to quench God's spirit and true holiness. In addition, the characteristic premillennialist expectations and hopes worked against the establishment of well-documented, institutional forms deliberately inscribed so as to provide a set of canonical norms. As one scholar points out, the conviction that the movement was supernatural in origin was enough to prevent its founders from documenting Pentecostal beginnings; only in recent decades have third-generation Pentecostals begun that historical work.[7]

Complete review of the roots of Pentecostalism is beyond the scope of this chapter. A brief history will be sufficient to get a view of the intertextual relation forged by women's practices in the folk Pentecostal communities. In what follows I propose a sketch of such a canon as it worked not simply in the early generations of Pentecostalism, but as it can still be presupposed by the independent holiness churches that characterize the women's performances described here.

Pentecostalism developed out of intensifying desires for purification or sanctification characteristic of nineteenth-century U.S. holiness movements. Fueled by Wesleyan versions of sanctification and the Reformed version as empowerment for service (Keswick holiness groups), believers with such desires flourished in camp-meeting settings. There much of this piety got its distinctive forms of worship.[8] A

---

tecostal communities would be more complex. Wacker notes that modernizing impulses displayed in the public prominence of faith healers of the late 1940s and '50s, culminating in Oral Roberts, for example, are signs of a new form of Pentecostal life and worship. Wacker, "Primitive Pentecostalism in America," 36–37.

[7] Spittler cites the book *Knowing the Doctrines of the Bible* by Myer Pearlman as exemplary of the few early efforts to write Pentecostal theology. Written in 1937, it has been widely used as a handbook for Pentecostal missionaries training ministers for evangelism. See Russell Spittler, "Scripture and the Theological Enterprise: View from a Big Canoe," in *The Use of the Bible in Theology/Evangelical Options*, ed. Robert K. Johnston (Atlanta: John Knox Press, 1983): 57–58.

[8] I draw heavily from the work of Grant Wacker here. See also Vinson Synan, *The Holiness-Pentecostal Movement in the U.S.* (Grand Rapids, Mich.: Eerdmans, 1971); and Edith L. Blumhofer, *The Assemblies of God: A Chapter in the Story of American Pentecostalism: Vol.1—To 1941* (Springfield, Mo.: Gospel Publishing House, 1989). For early forms of camp meetings, see Dickson D. Bruce, Jr., *And They All Sang Hallelujah: Plain-Folk Camp-Meeting Religion, 1800–1845* (Knoxville: Univ. of Tenn. Press, 1973). The Church of God in Christ (headquarters in Memphis) is largely black, founded in 1897 by Charles Price Jones and Charles H. Mason, former Baptists. A. J. Tomlinson, an itinerant preacher, organized the Church of God, Cleveland, out of a Camp Creek holiness church in 1907. Pentecostal Holiness Church (present headquarters, Oklahoma City, earlier in Franklin Springs, Ga.) was founded by Gaston Barnabus Cashwell. Assemblies of God was only indirectly connected to Azusa, but was shaped by Parham's followers (headquarters at Springfield, Mo.). Two groups of the period that incorporated later were the International Church of the Foursquare Gospel (Los Angeles) and the United Pentecostal Church (St. Louis).

vibrant expression in this worship was the display of spirit-filled behavior. An important contribution to the emergence of Pentecostalism
was an outbreak of speaking in tongues, sparked by holiness preacher
Charles Fox Parham at his Topeka Bible school in 1901.

The event accorded most significance in stories of Pentecostal origins, however, is the Azusa Street revival. The setting was a mission in
an empty livery stable in Los Angeles. The Azusa revival was inspired
by the preaching of William Seymour, a black holiness minister who
had learned from Parham. In the spring of 1906, Seymour initiated an
interracial, multiclass revival punctuated by tongues-speaking. The
revival lasted for three years.

Itinerant evangelists and preachers influenced both by Azusa Street
and Parham spread the practice of tongues-speaking as evidence of
Spirit baptism to locales already prepared for change by holiness
forces. A number of these communities eventually became churches
whose characteristic mark was to grant doctrinal status to glossolalia,
which had been an occasional practice until the early 1900s. Including
a number of smaller groups, the predecessors to the Church of God,
Assemblies of God, and Church of God in Christ announced that the
evidence of Spirit baptism by speaking in tongues was normative for
all Christians. Even if they speak in tongues only once—at this third
blessing of Holy Ghost baptism—all Christians must aspire to this experience of glossolalia in order to display the "initial physical evidence" of the Holy Spirit's work and reach full Christian maturity.[9]

In the midst of a variety of disagreements within late nineteenth-
century holiness traditions about the distinct stages of grace, Pentecostals' conviction that Christians must desire perfection was aligned
with holiness traditions, but distinct in its posture toward the signs of
that state. Pentecostals differed over the number of moments in the
order of salvation. Those with Wesleyan roots believed there are three
(justification, sanctification, and the Baptism of the Holy Ghost). Pentecostals with Reformed or non-Wesleyan roots allowed for only two
(conversion and sanctification are combined). Whether conversion or
justification of the sinner is separated from a second blessing or not—
the blessing of sanctification for the removal of actual sin—all Pente-

---

[9] Three important influences in the development of Pentecostalism were: (1) the Reformed emphasis on the power of God in Christian life; (2) the Wesleyan emphasis on
the real perfecting of Christian life; and (3) the camp-meeting revival setting where the
expressive, emotionally charged religion of new birth developed in the United States.
Equally important were the input of Baptist preacher Benjamin Irwin of "fire-baptized"
holiness fame, the network of faith-healing houses, and the apocalyptic eschatological
beliefs of the Plymouth Brethren. See Wacker, "Primitive Pentecostalism in America."

costals came to agree that the baptism of the Holy Spirit as an ecstatic sign of God's presence is a separate and required experience.

While few in holiness traditions would deny this baptism, what separates Pentecostals from their brothers and sisters in Wesleyan and Reformed communities is the belief that there must be physical evidence of the baptism in the gift of tongues or heavenly language.[10] This first feature of the canon, then, is the belief that the desire for God must issue in a separate experience that is the evidences of Holy Spirit baptism.

Tongues-speaking is not only a mark of Pentecostal forms of holiness, it is a status leveler for believers. As such it is crucial to the flexibility of qualifications for ministry, and therefore has great import for women. References to the Azusa Street revival often extol its liberating effects. The excess of the Spirit destroyed boundaries of race, class, and gender, and brought men and women of very different social locations together. Pentecostal faith was not a primarily egalitarian force in society, however. The leveling effects of Spirit baptism must be considered in the context of the presiding goal of the practice that characterizes this faith. Holy Spirit baptism is the effect of the aspiration to perfection. It also affords a unity with the divine that is qualitatively different from the relationship between believer and God claimed by the mainline Protestant traditions. The speaker becomes a "vessel" for God in a manner not duplicated by any other interpretive activities, nor, I would say, by Protestant understandings of the prophet. As David Roebuck says, because "tongues was a supernatural gift of God, the actions of the speaker were considered actions of God rather than actions of the human person."[11] The aspiration is for an experience of God, and the effect is religious ecstasy.[12]

In addition to this yearning for perfection as encounter with the divine, a second defining feature of the early years of Pentecostal religion was the premillennialism of the community (second-coming expectation). Any interpretation of the presiding purpose of Pentecostal faithfulness must acknowledge more than simply the desire for an ecstatic experience. The evidence of one's maturity in the baptism of the

---

[10]I thank Grant Wacker for this clarification. According to Wacker, about 30 percent of Pentecostals believe the order of salvation has three moments; 70 percent believe there are only two.

[11]David G. Roebuck, " 'Go and Tell My Brothers'?: The Waning of Women's Voices in American Pentecostalism," paper presented at the meeting of the Society for Pentecostal Studies, November 1990, pp. 8–10.

[12]Grant Wacker distinguishes this ecstasy from trance. "Primitive Pentecostalism in America," 18, 39–43. See Margaret Poloma on Pentecostalism as a protest against modernity in *The Assemblies of God at the Crossroads: Charisma and Institutional Dilemmas* (Knoxville: Univ. of Tenn. Press, 1989), xix, 3–20.

Holy Spirit is intended to serve as empowerment for increased motivation to witness to the gospel of salvation to the ends of the earth. The initial judgment included the mistaken assessment that tongues included the gift of xenoglossolalia, the ability to speak a foreign language unknown to the speaker. On the basis of this belief, numbers of Pentecostals were sent to do mission work overseas. Even the recognition that this gift was rare, however, did not undercut the zeal to testify.[13] Spiritual desire and compulsion to witness are fundamental to the community. Mission zeal finds a home outlet in expressiveness, emotional outpourings, shouting, dancing, falling out (or being "slain in the Spirit"), the characteristic accompaniment to worship witnessing in the narrative mode.

Despite what is in some ways an antiauthoritarian emphasis on the experience of the Holy Spirit and the ecstatic character of worship in the Pentecostal tradition, its canonical system is characterized by rigid doctrinalism. The desire to resist the accommodating worldly posture of mainline churches was not expressed as a desire to get rid of all belief. Strict adherence to beliefs about Holy Spirit baptism and scripture was required. The early rigidity was at its severest with regard to the practices that distinguished the Pentecostal community from the world. Thus, the aspiration to a sanctified life expressed itself in practices that forbade short hair and sleeveless dresses for women, Coca-Colas, movies, dancing, and a host of other cultural pleasures that seem innocuous only if one is not living in the end time. The rigidity of belief is tied to the pressing need to be "rapture-ready" at any moment.[14]

The adoption by many Pentecostal churches of more middle-class habits may blunt the eschatological edge. It would still be true for many communities, nonetheless, to say that the presiding goal of Pentecostalism (at least as defined in its founding communities) is witnessing to the saving grace of Jesus Christ, his imminent coming, and the

---

[13]The story of the origin of the tongues experience is that of the holiness preacher (sometimes faith healer) Charles Fox Parham. Parham prayed successfully for Agnes Ozman, a student at his Bible school in Topeka, Kansas, to receive the sign. He first claimed that speaking in tongues was the gift of foreign languages, designed to energize mission work. A number of early enthusiasts went to the mission field expecting to be given the gift of the native language, only to be disappointed. The reinterpretation of tongues recognized that the power to speak in other languages was not given to everyone.

[14]Many of these rules have been rescinded by official denominational decisions. The women preachers of my chapter, however, lived with the rules and are acutely distressed by their disappearance. Odine Morse is typical when she expresses how difficult it is for her to accept the wearing of pants, sleeveless dresses, and low-cut blouses by young Pentecostal women today.

necessity for the believer to participate fully in the gifts of the spirit, particularly the evidence of a second baptism of the Spirit.[15] As a whole, this discursive practice constructs a reading regime for Pentecostal scriptural practice that looks quite different from Presbyterian practice. It differs, too, from the regime of fundamentalism, with which it may appear to have more affinities.

How Pentecostalism differs from fundamentalism

When placed on a continuum between modernism and fundamentalism, a Pentecostal regime of reading, including its construal of scripture and exegetical principles for reading and practicing scripture, would appear to belong on the fundamentalist end. As a movement that decried the deadness of official, denominational religion, Pentecostalism spread most rapidly among lower, working, and lower-middle classes. Its appeal was not to an intellectual elite with interest in historical-critical method, for its spiritual ethos was defined precisely to avoid the kinds of skirmishes with modernism and historical criticism that characterized more mainline middle- and upper-class denominations like Presbyterianism. As historian Grant Wacker says, the basic ahistoricism characteristic of folk religion included an indifference to the criticisms of religion in the modern world.[16]

The rules defining Pentecostal reading assume a view of scripture that is in accord with the Protestant reformers, as Russell Spittler points out.[17] The Pentecostal urge to re-create the apostolic church, however, made "scripture alone" a rule for reading directly without the mediations of other Protestant denominations. The Assemblies of God, for example, refused to create doctrinal or faith statements at its 1914 Hot Springs conference because it was agreed that the Bible alone was to be the guide for all of life. In her history of the Assemblies of God, Edith Blumhofer explains the attitude to scripture by pointing to the restorationist influences on holiness that were designed to restore the living faith of the early church. It is fair to say that Pentecostals took the Bible alone as primary rule of faith in a more intense way than mainline Protestantism to avoid the imposition and taint of historic creeds.[18]

---

[15]Margaret Poloma points this out in *The Assemblies of God at the Crossroads*.

[16]Wacker, "Functions of Faith in Primitive Pentecostalism," 364ff.

[17]Spittler, "Scripture and the Theological Enterprise," 59. The original statement of Assemblies of God in 1916 did not include doctrines about Jesus such as virgin birth, bodily resurrection, or sinless life, but these were assumed.

[18]Restorationism is "the attempt to recapture the presumed vitality, message, and

However, Pentecostalism avoids some fundamentalist skirmishes. In certain respects living by the scriptures means bypassing its hermeneutic mediation via all the Fundamentals as well as the historic creeds. Although later developments in Pentecostal churches (and in the academy) move closer to fundamentalist principles, there are important indications that the Pentecostal position was much looser in the beginning. The rules for reading depart from fundamentalist accounts of biblical inerrancy at a point one might expect, given their identifying practice: at the point of the power and work of the Holy Spirit. Not only was inerrancy not part of the early statements of many Pentecostal churches, but the countering authority of the experience of Holy Spirit baptism had the effect of dislodging a certain kind of literalism. Pentecostals were frequently free of the literalism characteristic of a (later) evangelical Harold Lindsell, that is, the inerrant view of the plenarily inspired Bible, inspired "in whole and in part."[19] Until 1961, for example, the "official" position of An Assemblies of God "Statement of Fundamental Truths" puts it:

> 1. The Scriptures Inspired.
> The Bible is the inspired Word of God, a revelation from God to man, the infallible rule of faith and conduct, and is superior to conscience and reason, but not contrary to reason. 2 Tim. 3:16, 17; 1 Pet. 2:2.[20]

This statement avoids language of inerrancy, even though it speaks of infallibility.[21] The point here, and the debate among Pentecostals, cen-

---

form of the Apostolic Church." Blumhofer, *The Assemblies of God: A Chapter in the Story*, 1:18–22.

[19]The distinction between infallibility, inerrancy, and other variations comes later with evangelical scholarship. See Robert K. Johnston, *Evangelicals at an Impasse: Biblical Authority in Practice* (Atlanta: John Knox Press, 1978), chap. 2. Timothy Cargal finds more congruence between the Pentecostal biblical scholar's adoption of historicist assumptions and the modernism of fundamentalism. See "Beyond the Fundamentalist-Modernist Controversy: Pentecostals and Hermeneutics in a Postmodern Age," paper delivered at 21st annual meeting of the Society for Pentecostal Studies, November 7–9, 1991, pp. 1–7.

[20]This is how the statement read in the early 1950s. Spittler points out that later revisions brought it more in line with the National Association of Evangelicals by inserting the words "verbal inspiration." The statement read in 1961: "The Scriptures, both the Old and New Testaments, are verbally inspired of God and are the revelation of God to man, the infallible, authoritative rule of faith and conduct (2 Tim. 3:15; 1 Thess. 2:13; 2 Pet. 1:21)." Quoted in Spittler, "Scripture and the Theological Enterprise," 58–60. The NAE was founded in 1942 to create an alternative to the liberal Federal Council of Churches (later the NCC) on the one hand and the extreme fundamentalism of the American Council of Churches (led by Carl McIntire) on the other.

[21]Assemblies of God also issued a paper that defended inerrancy, published in

ters around the fear of "killing the work" by requiring certain interpretations of scripture or organization.[22]

Thus, whatever else it may mean, the "plain sense" of scripture for
Pentecostals assumes that the entire canon (King James and Scofield) is
God's written, inspired word. As such it is in line with Protestant understandings. In addition, that plain sense is literalist. The strict adherence to the sign of tongues with Spirit baptism, the distinction of sign
from gift, the claim about handling serpents — all these Pentecostal
emphases are the result of literal readings that were granted the status
of divine imperatives.[23] We find the differences of Pentecostal from
mainline Protestant understandings in the "rules" about how to negotiate what is invariably a heterogeneous text (whether a regime acknowledges this point or not), the authorization of that literalism —
which passages are more important, *who* can speak authoritatively,
and *who* can interpret. In early Pentecostalism this regime is characterized by a dynamism that distinguishes it from a strictly fundamentalist
view. This Pentecostal difference is absolutely crucial for the practices
of women.

In order to get at the canonical system and its implications for
women, the assumptions about biblical interpretation that hold for the
practitioner-pastor are most important. Despite the increasing complexity of Pentecostal hermeneutics in the years after their alliance
with evangelicals, including the use of modernist, historical criticism,
the precritical assumptions of the average preacher display an important difference from fundamentalism. These assumptions are
influenced by the deliberate avoidance of educational institutions

---

1970. Noted by Cargal, "Beyond the Fundamentalist-Modernist Controversy," p. 9,
note 21.

[22]See Edith Blumhofer, *The Assemblies of God: A Popular History* (Springfield, Mo.:
Gospel Publishing House, 1985), 39–53. Wacker stresses the continuity with evangelicalism. He argues that neither restorationism nor the Spirit baptism makes Pentecostals
any less rigid on doctrine; they simply avoided major detailed treatises on it. He points
out that within five months of Azusa, a credal statement was forthcoming indicating
this rigidity: "We are not willing to accept any errors, it matters not how charming and
sweet they may seem to be." He also attributes "inerrancy" to Pentecostal scriptural
positions and insists on the importance of "literalism." Wacker, "Primitive Pentecostalism in America," 28. The counter argument is that "inerrancy" was not in the earliest
positions, and the choice of literally interpreted passages is key.

[23]Wacker, "Function of Faith in Primitive Pentecostalism," 365–67. Blumhofer
points out that some restorationist views gave prominence to the literal interpretations
of passages about women's veiled heads and prohibitions against women's speaking.
Blumhofer, *The Assemblies of God: A Chapter in the Story*, 1:23. The Church of God,
however, allowed other literally interpreted passages more force. My argument is focused on the leeway allowed women by the authorizing power of Spirit baptism. This
view allows a different hermeneutical center in the weighing of the prohibitionary
verses about women.

of a mainline denominational sort (until 1970 for Church of God, Cleveland, 1973 for Assemblies of God). Another influence is the absence of official hermeneutical theories of the sophistication now found in evangelical distinctions between types of inerrancy and infallibility.[24]

Without a critical apparatus, the pastor can assume that a plenitude of meaning is mediated by a Spirit-led interpretation and not worry about a problematic hermeneutical gap created by critical-historical thinking. Sister Ruth Staples, Pentecostal preacher, puts it well: Even when a preacher is preaching on the same scriptural passage, she says, a sermon "is always so different, nobody would ever recognize it . . . because it's a different congregation, it's a different anointing, and God has a different message for everyone."[25] A Pentecostal reading regime assumes what Gerald Sheppard claims is characteristic of evangelicals—that "the meaning of any given text is contained . . . in a singular ancient author/redactor's intention." But it is arguable that this belief can be distinguished for many Pentecostals from the modernism of both historical critics and fundamentalists. In the anointing of the preacher, the spirit will open up the infinite possibilities for infinite numbers of "different congregations."

For the Pentecostal there is no need to argue for complex defenses of what the author/redactor's intention included. With no requirement to study at the middle-class institutions where the historical-critical battles were waged, the Pentecostal preacher has no need to worry that the plain sense of the text as ordered by Pentecostal beliefs might require some historical validation, or that it partakes of any historical relativity. The historicist assumption that authorial intention is objective and ascertainable is more akin to the fundamentalist's own "modernist" version of faith. Fundamentalism is characterized by the claim that something is true because it is historical—it really happened. This version of Christian faith appropriates the notion that a privileged kind of truth attaches to facts, data that are real insofar as they participate in objectivity. To define the truth of a biblical claim as its capacity to refer to an objective historical fact, however, is an injection of mod-

---

[24]See Joseph Byrd, "Paul Ricoeur's Hermeneutical Theory and Pentecostal Proclamation," paper delivered at 21st annual meeting of the Society for Pentecostal Studies, November 7–9, 1991. See also Cargal, "Beyond the Fundamentalist-Modernist Controversy."

[25]This quote comes from an interview given by Sister Ruth Staples to David Roebuck, available in videotapes housed at the Hal Bernard Dixon, Jr., Pentecostal Research Center.

ernist positivism into biblical infallibility that is totally inadequate to a Pentecostal reading regime.[26]

Such positivism is not faithful to the process or resources of the Pentecostal hermeneutical repertoire. For the Pentecostal preacher, the assumption that the Holy Spirit creates the bridge between that ancient inspired author's intention and the current meaning of that text is enough to make the text accessible, as Cargal points out.[27] Enough, that is, if the preacher allows himself/herself to be God's vessel. The "gap" for Pentecostals has simply not been a historical gap, a ditch to be negotiated by the tools of the educated historical exegete, or even necessarily by the fundamentalist proofs of scripture. The gap that does exist is a moral-soteriological one—it is the life of sin and absence of the Holy Spirit that prevents the practitioner from reading rightly.

Access to this Word is based, at least at first, purely on the Holy Spirit, who both worked through the original writers in the inscription of God's Word and works in the believer's life to enable a grasp of the spiritual meaning of scripture. Anyone can understand scripture, since grammatical and historical tools grant its apparent meaning, but the person does not thereby obtain its spiritual meaning. In the development of rules that require actual spiritual signs, we find one of the most decisive differences between Pentecostal and fundamentalist performances of scripture, and also between Pentecostal and more modernist Reformed-Presbyterian performances, as well. Both kinds of non-Pentecostal readings can occur without this kind of immediacy to God, which is seen in the physical evidence of the Holy Spirit.[28]

---

[26]Cargal, "Beyond the Fundamentalist-Modernist Controversy."

[27]Cargal indicates a number of accounts of Pentecostal hermeneutics that are laced with fundamentalist concerns. He points to Howard M. Ervin, "Hermeneutics: A Pentecostal Option," *Pneuma: the Journal of the Society for Pentecostal Studies* 3 (Fall 1981): 19. For an overview, see French Arrington, "Hermeneutics, Historical Perspectives on Pentecostal and Charismatic," in *Dictionary of Pentecostal and Charismatic Movements*, ed. Stanley M. Burgess, Gary B. McGee, and Patrick H. Alexander (Grand Rapids, Mich.: Zondervan, 1988), 376–89.

[28]Gerald T. Sheppard, "Biblical Hermeneutics: The Academic Language of Evangelical Identity," *Union Seminary Quarterly Review* 32:2 (Winter 1977): 81–94. Sheppard discusses some of the varieties and nuances in modern evangelical accounts of the authority of scripture. "Infallibility" is not as strong as "inerrancy"; the latter has its strength in its "referential (therefore, historical and factual) connotation" (p. 85). "All of evangelicals think the meaning of any given text is contained . . . in a singular ancient author/redactor's intention. Traditionally this sacred intention could be reconstructed by applying the historical-grammatical method" (p. 87). At one extreme is Harold Lindsell, who defines the mark of evangelicalism as the view of scripture's inerrancy (p. 89).

Dynamism of Pentecostal hermeneutics

Other features of a Pentecostal reading regime are significant for our reading of women's practices.[29] First, the site of hermeneutical practice: this Spirit-based hermeneutics comes to full expression in the worship service. In the view of one historian of the movement, the closest Pentecostals come to a belief in inerrancy is with regard to the practice of inspired preaching.[30] It is in preaching and testifying through the Spirit that the Bible is understood. These activities are the telos of the community's life of faith (on earth). Furthermore, this reliance on the Spirit is the basis for the distinctively oral character of folk communities. The focus on the setting of preaching-testifying for "right reading" in the place of intellectual/critical understanding of a biblical text is definitive for many contemporary independent Pentecostal churches, according to folklorists.

Interpretive practices, then, are not written texts, published books of exegesis, sermons, or systematic theologies, but the oral traditions of the Pentecostal service. The Spirit-led context of planned spontaneity forms the "institutionalization" of the uniquely Pentecostal regime of reading. The more felicitous description of the regime, then, is not reading, but performance. When I speak of a *performed scripture*, I do so out of respect for the oral character of this tradition, particularly as it is still practiced in mountain and rural churches (many of which are independent holiness churches).

There is an open-endedness to biblical interpretation in this regime that is a function of both anti-intellectualism and the refusal to impose credal constraints. Positively, that distrust of man-made doctrine is also the imperative to trust the Spirit to speak through the preacher or the testifier. (Heavy emphasis on education was precisely what killed the Spirit.) Such a canonical system allows for a good bit of hermeneutical leeway, and any text has multiple meanings.[31] Proper reading is proper performance, however, and so the openness of the text does not entail the possibility of any rendering, for interpreters have a stage for display and assessment. Also under inspection in the ethics of the

---

[29]Of two hermeneutical directions, one is aligned with evangelical readings that confine; the other is a more fluid possibility for the meaning of passages to be Spirit-directed.

[30]Harold Hunter, Church of God historian, in an interview at the Church of God School of Theology, Cleveland, Tenn., January 1991.

[31]Cargal also points out that the Pentecostal "method" has affinities with the narrative literal reading of Hans Frei and George Lindbeck. It is one of the ways a sense of the text is gotten without historical-critical method. Cargal, "Beyond the Fundamentalist-Modernist Controversy," 10.

community, the Spirit-filled performance gets its primary display in worship, where the uniquely dramatic signs of spiritual interpretations can be judged. Testimony, prayer, speaking in tongues, dancing, and shouting confirm the effectiveness of a scriptural performance.[32]

Like any other such system, the Pentecostal canonical system has implications for who is allowed to speak. The credentials of the preacher in a Spirit-authorized regime of scripture are the credentials required of every other believer. The regime, in short, (ideally) supports a radical leveling of access to authority. The Spirit-authorized character of the system levels access to the privilege of preaching; its rules about who can speak and who can interpret have been unusually egalitarian, particularly in the first decades of the twentieth century.[33] If God is to be the speaker in worship, then anyone, not simply the educated or the male adult, can be God's vessel or mouthpiece. As an early leader remarked, "God does not need a great theological preacher that can give nothing but theological chips and shavings to the people. He takes the weak things to confound the mighty. He is picking up pebble stones from the street and polishing them for his work. He is even using children to preach His Gospel."[34]

In one important sense, the dynamism of Pentecostal hermeneutics is the opening for women's performances of scripture. The effect of Pentecost was judged to be the new age when women could be the mouthpiece of the Lord. One of the earliest interpretations of the egalitarian character of the Holy Spirit insisted on the new gender arrangements after Pentecost:

> Before Pentecost, the woman could only go into the "court of women" and not into the inner court. The anointing oil was never poured on a woman's head but only on the heads of kings, prophets and priests. But

---

[32]I believe this is less true of more middle-class Pentecostal churches.

[33]Pentecostal women were ministers in these decades when other denominations refused to allow women to preach. It is often noted that many holiness women preachers, of whom Phoebe Palmer is one of the best known, had gone before. See Nancy A. Hardesty, "Holiness Is Power: The Pentecostal Argument for Women's Ministry," paper presented before the Society for Pentecostal Studies, 1983. Carolyn Rowland Dirksen, "Let Your Women Keep Silence," in *The Promise and the Power: Essays on the Motivations, Developments, and Prospects of the Ministries of the Church of God*, ed. Donald N. Bowdle (Cleveland, Tenn.: Pathway Press, 1980), 165–96. Also Letha Dawson Scanzoni and Susan Setta, "Women in Evangelical, Holiness, and Pentecostal Traditions," *Women and Religion in America, Vol. 3: 1900–1968*, ed. Rosemary Radford Ruether and Rosemary Skinner Keller (San Francisco: Harper & Row, 1986), 223–65.

[34]From "Back to Pentecost," *The Apostolic Faith* 1:2 (October 1906): 3. Quoted in Roebuck, " 'Go and Tell My Brothers,' " 6. This openness did not last, of course. A. J. Tomlinson in the Church of God determined that the gift of preaching was not given to everyone, even if the Spirit baptism was.

when our Lord poured out Pentecost, He brought all those faithful
women with the other disciples into the upper room, and God baptized
them all in the same room and made no different. All the women received the anointed oil of the Holy Ghost and were able to preach the
same as men. . . . It is contrary to the Scriptures that women should not
have her part in the salvation work to which God has called her. We
have no right to lay a straw in her way, but to be men of holiness,
purity, and virtue, to hold up the standard and encourage the woman in
her work, and God will bless us as never before. It is the same Holy
Spirit in the woman as in the man.[35]

Interpreting scriptural prohibitions concerning women

Pentecostal beliefs in the infallibility of the entire canon have important implications for the rules for reading. They implicitly require that
all scriptures that refer to women must be obeyed. The defining character of the premillennial pressure to witness, however, and the
sought-for evidence of tongues show that certain texts had more interpretive power than others — were "plainer" than others. The early
Pentecostal leaders judged that Joel's prophecy in Acts pertaining to
the prophesying of sons *and* daughters in the days of Pentecost was a
presiding warrant for women's prophesying roles. No one could prohibit God's Spirit from speaking through women. The verses that
commend women's silence (1 Cor. 14:34) could not be ignored; they
were simply interpreted to refer to some activity other than proclaiming the gospel.

In the case of the Church of God, the governing practices of the
community were interpreted as the gender-exclusive domain. The
Church of God (and, on and off, the Assemblies of God) prevented
women from sitting on the governance councils of the church and
from presiding over ordinances such as baptizing, foot washing, the
Lord's Supper, performing marriages, and taking in members.[36] Key
to the hermeneutics, however, are the narratives of Holy Spirit baptism (Acts 22:4, 10:44–46, 19:1–7, 8:14–24), as well as the passages re-

---

[35]"Who May Prophesy," *The Apostolic Faith* 1:12 (January 1908): 2. Quoted in Roebuck, " 'Go and Tell My Brothers,' " 7.

[36]See Dirksen, "Let Your Women Keep Silence," 165–96. Dirksen says, "The role of
women in the Church of God is a unique and paradoxical combination of unprecedented
access to the pulpit and almost unparalleled exclusion from administration." David
Roebuck shows, however, that women were speaking participants in the first General
Assembly, 1906. " 'Go and Tell My Brothers,' " 9–10.

garding the other gifts of the Spirit. These narratives provide hermeneutic controls over other NT prohibitions to women speaking. They contribute to the creative solution offered for other prohibitions—namely, the interpretation that no speaking in "church" refers to ecclesiastical ruling practice.[37]

In contradiction with its openness, the Pentecostal system entails explicit acknowledgments of the place of women. Women and men alike accede to the "biblically based" view that men should have authority over women. In the early defense of women's preaching quoted above, we find the argument for submission couched in the language of gender complementarity:

> The woman is the weaker vessel and represents the tenderness of Christ, while the man represents the firmness of Christ. They both were co-workers in Eden and both fell into sin; so they both have to come together and work in the Gospel. . . . No woman that has the Spirit of Jesus wants to usurp authority over the man. The more God uses you in the Spirit, the more humble and tender you are and the more filled with the blessed Holy Spirit.[38]

The discourses of proper masculinity and femininity are very important in the construction of subject positions for Pentecostal women. Such positions are defined by a culture that considers the hierarchical order of the family to be Bible-based. The chain of command—God over Jesus, over man—continues in the male-headed household, where the husband has authority over the wife and children.[39]

A less explicit feature of the system is the part of the regime that supports and reproduces the community and its practices. Remember that the full spectrum of a canonical system includes the material-institutional supports for its existence and reproduction. A logical parallel to the institutional supports that reproduced certain interpretive procedures in mainline denominational seminaries are the camp meetings, revivals, and Bible training schools that characterized the early decades of Pentecostalism. As compared to the socioeconomic status and power of the Presbyterian system, for example, these institutional supports and their homogenizing power were not as powerfully duplicated in Pentecostalism of the early years. This was in part a reflec-

---

[37]Roebuck tells of the "new light" received by Church of God overseer A. J. Tomlinson, enabling his exegesis of "church" in the Pauline passages to allow the crucial distinctions between preaching and governing. " 'Go and Tell My Brothers.' "

[38]"Who May Prophesy," quoted in Roebuck, ibid.

[39]Lawless, *Handmaidens of the Lord*, 5–6.

tion of the desire to remain rapture-ready, an automatic anti-institutional impulse, as much as the distrust of modern critical conversations that began to be imported from Europe into mainline denominational institutions of higher learning.

Intersection of the divine and ordinary life

An important observation about the hidden construction of a regime comes when we consider the cohesiveness effected by the Pentecostal view of the God-world relationship. The posture of Pentecostal world-resistance is an antimodern one. Pentecostals find God's agency, the agency of spirits, and the agency of the devil in every life occurrence. It is a world filled with supernatural power, imbued with the divine. Robert Mapes Anderson calls it animistic. Divine healings, resurrections, and miracles are ever-present possibilities. If God's supernatural power suffuses the earthly landscape of the Pentecostal, the opposition is no less personally real; the devil is at work with equal seriousness.

Beliefs about the intersection of the divine with ordinary life not only set Pentecostals off from other mainstream denominational practitioners, but put them at odds with the progressive structures of power in the nation. Such "at-oddsness" is important in the social reproduction of the regime. While it cannot be identified simply with class, opposition to modernity is clearly associated with subject positions outside of access to social power.[40] In a world where God and God's adversary can be identified as personally directing every event, one cannot so easily be of the saints and dwell with sinners.

More is needed, however, than a supernatural construction of the world. Although middle-class Pentecostal communities are reproduced by the relatively new educational institutions and monied institutes, the same cannot be said of rural and mountain Pentecostal churches, particularly independent ones.[41] The oral character of the

---

[40]Anderson calls the classic Pentecostals the "disinherited." For a fascinating study of early Pentecostals in the United States as basically marginalized, disinherited peoples, see Robert Mapes Anderson, *Vision of the Disinherited* (New York: Oxford Univ. Press, 1979). For complications of this view, see Grant Wacker, "Taking Another Look at the *Vision of the Disinherited,*" *Religious Studies Review* 8:1 (January 1982): 15–20. However the general argument is resolved, the connection between the marginalized social location of the women I consider and their faith practices is constitutive. This does not, of course, mean that one causes the other.

[41]See McCauley, "Appalachian Mountain Religion." The work of Lawless, Titon, William Clements, and Howard Dorgan confirms this focus on oral tradition as the

tradition is not only the place to develop hermeneutical insights, but the privileged discursive form of reproduction for these insights. "Folk religions" are identified by the phenomenon of oral tradition, the passing on of skills and knowledge by participation, imitation, and inspiration. This is reproduction in the sense that "folk religion" designates communities whose distinctiveness centers around affective, performed tradition.

The "power to move people," as Jeff Todd Titon puts it, constitutes the galvanizing and cohesive character of Pentecostal and independent Baptist faith practices. Affectivity is characteristic of the oral mode of the central identifying acts of the communities—preaching, witnessing, testifying, and speaking in tongues. These powerful oral practices are reproduced through memory and ritual repetition.[42] Carefully crafted memory passed on by imitation is a form of institutional reproduction; it is an alternative to educational institutions and written discourse. It is a form of religious life generally described as marginal, particularly as more prosperous forms of Pentecostalism have developed in the United States. For the rise of women preachers, however, the oral mode of reproduction has been crucial.

The final piece in an analysis of the reproductive aspects of this discursive formation is the link between the ritual performances of scripture and Pentecostal animism, the conviction that the world is saturated with divine presence. That link is found in the narrative discourse of Pentecostals. Telling a story is the way to concretize notions of divine guidance. It is a story of God and Jesus, but always a story that intersects the believer's life and must be told as a personal narrative. The narratives of call are exemplary of this practice—stories of lives punctuated with divine intervention and leading. Ministers have no monopoly on this form of storytelling, since every Christian must have a testimony, but ministers develop an expertise at the practice of retelling their lives in terms of their calling.[43] This telling can take the

chief locus of reproduction—a tradition that requires folks to remain in rural and mountain communities, I might add.

[42]Titon writes on a particular independent Baptist church, but finds his descriptions of their practices to be characteristic of Pentecostal rural churches as well. He draws on the work of other folklorists who share this definition. *Powerhouse for God*, 8–10. Regarding the folk character of the religion (its oral transmission), "traditional" refers to the autonomy of communities that pass on oral traditions. See Lawless, *God's Peculiar People*, x, 4. McCauley, "Appalachian Mountain Religion," 173–75, regarding verbal genres of the religion.

[43]Titon identifies this "narrative view of life" with the independent Baptist minister he writes about. *Powerhouse for God*, 408–456. See also Dell Hymes, "The Grounding of Performance and Text in a Narrative View of Life," *Alcheringa* 4:1 (1978): 138. Lawless finds these narrativizings in Pentecostal women ministers' call stories and identifies them as fictions. From a poststructuralist position, the distinction is not a helpful one,

form of analogical or typological readings of one's life in light of biblical characters or events, or the reading of seemingly trivial incidents as messages from God. Narrative, the ordering of reality as story, is a popular genre for theological analysis. What is distinctive about Pentecostal practice are the identification of supernatural guidance in the details of everyday life, the inbreaking of the Holy Spirit as cause in the life story, and the interpretive lens of biblical inscription to order that inbreaking.[44]

The continued existence of Pentecostal practices depends on confirmation of the truth of the gospel message, a point that is characteristic of all Christian practices in theory. There seems to be, however, a distinctive character to the oral, performative community of faith that grants to worship a kind of confirmational power. Truth is tested in a particular way in the oral folk community. The kind of reproduction that characterizes this oral, performance-based community is highly personal, face-to-face, and participatory. Whatever other institutional supports exist for the reproduction of Pentecostal practice, its continued power to persuade and be effective in the lives of its participants is surely the central force. Not only, then, is the reproduction of the community based on good memory and good performances by individual testifiers and preachers; it relies on a "social effect of truth." The performance is prolonged by the mutual reinforcement it engenders, and more persons are confirmed in the truth of the faith than simply the individual performer. The sharing of testimony and joyful witness to God's presence in individuals' lives are mutually confirming of the truth of the reading for subjects. This discursive formation is, by implication, intense and powerful in its affective elements, and simultaneously as fragile as its participants' continued experience of its promise. It is, after all, on the line every week.

---

because there is no "real story" of their lives to which their retelling can be compared as a less true version. *Handmaidens of the Lord*, 12–14. She notes that the expertise at narrativizing is found in those whose ministries have been most successfully developed. For narrative as a genre of oral communities, see a special issue on personal narrative in *Journal of the Folklore Institute* 14:1–2 (1977).

[44]Narrative is a category applicable to many personal interpretations of subjects' lives. It has been granted virtual ontological status with notions like the "narrative structure of experience." Stephen Crites, "The Narrative Quality of Experience," *Journal of the American Academy of Religion* 39:3 (September 1971): 291–311. Obviously, religious narratives are not all the same, and they differ not simply in content. Titon points out the difference in conversion narratives between Pentecostal and Baptist and "mainline" narratives, those of more highly educated Christians. *Powerhouse for God*, 386. With the exception of Wesley Kort, no one has taken a poststructuralist approach to religious narratives, a task that would take on the destabilizing features of the category. Wesley A. Kort, *Bound to Differ: The Dynamics of Theological Discourses* (University Park: Pennsylvania State Univ. Press, 1992), 125–34.

In sum, if there is a Pentecostal women's "performance regime" in which resistance can be found, it will be forged in relation to a canonical system that orders faithfulness in a world animated by God's Spirit. It is a system shaped by the surrounding culture's constraints on women even as it offers them a unique permission to speak. Its rules for reading are ordered doctrinally, but even these are distinctively shaped by the living presence of God. Thus it is in the commitments to an inspired scripture and to a definition of authority and Christian life as Spirit-indwelt that the force of doctrinal orderings for the question of women's practices is to be found.

The dynamism characterizing the rules of this canonical system is related to its social location, the significance of prophetic authority in the early years and, more recently, in communities not attached to the increasingly institutionalized, middle-class Pentecostal denominations. It is a prophetic rather than priestly authority.[45] The answer to the question "Who can speak?" is: Anyone who is qualified. At least through the 1930s, qualifications were fairly egalitarian. One merely had to be called by God and evidence that call by testimony and Spirit baptism.

The openness this created—its seemingly radical leveling of the hierarchies of the world—was not complete, however. The authority to speak did not carry over for women into the authority to rule or, in many cases, to preside over church ordinances. Submission to the man in this canonical system appears to be a doctrinairely held conviction, one not susceptible to direct refutation. The presiding telos of the practice of Pentecostal faith is a direct and intense relationship to God, one that offers a distinct participation in the sacred realm. If the participation in that realm in worship is, by implication, Pentecostal practice at its zenith, then exclusion from participation in ruling might be read by women as exclusion from a lesser activity.

Women's call stories: spiritual narratives

Three overlapping genres characterize the discursive practices of Pentecostal women ministers. The first is call narratives, which relate God's personal call to ministry. For many of the Church of God women I will discuss, that call story includes another genre, that of testimony. Following an analysis of these stories of spiritual history

---

[45]See Sheppard, who argues that this authority is one typically associated with new movements of reform and, according to sociological views, not expected to last. Sheppard, "Biblical Hermeneutics."

(or autobiography), I will consider the closely related discourse of women's sermons, the third genre. I will draw on the women's own descriptions of worship practices and the observations of Elaine Lawless. In light of the overlapping of the three genres, I will not consider field, tenor, or mode in each until all three are before us.

This analysis begins with the practices of Pentecostal women that rely on intertextual relations with their own canonical system. More indirectly, their practices have meaning in relation to the discursive formation of capitalist patriarchy; I will take up this relationship later.

From the outset we can assume that their practices will not involve direct or overt separationist strategies. The tight cohesiveness of the community that defines itself against the world gives Pentecostal women deeper connections with the men in their community than any connection they (hypothetically) share with women in other locations. The requirement that men rule is supported by the status of an infallible Bible. This suggests that gender resistance will not appear around the topic of women or women's nature. It is no surprise to discover that the issue of gender is not an explicit theme raised by these women's practices. If there are any possibilities for reading their practice as resistance to their constraints, these possibilities will be found in the most dynamic aspect of Pentecostal faith—the importance attached to God's indwelling of lives. This is signified most demonstratively in the practice of speaking in tongues.

Part of a generation of women ministers in the early days of Pentecostal churches, the women of my account were called in the 1930s and 1940s. All but one describe their families as poor. All the families were working class, and most included many children. These women came from religious families, most of them members of Baptist or holiness churches.[46] No other socioeconomic details are provided in these call stories, and the sociologist is bound to be disappointed. Data of place, family, career, love, which might fill most personal narratives, do not make up the substance of these stories. Most women

---

[46]The interviewer (Roebuck) asks all the women where and when they were born and how they came to associate with the Church of God. A few skip the first two questions and move immediately into their spiritual history. The twelve women are: Zoe Brown, b. 1905, Oklahoma; Ruth Staples, b. 1915 to a poor family with ten children; Lucille Turner, from an Alabama farm family with twelve children during the Depression; Mary Howard, b. 1921, St. Paul, N.C.; Odine Morse, b. in northern Louisiana, moved to Dunn, N.C.; Dorothy Murphy, b. Green County, Miss., to farmers, one of thirteen children; Tilda Anders Oxendine, b. Forrestville, N.C., to land-poor farmers; Pauline Lambert, b. 1912, Benton Township, Ill., to farmers; Bernice Woodard, b. 1926 on a farm in Illinois; Amanda Miller, b. to a grocer in Tenn.; Lucille Walker, b. Kentucky, Appalachian mountains; Mary Elizabeth Graves, b. 1917, Artesia, Miss., one of six children of the only local doctor.

barely mention these facts — a few skip them altogether. The call narratives of women ministers in the Church of God are spiritual histories constructing their lives from the time leading up to and following God's call to preaching ministry. The field variable of the self-narrations sets these life stories squarely in the context of a spiritual chronology of their lives, lives presented as directed toward and defined by God from the beginning.[47]

The women are prompted by the interviewer's interest in how they became ministers. Their accounts do not conform to the interviewer's questions as much as they display a logic of their own, following a pattern observed by many folklorists as a genre. In this genre three characteristics stand out.[48] First, the stories are constructed out of traditions of the Pentecostal community, even as they are creative versions of these traditions. This means that the stories represent religious personal narratives of the folkloric (read "oral") type. Offering minimal detail on family, the women focus on the origins of their salvation and their reception of the baptism of the Holy Spirit in the Church of God.[49]

A second feature of the call-spiritual journey stories comes from the particular relation of the narrator to the story. Call stories are frequently characterized by struggles, usually focused on conversion. For these Pentecostal women, this conflict is also articulated as a struggle

---

[47]Titon would disagree with my willingness to call these stories "fictions," for he wishes to distinguish between the controlled "history-focused" character of an interview and the interviewee-controlled account. I agree that the former is a construction; but the latter is as well, however much the interviewer strives to let the persons speak themselves. Titon is concerned that the ethnologist's role in the construction of folk research should be acknowledged and become a conversation. I applaud his wish for mutuality but disagree with his distinction between historical stories and fictions. These interviews contain elements similar to those identified in other Pentecostal stories of call/spiritual life. They are fictions. See Jeff Todd Titon, "The Life Story," *Journal of American Folklore* 93 (1980): 276–92.

[48]This point is important to folklorists, who have many conversations over the convergence of creativity and tradition in folklore. Thus Stahl goes to great lengths to show how a personal narrative such as a "memorate" is constructed from the tradition. My analysis of discourse assumes that discourses are not the expression of private or individual experience. See Sandra K. D. Stahl, "The Personal Narrative as Folklore," *Journal of the Folklore Institute* 14:1–2 (1977): 9–30.

[49]The stories are prompted by questions about how they came into the Church of God, how they received their call, what kind of preachers they are, and how they have dealt with the limitations on women in their community. Despite the obvious directing of their narratives by this setting, the stories contain most if not all of the marks of call stories recorded by Lawless. She reports a narrative that offers few personal details and focuses on when the woman was saved, received the baptism of the Holy Spirit, and the call to preach. *Handmaidens of the Lord*, 64–68. There are some similarities to Titon's accounts of Baptist conversions, as well, but these latter include more focus on conviction and sin prior to conversion. Titon, *Powerhouse for God*, 311–22, 382–407.

to accept God's call. It is not only the sin that the women share with all believers that stands in the way of accepting God's grace. The communities' gender restrictions, which the women have internalized, create a problem as well. Their stories recount victories in relation to these struggles, as God leads them again and again to overcome the obstacles and temptations of the world. The call story, then, is a dramatic life contest over which the narrator has gained control. She tells of a contest won. This logic of themes suggests that the woman possesses the skill of a "sagaman"—a narrator who tells of herself or himself as the protagonist in a heroic story.[50] The sagaman displays a certain sort of heroism as she grants a relation of closure and completeness between her identity and victories won.

A third distinct feature of the call story can be contrasted to personal experience stories, an oral form that relates a life from a secular point of view. These stories are "memorates," personal narratives about supernatural experience. This feature identifies their traditional nature; the call stories are discourses of a community. It also helps us distinguish Pentecostal women's discourse from that of other Christian women. What holds them together as Pentecostal narratives is not simply that God guides them, but that God supernaturally intervenes in that guidance.[51] God directs the minutest details of their spiritual journey, most intensely centered around the particulars of their (often reluctant) acceptance of God's calling to preach. These women are not secular heroines, but players who win in a divine and ultimate drama.

Two main tensions are set up in the first half of the stories. In the first type of tension, for some of the women who were already Christian, movement into the Pentecostal community was cause for a struggle. The lure of that community and desire for its special gifts and life conflicted with fear of the strangeness and fanaticism of Pentecostalism compared with comfortable, safe membership in another Christian community. Sometimes when that tension is minimal in an account, the second type of tension is stressed: struggle between participation as a Pentecostal Christian and the call from God to be a preacher.

In the second half of the call stories, the women recount the various subplots of their ministries. Most of the women pastored churches; one was a full-time missionary teacher overseas, pastoring only one

---

[50]The Pentecostal version of a sagaman is identified by William M. Clements, "The Pentecostal Sagaman," *Journal of the Folkloric Institute*, 17:2–3 (May–December 1980): 169–95.

[51]These are distinctions made by Stahl. A memorate "contains at its core a belief that is in nearly all cases collective." "The Personal Narrative as Folklore," 20.

year; some number were foreign missionaries in the early parts of their ministry and pastored churches in the United States for a number of years. Many traveled as evangelists, had tent ministries, and did street preaching. A number started new churches and moved a number of times as a result.

Not I but God: radical dependence as freedom

When the women tell of their calls, they highlight the ideas that legitimate their ministry. This legimating discourse is expessed in two dominant and integrally related ideas used to make sense of the calls: (1) submission to God and man, and (2) an absolute dependence on God rewarded by divine leading. In addition to the submission and dependence themes, the women express ideas that underline (even boast) the divine authorization of their calls, providing a subtext that creates an important tension with their humility. Although these other themes do not officially legitimate their calls, they offer a clue about what I read as the double function of the narratives: the display of total confidence in their call and utter pleasure in their role.

I begin with the themes of dependence and submission, which, despite their similarity, have different meanings in the discourses. The stories recount lives threaded with uncertainties and changes in circumstance. These lives are stitched together by God's special, personal guidance. God is not simply present in a general way in the events of Pentecostal women's existence. God provides specific messages or signs for particular crises or everyday decisions, as well. Sometimes the divine guiding occurs as God's refusal to leave a woman alone. Sister Staples heard her call at age five and brought a neighboring coal miner to the Lord with a sermon she preached as a child. Yet she avoided the call into adulthood, when God began speaking to her every night, bringing her to tears over her years of running away from his call.

Other accounts relate God's intervention as a response to a challenge the woman herself puts to God. Sister Brown, too timid to seek salvation at a Pentecostal meeting, asked God for a sign—in the form of directing her in a city she had never traveled in before. God provided the sign. Frequently the intervention is the supplying of need where no other resources seem likely. Sister Oxendine helped run tent revivals with her brother for two to five weeks at a time. When contributions were minimal, as they frequently were—sometimes fifty dollars was the offering total for three weeks—she and her co-evangelists depended on God to provide food and shelter: "The Lord just helped us and we ate where we were invited." Sister Howard narrates both kinds of guidance—fulfillment of basic needs and response to her request for a sign in accounts of God's miraculous healings of her own grave injuries from an accident with scalding liquid starch. Responding to her request for voice to praise Jesus, God gave her voice and healed her arm.

The theme of guidance is essentially connected with utter dependence, which the women claim consistently. The concern for money, resources, food, and material welfare is often disavowed in the narratives, as in Sister Oxendine's dismissal of the worry about food and the implications of only making nine dollars profit one year. Sister Brown tells story after story of God's supplying her needs, from providing her clothing to fixing a clock in depression times. The human posture that is inseparable with this kind of intervention—in fact is a condition of it—is one of trust and dependence. So sure is she that God will provide in response to her trust, Sister Brown tells of publicly pledging one hundred dollars a month to influence others to contribute for a new church, even though she knew she could not afford it. God came through. "The Lord has always took care of me" is a virtual litany in her story. Sister Lambert tells of her willingness to let her husband sell the family farm to go into itinerant ministry and travel across country in a trailer. This is one particular instance of utter dependence in her early ministry. This dependence is as much a part of her later years, as well. In her sixties she takes on volunteer work at a telephone contact ministry while living on poverty-level wages.

Often the divine intersects with the women's lives in miraculous ways. Glossolalia is the "ordinary" evidence of God's presence that they all report. Some tell of the incursion of God in their revivals and ministries in ways more stunning than that holy speech. Sister Brown speaks of her own pitifulness in the context of telling how God raised six from death at her revivals—all God's work, never hers. Sister Howard witnesses and participates in miraculous healings—of her own body, as well as of a dying man given up by medicine as hopeless, which was attended by her preacher mother-in-law. Sister Brown intervened in her own sister's brush with death. Given up for dead by doctors, this sister recovered from a gangrenous stomach in the presence of Sister Brown's prayer and trust in the Lord.

The most important idea around the topic of divine presence in their lives is the women's submission to God's will. Submissive, obedient alignment with God's will is the defining theme of their accounts of being called. Their calls come from *God*, and submission to that divine call brings a sense of utter security. As they tell it, nothing in their lives is more sure than their call. For some the call is immediate; for others it is drawn out over months or years. Once they realize it is

God speaking, the women report unwavering self-confidence in their
ministry. To be sure, self-confidence is never the same thing as self-
aggrandizement. It represents total submission to God's will. Only
God can authorize their ministry, according to their tradition. Thus
these Pentecostal women combine utter security in their vocation with
the denial that their will is the source of the call or that they amount to
anything without God's working through them.

The women's denials of self-aggrandizement are elaborated in a
number of stories about the ways they tried to avoid God's call, or
struggled with adverse situations, or even themselves thought women
should not preach. Sister Lambert tells of her feelings of distrust for
women in the pulpit, along with her dislike of masculine women.
With this as introduction, she tells of the paradox of her own acceptance of the call. So reluctant was she to put herself forward, she continues, that she would not accept the call until she received a sign from
God. She got it when a church member came up and volunteered to
Sister Lambert that God had called her to preach, a verbal assurance
confirmed by the electric feeling that passed through her at that
moment. Thus hers was a paradox with a purpose. If someone so
averse to female preachers is now one, she implies, it is clearly God's
will and not her own that is being acted out.

Sister Staples insists, "I wouldn't have chosen this as my profession
had it not been for God. . . . God just sorta pushed me into this."
Sister Murphy had no doubts in 1930 that her call was from God, and
she was unflappable in the face of male criticism and other discourage-
ment. "I said, well my call comes from *God* and I'm going to answer
him as to this." Sister Walker knew the call at once when the spirit
moved upon her in a night service. She testified and received the Holy
Spirit on the same night. In the face of fears that dogged her about
public speaking, her courage and surety came from the Lord's message, "That's the way I'm walking if you want to walk with me."
Sister Miller tells of making many vows never to be a woman
preacher; she told her daughter, "Honey, mother would backslide
before she'd be a woman preacher." It took a broken spine to bring her
to accept her call.[52]

---

[52]Lawless finds this denial of self and submission to God's will consistently in the call
stories of women she interviewed in *Handmaidens of the Lord*. She interprets this as a
limited strategy of freedom from male authority, as I will do in a slightly different way.
My difference from Lawless centers around our interpretations of the seeming contradiction involved. The idea that submission is freedom is puzzling to a folklorist. From a
theological perspective, however, it is a familiar if differently actualized central paradox

The theme of submission to God is told, then, in the first place as the legitimation of a woman's call to preach. It is God who must put his hand on his servant and choose her or him to be God's instrument. So high a calling is the call to preach for Pentecostals that there could be no other utterly trustworthy sign than God's selection. All of the women recount the important initial evidence of God's control in their lives as their first experience of baptism in the Holy Spirit and speaking in tongues.

The theme of submission also occurs in the self-denigrating pattern of speech that many of the women use. For some the self-denigration is largely in the discussion of who is responsible for their ministry; all share the submission language of submitting to God, submitting to the Holy Spirit. Others use more self-deprecating terms. When Sister Brown speaks of her timidity and how God took it away, she frequently adds the comment, "I'm so nothing it's pitiful." This self-denigrating pattern is part of the claim that God is responsible for their success, the souls they save, the power of their preaching. As Sister Murphy puts it, "I'm just a vessel." It is difficult to tell, however, where one kind of discourse stops and the other begins. Sister Brown, herself unschooled, tells of the wisdom she was able to impart to a college-educated young man who tells her she is like "Caleb" for him. She recounts the numbers of churches she built from the ground up, and the dying churches she brought back to life when men preachers had failed. But each narrated event of prowess and success is accompanied by the denial that the speaker is bragging.

The women's submission has another referent besides God. They attest to their submission or obedience to the biblically based construction of the family and male-female relations characteristic of the Pentecostal traditions. All of the women, with one possible exception, accept the biblical injunction for wives to be submissive to their husbands and to the men in the church (Ephesians 5). As they relate their stories of ministering, some for periods up to fifty years, an oft-repeated theme is the insistence that they were always appropriately submissive to the fully ordained male ministers.

Sister Staples puts it bluntly: "I respect man ministers as my superiors. . . . I really believe that women have limitations and I think we as women have an obligation. . . . We have to be more careful than a man. We have to be careful how we dress, how we speak . . . and I have always tried to be that, to do that," including being respectful of

---

of Christian faith. This particular form of it, in my view, simply does not extend the critical edge of refused loyalty to the status quo far enough.

her superiors. This form of submissiveness comes from the argument developed by the Church of God to deal with scriptures about submission, we remember, by interpreting them as prohibitions of women's access to governing authority. Sister Staples demonstrates her compliance by insisting that her entire ministry is under subjection. When pressed about the limits of their ministry by the church constitution, the majority express willingness—even satisfaction in most cases—to abide by the limitations on their functions and the need to be accountable to male overseers.[53]

The combination of subjection to God and subjection to the (male) church expands the field of ideas even further. The themes serve to legitimate publicly the women's faithfulness to biblical order. More creatively, they also use their submission to God to deflect criticism from folks who do not approve of women ministers. In the name of submission, these women stand up to men (or anyone else) who challenge their ministry. In response to a man's criticism about her being a woman preacher, for example, Sister Morse said, "He didn't think I was capable. I wasn't, it was the Lord that makes you capable! It's God that gives you the what to do and how to do and gives you wisdom and understanding, all those things you need. . . . The Lord gave me boldness to answer." Sister Brown says of the critics in the old days, "They just didn't mind telling you to your face. And I'd just preach anyway. And the Lord would always give me a place to preach." In fact, the Lord put her in the best churches he had, she says.

Sister Staples's insistence that she did not choose the profession is her defense against the people who tell her they "don't care for women ministers." In response she says that God is in charge, "and I just go right on, see I don't let it bother me." Some even warn potential husbands about God's prior claim on their lives. Sister Walker tells her future husband, "Now listen, if you just want a cook and housewife, I'm not it. I said, I have a calling. . . . The Lord has called me. And so if I go with you, we got to be partners, we got to be a team, we got to work together."[54]

---

[53]The interviewer asks more than once how the women felt about not being allowed to baptize, perform marriages, preside at the Lord's Supper, perform foot washing, or receive new members. Although one or two express disappointment at some of these exclusions, most insist that they are not bothered and that it is appropriate to be under the authority of the male overseer. One woman surmises that much of the exclusion is related to males feeling threatened by women. She points out that in the early General Assemblies, women could speak. All twelve think that they have plenty of work to do for the Lord without these ordinances.

[54]Lawless tells of the freedom gained by a Pentecostal woman minister in Missouri from her husband, who is not entirely happy with her full-time career. She visits her

The themes of submission and dependence are intricately related to those of self-confidence and pleasure, so much so that they are difficult to distinguish. Self-confidence is expressed in stories of accomplishments, echoing the tone set up by the sagaman-like character of the narratives. Although these accomplishments intersect with assurances that the woman is under submission and not bragging, they are notable all the same.[55] The women travel all over the United States and foreign countries, sometimes without their husbands or families. Sister Walker tells of leaving Tennessee as a young woman and traveling with another young woman to South Dakota, among other places, in the early 1940s. There they did evangelism in a variety of ways. They could not afford transportation, and so they walked to town, where they sang, played guitars, and preached in the street to attract crowds for night-time revivals. Sister Morse did this kind of traveling in Haiti and Brazil; Lucille Turner went with her husband to India for twenty-odd years. A sense of accomplishment and self-confidence is not a topic of focus, but it comes across inevitably as the women relate their travels and constant willingness to go to strange and new places, the starting of churches and renewal of dead ones, interventions in failed medical expertise, and the raising up of the spirit where male clergy had failed.

Not only does the assurance provided by their calls give them permission to do a variety of things, but this self-confidence sometimes breaks out in the form of contradictions with their alleged submission to men. Sister Staples recalls how she presided over a marriage ceremony for a couple who particularly wished for her to perform the rite. This was not a violation of the rules that exclude her from the ordinances, she insists, because "I felt the leading of the Lord."[56] In a discussion of her submission to the overseers, Sister Staples offers a spirited defense of the practice that is most dear to her:

> *Sister Staples*: I don't believe women should just take the lead in men, I never have believed that. I still believe that men, if they're godly men,

---

parishioners, does hospital visiting, preaches, and does all the other things pastors do. Thus she is gone from home for long periods of time. Her husband's incomplete acceptance of this "freedom" takes its toll on her, however. See *Handmaidens of the Lord.*

[55]These exploits fit the picture Clements paints of the "sagaman," a narrative performer adept at relating her own life as a story of prowess. What distinguishes the heroics of the Pentecostal sagaman is that they are attributed to God. See Clements, "The Pentecostal Sagaman."

[56]These are, obviously, not flip decisions for any of the women. With regard to baptizing, Sister Staples insists that "I respect man ministers as my superiors."

are our superiors and I respect them. I do nothing, I don't even counsel with anybody at our church without I first talk with our pastor.

Question: So you feel like your entire ministry is under subjection?

Sister Staples: Except preaching the gospel . . . what I preach; I will not allow anybody to tell me what to preach or how to preach it except God. . . . I will not even get in the pulpit there unless I am allowed to preach what God wants me to preach, or the way I feel to preach!

The freedom granted them by their radical submission is a freedom to rebel when their way is impeded. What is more, it is a freedom claimed without the stigma of rebellion.

Preaching: the pleasure of the spirit

The confidence of these Pentecostal women ministers is focused in a powerful way on the most important practice of their ministry: preaching. In their portrayal of preaching, the theme of confidence spills over into pleasure, for which they offer abundant imagery. That pleasure begins with the experience of speaking in tongues. They have already expressed admiration and desire for the happiness, the joy, the "difference" of Pentecostal communities, the yearning that brought many of them into the community. The outsider's apprehension toward this strange group of "holy rollers" is expressed by many of the women as the source of a curiosity that first drew them to revivals. Curiosity quickly turned to amazement at the happiness: worshipers slapped their hands, "they were dancing in the aisles and shouting and everybody prayed at one time and to me, I didn't know what I had gotten myself into," says Sister Howard of her first exposure. The energy and fervor drew Sister Miller, who attests that "many got happy. They talked in tongues and God was crazy in that service."

The women report intense delight in their experiences of Holy Spirit baptism. Many say it is the most wonderful experience of their lives. Sister Lambert speaks of being raised to her feet laughing with joy. Sister Howard volunteers an extended analogy of hunger satisfied to excess; not merely tongues, but Pentecostal faith in its entirety is "just one long, continuous feast." Sister Staples attests that her first experience of tongues was the most wonderful experience of her life; it came with a vision of Jesus, and the heavenly language poured from her mouth all day long.

A number describe the effect of God's Spirit in their lives as the creation of a hunger that becomes an intensified and permanent desire for more and more of God. Sister Howard says, "I never cease to be hungry for more of God. And I feel that any time I put my feet under his table he'll bless me real good. He feeds me abundantly." Sister Staples receives a "hunger" for the Word of God, and "for the things that I didn't even know about before or wasn't interested in." They know this hunger and pleasure draws other people to them. Speaking of her services, Sister Oxendine says, "It was the real power of the Lord that would just bless us and anoint us with so much of the power of God till people knew it was something that they didn't have. And it made them want it. And they'd say, I want that. Whatever that is, I want it!"

The special experience of pleasure associated with the "sweet Holy Ghost," as Sister Howard puts it, is the power of the Spirit that is given to these women in preaching. That power is called anointing. If anything, it is described with more intense pleasure than the joy of speaking in tongues. Anointing is the sign of their submission to God as evidenced in preaching. Anyone who would preach without it is in a rut, insists Sister Staples. She never gets in the pulpit without the anointing of God. With it, the women say that their preaching is from God and not simply their own words. With the anointing, their preaching is effective and becomes an experience of great joy and power. Says Sister Staples of her anointing, "I lost control and words just came." At a revival, she says, "I always wait a message until the Holy Ghost took over and then we just let the Lord plead for us." When she was anointed, Sister Lambert says, "I felt exuberant, I felt happy, I felt power. And I felt the Lord and the Holy Spirit witness through me."

Power is a word used frequently to describe the pleasure of anointing. Sister Murphy describes that power as a warmth; Sister Staples says that she feels "lifted out of myself." The anointing "is when that Spirit of God comes down on you and you wouldn't care if the house is full of rich people or poor people or who they are," says Sister Brown. "I mean, when you really get anointed with the Spirit of God, you don't pay no attention to what's around you and who's around you."

"There's been times that I just felt like I was going to be raptured," says Sister Staples, so great is the joy she felt. The overtones of sexuality in the discussions of power and desire—of excess, ecstasy, being satisfied, being filled, being overtaken—cannot be missed. The discourses combine the loss of control by women in their rapture and the images of an incessant hunger that is always filled but always recurring. This evokes the sense that God's relationship for the truly blessed is a total, almost erotic bodily event.

The anointing is a way the women understand that God is using them. It is what makes their preaching the living Word of God. The content of that preaching, of course, is scripture. All agree on that. As Sister Howard puts it, "If it's not in the Word, my word's not important. My opinion doesn't amount to anything. It's what 'thus saith the Lord.' " But it is through the anointing of the Spirit that her preaching becomes effective — becomes the Lord's Word and not human words. The manifesting of this power, and therefore the truthfulness of the preaching, is seen in its effects. Not only is it clear to the woman herself that she is anointed — her ecstasy is the sign of that — she must have another sign as well: the congregation's response. As several note, they could usually tell by the congregation "how things were going," as Sister Murphy puts it. Sister Woodard explains that when the Holy Spirit is behind the preaching, "the one who is delivering the message knows it and the one who is listening to the message knows it."[57] In the response of the congregation, her own joy and certainty at receiving the anointing is reflected back to her — a double signification of divine confirmation.

Call stories overlap with testimony

The field variable, the content of a Pentecostal woman's call to ministry, unfolds as a story of lifelong submission and dependence on God. These are stories of hard lives, but lives with intense pleasures in a world filled with God's incursions and guidance — lives of feasting and blessing. They tell of being chosen and responding faithfully to the call. As memorates the narratives are clearly distinguishable from the account a professional might give of her career choice, because they inscribe the individual's life in the divine purposes. They suggest overlap with another genre, as well: testimony.

Stories of call and spiritual journey contain some subgenres that are much like the testimonies found in Pentecostal worship services. There are, in fact, at least three kinds of testimonies: (1) Pentecostal straight testimonies, short accounts of the Lord's good blessing in the believer's life; (2) personal reminiscences that recall what God did in

---

[57]She continues: "The anointing . . . in the message is just further proof and further testimony to the fact that this is the word of the Lord."

the believer's life; and (3) homiletic testimonies.[58] The Pentecostal women's stories include all three. In addition to the small pieces of preaching that emerge in their tales (I will say more about this in a moment), the interviews are focused primarily on the second kind of testimony, personal reminiscences. The women also offer straight testimony all through their interviews as they speak about God's good work in their lives. Several women end their interviews with a striking short, straight testimony. Sister Morse, for example, turns her answer to a question about the church into a closing testimony:

> I feel, you know, very much impressed that we have some of the most wonderful leaders. And of course there may be some hard knocks and there may be some times when it isn't quite so . . . just what we think, but I do believe that the church is still progressing and going. And will be what God would have it be. I'm glad I'm a member of the Church of God and now I can say I'm glad I am a *minister* in the Church of God. I appreciate God's call to me. I love him. He is my faith, he's my help and my guide.[59]

The overlap of call stories with the genre of testimony points to the importance of the mode, a mode shared by both genres. Reminiscent of the earliest call to witness—"Then go quickly and tell his disciples, 'He has been raised from the dead' . . . " (Matt. 28:7)—call and testimony are best suited to the oral mode. The oral mode opens up the possibilities of communication of the good news, the ultimate subject of both genres.[60] In addition to the other-directed nature of these genres, the stories do important work for the teller. They reaffirm the teller's identity in a variety of ways and serve as self-assurances against

---

[58]These three types of testimony are described by folklorist William M. Clements from Pentecostal churches in Arkansas. See his "Public Testimony as Oral Performance: A Study in the Ethnography of Religious Speaking," *Linguistica Biblica: Interdiscziplinaere Zeitschrift für Theologies und Linguistik* 47 (1980): 21–32. See Lawless's analyses of women's testimonies in a Oneness Church, *God's Peculiar People*, 77–109. She discovers the mutual sharing of cares and burdens carried out by women in their testimonies.

[59]Compare this with Clements's examples of straight testimonies in a Pentecostal church in Arkansas: "Truly I love the Lord tonight. And I praise him for all that he does unto me. And I praise him because he saw fit one time to reach down and save my soul and fill me with the Holy Ghost and show me the way. You all just pray for me that I'll always do what God tells me to do." "I thank the Lord tonight for what he means to me. I thank him and praise him for each and everything. God's been awful good to me, and I do praise him for it." Clements, "Public Testimony as Oral Performance," 28–29.

[60]These interview responses were related verbally by the women and were not likely to have been written down beforehand.

a world of critics and doubters.[61] The testimonies recount the women's doubt and suspicion of the world. The women's speech includes reassurances to the listener that they are aware of the fanatical sound of some of the events they recount, particularly the miraculous healings. More than once, the women strike a posture of identification with the incredulous hearer, as if to offer thereby a personal authorization for the truth of their tale: If I, a doubter like you, now believe it, these events must have really happened; this marvelous God who disrupts the natural order must be real!

The combined effect of the oral mode with the content variable is to give these stories an importance that would be missed if they were treated simply as information attained from interviews for a historical archive. Through the stories, the Pentecostal women become sagamen who relate God's heroic exploits through their own deeds. They deploy ideas about their worthlessness and their submission to authorities through themes of victory and remarkable accomplishment. Through the stories, they tell who they are. This is what they do: they speak, they tell, they proclaim whole lives as journeys of struggles overcome. They proclaim God's mighty work at the same time they proclaim the intersection of that divine story with their "ordinary" ones.

Tenor of interpersonal witness

The (implied) hearer is obviously important to a testimony, and so we turn our attention to the tenor of the call stories. The distinctive character of tenor in this genre is found in the relationship with the hearer that the call-spiritual journey stories are meant to evoke. In distinction from the tenor of a didactic genre, these stories create the relation of interpersonal witness: of testifier to potential convert or fellow believer. The call stories are testimonies to what God has done in the women's lives, even as they also offer information. They partake of the dominant oral responsibility of the Pentecostal believer: to convert the hearer.[62] Titon's descriptions of the testimony genre among Appa-

---

[61]Titon observes that testimonies are distinctively identity-forming performances. *Powerhouse for God*, 369.

[62]Clements comments that many ethnographers have found that the Pentecostal (or evangelical) imperative to witness makes for an increased willingness by Pentecostals or evangelical believers to be interviewed by nonbelievers such as folklorists. Clements, "The Pentecostal Sagaman," 177.

lachian independent Baptists apply for these accounts as well.[63] Participating in the goal of all Pentecostal performance, their aim is affect—to move persons to deep emotional experiences. But it is affect with a clear goal, to bring persons to the Lord. As such, a relationship is evoked with the hearer that invites a more complex response than the passive reception of information. It evokes the response of edification or renewal of one's life. The tenor, then, is in part that of a testimony.

The tenor also adds a resonance of the communal character of their faith discourse to the meaning of the stories. The faith of such conservative groups is often interpreted as concerning solitary individual relationships to God. When tenor is recognized as the constitutive part of a situation of utterance and not just the content of the utterance, however, we can see that these speeches are designed for—in fact they require—a respondent. They address the hearer as a fellow traveler, one who can share the joys and assurance of the speaker. Thus they invite the hearer into a mutual reality. As edification they mutually confirm a shared faith; as testimony, they invite rededication or conversion to a communal faith. That nonindividualistic effect will be clearer in the setting of worship, but even as narrated interviews, these discourses invite and require a community, even if only a nascent community of two. (Insofar as the tenor of testimony is less prevalent in more liberal religious communities, their avoidance of individualism must happen in some other way.)

The overlap occurs, then, between testimony and call narrative. It is difficult for some of the women to maintain the sedate didactic tenor appropriate for information-provision throughout the stories. In the midst of recounting how they preach, a number of the women *begin to preach*. They cannot resist the move into telling about what God has done, rather than telling about the process of preparing sermons.[64] Even so, the stories also invoke another tenor than that characteristic of liturgical testimony. Recruited in a project to preserve the memory of the Church of God about its past with women, this discourse is not characterized by the full-blown tenor associated with

---

[63]Titon, *Powerhouse for God*, 192–212; chap. 8, "Testimony and the Conversion Narrative," 359–407; chap. 9, "The Life Story," 408–461. He distinguishes testimony from conversion narratives. The latter are obviously stories about being saved; the former recount what God is doing in people's lives.

[64]The interviewer (a man) is a Church of God minister, and they assume a fellow believer. Several of them react with surprise to his questions about their anointing. They question why he would not know exactly what they mean without elaboration. He has to remind them that he wants more detail for the oral history. One woman questions his credentials; in this sense their stories are related as the kind of sharing believers do.

preaching or worship testimonies. There the mode is more compli-cated than these sedate tellings, and the response expected is at a dif-ferent affective level. As such, the stories are told with more restraint than would be found in the register they most resemble.

The one-on-one telling of a life as intricately managed by God is a form that overlaps with the genre of publicly performed testimony and with the genre of preaching, but is not identical. Having sug-gested the implications of these overlapping functions, I conclude that it is still important for us to distinguish these call stories from all forms of testimony and its tenor, because of the restraint that characterizes them. Because in these cases the hearer is a fellow believer, we might say that as witness the response expected is one of mutual edification.

In order to appreciate the full range of registers possible in these women's practices, then, we must move out of the setting of interper-sonal narration and its restraint. The setting of utterance for Pentecos-tal women's practices, which can only be described in the call stories, directs us to their worship. Public praise of God is the setting where the most powerful registers of Pentecostal women ministers are dis-played. In that service we are drawn into a different setting of utter-ance, one characterized by the wide and transgressive semiotic range of Pentecostal women ministers. The descriptions in the stories are of bodily experiences but they are rendered in an oral mode. As part of a preaching service, where testimony and speaking in tongues accom-pany the message, the mode is bodily as well as oral.

Performing the word

The favorite homiletical topics of these Church of God women min-isters include the cross, salvation, spiritual adultery (Hosea), sin and hell, tithing, and sanctification. Elaine Lawless finds a spectrum of subjects in the sermons of Pentecostal women ministers she inter-viewed in Missouri. They pivot, she says, around two major themes: (1) total submission or sacrifice to the Lord; and (2) concern with re-pentance, salvation, and heaven. She notes the striking appearance of much maternal imagery in the women's discourse, an indication that their commitment to gender complementarity is creatively employed in their development of a distinctive take on the standard doctrinal themes of Pentecostal faith.[65] Rather than examining actual sermons, an exercise beyond the scope of this chapter, I will draw on descrip-

---

[65]Lawless, *Handmaidens of the Lord*, 111–42.

tions of the context of worship to fill out the variables of tenor and
mode, the most striking variables in Pentecostal women's performances.

In call stories, we found a genre that enabled the constitution of
identity. The call stories contributed to the legitimation of the women
preachers' authority as well as reaffirmed their heroic stance over
against the world. The intersection of this discourse with testimony is
not surprising, for the faith posture is an all-encompassing one. The
importance of affect and response connected to testimony, however, is
only hinted at in that setting. When we trace this overlap to Pentecostal women's actual practice, an intensity of both affect and response
contributes to the creation of another level of authority and pleasure.

The services of Pentecostal communities differ among themselves,
to be sure. Scholars who describe independent holiness services, independent Appalachian church services, Church of God services, and independent Baptist services rightly point out the personalizing of these
elements by different churches. Folk rural and mountain churches,
however, share many key elements. What outsiders usually find most
striking in the worship of these communities is the appearance of
spontaneity.

There is order behind the spontaneity, however. A typical order of
service includes greeting rituals, a song service, prayers, testimony
time, special songs, sermon, and altar call.[66] Many more performers
are involved in these events than simply the preacher. People volunteer the hymn choices; prayer services are contributions of the congregation; specials songs are sometimes accompanied by groups or
individuals from the congregation; and testimonies and healings can
be contributions of anyone in the congregation.[67] When women testify
from the congregation, they gain a stage that allows them an almost

---

[66]This comes from Lawless's description of rural Pentecostal church services, *God's
Peculiar People*. See her analysis of the schema of speech acts that make up a worship
service of a Oneness Pentecostal church, ibid., 62–64. Titon describes virtually the same
elements and order, *Powerhouse for God*, 23–57. Lawless says this pattern is characteristic
of most fundamentalist communities. Elaine Lawless, "Tradition and Poetics: Folk Sermons of Women Preachers," in *Comparative Research on Oral Traditions: A Memorial for
Milman Parry*, ed. John Miles Foley (Columbus, Ohio: Slavica Publishers, 1985), 275–
76. For descriptions of similar Appalachian services in Regular, Freewill, and Missionary Baptist churches, see Howard Dorgan, *Giving Glory to God in Appalachia: Worship
Practices of Six Baptist Subdenominations* (Knoxville: Univ. of Tennessee Press, 1987), 55–
85.

[67]This egalitarian participatory mode of worship has a long tradition in the United
States with important roots in camp meetings. I am assuming with Wacker that Pentecostals were not just the poor and down-and-out, but came from the "plain folk" —

unprecedented opportunity for virtuosity. For a skilled laywoman, this virtuosity at testifying can rival the preacher's role. Lawless and Titon underscore the importance of testimony for women, particularly in folk churches that do not allow women to preach. It is the chance for any woman to perform solo.[68]

It is no hyperbole to say that a woman gains a stage when she testifies. The participatory character of much of the service creates a distinctive tenor for the woman's worship discourses. Her testifying and preaching are verbal performances in the categories of the folklorist, not only because they are relatively formulaic and thereby recognizable as Clements's categories suggest, but because they are structured so as to invite and compel responses that will indicate their success.[69] As Sister Woodard and others remarked about their own preaching, the presence of the anointing is made clear by the way the people respond. The desired aim, of course, is to bring believers to the Lord, but there are intermediate signs preceding that moment of conversion. Not only are shouting and ecstatic verbal praise appropriate responses to hearing the Word preached, but responses to a testimony are coveted as well.

A number of possibilities exist for indicating the Spirit-filled nature of a performance: crying, chanting, stomping, clapping, waving of the arms, speaking in tongues, dancing and running around the church. Speaking of the shouting that her preaching elicits, Sister Howard says there have been times when "I wished they'd sort of calm down because I couldn't hardly hear what I was saying." Above all, however, an intensification of emotions is desired, as well as an uninhibited display. She goes on to admit that she really does not mind the uproar, for "if God wants this service for his glory, he wants to use someone else, thank you Lord." These responses are signs that God's blessing is being received in the service, just as the final test of the preacher's performance is in the response to the altar call. All the

---

"the great mass of ante-bellum Southern farmers and townspeople who were neither rich nor starving." See Bruce, *And They All Sang Hallelujah*, note 2, 4.

[68]Titon tells how some independent Baptist women take advantage of this opportunity. *Powerhouse for God*, 359–60. Lawless describes a situation where a male preacher can be virtually challenged by the virtuoso performances of women testifiers. *God's Peculiar People*, 106–9.

[69]Sister Howard is able to spot insincere performers, and tells a story of a woman who got ahead of God, being one of those who "feel like that they're obligated to shout." She would come up to the altar every night to be prayed for and fall out in her sister's arms. After putting up with this performance for a week, Sister Howard told the sister to sit down. She promised the woman that God would be her refuge if she went out again in the Spirit. This time the woman did not fall.

women wish to provide such anointed performances for their fellow
Christians.[70]

The tenor of verbal performance is intense and immediate. It creates a relationship characterized by authority for the woman as she
leads and the congregation follows. This is an authority reinforced
by rich, demonstrative feedback. The language of exhilaration the
women use in their call stories to describe their feeling of anointing is
a good indicator of their powerful experience of speaking in the Spirit.
The vessel imagery and the language of self-denial suggest a paradoxical trope of emptiness that is at the same time, by all indications, true
fullness, feast and ecstasy. The women are aware of the desirability of
their authority. Sister Oxendine speaks about the hunger and desire
that her own anointing stirs up in others:

> It was the real power of the Lord that would just bless us and anoint us
> with so much of the power of God till people knew it was something
> that they didn't have. And it made them want it. And they'd say, I want
> that. Whatever that is, I want it. . . . They said they wanted what we
> had. They wanted to be filled with the Spirit.

Clearly the mode of women preachers' discourse is more complicated in the worship setting than in interpersonal testimony. The
mode is intricately related to the tenor, responsible for the rich sense of
pleasure and authority the woman have. That tenor evokes mutuality
by inviting a response that is almost as intense as the utterance. The
response parallels the performance mode; it is intensely affective and
bodily as well as oral. The mode of worship performance is constituted by personally directed verbal and physical support for members
to evidence their experience of grace and the gifts of the Spirit.[71] The
uninhibited character of the entire Pentecostal folk service is a key to
its difference in mode from more formal mainline Protestant liturgical
traditions.[72] For the women as testifiers and preachers, however, this

---

[70]See Lawless's descriptions, "Tradition and Poetics." On the nature of audience
evaluation for each speech act, and the discourse rules of the different components of the
service, see God's Peculiar People, 62–63, 71. Lawless's work is helpful on the differences
in tone and oral style between women's preaching and testimony. See "Tradition and
Poetics," and " 'I Know If I Don't Stand and Bear My Testimony, I'll Lose It': Modern
Women's Testimonies," Kentucky Folklore Quarterly 30 (1984): 79–96.

[71]Clements describes this mutual support to testify as hard to resist. I agree.

[72]McCauley is the best source for the distinctions between "mountain religion" (Appalachian, mostly independent churches—Old Regular Baptist, Primitive Baptist, Freewill Baptist, holiness, Pentecostal, etc.) and the other denominational versions of these
churches. The autonomy of these churches suggests an important difference between
the possibilities for women preachers in mountain churches and those of Church of God

loss of inhibition takes on special significance. The oral mode of careful, modulated testimony in the call stories is raised in testimony and speaking in tongues to higher decibel levels and to a different kind of speech as well. It is rhythmic, sometimes chanted speech, and a unique form of orality in itself.

Each woman has her own preaching style. A number of the Church of God women ministers say they are emotional and "boisterous"; others describe themselves as "exuberant" but "not a shouter." Preaching mode is distinguishable from other directive speech in the service. A typical preaching style is described by folklorists as chanted and rhythmic, characterized by parallelisms and repetitions. It is not infrequently interrupted with personal addresses. The other distinctive oral mode of the service is speaking in tongues. The musical, rhythmic syllables of glossolalia give it a distinctive mode, not only because of its unintelligibility, but because the pitch is frequently intense and exclamatory. Glossolalia is an exuberant and powerful discourse that is an unmistakable addition to the fervent and joyful noise that is made to the Lord in a Pentecostal service.

The other mode essential to women's performance is the bodily. Movement by the preacher is typically a constant part of preaching. Most of the Church of God women admit they cannot stay behind the pulpit when they preach. The fact that few ever preach from notes is an important support for this freedom of movement. The raising of hands in prayer and the freedom of gesture-making contribute to a motion-filled performance. The practice of praying for the Holy Spirit involves laying of hands on the subject. Prayer for healing includes anointing with oil. In a service it is not unusual for all members to stand with arms uplifted, and for the preacher to come around touching oil on the forehead of each. Inhibitions against touching disappear as well when conversions in the service are followed by all-around hugging.[73]

The movement associated with Spirit-filled utterance adds bodily signifying of another sort. The Spirit-filled nature of their testimony and their preaching even when it does not issue in tongues supports uninhibited use of the body: "I had no control over it," says Sister

---

women ministers who are avowedly submissive to male overseers. Another difference is that the Church of God (Cleveland, Tenn.) is a kind of Pentecostal tradition that considers salvation, sanctification, and baptism of the Holy Spirit to be separate. McCauley argues that sanctification is not a part of the holiness-Pentecostal vocabulary in the mountains. Their order of salvation is conversion/salvation and Holy Spirit baptism. McCauley, "Appalachian Mountain Religion," 391.

[73]Titon, *Powerhouse for God*, 404–7. Dorgan describes the embracing and emotions surrounding communion and foot-washing services. *Giving Glory to God*, 113–52.

Murphy of what she felt at the anointing of the Spirit. The description of "absolute" loss of control, as Sister Murphy puts it, is one of the most frequent concerning the experience of this anointing with the Spirit. If the visible manifestations of the Spirit are the peak of the service, as Lawless says, then it is no surprise that the moment everyone is waiting for is that time in the service when controls are lifted.[74]

Touching and gesturing are increasingly found in other traditions attempting to loosen up a stiff liturgical style. The bodily freedom associated with glossolalia, however, transgresses normal social expectations for bodily restraints. The utterances of the Spirit are frequently accompanied by what Sister Howard calls "dancing in the aisles." They are the correlates to the conviction that "God got crazy" in a service, as another remarked. This holy language expresses itself with bodily significations of joy as well as celebratory tones. Women (and men) run around the room. They display the transformed experience of being "lifted out of myself," as Sister Murphy describes it, with their bodies as well as their voices. This loss of conventional bodily restraint is associated with the baptism of tongues. Sister Staples describes her first baptism as one that went totally against her prideful concern with her appearance. So powerful was the experience that she "cleaned the floor with her new suit" when she was slain in the Spirit.

Biblical practice: "I try to give them Bible, not just what I think"

The intense nature of worship performances, combined with the genre of preaching and the role of the Holy Spirit in these women's self-understandings, results in distinct practices of scripture. These women are mostly educated by life rather than formal schooling, although a number took courses at the Bible Institute. They do not use scholarly commentaries to prepare their sermons; when they use anything other than scripture, they are likely to use church literature. Their primary biblical practices are ordered by prayer, fasting, much time spent reading the Bible, and trust in the Holy Spirit, whose anointing they understand to be essential to the success of their preaching. Sister Woodard's comment was repeated almost to a person: "The Holy Spirit takes over in a way, he bring things to your remembrance that you hadn't really maybe planned to speak in that particular message

---

[74]Lawless, *God's Peculiar People*, 111–12.

but yet it is that that relates to the message. He oftentime takes over your thinking and adds to it." (This, she adds, is a beautiful, wonderful experience.)

In a fashion that parallels their denials of agency throughout their stories, the women do not understand their preaching to be their own word (which, as Sister Howard says, "doesn't amount to anything"). Anointed preaching is God's Word. As Sister Woodard points out, it was the Holy Spirit that inspired the Word of the Lord to be written. The anointing of the Holy Spirit in the message is further testimony to the fact that this is the Word of the Lord.

Such a view of scripture leads to a freedom of performance. It assumes a unity to scripture and its potential as a cipher available to read the world as God's.[75] Scripture is the source for preaching, the source of analogies for lives and events. It is the only authoritative source the women claim for their practice besides the anointing of the Holy Spirit. Scripture is the lens through which healing of bodies occurs. It is scripture whose center is narratives of the work and gifts of the Spirit (Acts, Joel), a center that is smoothly intertextual with the parallel miraculous transformations of the contemporary world, at least in the interpretive practice of these women.[76] This does not mean that they are more biblical than other communities; it does mean that they can appropriate scripture (selectively) with more immediacy than modern communities because the problem of historical distance is not their problem. The answer to any issue is found in scripture. This means that the kinds of issues that are raised are limited, because they are constructed by a particular doctrinal view of Christian faith that is designed to avoid conflict with competing world views.

The women are aware of their low status in the world's eyes because of their lack of education. This consciousness is not debilitating, however. What their communities count as evidence of a good interpretation is not scholarly expertise; it is rather something they are good at: performing for the Lord. Thus they are self-confident and

---

[75]The development of these women's use of scriptural analogy in their own lives would make this chapter overlong. Their stories of miraculous healings fit the tripartite structure of miracle stories that Bultmann finds in the New Testament. This is noted by Clements, "The Pentecostal Sagaman," 188. See Rudolf Bultmann, *Form Criticism: A New Method of New Testament Research*, ed. and trans. Frederick C. Grant (Chicago: Willett, Clark, 1934): 36–39.

[76]Titon describes the independent Baptist community as having an analogical mind for reading scripture. He also views the approach to scripture as one that comes from viewing life "as a potential source of narrative" with biblical analogies. *Powerhouse for God*, 390ff. See also Hymes, "The Grounding of Performance and Text," 138. I imagine this is true of Pentecostal believers who eschew modernist biblical methods.

free in exercising their exegetical skills. In response to a young man who challenged her about the scriptures that counsel women to keep silence, Sister Brown offers an interpretation that assumes some account of Paul's community and the problems it had with loud women. It is not a historical account, but a commonsense explanation, and her pleasure at the young man's respect for her wisdom is evident. It is fair to say that the rules for a good reading of scripture are focused primarily on the preaching and testifying performance.[77] When the women practice the art of praising God and bringing others to God, they excel at reading.

Tenor- and mode-dominant practice: tasting the feast in the here and now

The combination of field, tenor, and mode in the register of preaching and testifying in worship settings creates some important differences from other discourses. In the field variable of their discourse, the authority of the women ministers is highly focused on their dependence on God. This dependence continues to characterize their performance success, inasmuch as every aspect of their leadership of the service, whether as testifier or preacher or tongues-speaker, is legitimated by self-erasure and deference to God's control. The field variable's messages of God's love, of hell, and of moral oughts are not as important in capturing the distinctiveness of their practices, it seems to me, as the effects of the tenor and mode.

As oral practices, an important effect already distinguishes them even before consideration of the other affective aspects of mode and tenor. This effect is related to the different ways that reference works in oral as contrasted with written discourse. Oral discourse relies ultimately on a variety of possibilities for indicating that the reference of the speaker is part of a situation held in common with the hearer. Its reference relies on "monstrations" — a "this," a "that," indications of place and location, "now," "here" — and on the formal signifiers, "we," "I," "you." These indicators in oral discourse are successful when the participants of a situation perceive that situation to be a common one.[78] It is *this* "here" held between "us" of which "I" speak. The possibilities for effecting that shared situation in oral discourse

---

[77]Sermons analyzed by Lawless show patterns of interpretation, such as the use of analogy, typology, chains, and references. See *Handmaidens of the Lord*.

[78]Paul Ricoeur, *Interpretation Theory: Discourse and the Surplus of Meaning* (Fort Worth: Texas Christian Univ. Press, 1976), 34–37. Ricoeur says that references of oral

are increased: a gesture can back up a concrete description. The affect of the speaker, her face, gestures, voice, and exuberance, are all signifiers whose reference is the shared immediate situation of the community.

In written discourse, by contrast, the grounding of reference in the situation is broken; a gap is created between what Paul Ricoeur calls identification and monstration.[79] The definite descriptions—of the goal of God's love, of God's judgment, of Jesus' suffering in written discourse—do not necesarily refer to the reader's situation. The "I" and the "you," the "here" and the "now," are at a remove from the reader's context. This is true even if they are narrated in such a way as to restructure the conditions of a transferable ostensible reference, to make a permanent direct address to the reader's "absolute" experience.[80] The difference between written and oral discourse is the difference between an indirect reference and the ambiguity that is interposed between writing and its target—thus its possibility for endless and creative referring—and the meaning that a speaking face transformed by the joy of the Lord can convey.

This does not mean that oral registers are more successful at communicating an ostensible "real meaning" *because* they are oral. Nor does it eliminate the undecidability that attaches to all discourse. Ambiguity and mixed messages are part of oral reference as well as written. The hearer constructed out of different codes will not receive the message in the same way, notwithstanding oral monstration. The orality of discourse in the face-to-face context simply changes the impact of linguistic signifying when we look at folks who share the codes the women invoke. Ricoeur's point is to indicate that a channeling of reference is characteristic of oral discourse and the possibility for some direct references to be inscribed in immediacy. If the message is one of salvation and hope, the mode is not simply direct impassioned address, but touching and hugging and ecstatic celebratory noise. The reception of signifying processes is accomplished. Whether these significations indicate one's value, or indicate that one's soul is in danger, one is successfully and affectively addressed in the concrete—particularly if one is a Pentecostal believer who is constructed out of the Pentecostal discursive formation.

The tenor and mode of the setting of performance render the effect of oral reference even more significant for women's practices. The

---

language rely on monstrations; that is, they depend on a situation as perceived in common. (Writing shatters the grounding of reference in this common situation.)

[79]Ibid., 35.

[80]Ibid.

tenor of direct face-to-face relationships, set up by preacher to community and between members of the community, creates the possibility of immediate response to a woman's preaching. On the one hand, if the hearers did not share the codes, dissonance in such a setting would be intensified, perhaps beyond tolerance. On the other hand, a sharing of the codes makes for a heightened positive reception. The intensity of the response suggests that when the message is one of love and support, it is a *delivered message* received as such. Lawless points out how the testimonies provide women a way to speak to one another about the difficulties of life, to invoke mutual support through trials.[81]

When a woman is preaching, she frequently personalizes her points by naming persons in the congregation or speaking directly to them. Any possible ambiguity of the referent of oral discourse is lessened considerably when the touch and the name accompany it. The immediacy and situational character of this register are important to understanding the pleasure that accompanies this practice. The woman is confirmed by directly referring monstrations that she has reached and touched her listeners. More broadly, the communal perception that the situation being referred to is one shared—the distinctive feature of oral discourse—could be the discursive condition of a shared perception that the community is one where love and support, as well as judgment and criticism, are tangible realities. This does not guarantee a positive experience; what it underscores when the code is not contested is a *shared* experience, and the possibilities that this shared experience, if positive, might overdetermine the negative. (The obverse of this is, as Lawless points out, that the rearranging of power between genders that may go on in Pentecostal communities is temporary, ending when the service is over.[82])

The practices of Pentecostal women are manifested in a real contradictory discourse: the refusal to claim a will, an expertise, a forwardness, precisely along with the gaining of a place, a presence, an authority. It would be a crucial mistake to ignore that these themes—dependence and submission along with self-denigration, confidence, and pleasure—which appear contradictions in terms as a field variable have their fullness as a register in performance practices. The situational bodily, vocal semiotic alters the meaning of the ideas of dependence and submission considerably. Respect for the register of performance disposes me to conclude this summary of the practices by

---

[81]Lawless, *God's Peculiar People*, 107.
[82]Ibid., 77–109.

according respect to Sister Woodard's comment. When asked about her sense of exclusion in light of the church's practices and scripture's denigrating women, she states, "Well, I never felt that that meant that we were put down." Similarly, Sister Staples denies a sense of exclusion: "The only thing I just want [is] to be able to be free to preach the gospel and win souls. These other things, they're not important to me."

Assessing women's performances as a regime of resistance

The agenda here is not to make Pentecostal women feminists. They simply are not, if feminism is defined in terms of particular ideas. But if our interest is the effects of women's practices in relation to the pertinent discursive formation and the several subject positions it offers, then the practices of Pentecostal women merit another look. Typical assessments of the feminist possibilities in Pentecostal women's situation tend either to grant the ostensible egalitarianism in early Pentecostal practice an idealized status, or to emphasize the unliberated character of their situation given the obeisance to male authority that characterizes their posture toward the limitations on their ordination status.[83] By considering the intertextual relation of their practices with both their subject positions with regard to patriarchal capitalism and the canonical system out of which they produce themselves, I think more can be said.

Two dynamics have emerged in the Pentecostal canonical system from which the constraints and posibilities for something like gender discourse in Pentecostalism can be seen to arise. The first is the reliance on the empowering presence of God as Holy Spirit in human practice. The second is the inclusion in that canon of the belief that the entire

---

[83]Blumhofer thinks a more sobering assessment is needed for the situation for Assemblies of God women than offered by the Scanzoni-Setta and Hardesty estimations. See Blumhofer, *The Assemblies of God: A Chapter in the Story*, 1:355–72. See Scanzoni and Setta, "Women in Evangelical, Holiness, and Pentecostal Traditions," 223–65; Nancy A. Hardesty, Lucille Sider Dayton, and Donald W. Dayton, "Women in the Holiness Movement: Feminism in the Evangelical Tradition," in *Women of Spirit*, ed. Eleanor McLaughlin (New York: Simon & Schuster, 1979): 226–54. Lawless admits to moving from her initial approach that assumed this was a radically egalitarian community, to a view that assumed it was hopelessly patriarchal, then to a middle position. *God's Peculiar People*, 110–12. Susan Kwilecki finds "nonfeminist" gender views in her interviews with fifty-three Pentecostal women ministers. Kwilecki, "Contemporary Pentecostal Clergywomen: Female Christian Leadership, Old Style," *Journal of Feminist Studies in Religion* 3:2 (Fall 1987): 57–75.

scripture is inspired and available for use as literal prescriptions. This
second dynamic is a constraint on the radical possibilities of the first.
The dynamic aspect of authority does not impart to Pentecostal communities an "anything-goes" experiential religion of excess. The Bible
is unified by its Holy Spirit authorship. Whether the literalism practiced is fundamentalist matters little, for the doctrinal rigidity of the
community puts considerable control on the dynamism of its oral
notion of authority. When one scholar says that the closest Pentecostals come to inerrancy is in preaching, we must either assume that
these biblical literalisms are inscribed in the preacher or allow that this
flexibility is constrained by the granting of identity between certain
texts and God's will.[84] These two dynamics rule out a radical Spirit-
authorized women's regime of reading. At the same time, they open
up possibilities beyond the use of inspired prohibitions such as we find
in other kinds of fundamentalism or in the Princeton theology–
inspired position of Presbyterians.

Given these canonical constraints, Pentecostal women display considerable, distinctive performative power. We see that first in their
preaching, their prophetic status. Public speaking was for a long time
the forbidden territory for women of mainline denominations. Associations of women with the private and domestic sphere and the pro-
hibition of women from the sacred have been strong and long-lived
forces in mainline Protestant denominations. By contrast, the early
openness of Pentecostalism to women is attested to by the extraordinary range of activities in which women engaged as they exercised the
privilege of proclamation. Women founded two Pentecostal denominations, the Apostolic Faith and the International Church of the Foursquare Gospel. Women were traveling evangelists and missionaries;
they preached, taught, founded churches, led revivals, wrote tracts
and literature. Underlying this broad expanse of terrain for their witness is the privilege of "speaking" for God. Dress restrictions do indicate that some danger is attributed to women's bodies in the
Pentecostal system, but they are not evidence of the misogyny or dis-

---

[84]Although there is a difference of opinion over the nuance, some contend that Pentecostals have resisted the modernism of evangelical fundamentalism (the NEA) in important ways. Despite Wacker's persuasive and vigorous argument that Pentecostals
were as literalist and fundamentalist about biblical texts as any non-Pentecostal fundamentalist, the primary way in which women have negotiated space for themselves has
been in relationship to the dynamic canon of the Spirit-possessed performance. Thus,
depending on which group of scholars one takes to be correct, women will prove to be
either more transgressive (if Wacker is correct) or to have taken advantage of an early
dynamism that was essential to their system.

dain that disqualifies the female body as a public signifier of the holy.[85] As tongues-speakers and preachers, women are on public display; they are vessels for the divine.

Considering the nature and status of preaching, it is no small admission that the canon acknowledges women's public performing as holy speech. My first observation is that women ministers' practices are congruent with a canonical system that relies on the empowering, actual presence of God as Holy Spirit in human practice. Although this is discursive repetition of the system rather than resistance, the practice of liturgical performance signifies a status granted women that is belied by their conservative gender discourse. In communities where women's preaching practices still occur, the centrality of oral performance and aural reception makes women's access to this register doubly significant.[86] First, the doctrinal valorizing of speaking, whether in testimony, glossolalia, or biblical preaching, means that a Spirit-filled believer is understood to be a vessel for God's Word.[87] Second, this register is significant because oral tradition is a primary institutional form for this particular social location—rural or mountain folk churches. Thus, despite their exclusion from governance, these women preachers pass on the religious practice and thereby qualify as official transmitters of the faith.

Reading regime: peculiarity as resistance

Pentecostal women's practices include a combination of call stories and performance genres for which the mode is the most striking variable. Although these practices comply with the system's rules for reading, they constitute a reading regime that stretches women's potential for claiming and benefiting from the status of the ministry. First, their community is characterized by rules for reading that are famous for their openness on the question of who can read. The

---

[85]Sister Staples: "I really believe that women have limitations and I think we as women have an obligation, we have to be more careful than a man. We have to be careful how we dress, how we speak. . . . " But this same woman relates how she "cleaned the floor" with her new suit at her first tongues experience. This is a complex view of the public display of the female body, it seems to me. See Lawless, *God's Peculiar People*, 82–83.

[86]I make this qualification because of the drop in numbers of women ministers since the 1960s and the move of many Pentecostals into the lower-middle to middle class, which I believe is related to the moderating of the affective aspect of the services. Roof and McKinney, *American Mainline Religion*, 107–117.

[87]Byrd, "Paul Ricoeur's Hermeneutical Theory," 1.

answer is not gendered, nor is it limited to "the professional"—the academically trained. This canonical system opens up the qualifications for authoritative reading. The authoritative subject position is available to the spiritually reborn, the Spirit-baptized. This is the significant difference between Pentecostalism and the mainline denominations, with the exception of the United Church of Christ. None of the mainstream denominations ordained women in the first decades of the twentieth century; all had gendered rules for reading.

Second, the Pentecostal set of rules removed class restrictions as well. An important feature of the rules for reading was the avoidance of critical disciplines that were taught in mainstream educational institutions. This feature distinguishes this regime from the modernist versions of the shift that appear in Presbyterian reading regimes. The Pentecostal women practiced their craft with "precritical" notions of authority that relied on the charismatic character of Pentecostal experiences and interpretations of authority. For the communities of women I have portrayed, the rules for reading did not include historical-critical interpretation and did not require that official interpreters be educated in middle-class ways. The gap between biblical times and now was not taken as a historical gap but a spiritual one, and the spiritually fit were optimally qualified to interpret the Bible and to probe for its "deeper" meaning. Thus both the authority of the women's subject position and their self-confidence were reinforced by their ability to preach and interpret scripture and be lauded as experts. The knowledge that they were nobody in the eyes of the educated world was no barrier in the face of the God who provided the Words to those willing to spend hours in earnest fasting and prayer.

The intertextual relation of women's practices with the Pentecostal canonical system is also indicated in the contradictory nature of the discourse. This contradiction, presented in their self-denigrating dependence language, comes from the aspect of the canon that construed scripture as containing divine constraints on women. Thus biblically ordered submission to male authority constructs a subject position of female *place* for these women. This canonical discourse of place is not displayed as an honoring of women, a romanticizing of the female nature or the domestic, but is defined by exclusion from governance. It is a place the women accept gladly, and we hear about this submission in their practices of self-denigration, which are part of their attributing to God all that they do. They are eager to assure the audience that they keep their proper place, that they do not do things without the authority of the male overseer. For a few, this even includes denials that they are unfeminine.

The discursive genre of the call story has an intertextual relation with the canon and with the contemporary culture in more ways than simply as a reinforcement of women's submission. When viewed as intertextual with the antiwoman discourse of their community, the self-denigrating practices of Pentecostal women can be read as resisting registers. In this discourse of submission and dependence, paradoxically, they construct a place of honor outside the home for themselves. They legitimate their authority even when men oppose them. The women are sagamen or heroes not only because they tell of God's victorious exploits through their lives, but because these stories get them out of their traditional roles.[88]

The field of discourse against which these call stories get their meaning is not just the theological ideas of Pentecostalism. The lingering challenges to the status of the register these women have appropriated are also invoked. In other words, the stories as a genre are intertextual with the restrictive view on women's place. To have a call story is to respond to the pieces of the Pentecostal canonical system that subordinate women. To have a call story is to resist criticism by claiming the ultimate authority for one's practices—God. It is also, as Lawless says, to "rescript" one's life in a radical way. It is to craft a calling that allows a woman the freedom to travel and lead and to be the object of holy envy, to perform and know that others want what she has. This self-scripting is very different from these women's own comments that women's place is to take care of the children and husbands in the home, as passive and meek homebodies who keep silent and powerless.[89]

The affective performances of preaching and testifying display this contradiction as well. The same woman who insists that women have limitations ("We have to be more careful than a man. We have to be careful how we dress, how we speak . . . ") is the one who says she "cleaned the floor" with her new suit when she spoke in tongues for the first time. The affective transgressions that occur with their performance, from such uninhibited bodily display to the way in which

---

[88]This does not mean there is no valorizing of the domestic among the female in these communities. It simply does not appear in the women ministers' self-descriptions. Lawless develops the theme of the value of the feminine-domestic from the sermon themes she identifies in *Handmaidens of the Lord*.

[89]Lawless writes of the reaction to her accounts of this freedom by one of the women she interviewed. Sister Anna decidedly did not understand it the way Lawless did. Thus it is important to reiterate that this is a *reading* of their discourse, not their self-understanding. Lawless, " 'I was afraid someone like you . . . an outsider . . . would misunderstand': Negotiating Interpretive Differences Between Ethnographers and Subjects," *Journal of American Folklore* 105 (1992): 307–9.

women testifiers can take control of a service even when the preacher is a man, signify excesses that belie their descriptions of humility and submission. The vocabulary of self-denigration is, then, not the language of self-hatred. It is the language of one's true identity, an identity that is a powerful one for these women.

These stories of Pentecostal women's call to ministry are "rescriptings" that depend on intertextual relations not only with their conservative communities' place for them, but also with the world's estimation of them. In addition to the double referential target of their practices—the canonical system, its continued constraints on them—the women's discourse must be read in relation to the processes of the social formation they resist. The field of cultural discourse disdains rural, farm, and mountain folk of their social class and educational level. The subject position occupied by the majority of the Church of God women has been working-class or lower-middle-class. All but one came from families described as poor. The dependence constructed for women in these locations is not the same as that of Presbyterian Women, whose subject positions were dependent and vulnerable but privileged economically. For these Pentecostal women, dependence impacts the construction of access to the means of survival and well-being.

Out of the various ways that patriarchal capitalism idealizes and reproduces dependence as female, the subject positions constructed for these women are not focused on the idealization of a personality structure, although that image is there. Nor is it found primarily in an eroticized physical image or an ideal of beauty—the subject position for a woman with more income at her disposal. This latter kind of dependence, even if they could afford it as an ideal, is ruled out on the basis of Pentecostalism's moral rigorism. The ethos of Pentecostal communities would support the assumption that women should be economically dependent in the mode of idealized domesticity, but these communities cannot afford for women to stay home. Although poor and working-class women are subjected to discourses that construct the homemaker's dependence similar to that which characterized Presbyterian Women, their dependence is more likely to have to do with access to means of survival.

These Pentecostal women are near the bottom of the economic ladder, where the processes of the entire social formation work to undermine access to goods and services, from education, health care, and public dignity, to political participation. Even when they are not poor but lower-middle-class, capitalism reproduces dependence in the form of lower-paying service jobs or part-time employment. Although these women do not relate situations of abject poverty, their livelihoods as preachers were scanty at best. Sometimes they lived on church contributions. Several refer to fill-in jobs in factories, offices, or at the local discount store.[90]

The significant intersection of capitalist patriarchal sign systems on these women's reality occurs with the continued effects of public-private spheres, definitions of gender, and the force of gender contructions on job training and access. But more particularly, the social formation intersects with their lives in the role of their own class situation to keep them outside of access to education and power. Consequently the discursive process of capitalist patriarchy constructs subject positions of nonpersonhood for Pentecostal women both in relation to socioeconomic and cultural power and because they are considered members of a fringe population of religious fanatics.

The intertext of these women's practices with such a socioeconomic situation would seem to construct oppression-liberation issues as survival issues. Such a diagnosis is complicated, however, by their canonical system and its posture toward the world. They do not identify their needs as physical or as desires for goods and services and rights. Their stance toward the "things of the world" is informed by the expectation of rapture and the related moral rigorism required to be rapture-ready.[91] As Sister Howard puts it, they are a community of the different: "We are separate." They volunteer no discourse about lusting after worldly goods or power. This separateness means that God will give them everything they need. The muted text in these stories is how difficult it has been to get by without assured food supplies (a difficulty sometimes signified by a reference to the temptations of the devil).[92] The clearest affirmation, however, is that God gives what they need: salvation, sanctification, the indwelling of the Holy Ghost, the interpretation of tongues, healing for the body. "Everything I needed" was provided, as Sister Howard says; "I found a full table. It was bountifully spread."

---

[90]Most of the Church of God women ministers do not mention their husbands' occupations unless they were itinerant evangelists with their wives or ministers who moved with them in overseas missions or from church to church in the United States. Lawless's interviewees had husbands who worked in the marble quarries or whose occupations were not named. Their status was working class at best. *God's Peculiar People, Handmaidens of the Lord.*

[91]Sister Staples says of poverty in Brazil that she knows that just saying "Jesus loves you" is not enough for children who are hungry and need clothes. But the goal is to allow "God to make them see that God is the source and to depend on him."

[92]One story comes closest to describing a period of great uncertainty with regard to basic needs of food and shelter. This is related by way of a vision from Satan that urged Sister Lambert to break the moral codes of her faith flagrantly so that she could better testify to forgiveness and grace.

In light of the scarcity of goods and power, the speeches about pleasure and feasting and fullness are worthy of remark. The world's constructions of these women as fanatics (a view to which they all allude), the disdain society has for them (of which they are aware), and the socioeconomic difficulties of their lives are texts to which their self-denigrating discourses signify. As a Pentecostal historian remarks of the prominence of "I am nobody" discourse, this is true language, "this is who we were—nobody."[93] Intertextual practice with this world-disdain is discourse of their value. The "world" as the social text for these women offers no sustenance. The self-denigrating dependence language is, paradoxically speaking, language about their value. This discourse is, then, where the strain in their oppression is a signification. It is the contradictory route traced out of biblical texts that wrests a flow of nourishment. This self-denigrating discourse is a graf(ph)t on biblical texts that are nourishing not by virtue of an offer of language about the goodness of femaleness, nor by valorizing their identity as women, but insofar as they inscribe the women as vessels of God.

The form the women's discourse takes in relation to their low status in society is constructed by their cohesiveness as a marginal community much more than by any commonalities they might seem to have with other women. They understand themselves as "a peculiar people," as Sister Howard puts it, who are called by God to resist the worldly accommodation to the devil. This subject position entails a bond with the men of the community. That identity of separateness means that we must read their self-empowering practices as graf(ph)ts which route away from the sustenance that might come from a subject position of social success, but which route around discourses of egalitarian gender relationships as well.

Graf(ph)ts out of patriarchal tradition

Pentecostal women are nourished by refusal of the world's estimation of them, and thus their resistance is not aimed at patriarchy's estimation. But it is a nourishment that is erotic (in the sense that being fulfilled bodily is erotic) and pleasurable to (controlled) excess. Sister Howard, whose elaboration of the joy of this life is an extended de-

---

[93]Comment of historian David Roebuck, Church of God School of Theology, Cleveland, Tenn., January 1992.

scription of feasting and fullness, goes on to explain what it means to be "peculiar":[94]

> When God saves our soul, he doesn't take us out of the world, he takes
> the world out of us. By that I mean, he separates us from the sinful
> things of the world. He helps us to find joy in the things that before
> didn't appeal to us at all. And things that once delighted us—I've never
> danced since God saved my soul. I'd leave the dining table to dance. I
> loved to dance! And I never seen any harm in it. The only time I ever
> dance now is when the Holy Ghost orders it.

That means that the women's practices which occupy and expand an authoritative place, their pleasure-filled performances, are signifying processes that resist modern secular hedonist society's assessment of them.[95] But they stretch and resist the patriarchal household envisioned by their own community at the same time.

If, then, these women's practices repeat but resist the canonical system, if they also resist the sinful society's contruction of them as marginal and crazy, Pentecostal women are neither utterly oppressed by patriarchal arrangements, nor have they resisted in completely successful ways. Furthermore, they have not identified gender as a problem. As always, their practices can be identified from a feminist theological position as displays of the sinful constraints and limitations of their religious tradition and their social location when we look at their linkages to power and desire. I have argued that the contradictions of a discourse are indications of socially reproduced finitude and the possibilities for sin and its constraints/denials. Thus, even the possibilities for pleasure and celebration of their goodness signify places where desire and pleasure have been rerouted by gender oppression and overdetermined by other social processes—where they produce graf(ph)ts out of patriarchal biblical traditions. Their "oppression" is overdetermined, not simply by religious traditions that grant asymmetrical gender status to participants, but by the hardships of life and

---

[94]Lawless uses this expression for the title of one of her books, *God's Peculiar People*.

[95]Titon is adamant that these communities should not be reductively explained by their social location. "I have argued throughout this book that religion at the Fellowship Independent Baptist Church is not a compensation for powerlessness and poverty, but that it involves the deliberate use of inherited traditions to make life meaningful." *Powerhouse for God*, 448. I do not disagree with him. As a theologian, however, I assume that every religious tradition's practices involve compensation, if that means they entail the denials and idolatries that come with human finitude and its display as social sin. As a folklorist, he reads "compensation" as a functional explanatory category, and I do not.

the outsider status of their class and religious practice. Their liberating practices are found in the cracks where discourses of self-worth can be forged and where new lines of life-giving flow can still be found on an old plant, the Pentecostal system.

The personalizing and acceptance of patriarchal capitalism by the women is a form of domination accomplished by means of the discourses of their religious community and the channeling of desires that it affords. Interestingly, the channeling of pleasure allows for them to be co-opted into their own oppression and to display otherwise nonacceptable female behavior. Their participation in the restrictions on women's dress—no sleeveless dresses, no short haircuts, no pants or low-cut attire—implicates them in a moralistic victim-blaming posture toward women. They do blame other women for inciting lust by their dress. As Sister Howard says, "Dress modestly, not expose my body, as I was taught that's what causes lust of the flesh so many times. And divorces and heartaches. Women bring a lot of things on themselves." These Pentecostal women are disciplined—not by endless beauty routines, but by the need to cover the body and diminish its garish and colorful decoration. They are constructed into subjects who reproduce women's self-policing of their own bodies. The pleasures of being good women, of pleasing the Lord, reinforce this self-subjection.

At the same time, even this form of discipline includes a refusal of another form of patriarchal domination: the eroticization of women's bodies. While it cannot be claimed as a new feminist "style of the flesh" enlistable to resist the patriarchal feminization of bodies directly, it is still a refusal of an oppressive patriarchal disciplinary technique that dehumanizes women and endangers them. Given these contradictions, it would be misleading to read Pentecostal women as simply effaced as bodily agents or to read them as disciplinarians themselves. Their behavior is not completely controlled by ideals for domesticated femininity or commodified female sexuality.[96] Their worship behavior is neither constrained, passive, and demure, nor is it modulated, quiet, or even intelligible (by modern standards). Their acceptance of dress codes comes with their powerful gifts of

---

[96]Sandra Bartky is right to identify the role of beauty regimes that discipline female bodies. As far as I know, however, the subject of Christian or religious postures toward this form of oppression is not tapped by her or anyone else. The fact that other forms of male dominance accepted by such women may dampen the "feminist" character of this refusal does not invalidate it as a refusal. Sandra Lee Bartky, "Foucault, Femininity, and the Modernization of Patriarchal Power," in *Feminism and Foucault: Reflections on Resistance*, ed. Irene Diamond and Lee Quinby (Boston: Northeastern Univ. Press, 1988).

performance—the development of expertise at uninhibited bodily practices that God authorizes. The idealization of dependence as female is somehow altered in their practices, in that they do not comply with the standard stereotypes of women's body control, posturing, and bodily restraint. The transgressions of worship practice, particularly its bodily and oral modes, are temporary, perhaps, but they *are* countersignifying processes to the compliant femininity the women espouse. They are countersignifying processes to the demure, dependent, eroticized body that feminists also resist.[97]

There is pleasure and self-respect in these women's practices. I read their language of self-denigration as only partly signifying a subject position shaped by gender oppression. It would not be accurate to discount the fullness of their pleasure, particularly with regard to the places of authority their reading regime has constructed. It is not a regime for which gender resistance is a theme, nor is it a regime dominated by feminist registers. The subject position of Pentecostal women who are part of rural and mountain communities in economically distressed areas is a part of consideration of their practice. When we read their practices as overdetermined, as constructed out of a social order that minimizes their socioeconomic worth and gives them no status at best, and brands them as religious fanatics at worst, then the target of their practices seems to be the world estimation more than their gendered status in their own communities. Even then, they are not able to challenge the larger processes of society and the unity of their various commodifications. Although their practices refuse the "modern world" in a way that converges with some feminist interests, they refuse a directly political character to their faith.

Their regime, however, displays the important gospel effects that spirit-focused uses of Christian tradition can create, the richly affective transgressions that spirit-authorized Christian practices can support, and the importance of face-to-face tenor and oral mode for women's sense of well-being. The effects of their discourse are found in their oral and performed character, the power of referentiality of an immediate situation, and the support that oral referentiality delivers for persons in an ongoing set of relationships. It is a regime that constructs grace for these women outside the accommodating pressures of more affluent contemporary life that will never offer them recognition. No matter; part of the grace of their peculiar practice seems to be that they

---

[97]Lawless speaks of the threat males sometimes feel when women perform to excess. *God's Peculiar People*, chap. 4, 77–109. I. M. Lewis discusses the "veiled protest" that these kinds of women's practices entail. *Ecstatic Religion: A Study of Shamanism and Spirit Possession*, 2d ed. (New York: Routledge, 1982).

do not want that recognition. They would not read the ingenious re-placement of subject-language with subject-effacement as evidence of their lack of worth. As Sister Lambert puts it with stark elegance: "God knows who I am."[98]

The Father-God: oppressor or author of freedom?

Pentecostal women's practices do nothing to challenge the reproduc-tion of complementary binary genders where the very being of one gender is a dependence characterized by the features of commodifica-tion. I do not mean to underestimate the oppressive character of dis-course of submission in a social formation where violence against women is part of the commodification of eroticized dependence. I wish to close my reading, therefore, by considering the multiple sig-nifying possibilities of Pentecostal language of self-denigration and Father-God dependence. Even if I am correct that the situation refused by their targets of dependence language can as easily be the derogatory subject position constructed by the social formation, this does not erase the ambiguous, negative work such discourse can do. The dis-course of submission is not simply to God, but to husbands as well. The semiotic interchange between the signs for God and male head of household are indisputable. My argument has focused on the overde-termined nature of signifying and its muting effects on the communi-cation of certain possible meanings of gendered discourse. One of the most prominent oppressive outcomes of such discourse is the willing-ness of women to stay in battering situations. Women's willingness to be battered is often linked to the kind of ecclesiastically supported lan-guages of submission that appear in Pentecostal women's stories.

The subject of wife-battering did not come up in the interviews with these women. The undecidability of this discourse of depen-dence, however, is suggested by the testimony of another Pentecostal woman, whose poetry of joyous dependence opened this chapter. For

---

[98]It would be romanticizing to suggest that their communities avoid the oppressive cultural processes of commodification. At least in the persistent semi-isolation of some folk churches, however, perhaps some of these processes are avoided. By definition, a commodity is something that has been removed from the social relations and context of its use. We would expect the effect of such a process on gender to be the commodifica-tion of women's bodies, of beauty, of personal relations, of the women's movement itself. The removal of an entity from its context of use and social relations is an invita-tion for exploitation, the denial of ambiguity, of corporate relationships, of change, of death, the refusal of finitude, tragedy, and complexity. The ways folk churches have avoided these forms of commodification would be an interesting subject to pursue.

Clady Johnson, whose life has been spent in the coal-mining mountains of Virginia and whose self-denigrating language mirrors the discourse of Pentecostal women ministers, the convergence of Holy
Spirit guidance and God's intimate involvement in her every life situation are threads in an existence lived in subjection to a man who
abused her for fourteen years. Reliance on the Holy Spirit's leading,
and her complete trust in the Father, however, are the discourses of her
escape, and cannot be neatly separated out as the oppressive patriarchal
discourse that kept her submissive. Her testimony to her worthiness is
a discovery that God is there always to pick her up; it is never a discovery that she can do it on her own: "The Lord gave me the words
an' He give me the song."[99]

The testimony of empowerment is one in which her conviction is
that certain promises of this Father God are more powerful than anything 1 Timothy or Ephesians says about submission. "God promises
He will never leave us or forsake us," insists Sister Johnson. In response to the biblical passages that preachers use to silence women,
she insists that she fears God, not men. And if that God called her
to preach, nothing would stop her. Sister Johnson understands the
dominating attitudes of some mountain men in her area to be cultural—"the type of thinking—men either keeps a woman pregnant or
bare-footed so she can't get out." Biblical calls to submission and dependence, which she values in her own relationship to God, are not
appropriate in many cases: "What if your husband is a drunk, a dope
addict? How you gonna ask that husband and get the true answer?" It
is God the Father upon whom she totally depends, whatever the situation, not men. It is this God who concurs with her own self-preservation.

Telling of years of abuse living with an alcoholic spouse, Sister
Johnson assesses the impact of a husband who "led me to think that I
wasn't capable of doin' hardly anything. And after you been told that
for so many years, then you get to believin' it yourself." Yet her discourses of Pentecostal belief in God's intensely personal guidance in
her life and her move to work in a community ministry produce resistance. Sister Johnson's construction of the good news of the Bible
converges with her common sense. This self-described uneducated
woman with her "survival or commonsense kind" of education comes
to some dramatic conclusions. When her husband, the father of her
four children, had shot at her and the children, had cussed and beat her

---

[99]The song and events related here come from my tape-recorded interviews with
Clady Johnson, Trammel, Va., November 1991. Recounted with her permission.

and locked her out of the house, she decided to get out. "The whole side of my face was numb from where he hit me—I said, why are you taking this? You know, God put us here and we supposed to turn the other cheek, but we're not supposed to sit down and let people kill us." She got a restraining order against him and was awarded custody of her children.

The graf(ph)t of this social location with its hardships produces a text where 3 John 2 has more significance than Ephesians 5: "God wants us to prosper and be in good health," Sister Johnson says. The graf(ph)t of life in a devastated coal-mining town on an intense relationship with the Holy Spirit produces a text about a God who "never leaves us or forsakes us," a God who "lives inside our bodies" and "has dried our teary eyes." A subject position constructed out of forces that make survival an issue is graf(ph)ted onto religious discourse of a God who gives us the words and the strength. A life whose subject position is fragmented by forces that convinced Sister Johnson that she was not worth anything produces poetry and song that she knows offer blessings to others. These convergences graf(ph)t nourishment out of thin soil and produce a song of praise where, as Clady Johnson says,

> Without your love, Holy Father,
> There is no other way.

This is a faith that speaks of receiving everything, but is anything but passive.

6
Chapter

Christianity as Patriarchy: Discourses of Parody and Politicization

> Holy One, Thy Kingdom come, Thy will done on earth. All shall sit under their own vines and fig trees and none shall be afraid. The lion will lay down with the lamb and the little child will lead them. A new thing is revealed; the woman will encompass the warrior. Thou shalt not hurt, thou shalt not kill in all my holy mountain. The Shalom of the Holy; the disclosure of the gracious Shekinah; Divine Wisdom; the empowering Matrix; She, in whom we live and move and have our being—She comes; She is here.
>
> —Rosemary Radford Ruether

The investigation of women's biblical practices brings me back to the matter of feminist liberation theology. From an argument about what feminist theology cannot be (namely, reflection of women's experience), I come full circle to think again of feminist theology itself on the terms of discourse theory. My intention is not merely to offer a language theory to address differences between women's faith practices, but to develop further the capacity of feminist theology to analyze its own embeddedness in the distortions of patriarchal capitalism. Discourse analysis helps in this latter purpose.

An intertextual reading of feminist theology

This chapter treats feminist theologies as practices in much the same way that the previous two chapters treated Presbyterian Women's literature and Pentecostal women's performances as practices. In it I offer a reading of two examples of feminist theology as an academic regime that is both intertextual with and resists a canonical system. I will explore Rosemary Radford Ruether's *Sexism and God-Talk* and Mary Daly's *Beyond God the Father*, no longer reading them as (unsuccessful) expressions of universal woman's liberationist intuition, but as discursive practices that have distinctive meaning effects, intertextualities, and targets of resistance. By doing so, I will highlight the constraints, pleasures, and possibilities of academic feminism as a subject position.

Unlike the women's practices I have considered, feminist theologies are explicitly about the complicity of Christian theology, its traditions, authorities, and the practices of its communities in the oppression of women. Feminist theologies not only identify this complicity, they also speak of the goodness of woman, her agency, her capacities for creativity. They call for transformations of the hierarchical gender relationships that are rooted in the deconstructive effects of the idolatry of maleness. Feminist critical judgments are ordered by the feminist vision of the good society, of the kingdom or realm of God as one in which right relation to God entails a communal subject, a world social order constituted by relations of mutuality rather than domination.

This summing up of the ideas in feminist theology does not go far enough if our concern is to investigate the issues and conditions of different discourses in relation to different constructions of "woman." We must identify register, intertext, and canonical system to help locate these ideas in practices lodged in the social formation so as to focus their targets and limitations. Feminist commitments are shaped by their situation of utterance as are the ideas of Presbyterian or Pentecostal women. Thus my first inquiry is with regard to the dominant genre or register of feminist theology. Feminist theology is written in a variety of ways, from women's stories to topical or thematic essays. It also takes place in consciousness-raising processes in such communities as WATER (Women's Alliance for Theology, Ethics, and Ritual), change-oriented women's communities, and as liturgical practices of women's spirituality. For the purposes of identifying the intertextal relationship of feminist theology with its academic communities of discourse, I will treat feminist theology as written texts, the dominant practice of the academy as these (if not their authors) are presently (and lamentably) separated from feminist activism.

Of these texts, the most useful with which to focus on academic feminist discourse are those feminist theologies that employ the form of much traditional theologizing: systematic thinking. Two works by the founding mothers of feminist theology that are exemplary in this regard are Mary Daly's *Beyond God the Father* and Rosemary Radford

Ruether's *Sexism and God-Talk*. Not only have they been ground-
breaking feminist theological texts, but they provide the intersection
of feminist practice with those firmly embedded in academic/church
theological institutions that will allow me to return to the question:
How can feminist theology be a liberation theology that acknowledges and addresses its location?

Field dominance of feminist theology

Feminist theology is distinguishable from the discourses of Presbyterian and Pentecostal women not only because it is overtly feminist,
but because it is self-consciously theology. Although this is an obvious
distinction, the implications of the difference between producing theology and producing practices of self-world transformation or worship performance are hardly trivial, as the remainder of the chapter
will show. Theology is a field-dominant genre. That is, it is a discourse type in which the most prominent feature is a domain of meaning, a subject matter and its articulation as ideas. When field is the
dominant variable in a genre, its communicated meanings are automatically different from, for example, a genre where tenor (the power
relations between partipants) or mode of a discourse is its characteristic variable.

These distinctions are in some ways artificial. It is possible for more
than one of the variables to characterize a genre. The contrast, however, is helpful. Highlighting the field dominance of feminist theology
reminds us that theological discourse has affinities with such discourses as the field-dominant genres of science or the professional
jargon of law or medicine. What identify this genre to the outsider are
its ideas or subject matter, particularly its jargon-laden presentation of
that subject matter.[1] Feminist theology is a field-dominant register because it is about the ideas of Christian theology, conceived as a scientia
of "divine things."[2]

Although not unconnected to the language of the layperson, theological discourse (like medicine and law) contains a set of ideas and a

---

[1]John Frow, *Marxism and Literary History* (Oxford: Basil Blackwell), 69–71. To be
identified as a field-dominant genre, theological discourse might be characterized as creating a certain kind of tenor: authoritative ideas rendered to an audience of readers. It is
constituted in the written linguistic mode. Although the mode and tenor are not incon-
sequential, they will merit our attention later in the analysis.

[2]This term comes from Edward Farley, *Theologia: The Fragmentation and Unity of
Theological Education* (Philadelphia: Fortress Press, 1983).

vocabulary that are restricted to a professional elite. As such, feminist theology is a genre relative to a particular situation or institution. (Some genres, like political debate, are not tied to particular settings; others, such as investitures or liturgy, are.)[3] Its texts are part of a practice carried out in the setting where knowledge is produced and appropriated for the training of those who attend institutions of higher learning. Like legal or medical jargon, theology exists in some important relation to the professional practices for which the production of knowledge is ordered, but is not the same thing as those practices.

As a field-dominant genre, feminist theology is associated with the academy, which means that it helps define the nature of knowledge in a setting characterized by professionalization. This is so whether theology is officially part of the education of those who are training for Christian ministry or is incorporated into the general enculturation process of liberal arts training. Theological discourse is associated with "experts" and with the structures that legitimate experts in the late twentieth-century social formation. Those structures encompass the accrediting, degree-granting educational institutions and church bureaucracies for denominational authorization of theological education.[4] As an academic and professional discourse, feminist theology is distinct from the other women's discourses because it constitutes (or intersects with) official cultural writings and is granted an authoritative status in the institutions of academy and church.[5] It is, in short, a practice charged not only with the task of disseminating knowledge in an official capacity—educating persons—but with authorizing and producing it as well. This fact embeds it in power in certain distinctive ways, as I shall discuss. Even though feminist writings are marginal

---

[3]Some would argue that the reflective life of the faithful also constitutes theology. There is, though, a significant difference between a form of reflection that is institutionally validated and that of individual persons.

[4]Frow, *Marxism and Literary History*, 70–71.

[5]The culture out of which it is produced is a professional one, whether we locate feminist theology in divinity school, seminary, or religious studies program, because the culture of professionalism includes the university and any accredited institution of higher education. This culture is identified by the creation of services/expertise and their channeling by means of monopolies of competence. Education provides the monopolies. This will be further discussed later. See Burton J. Bledstein, *The Culture of Professionalism: The Middle Class and the Development of Higher Education in America* (New York: W. W. Norton & Co., 1976). While divinity was one of the original three professions in the United States, its fate as a profession is somewhat different from the more directly market-defined professions by the late nineteenth century. Many of the features of professionalization still apply to it, however, because of the necessary role of the university. Larson notes the role of the church bureaucracies as paralleling some of the monopolistic credentialing processes. Margali Sarfatti Larson, *The Rise of Professionalism: A Sociological Analysis* (Berkeley: Univ. of California Press, 1977), 121–22.

and contesting writings in that official realm of production and authorization, they are still part of it—part of the practice of defining what counts as true in the knowledges of Christian and secular cultural worlds.

Feminist theological writings are *certifying discourses* for the academy and church. This means they are "socially endowed with the authority required to establish the 'reality' or 'unreality' of the designatum of each item introduced in their lexicon."[6] This establishing force does not serve, of course, to create the reality of God or things divine such that to acknowledge this requires reduction of theology to such functions. Rather it defines the boundaries of the thinkable, allowable designata of that discussion. Certifying discourses, then, are those discourses and the institutional forms to which they are graf(ph)ted that define what can count as true about these matters and the limits of these discussions. This means that, even when feminist theologies claim to be about women or the social situation, one of their primary subject matters is other certifying discourses—the academic practices of the institutions and, most explicitly, other texts.

As certifying discourses, feminist theologies have an intertextual relation to a canonical system, namely, theology as an academic discipline.[7] That system differs from the faith traditions that constitute religious communities, such as Pentecostal or Presbyterian canons, both of which incorporate rules for liturgical and ethical practice into rules for reading scripture. Theology proper—systematic theology, or theology as a field in the contemporary system of theological (seminary and divinity) education—is not strictly speaking subsumable under the notion "readings of scripture." It is still decipherable by means of my categories of intertextuality, reading regime, and canonical system, however. Its rules are simply configured differently than those that are ordered around reading scripture. If we follow through with these categories in examining the graf(ph)tedness of feminist ideas

---

[6]Communities of faith and their ecclesiastical boards and agencies contribute to this construction of knowledge. If these institutions substitute in some ways for the monopolies created by market-driven professions, however, their role in producing knowledge is indirect. The primary impulse in production is still the academic setting. It is true that theology is read in a number of settings, not all of which are academic institutions. Again, however, the kind of learning that goes on in the latter is channeled more specifically by institutions (of accrediting, credentialing, etc.).

[7]It is akin to the certifying work of a geographical atlas, which one consults to discover what is a "real place." Didier Coste, *Narrative as Communication*, vol. 64 in *Theory and History of Literature* (Minneapolis: Univ. of Minnesota Press, 1989), 98–100. We should note that Daly's *Beyond God the Father* did not function for her as a certifying discourse in her own institution.

with social relations and their possibilities and limitations, some of the contradictions that can be openings for change will appear.

Canonical system: certifying theos-logos

Of the many possibile ways to define systematic theology as a canonical system, the salient features for feminist theology are those that characterize critical modern or revisionist theology. Revisionist theological positions are found in the work of such inheritors of the Tillichian modern theological legacy as Schubert Ogden, Edward Farley, and David Tracy, who provided the contrast with feminist theologians' work in chapter 1. Although the positions feminists challenge cannot be restricted either to these particular theologians or to critical modernist theology as such, the theoretic practices of these contemporary thinkers provide a striking intertext for the feminist challenge. As always, the canonical system is not simply identical with the ideas put forth by such theologies, or with theology as texts, but includes the discursive formation of power in which critical modern theology is validated as knowledge. It will be treated in this way.

Modern theology, broadly speaking, is the attempt to articulate Christian faith in response to the challenges of Enlightenment versions of certifying discourse in the modern university. Prominent among these, the Kantian shift to the subject rendered the classic metaphysical claims of theology problematic for the modern theologian. With the addition of the notion of "critical" to "modern," theologians indicate that after Sigmund Freud, Karl Marx, and Friedrich Nietzsche, the "subject" is a problematic ground for claims as well. For the critical modernist, the norms of modernity cannot be uncritically embraced by the theologian, even as he/she cannot return to the premodern faith world. David Tracy has called this postmodern project postliberal, or critical correlationist theology. Edward Farley calls it critical theology.[8] A number of its features can be drawn from representative theologians Tracy, Farley, and Ogden.[9]

---

[8]David Tracy, *Blessed Rage for Order: The New Pluralism in Theology* (New York: Seabury Press, 1975), 32–42. See Edward Farley's defense of critical modernism in "The Presbyterian Heritage as Modernism: Reaffirming a Forgotten Past in Hard Times," in *The Presbyterian Predicament: Six Perspectives*, ed. Milton J. Coalter, John M. Mulder, Louis B. Weeks (Louisville: Westminster/John Knox Pess, 1990), 49–66. The critique of the "House of Authority" represents critical modernism. See Farley's *Ecclesial Reflection: An Anatomy of a Theological Method* (Philadelphia: Fortress Press, 1982), 3–170.

[9]Were I to develop further connections, I would need to identify theologians according to the distinctions *liberal* and *postliberal*. One can also speak of responses to the prob-

Critical modern theology continues a set of practices that has long governed the theological enterprise, even as it alters them. Theology has long appropriated the concerns found in the Anselmian claim that it is *"faith* seeking understanding." This formula often assumes the rootedness of Christian theological reflection in historical particularity—the faith of Israel, the life, death, and resurrection of Jesus of Nazareth, and witness to these events. It is a knowledge of "divine things," understood to have the character of gift; the one who strives to understand is already in the posture of faith. For the development of this witness as a theological task that involves the pursuit of authorized/certifying knowledge, this dictum stands for the ancient sense in which the scientia of theology encompasses both a habitus of knowledge that transforms the knower and a rigorous pursuit of reality as such.[10]

In its genuine noetic aspects, scientia requires the ordered, disciplined appropriation of content. It is content in the forms of the authoritative scriptures and traditions of the church, but it also includes the systematic relating of the themes of these literatures, a practice begun as early as Justin Martyr's use of logos to order the literature of Christian faith. In addition, that disciplined pursuit of knowledge occurs as scrutiny of reality as such, whether through the Neoplatonic metaphysic of an Origen or the Aristotelian causality of a Thomas Aquinas.[11] Theology orders itself by means of a witness and knowl-

---

lematizing of modernism in terms of the recuperative reactionary postmodernism associated with such figures as George Lindbeck and Alasdair MacIntyre, and some other form of postmodernism (employing poststructuralism, for example) illustrated by deconstructionist a/theologies, of which Mark C. Taylor is the best known. See also Kevin Hart, *Trespass of the Sign: Deconstruction, Theology and Philosophy* (Cambridge: Cambridge Univ. Press, 1989). Wesley A. Kort's *Bound to Differ: The Dynamics of Theological Discourses* (University Park: Pennsylvania State Univ. Press, 1992) is the best, most succinct proposal of the constructive stakes of postmodernism for theological discourse.

[10]This account draws from Edward Farley's work on the history of the concept of theology or "theologia." He identifies it as a form of scientia or episteme—true knowledge, an organized body of knowledge, and deliberate inquiry producing it. Theologia can be a habit of the soul, "a history of the church's claim that faith facilitates an individual cognitive act," and "a history of interpretation (inquiry, argument, scholarship) in the church." Farley, *Theologia: The Fragmentation and Unity of Theological Education* (Philadelphia: Fortress Press, 1983).

[11]Theology, or theologia, has taken two forms in the history of the church from the twelfth century to the Enlightenment. The first, *scientia* (the Latin for Aristotle's *episteme*) is a transformative sapiential wisdom, the understanding that this knowledge-seeking is inseparable from the process of salvation itself. The second is an increasingly developed version of the rigorous pursuit of knowledge through interpretation and attention to methods. Insofar as the telos of knowledge shaped the knower in such a formulation, theologia was a habit of the soul, an understanding best nurtured by

edge of content, as transformative habitus, rigorous intellection, systematizing—all general determinants of its boundaries.[12]

These traditional theological concerns do make an appearance in the work of critical modernist theology. These theologies concede that a primary source of the content of theological reflection is to be found in the Christian community's memory of its founding, a memory that expands from interpretations closest to those saving events to include those that span its entire history, namely, scripture and other traditions. Theological content is found as a set of interstructured meanings, as well; theology is, for these thinkers, still a systematic mode of relating central topics in that tradition. Schubert Ogden defines Christian theology as a "fully reflective understanding of the Christian witness of faith as decisive for human existence." The temporal vector of this process is rooted in the past, for theology reflects upon faith as a given, the Christian witness as found in the events of the origins of Christianity. Ogden calls this given the "datum discourse," and its texts and traditions are brought to bear on the contemporary situation of human existence. Of the two poles to which theological reflection must be adequate, faithfulness to the datum discourse fulfills criteria of "appropriateness," whereby theological judgments explicate the content of Christian witness.[13]

It is in the historical-ideal moment of theological portraiture that Farley directly appropriates the content of the historic tradition. That appropriation is a judgment regarding the (ideal) essence of social existence that is ecclesial or redemptive Christian life. This dimension incorporates into the theological enterprise the memory of Christian origins through its canonical and postcanonical traditions as an essential aspect to the discernment of God's contemporary mode of redemptive presence.[14] Likewise, Tracy insists that theology's task is not

---

Augustinian and monastic orders. This is clearly a much abbreviated account of the number of theological concerns—dogmatic, apologetic, exegetical, and so on. I have also ignored distinctions between fundamental or foundational and positive theology.

[12]Systematic theology, or theological writings that include a set of theological loci or doctrinal topics, is a result of the fundamental relationships between theology (God), Christology, anthropology, ecclesiology, and eschatology. Even though we may understand by these themes a discourse found in particular theological texts, these are subjects that are dispersed throughout the other theological disciplines as well.

[13]According to Ogden, "appropriate" means that a theological statement "represents the same understanding of faith as is expressed in the 'datum discourse' of the Christian witness." The other pole, "understandability," means that a claim "meets the relevant conditions of meaning and truth universally established with human existence." Schubert M. Ogden, "What Is Theology?" *Journal of Religion* 52 (1972), 25–26.

[14]The first two dimensions of ecclesial reflection are most fully developed in Farley's *Ecclesial Reflection*, 193–216, 301–320.

only "philosophical reflection upon the meanings present in common human experience," but "the meanings present in the Christian tradition" as well. Theology is thus required to explicate Christian texts, and, furthermore, to be accountable to "the Christian fact."[15]

These traditional features of the theological task appear, then, but with a critical modern twist. The dimension of tradition, or the Christian fact, and its content undergo the scrutiny of critical consciousness. This marker of theological discourse is an aspect of scientia that takes the theologian outside the bounds of tradition. Although the practice of rigorous critical scientia is not peculiar to modern or postmodern theological reflection, what is distinct about this form of critical consciousness is that theological postures toward the givens of the faith are taken up "outside of the House of Authority." Edward Farley's phrase, the collapse of the "House of Authority" is a metaphor widely accepted by such theologians to represent a critical theological posture toward the founding events and toward formerly absolutized forms of access to those events. This posture includes the contextualizing force of historical consciousness on the traditional authorities (scripture, doctrine, tradition). It permanently disrupts versions of the theological task that depend on mimesis of Christian authorities. Its critical scrutiny courts a scientia threatening to the faith conceived as divine deposits of revelation.

The critical posture accounts for the fact that theological reflection is multidimensional reflection for these theologians. This is distinct from either the Calvinist systematic deliverances of scripture, or a Thomistic articulation of the relation between the truths of revelation and those of natural reason. For Ogden, theology refers to a unifying rubric that can be broken down into a three-dimensional process. These three dimensions come from three disciplines—historical, systematic, and practical—each of which provides criteria for making particular claims. In Farley's work, theology is constituted by three dimensions of ecclesial reflection: portraiture, ecclesial universals, and praxis or situatedness. Tracy also divides up subdisciplinary moments of theological reflection, including the fundamental task, the systematic, and the practical. While not all the various tasks are the product of critical modernists, their linkages to the criteriology of a multiplicity of publics and human sciences are.

---

[15]See Tracy's succinct definitions in *Blessed Rage for Order*, 34. His longer definition of revisionist or critical correlationist theology: "the dramatic confrontation, the mutual illuminations and corrections, the possible basic reconciliation between the principal values, cognitive claims, and existential faiths of both a reinterpreted post-modern consciousness and a reinterpreted Christianity." Ibid., 32.

Done outside the House of Authority, contemporary Christian theology assumes a modern world characterized by what Jürgen Habermas calls the autonomy of spheres—scientific, moral, and aesthetic. Theology of this type also mandates that reflection be negotiated in part with criteriology beholden to these disparate spheres of knowledge.[16] Although such knowledges are subject to criticism, they are necessary to theology's understandability. Ogden, for example, requires that theology be subject to the "relevant conditions of meaning and truth universally established with human existence." David Tracy's version of this critical posture is a focus on publicness, a more complex explication of criteria for meaningfulness and truth. Contemporary theological reflection, he says, must reject the privatism that characterizes theologies which avoid attention to shared criteria for meaning and truth that Christians have with other publics. Tracy's concern is that the many and conflicting criteriological worlds with which theology has to do be acknowledged and that criteria for adequacy be addressed by the theologian for the three dominant publics (church, academy, and society) to which she/he is accountable.[17] "Publics" are spheres defined by "criteria of adequacy, . . . evidence, warrants, backing," according to Tracy—a construction of knowledge modeled on Stephen Toulmin's image of reason as argument. Although Tracy's later work portrays the work of theology as conversation rather than argument, the need for warranting does not disappear.

In short, a distinguishing feature of critical modern theology is its focus on epistemological projects. One of theology's key dilemmas on Ogden's terms is legitimating "its right to exist" in the face of modern critical reason. Tracy identifies that concern as the "crisis of cognitive claims." Attention to the crisis focuses these theologians' writings on the negotiation of criteria of intelligibility from historical disciplines

---

[16]Jürgen Habermas, *Knowledge and Human Interest* (Boston: Beacon Press, 1971); *Legitimation Crisis* (Boston: Beacon Press, 1975).

[17]Ogden, "What Is Theology?" 25. *Publicness* is a term that belongs to a model for thinking about theological reflection as structured by rational argument on the model of Stephen Toulmin's elaboration of the structures of argument (although not with the naive notion of reason attributed to the Enlightenment). Tracy defines it as "the search for criteria of adequacy, the demand for evidence, warrants, backing (in a word, for publicness)." David Tracy, *The Analogical Imagination: Christian Theology and the Culture of Pluralism* (New York: Crossroad, 1986), 18, 1–46. Tracy specifically rejects the model of argument as the adequate rubric for theology, however. Rather it is a subcategory under the more capacious model of "conversation." See *Plurality and Ambiguity: Hermeneutics, Religion, Hope* (San Francisco: Harper & Row, 1987). See Tracy's short, succinct version of the role of publics in the various subdivisions of theology in David Tracy and John B. Cobb, *Talking about God: Doing Theology in the Context of Modern Pluralism* (New York: Seabury Press, 1983), 1–16.

brought to bear on the founding events of the faith, from social sciences as brought to bear on readings of the contemporary situation, and on the problem of defining such a multiply warranted thing as theology as a practice in its own right.[18] Critical modern theologies are thus characterized not simply by historical consciousness, or even ideology critique, but most of all by a compulsion to attend to the publics that are accepting of science and secular disciplines because these publics and their knowledges are perceived not only as sources of knowledge that Christians must appropriate, but as potential and actual challenges to traditional forms of Christian belief.

A critical realist posture

Underlying this concern with public criteria is a critical realist posture that presents theological claims as credible intellectual pursuits committed to some understanding of the way things really are.[19] Insofar as saying something true (in the trivial sense) characterizes all discourse, the important feature of this realist posture—where it goes beyond that trivial sense—is seen in the appeal to ideal knowers. The critical modernist is not content to say with poststructuralism that reality is constituted through discourses, a comment that I have maintained is not identical with the claim that reality has no existence outside of our signifying practices. Instead, this kind of theologian commends a certain form of access to objects, one that ostensibly transcends the locatedness of discourse by being universally available under certain conditions. That access is a subject position for which the conditions include (particularly for Tracy) the qualifier "reasonable" and which bears a status of truth that appears fundamental to the theologians' ca-

---

[18]One of the epistemological battles is the continued lack of consensus on the legitimacy of theology—for instance, in religious studies departments. Detractors contrast its confessional character with the "objectivity" of a phenomenological or history-of-religions approach. The articulation of the faith discourse of a particular community as a subject with academic credibility is still contested.

[19]Farley has always carefully qualified the character of "universal." It is not a static thing or an anthropological a priori. Edward Farley, *Good and Evil: Interpreting a Human Condition* (Minneapolis: Fortress Press, 1990), xviii. Not only is the ecclesial universal a structure modified by the determinacies of Christian faith, but the universal structures of "reality" that access "how the world is" are intersubjective, not "global or worldwide." *Ecclesial Reflection*, 305–7. More recently, he defends the ontological project in the form of reflective ontology, acknowledging its unpopularity, in response to liberationist and postmodernist criticisms. *Good and Evil*, 1–26. David Tracy connects the publicness of theological discourse with analogical languages, a position I find quite promising. See Analogical Imagination.

pacity to certify — to vouch for the reality-defining categories of his/her own writing.

This is so, not because these theologians are unwitting proponents of an unlocated Cartesian rationality, but because universal conditions of access are the prerequisite for devising criteria that qualify as legitimate warrants for claims. True judgments come from references to "what is the case," whether in fact or in structure, says Farley. Even though this "as suchness" is not granted permanence, it concerns a claim regarding " 'how the world is,' in its as-such or universal availability," a condition that must be fulfillable for this dimension of theological reflection to be of any use.[20] In Ogden's terms, fulfilling criteria of understandability means that a statement "meets the relevant conditions of meaning and truth universally established with human existence."[21] For such criteria to exist there must be a correlate subject position of (hypothetical) universality.

Tracy's version of this critical realism requires the notion of theoretical publicness in order to conceive of theology at all. While publics differ, their importance is to provide the ideal of shared criteria of adequacy to legitimate forms of reflection. It is this lack that prevents theology (along with psychology, anthropology, and religious studies) from becoming a "compact discipline." Because it does not have an organized public ideal community that will accept the same standards of evidence, warrant, and backing, theology lacks the credibility of those disciplines that do.[22] When theology has such a public, it is populated by the "ideal reader" or adjudicator of theological claims (in the public of the academy), namely, the "reasonable, thoughtful person." The subject position under which such "is the caseness" becomes available is one that will be altered by the other dimensions of theolo-

---

[20]Farley, *Ecclesial Reflection*, 306. The distinctions Farley makes between the different dimensions and moments in theological judgment are too complex to go into. My quarrel is not with his observation that all knowledge is abstraction and that continuities have to be claimed. My quarrel is with his failure to pursue the implications of admitting that the subject position of abstractions is part of knowledge. Poststructuralism does not simply imply that he cannot forge transient "universals" but calls him to account for the meaning effects of his own discourse. Thus he misses the target when he criticizes liberationists and poststructuralists for making use of the noetic moves he thinks they criticize. Farley, *Good and Evil*, 1–26.

[21]Ogden, "What Is Theology," 35.

[22]Tracy, *Analogical Imagination*, 14–21. Tracy identifies Nygren, Ebeling, Pannenberg, Ogden, Harvey, Kung, Kaufman, Gilkey, and Metz as theologians dealing with the public character of theology. Moreover, he claims that "despite some confused disclaimers to the contrary, all theologians are in fact involved in publicness." Ibid., 16, 20. Tracy's recent work is sympathetic to a Habermasian sense of public.

gia, each of which has its own criteria of adequacy, but is capable of being theorized outside of them.

Again, these theologies are not naively modern, invoking an acontextual or asituational theological knowledge. In addition to the hallmark of intellectual honesty characterizing this tradition of theological thinking, Sharon Welch notes its adeptness at explorations of "the disparity between the limitations of their categories of knowing and the richness of their subject."[23] In response to liberation theologies, these theologians acknowledge the impact of power, fallibility, and human locatedness on theological reflection. They are not, however, taken with poststructuralist challenges to representation or to humanism; or, in the case of Tracy, they appropriate them into support for plurality and the project of rediscovering "the contingency and ambiguity of history and society."[24]

Failing to pursue the implications of the poststructuralist claim that discourse produces meaning effects, they are unable to problematize their own writing other than to note its fallibility. Instead their attention is directed to defining theological reflection without the special pleading of traditional (and postliberal) theologies, which attempt to avoid the criteria of modernity. However transient its criteria, one *can* articulate reality critically—link arms with other disciplines—they argue, without losing the specificity of faith.

Although less explicitly addressed in critical modern theologies, the other of the two classic ends of theologia, the transformation of the knower, is shaped by the focus on rigorous intellectual pursuit of reality. These theologians are reluctant simply to reassert an unmediated soteriological relation of the individual soul to God. No strict parallel exists, however, between notions of Enlightenment rationality and these theological proposals, which take their challenge in large part from the call to divest modernity of its corrupt versions of instrumen-

---

[23]Although she is appreciative of these theologians (a group in which she includes Gordon Kaufman, Langdon Gilkey, and Van Harvey, in addition to Farley, Tracy, and Ogden), Sharon Welch shows vital connections between this kind of theological sensibility and cynical despair. She even notes that Tracy has come to recognize that the "crisis of cognitive claims" is overshadowed by that of the global realities of massive suffering. He still refuses to reduce theology to the latter, and argues that truth has disclosive aspects as well as transformative, thus requiring the attention to criteria, warrants, cognitive legitimating. See Sharon D. Welch, *A Feminist Ethic of Risk* (Minneapolis: Fortress Press, 1990), 103–122.

[24]Tracy, *Plurality and Ambiguity*, 65. Both Tracy and Farley respond to some forms of poststructuralism, but dismiss it (Farley) and domesticate it (Tracy) too easily. Tracy, *Pluralism and Ambiguity*, 52–65; Farley, *Good and Evil*, 18–26. See Terrence W. Tilley's review of *Good and Evil* on this subject in *Theology Today* 48:4 (January 1992): 485–88.

tal reason. Although they do want redeemed reflection of some sort, it is difficult to figure out its critical modern form.

Farley speaks of the redemptive transformation of social spaces as the telos of ecclesial reflection, portraying a characteristic interest in the need to incorporate social structures in contemporary notions of redemption. His ideal is a habitus, a form of wisdom that accompanies theologia, but it is clearer that habitus is cognitive insight than that it is salvific.[25] Critical modern theologies seem best at refusing the neutral ideal of reason that funds the research model of knowledge and at expressing concern for a fuller account of theologia. Given, however, their interest in cognitive crises, it is not surprising that they have less to say about how criteria of intelligibility can be rooted in transformed communities of "knowers."[26] The possibilities of construing a transformed character (or subject position) as essential to the producer of theology and her context are not part of discussions about the pursuit or conditions of theological knowledge.[27]

The focus of theological knowledge on epistemological issues and the legitimating tasks of reflection sets the parameters of knowledge in certain ways. Although it is not simply the pursuit of scientia as demonstrative undertaking that concerns these theologies, their primary form of that pursuit is the development and integration of criteria of rational intelligibility. This means that the salvific dimension of theologia is present in relation to the epistemological issues — that is, in the form of a set of refusals. Theology is never reducible to some other knowledge; and even though it requires their input, theological reflec-

---

[25]Craig Dykstra notes that Farley moves from defining habitus as "a state and disposition of the soul which has the character of knowledge" in *Theologia* to a more cognitively focused definition, "the reflectively procured insight and understanding which encounter with a specific religious faith evokes" in *The Fragility of Knowledge*. See Dykstra, "Reconceiving Practice," in *Shifting Boundaries: Contextual Approaches to the Structure of Theological Education*, ed. Barbara G. Wheeler and Edward Farley (Louisville: Westminster/John Knox Press, 1991), 64–65, note 27.

[26]One casualty of modernity, already noted, is the conviction that the character of the knower is inseparable from knowledge, as Timothy Reiss put it. Endangered by the model of reflection for which the telescope is a primary trope for methodology, the various ahistorical Cartesian and Kantian construals of the consciousness solidified this objective/unlocated subject. Reasoned reflection, like the telescope, is understood to provide sure access to the reality it would describe. See David H. Kelsey, *Between Athens and Berlin: The Theological Education Debate* (Grand Rapids, Mich.: Eerdmans, 1993).

[27]The idea that there would be moral conditions for the producers of theological knowledge is not discussed. Nor is it typical to find discussion of the etiological role of the theologian in the production of knowledge or his/her construction out of the institution that produces theology, except in some marginal discussions about whether a theologian has to be a believer. An exception is Mark Kline Taylor, who insists on the social location of the theologian. Tracy talks about accountability to the publics of church, academy, and society, but that is not the same thing.

tion is not legitimated by other disciplines. A prominent way to indicate that theology is something for which the purpose is other than worldly wisdom is recognition of its fallibility and alteration by location, exemplified by Farley's theocentric principle ("theonomous criticism") for all knowledge.[28] Such a principle shapes the parameters of Tracy's identification of the mode of knowing: fallible, plural, and ambiguous conversation.

The inscribing of the soteriological dimension of theologia as various forms of theocentric fallibility is not yet displayed in the attention to knowledge/power relations that pertain to a knowledge-producing institution, nor does it dissuade these theologians from appeals to standards of intelligibility.[29] In summing up the constructive posture toward theologia as salvific knowledge, we might say that the notion that some interplay of inquiries which rigorously interrogate dimensions of reality must occur is linked with the insistence that a self-critical Christian vision needs to order those knowledges. Despite the formal attribution of fallibility to their own work, their failure to pursue the discursive effects of their epistemological projects suggests that these theologians operate with representational notions of their own discourse.

The place of liberation specifics in this vision is rather formal. Critical modern theologians are convinced of the continued vital character of the cognitive crisis. They also consider the liberationists and theorists of knowledge/power connections as important, noncontradictory further embellishments of this task, not as substitutes or alternatives to it. The "crisis of cognitive claims," as Tracy puts it, however more complex as a result of the challenges of liberation thinkers ("the crisis of ethical claims") cannot be replaced by the latter.[30] Theoretically the features of the certifying character of theological discourse—what counts as "real" on its terms—include criteria of intelligibility brought to bear on both its traditional content and the

---

[28]Farley, *The Fragility of Knowledge*, 21–23. Milbank is the only theologian of whom I am aware who attempts to alter other "disciplines" with an encompassing narrative from ecclesiology. See John Milbank, *Theology and Social Theory: Beyond Secular Reason* (Cambridge, Mass.: Basil Blackwell, 1990). Farley's notion of the ecclesial universal is a claim about such alteration, but he has not developed the idea that the church is a social theory.

[29]Tracy's books continue to be about the fallible character of theological conversation, but his analysis never looks at the practice itself. *Plurality and Ambiguity* comes as close as any I have seen to calling for certain changes; he even mentions the knowledge/power dimension of academics in passing. See *Plurality and Ambiguity*, 61–62.

[30]Tracy insists on this repeatedly. See *The Analogical Imagination*, 21, note 74; 41, 69–79. Farley refuses the reduction of theological claims to pragmatic or political ones. See *Ecclesial Reflection*, xviii–xix.

transformative character of this knowledge. The latter noetic practice is accountable to (relatively formal) concerns of social liberation as well.

As a consequence, there is a remarkable capaciousness, a stretching of boundaries in critical modern theologies. It is paradigmatically displayed by Tracy's commitments. He positions theological conversation such that its cognitive tasks are challenged and corrected by the voices of the oppressed. At the same time, he aspires that theology approximate what he calls a "compact discipline," characterized not only by collective goals, from which demands, discipline-defined "reasons," and professional forums are correlated, but from which "criteria of adequacy" for judging arguments are determined. This aspiration is a response to the two lacunae that make theology a "loose discipline"—lack of disciplinary direction and cohesive professional forums, with the resulting lack of a "clear set of criteria" for adjudicating arguments.[31] Inasmuch as the goal is supporting a community with shared criteria of adequacy, or at least basic shared assumptions with some shared criteria, such a wide casting of the net would seem to imperil any hope of compactness. Tracy's publics include not only academy and church, but (implicitly) the oppressed. This discipline would be populated not simply by the ideal "all reasonable persons" and what they would recognize as reasonable, but by the criteria shared by ordinary Christians and what he conceives as the plaints of the marginal as well. It is an ambitiously conceived project befitting the very notion of critical modern theology.

A summary of the features of critical modern theology suggests a canonical system with the following components. Theology is a form of reflection that serves to unify the knowledges that make up the study of God (logos-theos). That knowledge is rooted in the content

---

[31]These definitions of a discipline come from Toulmin: (1) The activities involved are organized around and directed toward a specific and realistic set of agreed collective ideals. (2) These collective ideals impose corresponding demands on all who commit themselves to the professional pursuit of the activities concerned. (3) The resulting discussions provide disciplinary loci for the production of "reasons," in the context of justificatory arguments whose function is to show how far procedural innovations measure up to these collective demands, and so improve the current repertory of concepts of techniques. (4) For this purpose professional forums are developed, within which recognized "reason-producing" procedures are employed to justify the collective acceptance of novel procedures. (5) Finally, the same collective ideals determine the criteria of adequacy by appeal to which the arguments produced in support of those innovations are judged. Tracy thinks the two important "divergences (applicable to . . . psychology, sociology, anthropology . . . religious studies, and theology) are: first, a lack of a clear sense of disciplinary direction . . . ; second, a lack of adequate professional organization for the discussion of new results." Quoted in Tracy, *Analogical Imagination*, 17–18.

of Christian origins, its authoritative scriptures and traditions, but rules out uncritical reliance on those givens. Theologies appear to transcend denominational or other more specific forms of Christian tradition. In the place of such local traditions, the pursuit of theology as rigorous intellectual inquiry appropriates other modes of understanding, and it attends to a number of publics and their criteria of adequacy or warrants for meaning and truth. Theology does this because it intends to be intelligible and about reality—ostensibly thereby ruling out "unintelligible" accounts of reality.[32]

Critical modern theology (ideally) has a presiding telos of some sort. The appropriation of content is not simply for cognitive purposes but is also for the life of faith, a life where change, conversion, and transformation are taking place. Finally, the claims of the oppressed are stitched alongside the claims of the reasonable and the faithful. Thus critical modern theology excludes a simple rationalism/intellectualism by virtue of the latter's failure to approximate the soteriological breadth of theologia, and its inadequacy to the social liberationist dimensions of the wisdom that is saving God-knowledge. If its commitments seem a bit overextended, it is not because of their unintelligibility, but the more hidden aspects of the canonical system. To these we now turn.

Graf(ph)tings in the contemporary theological institution

In addition to the general "rules" characteristic of this discourse (rules for what counts as real theological knowledge on the terms of critical modern theologies) institutional arrangements support the production and dissemination of knowledge. Proposals for theologia are graf-(ph)ted on definitions and distributions of knowledge in the contemporary theological institution that are not entirely or uncontradictorily supportive of the ideal theologia. The ideal unity envisioned by each

---

[32]The rationale for intelligibility and criteria outside of the faith community is complex. It certainly involves inner-doctrinal warrants, as Tracy would say—doctrines of creation, the theocentric character of theology. It has to do with the transformational purpose of theological reflection, praxis. *Plurality and Ambiguity*, 47–49. It is also related to the less easily identified pleasure in legitimacy in the variety of modern publics to which the theologian would speak—the desire to be accorded more status in an academy and to shake its reputation as what Toulmin calls a "soft discipline" or a "diffuse" and "would-be" discipline. Ibid., 17–18. See Stephen Toulmin, *Human Understanding*, vol. 1: *The Collective Use and Evolution of Concepts* (Princeton, N.J.: Princeton Univ. Press, 1972), 379.

of the examples I have given—intersecting publics for Tracy, transformative wisdom presiding over disciplined inquiry for Farley—is more likely to be graf(ph)ted on the institutional leftovers of modern epistemological issues that have shaped the social formation of which theologia is a part. The structuring of knowledge is characterized by sedimented responses to Enlightenment epistemological challenges, residuals of older battles.[33]

The concern to represent Christian faith apologetically in relation to the modern historical and scientific consciousness, for example, is institutionally displayed in the division of subject matter into fields that get their criteria by and large from secular disciplines. The resolution of the Enlightenment challenge to the scientia of divinity adopted by many U.S. versions of theological education was that of the German University and Friedrich Schleiermacher's proposal to make the education of clergy the unique purpose of this education.[34]

The question of this institutional matrix is a complex one. By insisting that theology as a form of reflection is graf(ph)ted on the seminary or divinity school complex of institutional practices, we are reminded that it cannot be separated from the subject position of those who produce it. Although, strictly speaking, the Derridean notion of graf(ph)ting is useful for joining text and context, I think it possible to use the trope in this extended setting within my broadened definition of the canonical system. That system becomes the discursive text against which a resisting regime must be understood. The project of critical modernist theology to develop public theology is another text

---

[33]This structuration has led to two false divisions in theological schools, says Farley: that between academic and "practical" disciplines, and the ordering of the "fields" around borrowed criteria of adequacy. Farley, *Theologia*, 99–124, 127–49. The strain is also indicated in the attempts to fit some modern version of the transformative "habitus of the soul" into secondary parts of theological education such as field education and spiritual direction curricula. These attempts are intended to make up for an overly cognitive model of education and gesture toward the "formation" of students. By and large, however, "transformation" is individualistic. Often the more easily discerned qualifications for practicing a profession have developed in place of figuring out an account of the redemptive transformative telos of scientia.

[34]Farley has done important critical work on the structure of disciplines in divinity schools as a result of the Enlightenment. Farley and others criticize this "clerical paradigm" of theological education. See Barbara G. Wheeler and Joseph C. Hough, Jr., eds., *Beyond Clericalism: The Congregation as a Focus for Theological Education*, Studies in Religious and Theological Scholarship (Atlanta: Scholars Press, 1988). It is a solution to the Enlightenment challenge to theology offered by Schleiermacher. The ancient professions, medicine, law, and theology, justify their presence in the modern university by virtue of their contribution to the good of society. There are those, however, who defend the paradigm. Joseph C. Hough, Jr., and John Cobb, Jr., argue for the reflective practitioner, in *Christian Identity and Theological Education*, Studies in Religious and Theological Scholarship (Altanta: Scholars Press, 1985), 77–94.

of sorts, and the intersection of that text with the so-called context from which it is constructed is the academy. Thus we speak of the graf(ph)ted nature of the practice of theological reflection with the codes of the institutional matrix. To get at the way in which the academy is itself coded, we must ask who and what is the subject position that it supports. Graf(ph)t, as Laura Donaldson says, allows us to focus on "the intersection of belief systems and political power."[35]

Of the possibilities that might constitute a definition of the social relations of academic theology, my interest is in the "points of juncture and stress" that are, as Donaldson says, "where one scion or line of argument has been spliced with another." The graf(ph)ting occurs at the juncture where the codes of the academy match up with or seem most significant to the project of critical modernist theology in its commitment to the values and concerns of intelligibility. Although critical modernist concerns have arisen in response to the errors of other theological practices (thus so-called "public" warrants arose to refute ecclesiastical hegemonies), we expect to find critical modernist commitments allowing sustenance to some interests, just as it makes possible the ignoring of others. The graf(ph)ting of the cognitive project onto the institution, then, is materially rooted in certain social relations that characterize modern education, that "feed" it. Since any particular graf(ph)tings exclude other possibilities in the text, we expect also to find lines of stress and contradiction in this practice around those excluded issues.[36]

The project of addressing the cognitive crisis is graf(ph)ted onto the professionalization of knowledge. In other words, reading the theological text as critical modernists do aligns them (wittingly or unwittingly) with certain social relations that construct the modern institutions of higher learning. This relationship is like a living graf(ph)t; it sustains and materially roots the project, and it shuts off certain lines of flow or fertilization. The professionalization of knowledge characterizes the pertinent subject position for critical modern theology, and it applies whether an institution defines its end as the provision of expertises toward the receiving of credentials for a professional career in ordained ministry or not.[37] The modern North American

---

[35]Laura E. Donaldson, "The Con of the Text," in *Decolonializing Feminisms: Race, Gender and Empire-Building* (Chapel Hill: Univ. of North Carolina Press, 1992), 59–60.
[36]Ibid., 57–58.
[37]The subject of professionalization of theological education has been much discussed and written about. There are many critics and some adherents. Beverly Harrison is one of the few who speak to the continuous reproduction of certain class affinities. Stanley Hauerwas speaks of the formative (and deforming) influence of graduate edu-

university is the preeminent institution in the creating and sustaining of what Burton Bledstein calls the "culture of professionalism." The production and channeling of knowledges in the university creates the key institution for passing on "mid-Victorian" or middle-class values, and it is these that continually flow through the lines of the graf(ph)t.[38]

While it may seem odd to say that the contemporary educational institution (seminary or university) creates faculty instead of just graduates (the latter being the embryo of the former), the production of theology is first and foremost about the production of certain kinds of subjects or speakers as authorities. Theologians, the authors and faculty of the knowledges that are produced in these institutions, are middle- and upper-middle-class subjects. Whether they are located in institutions of learning supported by private or tax monies, by denominations or the state, whether they are in church-related universities or freestanding seminaries or public universities, theologians are not able to escape the culture of professionalism that has shaped North American education. This culture is key to the production of theology as a form of faithful reasoning, a crucial constitutive feature of the practice of theology.[39] Certain relations of power/knowledge obtain in the production of theological knowledge related to the impulses and pressures of such institutions. However different these institutions may appear on the surface, they legitimate similar subject positions in late twentieth-century capitalism, those occupied by the professional managerial class.[40]

---

cation on the theological knowledge produced by this class of theologians. Stanley Hauerwas, "The Ministry of a Congregation: Rethinking Christian Ethics for a Church-Centered Seminary," in Wheeler and Hough, eds. *Beyond Clericalism*, 131, n. 14. Beverly Harrison, "Toward a Christian Feminist Liberation Hermeneutic for Demystifying Class Reality in Local Congregations," in Wheeler and Hough, eds., *Beyond Clericalism*, 137–51.

[38]I am using "university" in the sense of higher education. Bledstein, *The Culture of Professionalism*, 121.

[39]See John Cobb's excellent criticism of the construction of disciplines in the modern university and the resulting protection thereby afforded them from serving desperate social problems. John Cobb, "Theology against the Disciplines," in *Shifting Boundaries*, 241–58. See Tracy's comments on the academic publics of the theologian in *The Analogical Imagination*, 14–21.

[40]Barbara and John Ehrenreich, "The Professional-Managerial Class," in *Between Labor and Capital*, ed. Pat Walker (Montreal: Black Rose Books, 1978), 5–45.

Theologians in subject position of the professional managerial class

As distinct from the ancient professions (law, divinity, and medicine) the organizations of craft guilds, and other groups of artisans and workers, the professional managerial class (PMC) is a relatively recent grouping brought into being by industrial capitalism, as we saw in chapter 4. The PMC are "salaried mental workers who do not own the means of production and whose major function in the social division of labor may be described broadly as the reproduction of capitalist culture and capitalist class relations."[41] Typically theologians mourn the rise of professionalization because they associate it with technique-oriented practices and the distortion of ministry by marketing agendas. The PMC, however, is the subject position occupied by the very theologians who deride the transformation of the tradition of learning into the creation of church bureaucrats. This position encompasses more than simply those who go into parish ministry or other specific vocations because of the possession of expertise that sets it off from other classes.

The professional managerial class is a recognizable (though derived) position in the social formation because it is characterized by antagonisms with both the working and capitalist classes. The PMC population includes those with whom theologians and academics may least identify—"middle-level administrators and managers, engineers and other technical workers whose functions . . . are essentially determined by the need to preserve capitalist relations of production." The group with which theologians most clearly have affinities is characterized by a function that most of us would want to say we resist—namely, supporting the status quo. This latter group, comprised of workers "directly concerned with social control or with the production and propagation of ideology (e.g., teachers, social workers, psychologists, entertainers, writers of advertising copy and TV scripts, etc.), is distinguished by a functional relation to the capitalist mode of production."[42]

The most obvious reason to place theologians in this subject position is that we produce ideas. However much we would dissent from functional descriptions of the class by appealing to the distinction of

---

[41]Ibid., 12.

[42]The need for this class arose when the development of enormous economic surplus and the increase of violence between capitalist and industrial working class emerged, creating the need for "capitalist rationalization of both productive and consumptive processes." Ibid., 12–15.

religious faith from status-quo forms of culture, when looked at from
the view of the power of the state and the institutions that it protects
and supports, the academy—and therefore *we*—are so constituted.
The affinities of theologians with this class are more significant, however, than simply the mental character of our labor. The relation of the
PMC to the working class is characterized by the appropriation by this
emerging class of knowledges and wisdoms provided by the indige-
nous culture itself before the impact of industrialism. The provision of
expertise by emerging professions came with the breakup of the in-
digenous working-class culture from 1890 to 1920. Although the professional managerial class has the potential to form alignments with
the working class in antagonistic relation with the corporations/
capitalists, it exists in the contradictory position of providing services
for and managing the working class.[43]

The PMC "knows better" than the working class in ways that vary
on a continuum ranging from the more pronounced forms of control
in managerial positions over semiskilled workers to the benign forms
of power displayed in social services, educational endeavors, and
every other helping profession. A relation of control is at the heart of
the PMC, control that is frequently benevolent and expressed in the
manager-worker, social worker–client, and teacher-student relation.
The university and its cultural production is at the center of the PMC;
the theologian as teacher is a member by virtue not only of her or his
specialization in mental labor (a labor that is concerned with the symbolic capital of the social order), but by her or his position in the ecclesiastical and secular world as "expert."

It is useful to recognize academic theologians, myself included, as
members of this class because to do so highlights the social relations at
the heart of its credibility and cohesiveness. The "only guarantee of
security for the PMC," say Barbara and John Ehrenreich, was and is
corporate action; "the characteristic form of self-organization was and
is the *profession*."[44] A profession is the organization of a knowledge. Its
most important moment involves the creation of standards to define

---

[43]My argument here is dependent on the Ehrenreichs' analysis, ibid. Regarding the
appropriation by the "experts" of skills and culture from women of several classes, see
also Barbara Ehrenreich and Deirdre English, *For Her Own Good: 150 Years of the Experts'
Advice to Women* (Garden City, N.Y.: Anchor Press/Doubleday, 1978).

[44]Ehrenreich and Ehrenreich, "The Professional-Managerial Class," 26. Regarding
the development of this monopololy of competence, see Larson, *The Rise of Professionalism*, 208–45. For a view of professionalization that is overly rationalist in my estimation (and critical of Michel Foucault and the Ehrenreich theses), see Eliot Freidson,
Professional Powers: A Study of the Institutionalization of Formal Knowledge (Chicago: Univ.
of Chicago Press, 1986).

its adequate practice, and control of that process by means of defining and limiting access to its knowledges. This control takes the form of credentialing and control of the standards of credentialing. Pierre Bourdieu identifies the site of the professional academic in terms of its accumulation of "cultural capital," such as prestige and social and economic power.[45] Despite a real difference in social power and prestige among them, all three of the oldest professions are supported not simply by the valuable "goods" they provide, the special knowledges and expertises they offer for the good of the social order, but by the supports that legitimize and reproduce their proper practice.

All three professions underwent shifts when they had to professionalize services that were once dispersed more widely in the social order and valued in terms of direct service.[46] The effect of a commodity-ordered market society on this labor, although slightly different for each profession, was to create one of the prominent features of modern professions, which no longer deal in value assessed by use in direct service. To create and sustain the value of M.D.s' and lawyers' services—to create a preference for their services over that of midwives or barbers, or the minor court officers who did legal work before the legal profession was formalized—the public must be convinced it needs the product. This happens for all three professions in large part through the institutionalization of criteria and gate-keeping, which offer "objective" testimony to the better quality of the service. While the clergy did not depend on the market in the same way other modern professions did, the church bureaucracy and (inevitably) educational criteria served parallel functions of warranting their product with the status "professional." It is a warranting that creates, as Margali Sarfatti Larson puts it, a "monopology of competence."[47]

The important feature of this class position for the theologian is not its more crassly profit- or prestige-driven professionalism. The history of the production of theologians is more complex than a market-driven account suggests. A full account would require consideration of its credentialing in relation to church communities and their deliberations. What we theologians undoubtedly share, however, is the position of expert, a position that puts the egalitarian impulses of its self-

[45]Bourdieu's study analyzes academics in France. Pierre Bourdieu, *Homo Academicus*, trans. Peter Collier (Stanford, Calif.: Stanford Univ. Press, 1988), 36–38, 73–127.

[46]This history is detailed in Larson, *The Rise of Professionalism*.

[47]Larson does not detail the history of clerical professionalization. She sees its non-dependence on market-driven forces as a feature distinguishing it from law, medicine, and the new professions. She does make the point about the church bureaucracy effecting parallel monopolies. Professional criteria are practices that are publicly defended as those which will protect both the "client" and the practitioner.

critical instincts in a contradictory relation to its awareness of the potentially hegemonic character of benevolence. Theologians are educators who seek to produce "reflective practitioners," according to Joseph C. Hough, Jr., and John B. Cobb, Jr.; they produce texts for their peers and for the churches; they produce better-educated religious thinkers; and they produce other professionals. These ostensibly better professionals replace the unlettered practitioners such as Pentecostal women ministers.[48]

Stress lines appear in the graf(ph)ting of theologia as scientia onto the professional culture of the institution of higher learning. They lie around the contradiction in the system of discourse that is critical modern theology. That contradiction is found in its commitment to incorporating the public of the oppressed and its material rootedness in social relations that require the power of monopolized competence. The lines of the splicing include the concern with the marginalized; the flow of interest, however, routes this theology around other possible readings of the theological project and grants the power to define that concern with the PMC.

To recapitulate, by virtue of its turn from the precritically understood objectivities of faith to the constituent features of the human subject, critical modern theology is concerned with developing scientia as a capacious epistemological science, one that addresses publics with the criteria of academy, church, and the social issues of the oppressed. The capaciousness of this project has shown signs of strain, which I noted in the incompleteness of the judgment regarding the formative character of theologia as a habit of the soul, the incompletely developed vision of the importance of moral formation on cognition unilaterally recognized by modern theologians.[49] I judge that the dominant focus of modern theologies is not simply that discipline. Insofar as the crisis of cognitive claims does hold the attention of modern theology, however, it has not moved completely out of a culture of certainty.[50] That culture of certainty may very well rely on

---

[48]Hough and Cobb are aware, however, that the temptation of the expert is to disempower the client; they offer a brief warning against it for clergy. Joseph C. Hough, Jr., and John B. Cobb, Jr., *Christian Identity and Theological Education*, Studies in Religious and Theological Scholarship (Chico, Calif.: Scholars Press, 1985), 78–94, esp. 87–88.

[49]Tracy and Farley defend the importance of the cognitive claims project in response to liberation theologies' critiques of academic theorizing. I do not disagree with them that the academic project is defensible, but I am arguing that the academic project is insufficiently identified in its political rhetoric and social relations. I hope for changes in the academy, not its dismantling.

[50]This expression is Wesley Kort's. See *Bound to Differ*, 134–41.

the more graspable authorizations of professional criteria than those liberation–soteriological criteria that it needs to invoke to protect its distinctiveness.

Because I read the practice of theology as one for which the boundaries are wider than the stated ideas and ideals, new contradictions are graf(ph)ted into the practice by the addition of the subject position to the rules that characterized critical modern theology. The ideologies about combinations of publics, "reasonable persons," and criteria of adequacy may be in potential conflict with a critique of the power of expertise. There is, in fact, a crack perceivable in the edifice of certification, when what is "really" theology is defined in relation to the criteria of a host of publics invested with certain kinds of power, including the critique from the marginal. The presence of the marginal in articulating believable, warranted claims has yet to be described. The dynamics of the graf(ph)t, like the sustenance of a natural cutting, would appear to favor publics with expertise, leaving the "other" voice—the public of the marginalized—to wither like a false hybrid.

An account of the role of power in this discursive formation is incomplete without construing the subject position more specifically with regard to its constraints and possibilities. After considering the intertextuality of feminist writing with the practice of critical modern theology, we will return to those issues of the production of theologians as subjects by the disciplinary power of educational institutions, the resulting pleasures and occlusions that productive power creates, and the ways feminist theology resists.

Feminist theologies: discourses of resistance

A turn to feminist theological texts shows a simple level of dependence that one might call intertextuality. Simply to attend to the host of theologies and disciplines appropriated by these feminists, to define their intertexts as thematic sources, could keep us quite busy. Mary Daly, for instance, appropriated the discourse of Paul Tillich in *Beyond God the Father*, finding his employment of the philosophical language of being, essence, and existence to be eminently more to her liking than the personal anthropomorphic language of deity found in much traditional theology.[51] Similarly, Ruether employs existentialist vo-

---

[51]Mary Daly, *Beyond God the Father: Toward a Philosophy of Women's Liberation* (Boston: Beacon Press, 1973), 21. She employs this language in order to offer an alternative to the male-dominant symbol system of Christianity that she labels patriarchy.

cabulary for a feminist anthropology, developing the categories of
Simone de Beauvoir and Jean-Paul Sartre for an analysis of the origins
of patriarchy.[52] Both assume historical-critical consciousness.

It is not the ideas, however, that provide the distinctive resisting
register for an academic discursive practice. Such an exercise would be
nothing more than ordinary theological criticism within the parameters of the current certifying discourse. Read simply as the legitimation of their ideas with the appropriation of theological and
nontheological ideas, feminist theology cannot be seen as a practice of
resistance, except to say that it competes in the marketplace of ideas
like every other academic theology. Read intertextually with critical
modern theology, Ruether's and Daly's "systematic" texts create registers of resistance that are easily missed when they are deemed to represent women's experience. These registers come into view with a
careful examination of feminists' academic practice as it intersects with
the rules assumed by critical modernists and their subject position.

The feminist literature itself hints at its failure to comply with the
scholarly norms for offering ideas. Not only the ideas but the presentation are too outrageous for many non-feminist readers to accept.
Mary Daly piles one claim upon another in displaying her fundamental thesis that Christianity is patriarchy. To make the case that Christian symbols can do nothing but oppress women, she argues in only
two-and-one-half pages that Jesus imagery creates scapegoats of
women; she elaborates an account of the function of male God-lan-
guage in a few sentences. Similarly, Ruether combines brief anthropological data with an existentialist account of the origins of patriarchy.
These vast, universalizing claims are presented as descriptions of reality. Too abbreviated for the kind of warranting and argument that
characterizes the discourse of the scholarly essay, these texts almost
beg to be read a different way. That different way will require attention to their employment of registers that challenge the rules of the
canonical system of modern theology. As strategies that appropriate

---

Her search is for a "new language of transcendence," "a different semantic field" than is
possible with the religion with a male savior, male God, and male priesthood.

[52]Rosemary Radford Ruether, *Sexism and God-Talk: Toward a Feminist Theology*
(Boston: Beacon Press, 1983). The existential categories are found in chapters 4 (anthropology) and 7 (evil and sin). Ruether's text reads like an abbreviated typology of feminist social theory, as she considers a number of nontheological discourses of gender
analysis (liberalism, romanticism, socialism) as sources for feminist theology. Her typology comes from the many extratheological sources she uses, including "critical post-
Christian world views such as liberalism, romanticism, and Marxism." They get
reviewed particularly in the chapters on anthropology and redemption. Ibid., 22; chaps.
4, 9.

the rules of modern theology only to bend and disrupt them, Ruether's and Daly's systematic texts display and simultaneously dislocate
a number of the features of critical modern theology.

These writings share with other theological texts some teleological
account of the end toward which theological reflection is ordered. As
I defined it earlier, feminist liberation theology is initiated by a social
fracture (the oppression of women) and is a reading of the social situation, both religious and sociopolitical, that is defined by resistance to
that oppression.[53] Thus the feminist vision is the transformation of patriarchal arrangements in church and society. The "good" society requires right God/ess-relation—a theo/acentric form of existence. This
"good" is the reason that feminist theology refuses to treat the traditional authorities as givens. Although this is a theological rule it shares
with critical modernists, feminists go further in their refusal to identify that form of existence with a normative Christianity or its embod-
iment in institutional church. This suggests two things about the
intertextual relationship: (1) that the nature of theological reflection as
well as its institutional conditions are fair targets for feminist criticism;
and (2) that the criticism has a vision of the "good," even if only a
proximate one, that supports some departure from the traditional
theological enterprise.

Ruether's and Daly's texts take up the conventions of theology as
certifying discourse in a number of ways. Right away we are clued
that feminist theology is a systematic enterprise. Both texts are written with chapter divisions corresponding to the familiar doctrinal loci:
God, revelation or method, anthropology, Christology, and so forth.
In the place of apologetic or fundamental theology as prolegomenon
for the enterprise, however, Daly and Ruether offer alternative opening frames. The introductory discourse of both *Sexism and God-Talk*
and *Beyond God the Father* puts us on notice that something strange is
afoot.

In the place of arguments for the intelligibility of the enterprise,
both feminists offer tropes of the unacceptablity of the enterprise as it
has traditionally been done. Ruether retells the biblical story of origins
and eschaton. Her text begins with a feminist midrash in three acts.
The first, "The Kenosis of the Father," presents the musings of the
God of Heaven, Father and Lord of all, on the events of Genesis 6, the

---

[53]Of course, resistance is not identical with the discourse of Christian institutions or
the discourse of liberal institutions. "Woman-church" is located somewhere in between
as well as within and without denominational Christianity. Its vision of the good is constructed out of the Judeo-Christian tradition, but feminist theology questions traditional
distinctions between orthodox Christians and everybody else.

rape of the daughters of earth by the Sons of Heaven. From the Father God's reflection on the cause of earthly trouble, the seductive daughters and their mother Eve, to his conversation with his repressed Mother, the Queen of Heaven, we have a pretemporal enactment of the struggle within God over the meaning of divine power. A mental flash of the image of the coming fatherless child reminds the Father God of a nonhierarchical possibility in his divine nature. The next two acts present similar rewrites of the contemporary conflicts in Christianity by locating them in the very beginning—conflicts between ideals of domination represented by male disciples and the alternatives presented by the "Iconoclastic Teacher" and the vision of the women at the tomb. The drama closes with the foreshadowing that relations of domination have won out, however temporarily, as the woman's version of Jesus' message of the new way beyond relations of master-slave, ruler-subject, is silenced by the men.[54]

Ruether closes her systematics with an interpretation of the divine Shekinah, or Wisdom of God, presented as a vision of the end, when subjugation of womb, labor, and the earth and its peoples are overcome. Through it we are offered a frame that retells the story of God's saving events with God's people such that its patriarchal deformation becomes the lens for rereading salvation history. These are not simply myths accommodated to the systematics of a Christian theology, because both pieces of the frame take up biblical imagery and language in the new telling of a gospel and an eschaton. A new "biblical" discourse emerges—not the rejection of the canon but its rescripting.

The gospel is ripe with the promise of something beyond patriarchy; the last things are its glorious image. The Divine Wisdom, She, the repressed of the Father God, is come. There is no way to mistake the addressee, a subject position on the intersection of old and new, between patriarchal church and woman-church. The counterposing of discourses (Matt. 6:9–10, 2 Kings 19:31, Isa. 44:18–19, Isa. 65:25, Acts 17:28) bears remarking:

> Babies grow in wombs without help from computers. The sun rises every day. Con Ed sends no bill for sunshine. The harmony is still there, persisting, supporting, forgiving, preserving us in spite of ourselves. Divine Grace keeps faith with us when we have broken faith with her. Through the years of alien madness, she did not abandon us; she kept the planets turning, the seasons recurring, even struggled to put the

---

[54]Rosemary Radford Ruether, "The Kenosis of the Father: A Feminist Midrash on the Gospel in Three Acts," in *Sexism and God-Talk*, 1–11.

upside down right side up, to cleanse the channels of the garbage, to blow the smog out to sea. To return Home: to learn the harmony, the peace, the justice of body, bodies in right relation to each other. The whence we have come and whither we go, not from alien skies but here, in the community of earth. Holy One, Thy Kingdom come, Thy will done on earth. All shall sit under their own vines and fig trees and none shall be afraid. The lion will lay down with the lamb and the little child will lead them. A new thing is revealed; the woman will encompass the warrior. Thou shalt not hurt, thou shalt not kill in all my holy mountain. The Shalom of the Holy; the disclosure of the gracious Shekinah; Divine Wisdom; the empowering Matrix; She, in whom we live and move and have our being—She comes; She is here.[55]

Daly's prolegomenon is actually a double text. The original Introduction takes up epistemology and revelation via the cognitive issues of "Problem, Purpose, and Method." The "cognitive crisis" to which she speaks is the patriarchal theological project itself, which continues to make woman the "other." Daly locates feminist theology "on the boundary" and relies on the power of women's consciousness to effect a transformation. To do this, theological discourse must engage in "methodolatry," because traditional theological method obscures women's questions as it continues to legitimate the male hegemony. To de-reify the symbol system of patriarchy, to penetrate the false consciousness it produces and sustains, and to effect liberation, a new method must castrate the "phallocratic value system imposed by patriarchy" and allow women to exorcise the false consciousness. Feminist method, according to Daly, effects an intertextual relation of "liberation-castration-exorcism" with mainstream theological method.[56]

The second part of the double text that creates the prolegomenon is a new Introduction Daly added in 1985. Departing from the practice of revision, Daly creates another layer of text, an "Original Reintroduction." This new voice forgoes the task of rendering theological discourse intelligible, and offers its own rereading of the text. The reintroduction locates the text in an ongoing history of women's jour-

---

[55]Ruether, *Sexism and God-Talk*, 266. One possible reading of this frame is that it is a midrash on the pre- and posthistory of salvation, one that corrects the patriarchal traditions of Christianity. If we ask about the voices that construct it and its domains of meaning, we have a more complex grasp of its relation to the canonical discourse. A number of other features of critical modernist theology appear only to be transgressed.

[56]Mary Daly, *Beyond God the Father*, "Original Reintroduction" (1985), xi–xxxii; the first introduction (1973), 1–12.

ney, posing as a tradition-history that calls attention to itself. From it a clearer-eyed "Daly" speaking from a new space-time calls for a new spiraling movement "Beyond Beyond God the Father."[57]

She warns that the movement to resist patriarchy to which the first text contributed has assumed failed forms, as patriarchy is able to co-opt it. The dangers for women have increased in the twelve years since the writing of the text, and increased vigilance against the "stagnation" of patriarchy, the state of bondage, is called for. Although the bursts of transforming energy in women's spirituality that have occurred since the first publication testify to the success of de-reifying the God of partriarchy, she says, the move to a new naming of "Being as Verb" and the alternative vision of "ultimate/intimate reality" that attends it cannot be taken for granted. Patriarchy co-opts God-ess speakers from the active process of empowering wild women. *Goddess* has become a noun, masquerading as a feminist critique when it is actually one of many token versions of the Christian God. Despite the appearance of feminist credibility, in fact, it serves "the cockocratic establishment perpetuating the status quo."[58]

Daly's reintroduction signifies the fallible, open character of the analysis of *Beyond God the Father*, and implicitly of any analysis. Because it does not "take back" the text, the prolegomenon lays out the impossibility of any verbal victory, given the ever-expanding necrophilic reach of patriarchy, always capable of more sophisticated ways to spread its phallocratic rule. The process of naming is an ongoing, ever-changing task, Daly says; some of the language of the first journey *Beyond* included "transitional," even "self-liquidating words" like *homosexuality* and *androgyny* (p. xxiv).

The reintroduction runs riot with punning and poetic invention as the new images of living on the boundary for lusting, wicked, metapatterning women spill out on the pages. It is a war of words, as "rhymes, alliterations, alteration of senses—all aid in the breaking of fatherland's fences"; it is a re-membering; it is a "Race of Wild Women," a reversing of reversals. It is a "quantum leap into Tidal Time" and a "jumping off the face/foreground of the impoverished doomsday world," an exit from the poorhouse of patriarchy. Its impetus is not simply to empower women's courage and biophilic bonding. Like Ruether's midrash, the closing attribution echoes Acts 17:28:

---

[57]There is, in effect, an implicit decentering and multiplication of the subject "Mary Daly" here. Which one is the "real Mary Daly"? I do not think it would suffice to say that the real one is always the most current, particularly when we are attending to theological discourse and its effects.

[58]Daly, *Beyond God the Father*, "Original Reintroduction," xviii.

"The Journey can and does continue because the Verb continues — from whom, in whom, and with whom all true movements move" (p. xxix). Religious faith in a radically new display will construct the new time-space of liberation.

The intertextual relation effected by feminist prolegomena with modern theological apologetics reorients the moral crisis. It is the crisis of patriarchal Christianity itself, not a "crisis of cognitive claims," that must galvanize the community into new practices. Introductory frames are only the beginning strategies, however, in this dislocating of traditional and modern patterns of theological reflection.

Although the familiarity of feminist theological claims may have begun to dull our sensibility to the work of its language, the nominalization of traditional words effected by Ruether and Daly is a strategy in itself. To understand the way in which their language is an intertextual strategy, we must return to the writing of modern theology, particularly with regard to the style of this field-dominant genre.

Intertextual strategies of language/style: politicizing tropes versus civil discourse

The language of much theological writing is that of the serious essay (the language of my own argument, as well). The purpose of the critical modern theological project is to display the intelligibility of Christian faith, and so it is no surprise that discursive strategies of argument and tight logical reasoning are likely to dominate. Through the dominance of this style of argumentation, theological discourse aims to effect objectivity. By objectivity, I do not mean the subject matter of theology. No subject matter is, strictly speaking, objective. The subject matter of science is as permeated with valuation as is theological subject matter, however differently we might want to define particulars. Nor does "objectivity" refer here to the language of theology — the linguistic signifying process itself. The attempt to rid language of its figurative character is as futile as the attempt to articulate the view from nowhere. Tropes, as Paul De Man reminds us, are part of even the most abstract, conceptual philosophical language.[59]

---

[59]De Man shows the ubiquity of trope with the example of John Locke's argument that tries to deny metaphoricalness yet must employ it to make his case. Paul De Man, "The Epistemology of Metaphor," in *Language and Politics*, ed. Michael J. Shapiro (New York: New York Univ. Press, 1984), 195–214.

Theological arguments cannot be presented in purely objective language because there is no such thing; moreover, the subject matter, *theos*, is defined by a long tradition of negative theology to mark its ungraspable character. "Divine things" inevitably invite imaginal and highly figurative expression, and it is difficult to use solely technical, bloodless language to describe such matters. Theological arguments employ the domains of biblical and concrete imagery of the faith tradition, evoking the poetic and utopian imaginative registers. Thus theological discourse is rarely able to confine itself completely to the domain of the philosophical and abstract.

Despite its inevitable employment of the poetic, however, theological discourse can effect an objective style. It does so with the use of certain linguistic forms. Not surprisingly, the style of theological argument is designed to create the effect of the credibility and rightness of its claims. Objectivity is an important ethos to evoke in support of this end, even if it is used to describe a situation of radical interest or commitment, as theological discourse inevitably does. One example of the stylistic features that help construct this effect is the attributing of agency. Agency can be hidden in an account in such a way that the givenness of an object under discussion is implied. Subject matter is presented in theological arguments so as to mute the role of the theologian in constructing the argument. Theologians may never use the construction "I" in their arguments; or we may appear as the enunciator of our discourse yet seem to have minimal impact on the course of events as in my style here.

Passive constructions are frequently used to invoke a sense of the inevitability of an argument and its conclusions. When events are simply occurring, logical relations appear to obtain without any directing or positioning by the author. This grammar of agency can give the reader the sense that the theologian is simply describing and reporting reality as it is—not viewing it from a vantage point or selectively representing and valuing it. A use of such forms to heighten the givenness of the claims fits the goal of credible reasoned argument. It can also diminish the rhetoric of persuasion and advocacy—of being too heavily invested in one's subject—that attends the inevitable move into confessional language.[60]

---

[60]See Michael Shapiro for examples of the "grammar of agency" in "Literary Production as Politicizing Practice," in *Language and Politics*, ed. Michael Shapiro, *Readings in Social and Political Theory*, ed. William Connolly and Steven Lukes (New York: New York Univ. Press, 1984), 231–39. Daly identifies another strategy of hidden agency— the attribution of oppression to abstractions: " 'forces,' 'roles,' 'stereotypes,' 'con-

Another opportunity to evoke objectivity occurs in the tone of the address, the implicit and explicit ways that the reader is solicited or spoken to.[61] The more formal language of the theological scholarly argument requires or depends upon getting the reader's consent at key points; it achieves this with more or less explicit solicitations. Typical of an objective style is address that tones down the rhetoric of persuasion when making points the author does not want to argue. For example: "In laying out the cognitive crisis of contemporary theology," Tracy must foreshorten the task of convincing the reader of the crisis, that all is not well with traditional formulations of the faith:

> The reality of the situation is both more simple and more basic (than a mere desire for "relevance"): when all is said and done, one finds that he can authentically abandon neither his faith in the modern experiment nor his faith in the God of Jesus Christ. Anyone who experiences at all such a seemingly unenviable condition finds the attempt to theologize pure necessity. For anyone who correctly understands the full dimensions of that experience, neither traditional Christian self-understanding nor recent modern self-understanding nor any combination thereof will suffice to resolve that dual dilemma. Only a basic revision of traditional Christianity and traditional modernity alike would seem to suffice.[62]

Tracy's style moves the reader along in such a way that even unargued points come across as credible scholarly convictions rather than mere opinion or distorting prejudice.[63] We see this in the formal vocabulary of address. Tracy typically employs the "I" in his discourse; he is not invisible in the text as the author, the ultimate in objectifying styles. The appeal in the above-quoted claim, however, is a strategy for evoking agreement that underscores the objective character of the

---

straints,' 'attitudes,' 'influence.' " *Gyn/Ecology: The Metaethics of Radical Feminism* (Boston: Beacon Press, 1978), 29.

[61]For interesting comments on different academic writing styles and their function with regard to the creation of objective effects, see Bourdieu, *Homo Academicus*, 21–30.

[62]Tracy, *The Analogical Imagination: Christian Theology and the Culture of Pluralism* (New York: Crossroad, 1986). Tracy and Farley would argue that this appeal to the criteria of intelligibility is not simply a function of modern theology, but was always an aspect of theologia as a scientia. If Reiss is correct, however, modernism is a discursive formation where the criteria of intelligibility are radically altered from those where analogical thinking could connect heavenly realities and textual and other earthly realities. One of the differences is in the implications for unacknowledged power. Timothy J. Reiss, *The Discourse of Modernism* (Ithaca, N.Y.: Cornell Univ. Press, 1982).

[63]Tracy incorporates the insights of Hans-Georg Gadamer into his definition of theology as conversation/dialogue, so I do not mean that he fails to acknowledge that the "prejudice" of preunderstanding is part of any interpretation. He, like other critical modernists, tends to treat his own discourse as representational.

logic. It does so by implying that the common state of things may be taken as a given by "anyone"—anyone who experiences, who correctly understands. The reader whose consent is invoked here, rather than won by argument, is not "anyone," of course. It is not the Pentecostal mountain woman. She might well take issue with the one who cannot "authentically abandon . . . his faith in the modern experiment." It is some other reader population that is addressed, carried along, persuaded by the codes of the "one" who is unable to give up on modernism.

My point is not that Tracy is unaware that his readership is selective; the point is that the discourse creates an inexorable logic that moves the argument along. It does so by invoking an unnamed but coded audience of agreement. It invokes that agreement in such a way that the moves do not disrupt the "objective," reasonable character of the argument.

Such devices heighten the sense that even the ultimate undecidable, the antithesis to the publicly available—the transcendent subject God—can qualify as an object of serious reflection. Faith can seek understanding such that the latter is intelligibly rendered without the distorting effects of the passion of religious faith or the clouding influence of belief. Literariness, an effect created when language draws attention to itself, is underplayed in this kind of writing in the interest of pointing beyond itself to the subject matter.[64] Such a literary style, which Bourdieu calls "writing too well," is avoided in most disciplines because it would undermine the impression of "scientificity." This is the case in theology as well.[65] Critical modernists, we remember, do not attend to the meaning effects of their discourse, but choose to treat language as if it were representational.

We have already seen that the form/style/devices of both feminist texts display crises that are signified in the prolegomena in similar ways. These initial protests of the rules of theological discourse become more striking when we trace out the appearance of the rest of the critical modern theological conventions in feminists' strategies. The next strategy is the argumentative practices of Ruether and Daly, which take on a heightened significance in relation to the kinds of literary practices that characterize academic critical modern theology.

Neither Ruether nor Daly eschews the use of an objective style. Whenever a discourse makes claims that point beyond itself, it almost

---

[64]The use of the term *literariness* to indicate a language that draws attention to itself is Shapiro's. See "Literary Production as Politicizing Practice."
[65]Bourdieu, *Homo Academicus*, 29–30.

inevitably employs a style that gives the reader a sense that an objective description of reality is being offered.[66] It is no surprise to find plenty of examples in both feminist authors of the prose of scholarly argumentation. Ruether documents the treatment of women and the function of various religious symbols throughout history, for example, in this objective style: "From archaeological evidence one can conclude that the most ancient human image of the divine was female," she reports. She then cites the authorizing sources for a case built on the legitimacy of anthropological and historical data.[67]

Feminist discourse counters this style, however, with vocabulary that draws attention to itself. While the feminist term for the problems of sexism — *patriarchy* — is familiar enough, its discursive effects are key to the power of feminist theological practice. As a description of the corrupting forms that Christian doctrine takes, the term juxtaposes the language of political ideology with the language of Christian truth: the "patriarchalization of Christology." Mary is the "patriarchal feminine."[68] This vocabulary calls attention to the nonabsolute, nonessential nature of authoritative formulations of Christian truth by focusing on their relation to corrupting social forces. The creation of nominalizations, "hierarchicalism, abstractionism, consequentialism," calls attention as well to the deposit of Christian truth as a process of political advantage/subjugation. Instead of being treated as a thing, a phenomenon with the solidity of an enduring entity, Christian truth is de-reified and acknowledged as a situational entity characterized by flux and social interests. Feminist vocabulary destroys the smooth reading of rational theological reflection. It exemplifies and perhaps outruns the literariness that calls attention to itself. Its effect is an angry cacophany that could not create more contrast with the distanced and dispassionate scholarly apologies of critical modernists' arguments to the various criteriological publics.

The shocking, alliterative vocabulary of Mary Daly is even more striking than Ruether's. Daly's transvaluation of a vocabulary of mi-

---

[66]There is probably an exception to this in modern literature, perhaps in the modernist text of Roland Barthes, *S/Z* (New York: Hill & Wang, 1974).

[67]Ruether, *Sexism and God-Talk*, 47.

[68]I am assuming Didier Coste's definition of referentiation here. "Referentiation is the operation by which signifieds belonging to different textual areas are related. . . . Reference is to referentiation what significance is to signification, the result of a process of globalization." The analysis of discourse as a process of referentiation redirects attention away from the notion that these discourses refer to some entity outside of signifying processes and to the discursive constructions of our practice of the faith, to the referentiation that places the signified of one discourse with the signifieds of another and their meaning effects. I will discuss how this is "*theo*-logical" in chapter 7. See Coste, *Narrative as Communication*, 107.

sogyny has been noted in chapter 2; her later work is a virtual exercise in vocabulary production. The strategy of politicizing theological terms begins in *Beyond God the Father*, however. Such phrases as the "castration of God," "phallocentric morality," the "sisterhood of man," and "Christolatry" are extensions of the use of the politicizing term "patriarchy." They do not simply create the tensive contrast of a metaphor, but juxtapose the discursive realm of authoritative or revelational truth with semantic realms of ideology and violence. Daly identifies contemporary society as a "gynocidal society"; she identifies male symbol-based Christianity not simply with patriarchy but with a "phallocracy" that extends "its organs everywhere." Thus she joins meanings associated with redemption, divine truth, and the salvation of human creation with those evoking the subjugation and destruction of half of that creation. (Redemption and salvation are constructed as exorcism and castration.)

Read as labels referring directly to reality, these tactics are easily dismissed by unsympathetic readers as outrageous and "too angry" or man-hating. If we read feminist "hyperbole" as a discursive practice that constructs an intertext with the objective, abstract style of critical modern theology, however, its strategic effects are more complex. The force of these signs is transgressive when perceived as strategies of de-reification. They create consciousness of the political (i.e., nonnatural) character of the realities they appear to name. More accurately, this style opens up what poststructuralist accounts would describe as the realities of theological reflection as politically *produced*, discursive objects.

The (potentially) politicizing force of feminist terms can be compared to the effects of Michel Foucault's signifying practices. Because knowledges are always embedded in power, any look at a discourse must include an analytics of power. Foucault calls attention to the power landscape of the modern prison, clinic, and sexuality with politicized tropes designed to expose the connection between ostensibly natural or benign realities and social practices that construct them. Thus, to reiterate, he calls into question the humanist purpose of liberal reform of prisons that replaced the barbaric practices of public torture and execution with more "humane" practices. He judges that the resulting disciplinary procedures of the modern prison produce a different and more technically comprehensive kind of power than the seemingly more horrendous power of monarchical oppression.[69] The

---

[69]Michel Foucault, *Discipline and Punish: The Birth of the Prison,* trans. Alan Sheridan (New York: Pantheon Books, 1977).

self-description of these reforms, however, conceals the social practices that produce them, and that is what Foucault's significations break open.

From identifying the oppressive disciplinary power that constructs the prison, Foucault uses incarceral discipline as a trope for a number of other "humane" practices, thereby calling attention to the social practices that produce seemingly natural objects. Schools are disciplinary mechanisms, for example. The work of medical science constructs new sexualized subjects as objects of the "clinical gaze." The notion of "populations" is not a natural entity merely discovered by social science, but the production of quantifiable objects of control in Foucault's analytic of power—objects constructed by social practices. In other examples of politicizing tropes, Foucault identifies various practices such as the talking cure of psychiatry and production of the sexualized self as disciplinary; feminists call women's practices to beautify their bodies a "disciplinary regime." The terms of incarceral functions do not simply shock and arrest the reader's attention, but signify political and oppressive workings.[70]

Daly's and Ruether's vocabularies of patriarchy have similar effects when we see how their devices overlap with those of modern theological discourse. We saw that theological "objects" are typically presented as given, either as logical-intelligible in critical modern theology, or as divinely given and therefore objective realities. Feminist vocabularies contest this givenness by highlighting the fact that theological "objects" are predicated on human practices. In addition, they signify that human practices are about concealment, distortion, and domination, as well as grace and redemption. Feminist vocabularies counter the restrained and objective style of modern theological arguments and go beyond the poetic language of symbol and imagery that any theologian must use. Thereby feminist theologians move to a language that juxtaposes the symbols and doctrines of Christian faith with discourse that grants not just social agency, but complicit and oppressive social agency to truths heretofore conceived as "natural."[71]

---

[70]Michael J. Shapiro is helpful on this topic and extends his analysis to photography as well. In addition to his article in *Language and Politics*, see his *The Politics of Representation: Writing, Photography, and Policy Analysis* (Madison: Univ. of Wisconsin Press, 1988).

[71]"Natural" here does not mean that theologians who espouse these givens consider them given with nature, but that they reflect reality, either divinely given or discovered via theologia's reflection.

Intertextual strategies of authorization: voice, argument, and scholarly apparatus

There is more to feminist practice than politicized vocabulary, which by itself does not adequately link it intertextually with critical modern theologies. Ruether's and Daly's texts also portray the features of systematic theology and the traditional forms of argument characteristic of faith seeking understanding. The question of authorization, both explicit and implicit, is key to links between these feminist theological texts and those of critical modern theologians. To explore these links we must look at the modes of authorization that enable the appropriation of the historic traditions of the faith community, a procedure whereby appeals to scripture or doctrinal formulations define authority, and at other implicit strategies as well. Feminists' intertextual practices of authorization require brief consideration of the appearance and arrangement of different voices in theological argument and their effect.

We saw previously that appropriation of the memory of the Christian community is a fundamental aspect of authorization for these theologies. Critical modern theologies authorize their proposals by way of fairly similar approaches to the historic tradition. They require scripture and tradition, even a normative account of core Christianity. Where they differ from other theologies is in insisting that tradition be filtered through and altered by the discernments of reality accessible to the critical modern theologian.

The intertext of feminist theologians with these critical uses of the tradition requires more than a look at what they say about scripture and creeds. We need to look at the discursive display of arguments. How do they authorize their proposals? A first category for this is the use of voice, an important strategy of the essay or the scholarly piece in evoking the authoritative certifying ethos.[72] Voice refers to a discourse within a text and answers the question, Who speaks? Voices in a novel, for example, are traceable to the characters who act out the plot. In this type of text the origin of voice is not hidden or mysterious. A discourse can be presented directly when a voice (a character) "speaks for itself," or it can be reported in the form of indirect discourse. Voice is not limited to what characters say or do or what is

---

[72]Voice, according to Coste, is "the product of the reader's quest for the origin of the text. . . . [It] is the vague, empty answer that we must give to the question of 'who speaks,' at least until we can describe more or less correctly the situation at the other [sending] end of the act of communication." See Coste, *Narrative as Communication*, 164, 165–205.

reported about them, however. Voice simply requires that a discourse can be traced back to an origin. Another example besides that of a character is the voice of the narrator. The narrating voice provides a discourse that has important effects on the signifying processes of the text. Still another type of discourse is created when the narrating and authorial voices are different. This strategy frequently adds a more subtle and authoritatively significant layer of complexity to the conversation.[73]

Theological essays are not novels, and so it may seem unimportant to identify voice. This device is not confined to the sense of voice found in a novel. It is, in fact, a particular form of an intertextual relation. All texts can be read as dialogical, because they are constituted by voices that are being responded to, whether they are prominently displayed in the text or submerged. A theological text is dialogical because it contains more than one voice or discourse, whether it displays those other voices prominently or not. On this point it differs from a novel only in the way the discourses are present. As rational arguments, modern theological texts will be populated by discourses, as it were, in a variety of ways. One example is the presence of historic and normative Christian faith as an authorizing voice, although a critically sifted one.

The way a voice appears in a discourse tells us much more than simply what will count as an authorizing source. Theological discourse, at least of the modern academic kind, displays its voices most directly as positions in an argument.[74] In an argument in an essay, voices can have varying degrees of presence. Generally, they are presented as indirect. They do not usually "speak for themselves" in the form of characters. They are generally recognized as distinct discourses over against the author's voice, however. The logic of an argument requires that an opponent be acknowledged.

Another feature of the presence and arrangement of voices is the impact of the voice that is potentially dominant in any discourse: the author's. Because she or he is the transcendent voice, an author inevitably subordinates other voices in one way or another. The author transcends the characters of a story, for example, by knowing the plot—an ominiscient location sometimes displayed in the text by the

---

[73]Coste points out that there "is no such thing as a non-narrated story, although the receiver may lose consciousness of the act of enunciation." When a non-narrated effect is created it is because of textual devices that create "the illusion of pure mimesis." Ibid., 167.

[74]Although David Kelsey is the theologian who has popularized Toulmin's account of argument, it seems a model of reflection that characterizes many more modern theologians than those who might give Toulmin credit. See Stephen Toulmin, *The Uses of Argument* (Cambridge: Cambridge Univ. Press, 1958).

author's provision of access to the consciousness of a character. A theological text subordinates other voices in a distinctive way for the purpose of the discourse—to resolve the conflict between voices. The transcendence of the author's voice is rarely indicated by access to the consciousness of the other agents, of course, but other forms of transcendence serve the goal of the discourse. A scholarly essay presents its alternative discourses as either supports for or antagonists of the position advocated by the author. This means that their presence is distinct from the author's, even if not totally represented.

"Precritical" theologies that are authorized by scripture, for example, are minimally present in Ogden's text, but they are there and easily opposed and dispensed with. Theologies in the "House of Authority," Farley's version of precritical theology, take up more space in the argument, but appear in the form of an anonymous phenomenological description that is carefully dissected and discredited.[75] The force of the transcendence of the theological author's voice is displayed in the subordination of these discourses, as the various voices move steadily toward unification. As the inadequacies of a number of voices are gradually exposed, they are either vanquished or remade. In short, differing discourses are presented in the light of a winner of the argument. Ogden's and Farley's opponents (and mine, for that matter) are defined by these narrators' concerns. Thus instead of a dialogical heterogeneity of discourses—a multiplicity that is left unresolved or ambiguous—a critical modernist theological style resembles a controlled and dignified progress toward unity. It is a progression that can resemble a consensus, but it may in fact be more like a monologue, given the presiding discourse of the theologian/author.[76]

---

[75]I am influenced here by the work of Mikhail Bakhtin and his notion of the utterance as dialogical, which is similar to my contention that all discourse is intertextual. The notions of direct and indirect discourse are helpfully defined by V. N. Volosinov, *Marxism and the Philosophy of Language*, trans. Ladislav Matejka and I. R. Titunik (Cambridge: Harvard Univ. Press, 1929, 1973). Once thought to be written by Bakhtin, this work is most likely a product of the Bakhtinian school. See Mikhail Bakhtin, *Problems of Dostoevsky's Poetics*, ed. and trans. Caryl Emerson, vol. 8 in *Theory and History of Literature* (Minneapolis: Univ. of Minnesota Press, 1984). For the concepts of Bakhtinian monologue and dialogue, see Tzvetan Todorov, *Mikhail Bakhtin: The Dialogical Principle*, trans. Wlad Godzich, vol. 13 in *Theory and History of Literature* (Minneapolis: Univ. of Minnesota Press, 1984).

[76]I do not mean to say that voices in another kind of text—a novel, for instance—are not controlled by the author. But the penchant for smoothing out the contested discourses in a theological argument, representing them as ordered by the logic of the winning view, is dramatically different, for a variety of reasons. All discourse is dialogical according to Bakhtin (at least this is a prominent Bakhtinian theme). One presents a discourse as monologue when attempting to create "scientific" effects or when studying a discourse looking for its patterns and regularities. One opens it up when one treats it

The register of argument is not distinctive of the modern theological essay alone. Theologians throughout the centuries display arguments and move to conclusions that smooth out the conflicts of contesting voices. Readers of Martin Luther and John Calvin can attest not only to the intensity of the rhetoric of these discourses but also to the highly polemic presentation of the enemy's perspective. Other voices appear frequently not only as named (the Pope, the Catholic church, Johann Eck, Servetus) but as vilified (simpletons, coxcombs, Popish flatterers). In comparison, the highly civil tone of modern theological presentations of contesting voices is noteworthy. This civility may suggest a distancing from the stakes of the argument; at the least it implies that criteria of intelligibility of a certain sort dominate.

The goal of consensus, of unifying the discourses, is further supported by another way modern theology as certifying discourses creates authoritative effects. The goal of modern theologies to achieve "publicness," to respond to the requirement for warrants, backing, criteria of adequacy (Tracy) or the criteria of intelligibility (Ogden), is aided by another distinctive kind of voicing. In addition to the indirectly presented voices in an argument, the theological essay is characterized by authorizing voices found in the practice of footnoting.[77] The theologian is the voice presiding over the progression of the argument, using forms of speech and appeals to logical progression to legitimate the points to be scored. The voice of the narrator/author is itself warranted, as her/his claims are separately backed up with the citation of ostensible expertises of other researchers. The cumulation of these effects—the variety of voices, their mode of presence, their subordination to a unifying logic—contributes to the sense that the Christian tradition and the intelligible reading of reality converge in a theologia that is a development of one of its historic aspects, scientia as a rigorous and unifying reason.

---

as a dialogue. See Todorov, *Mikhail Bakhtin*, 60–74. For Bakhtin's comments on the problematic notion that consciousness is monologic, see appendix 2, "Toward a Reworking of the Dostoevsky Book" (1961), in Mikhail Bakhtin, *Problems of Dostoevsky's Poetics*, ed. and trans. Caryl Emerson, vol. 8 in *Theory and History of Literature* (Minneapolis: Univ. of Minnesota Press, 1984), 283–302.

[77]Bourdieu's comments on the tools of intellectuals seem appropriate in regard to footnotes: "Intellectuals are prepared by the whole logic of their education to treat works inherited from the past as a culture, in other words, as a treasure that they contemplate, venerate, celebrate, by the same token giving themselves added prestige by that very fact—in short, as accumulated wealth destined to be exhibited and to produce productive capital that you invest in research, in order to produce effects." Pierre Bourdieu, "Fieldwork in Philosophy," in *In Other Words: Essays towards a Reflexive Sociology* (Stanford, Calif.: Stanford Univ. Press, 1990), 29.

Strategies of authorization in Ruether and Daly

When we return to feminist texts, the strategies of theology as civil
and intelligible scientia appear in a new light. The system of theological doctrinal loci, as mentioned earlier, creates the chapter divisions of
each feminist text, and the authorization process is dislocated from this
point on. Ruether moves from the loci of revelation, God, creation,
anthropology, Christology, Marian doctrine, evil and sin, ecclesiology, to the world and eschatology. Daly's order is similar, though less
complete, moving from method (revelation), God, Evil, Christology,
ethics, ecclesiology, to the world and eschatology. Daly's chapter titles
are reminiscent of the challenge of individual words and phrases, but
now displayed at the level of the system itself. Method is defined as
"methodolatry," the process of castrating theological method of patriarchy; the doctrine of evil is represented as exorcism of evil from Eve.
The doctrine of God is a postmortem of sorts—"After the Death of
God the Father"; ecclesiology is "Sisterhood as Antichurch."

A process of transvaluation, as Daly says, is carried out in relation
to the subject of each doctrine. There is a reorienting of the temporal
or axiological logic of themes.[78] Liberation of the doctrine of the fall
for women means a "Fall into Freedom." Ethics for a religion liberated from patriarchy is the end of ethics, or at least of the "phallic Morality" of patriarchy. A redeemed Christology for the new time-space
of liberation is one that refuses "Christolotry" and creates "A World
Without Models."[79] Daly's process replaces the doctrines that patriarchal Christianity has dislocated.

Daly dislocates the implicit strategies of authorization as well. To
be sure, the voices of experts are present in her use of academic textual
format (although she frequently is citing examples of misogyny). The
real twist on the practice of academic citation, however, is her footnoting of conversations with women. Women's unpublished opinions
are thus granted the status of warrants that justify claims. *Only women*
are cited in the notes from the new time-space in the Original Reintroduction. Clearly this practice departs from the usual theological

---

[78]Daly, *Beyond God the Father*, 1–12.

[79]Meaghan Morris identifies Daly's treatment of vocabulary in *Gyn/Ecology* and her
later books as constructing a decoding procedure that reads Christian codes "backwards," focuses change on fixed meanings residing in words, and creates a closed category of good women that is placed in relation to a new "other," bad women (fembots).
Beyond God the Father treats not just words, but the systematic frame and method. It also
offers a transvaluation that allows for more discursive openings for women than the
good versus bad. See Meaghan Morris, *The Pirate's Fiancee: Feminism, Reading, Postmodernism* (New York: Verso, 1988).

reliance on written and recognized academic texts and, in the case of the reintroduction, on sources (ostensibly) without regard for gender. This use of unconventional authorizations counters the patriarchal scholarly authorizations that have long compounded the layers of silence over women's voices. It represents a singular device in its own right.[80]

Ruether's text appropriates and dislocates the conventional scholarly authorizing of theological claims, as well. She effects the dislocation of the traditional certifying of Christian faith that is associated with appeals to a position's continuity with the tradition, whether of orthodox or critical modernist variety. Ruether adopts theological authorization in citing biblical traditions and watershed creeds and church fathers in her systematics, a procedure that identifies her work with traditional systematics. In place of the hyperpoliticizing vocabulary of Daly, however, Ruether moves to a counteruse of this tradition. She appropriates the traditional sources in a more conventional way than Daly, but that use is constructed around a twofold insistence: (1) that the full humanity of women will be the central critical principle, and (2) that the failure of the Christian tradition to affirm that principle requires that other sources be deployed. She defines the Hebrew and Christian scripture and the "primary theological themes of the dominant stream of classical Christian theology" as the authoritative sources for feminist theology, and then pronounces them insufficient. Heretical traditions, religious traditions of the Ancient Near East and Greco-Roman religion and philosophy, and "critical post-Christian world view" (romanticism, liberalism, Marxism) are authorities as well.[81]

Ruether's presentation of systematics, then, turns out to be a redefinition of the Christian tradition. Each theological locus is articulated with a failed history and a counterhistory. Instead of appropriating the creeds and church fathers as voices of truth and wisdom, Ruether cites litanies of the tradition as violations of truth, of error and oppression mixed in with the passing on of the treasure. By appropriating heretical traditions, her counterhistory widens to include a story of sup-

---

[80]Original Reintroduction: n.1, telephone conversation with Linda Barufaldi; n.22, Suzanne Melendy, Emily Culpepper. Preface, n.1, Jean MacRae. Chap. 1: n.4, Janice Raymond; n.32, Linda Barufaldi; n.54, Emily Culpepper. Chap. 3: n.18, Emily Culpepper; n.34, Emily Culpepper; n.35, Jean MacRae. Chap. 4: n.50, Emily Culpepper. Chap. 6: n.11, Pauli Murray; n.24, Janice Raymond; Chap. 7: n.1, Linda Barufaldi. (See her explanation in *Gyn/Ecology*, 27.) Daly later produces more transgressive academic practices. Her *Websters' First New Intergalactic Wickedary of the English Language* is written "in cahoots with Jane Caputi" (Boston: Beacon Press, 1987).

[81]Ruether, *Sexism and God-Talk*, 12–46.

pressed insight and vision—as the Chalcedonian patriarchalization of Christology subverts not only the iconoclastic spirit of Jesus, but a variety of charismatic and androgynous Christologies as well.[82]

With these "anti-appeals" to the church fathers, feminist theological method counters the objectivity of style and muted signifying processes of modern theologies such as Tracy's or Ogden's. It also politicizes the apparatus of traditional warranting from the church's historic memory. If Ruether's accounts of the patriarchal character of each doctrinal theme are read as representational descriptions, they can be quickly dismissed. Her evidences and sources are minimal and the account thin by the standards of contemporary historical work. Moreover, a reading of the history of gender oppression as uniform as hers has been criticized as essentialist. Read as discursive practices that create their meaning in relation to other theologies, however, Ruether's text is a feminist litany of protest. Its target is the failure of traditional and modern theologies to acknowledge their own grounding in political practices.

Ruether's politicized litany of Christology and doctrine of God as patriarchalized through the ages constitute a strategy about the tradition. This strategy foregrounds the concealment at work when the tradition is treated as a fixed, unchanging entity that exists simply to be appropriated as truth or norm. Her litany is subversive not because it replaces the false history of doctrine with the true feminist discovery of the misogyny that was actually signified. It is subversive when read as referring to the apolitical renderings of theological use and construal of authorities.

My analysis of Ruether's and Daly's systematics has moved from strategies of vocabulary to strategies of discourse, where a frame of meaning and method are invoked and dislocated by means of the literary strategies of feminist critique. The effects of their work highlight the production of the objects of discourse and the way in which women's oppression has occurred in theological worlds. There is more to this practice than highlighting, however. By moving from the juxtaposition of domains of meaning around single terms and short phrases to larger units of discourse—the genre of systematic theology—a distinct form of challenge can be constructed with these texts. There is subversion going on (what Meaghan Morris calls "subverting the code"). By taking this discourse as an intertext with critical

---

[82]Ibid., 116–38.

modern systematic theology and reading the larger units of discourse, we can see that more is subverted than individual words or phrases.[83]

That "more" can be found by moving to a final observation about the dissent employed by Daly's and Ruether's systematics. From it we can conclude that an intertextual register is to be found here that characterizes feminist theology as a distinctive certifying discourse. We can get at the nature of its resistance, as well. It is, in other words, a reading regime, a set of intertextual strategies that have a cohesiveness as a distinct practice of resistance.

Feminist regime: politicizing parody

Another voice is present in these texts, a voice not distinguished from that of the authors. That voice is the genre of systematic theology itself accompanied by the authorizing voices of the tradition. By using this larger organizing discourse of systematic theology and its traditional warrants to present the dissenting feminist voice, Daly and Ruether turn systematic theology into an altogether different kind of exercise than a scholarly essay rendering faith into understanding. They use the genre not simply to state a new truth, but to call attention to the vehicle itself, even to make fun of it. In short, these feminist practices are *parodies*. They are parodies of a solemn tradition that protects itself from innovation and thereby refuses women and disorderly "others." They are also parodies of the civil and earnest theological discourse of modern theologies that are avid for change, but only civil and intelligible change.

The organizing strategy here is parody, not simply criticism of traditional or critical modern theology. On one level Ruether's and Daly's dissent is simply *polemic*—an antagonistic dialogue where the other partner actively influences the author's discourse, either in an

---

[83]If Christianity is read as a collection of vocabulary, each unit of which contains a sexist meaning, then her critics would be right that at least Daly's strategy is a closed system. Daly's dictionarylike approach to the semantics of Christianity is problematic, as Morris insists. The problem is her posing of dichotomies in the later texts between strong feminist women and lobotomized women or painted birds. I don't think that dichotomy is fixed in *Beyond God the Father*, nor do I think the strategy is aimed simply at words. This does not contradict my earlier critique of the essentialist impulses in Daly. I am reading Daly intertextually to find this alternative strategy. Morris, *The Pirate's Fiancee*, 31–32.

overt or hidden way.[84] More is going on than antagonistic argument, however, and this is where systematics as a distinct discourse comes into play. In the discourse of polemic, other discourse may be derided, accosted, criticized, and even caricatured, but the opposing discourse is distinct, even if it does not appear in a text. Parody, unlike polemic, takes the other discourse and uses it for its own purposes. This is precisely what feminist dissent does.[85]

Parody is not concerned with setting up a distinction between two discourses, whether to represent the object faithfully or to use other voices to get at a correct and winning reference. Parody is concerned with the act of imitation itself. In the hands of liberation feminists, parody employs the genre of traditional theological presentation. Feminist parody does not controvert the systematic genre; it does not argue with it directly, nor is it influenced by it as by an invisible opponent who is "present" as the unheard voice. Feminist theology uses the voice of systematics to subvert theological discourse as usual.

Parody subverts by imitation that leads to excess. Operating on a different field than argument, parody takes a discourse that is part of the common memory (in this case the theologians' memory) and speaks through it in order to take that discourse to its limits. Daly's chapter titles turn systematics upside down, dislocate it, reorient it. Ruether parodies biblically-based theology by beginning her system with a story of God's angst over patriarchy. When Daly says that Christology is Christolatry, that Jesus is the original scapegoat, she parodies the notion that the topic of Christology must either move in the rarefied air of *ousia* and *physis*, or negotiate questions about the "historical Jesus." She parodies the idea, in short, that Christology is not about its effects in human lives. It would be mistaken to read this as the rational disproving of the truth of Christology. The discovery of what is wrong requires — is parasitic upon — the discourse itself.

Through parody, feminist theologies counter the presentation of critical modern theology, which, despite its occasional utopian figures, retains the serious tone of an intellectual enterprise with reality as

---

[84]Ruether's and Daly's direct criticisms are for "liberal" male feminists as well as the conservative traditionalist. Bakhtin defines the polemic, hidden and overt, in relation to parody. See *Problems of Dostoevsky's Poetics*, 193–99.

[85]I follow Bakhtin's definitions here, which distinguish the degrees of presence of voices in this way. Parody falls in the category in which the other's discourse is not acknowledged as such, but is "summoned forth" because it is "in the collective memory of a given social group." "Here one language only is actualized in the utterance, but it is presented in the light of another language." Todorov, *Mikhail Bakhtin*. Also, Bakhtin, *Problems of Doestoevsky's Poetics*, vol. 8, 185–86, 197–98. See his charting of the various ways other discourses are present, ibid., 199.

its subject matter. Daly and Ruether display the disrespect of parody, the exaggeration of parody, and sometimes even the carnivalesque grotesque of parody.[86] Something like carnival appears in the short parody that closes *Beyond God the Father*. The story of Christianity as patriarchy is told in a vignette of the "Looking Glass Society" where the distortions of patriarchy view everything backward. Continuing in the tradition of the first male's robbery of the first woman, this society produced a priesthood that spiritualized the powers of women in order to appropriate them as male property, initiating a practice that would continue to characterize Western history. The Male Mothers created fancy dresses to mark their high calling. They created supernatural functions out of each of women's daily practices, ritualizing them while denigrating the material version still carried out by women. Feeding was spiritualized as Holy Communion, washing as baptism, consolation as Extreme Unction.

These spiritual "transsexuals" became "Supernatural Mothers called Fathers" and set in motion a males-only club characterized by a persistent inverting of all reality—where one fights to bring peace. In this club, women are mirrors who continually reflect back the inflated image of men. The ruler of this society bent on self-destruction is God the Father, who, "gazing at his magnified reflection, believes in his superior size," yet struggles with the fear that he is diminished by making "a renewed act of faith in Himself." This story resembles nothing more than the inside-out logic of carnival, where the oppressive rules of rank and hierarchy are rendered ridiculous.[87]

The disrespect and inside-out logic of parody do not disqualify feminism as a theological practice. Although it can be grim or cruel, parody as we find it in feminists' work is full of laughter. Subversive humor gives courage to the folk who need to display the "truth" about a dominant regime that refuses to tell it. The priesthood *is* a club of spiritual "transsexuals" when seen from the subject position (woman) that is defined by that club as an improper icon of the holy; to say so is a parodic chuckle. This logic is analogous to the parodic religious feasts of the medieval peasants, a custom that worked to puncture the rigid caste barriers of the medieval social order and the rank-obssessed ecclesiastics and turn that hierarchy topsy-turvy.[88]

---

[86]Bakhtin has written a great deal on carnival, a parodic discourse that was a prominent feature of Renaissance writing, particularly that of Rabelais. See *Problems of Dostoevsky's Poetics*, 126–28.

[87]Daly, *Beyond God the Father*, 194–98.

[88]According to Bakhtin, parody is a vehicle of laughter in medieval and Renaissance folk culture; romantic and modern parody are defined differently. See Mikhail Bakhtin,

Daly's most transgressive imagery, the use of castration and exorcism as terms for liberation, like her introduction of hags and wild women into the discourse of the worthiness of women, are giant belly-laughs—somewhat like the grotesque carnival humor that included bodily excretions and such bizarre images as the senile, pregnant, laughing hag. As is said of the parody of medieval and Renaissance carnival, these feminist practices are about opening up another order, about reviving and renewing possibilities.[89]

This intertextual reading provides a view of parody as a genre, a view that a "realist" or "literal" account of feminist theology misses. The parodic register displays a set of practices—systematic theological loci, the various forms of authorization, the civility of theology as reasonable discourse—as the fallible deformed reifications of transforming faith that they have become. Instead of offering a fixed system in the place of that flawed model, instead of putting forward the correct version on the discursive terrain of intelligibility, a parodic register evokes laughter at the pretensions of the project.

This is not to say that feminist theology as parody names no vision, or that the parody is not driven by hope for the emergence of God/ess' realm. The use of systematic loci and tradition as a framing genre offers hints of new images with a theo/a-logic: iconoclasm against the Father God gives way to a God beyond, the transforming power of be-ing, Verb; parody of anthropology/sin gives way to imaging of woman as good. The ultimate cause is "the creative drawing power of the Good Who is self-communicating Be-ing, Who is the Verb from whom, in whom, and with whom all true movements move." This last quote echoes Ruether's vision of "the gracious Shekinah; Divine Wisdom; the empowering Matrix; She, in whom we live and move and have our being." It is a vision formed by Christian memory, but displayed as the radically new hope that it must become.

The dominant intertextual relation—the feminist register that constructs a politicizing parody of critical modern (and to some extent traditional) theology—is the best argument against the reading of Daly's as an anti-Christian position; she is typically categorized as a "rejec-

---

Rabelais and His World, trans. Helene Iswolsky (Bloomington: Indiana Univ. Press, 1965, 1984), 37–58.

[89]I follow Bakhtin here, who discusses the threefold form of medieval and Renaissance folk humor—as ritual spectacles (such as the shows and pageants of carnival), comic verbal compositions (such as Latin sacred parodies), and genres of billingsgate (such as oaths and curses). See his introduction to a treatment of the carnivalesque humor of Rabelais, ibid., 1–58.

tionist."[90] Even a nontheological reader of Daly's later works judges that she has created a closed register by creating a replica rather than a parody of patriarchy. The effect in *Beyond God the Father* of the theological grammar, however, is to undermine the potential for a rigid coded binary, a universe populated by only two kinds of women: "real women" and "painted birds." *Beyond God the Father* offers a fluid set of subject positions from which persons are assessed and to which they are invited.

My reading of these feminist texts as politicizing parody is designed to portray them as a resisting practice in the sense that Presbyterian Women's literature or Pentecostal women's performances were resisting regimes. The rules for reading that organize these feminist discourses are the implicit rules that I find in critical modernist accounts of what theology is. This theological reading regime makes its mark in relation to feminist theologians' vision of a social order participant in the kingdom of God, a reality characterized by justice, radical love, the refusal of hierarchy and domination in religion or politics. In light of that vision, feminist theology invokes a humor and disrespect with its subversive parody of modern theology that can open up an imaginative space for alternative redemptive practices. I propose, in short, that this parody is antitheology in a good sense. It aids in a move toward a contemporary version of theologia as transformative practice, rather than simply rigorous inquiry.

More is needed in this account, however. Not only am I reading the texts in a different way than their authors, but it is insufficient simply to find alternative hopeful images generated by the parodic use of the systematic frame. The parodic, politicizing register calls the project of critical modernist reflection into question; it leaves us with a crack, a contradiction, that cannot be smoothed over. We must trace the category of resisting regime further, determining its effectiveness and limitations in the social formation. We need to see how it is engraf(ph)ted in social relations that are not directly evident in the regime itself.

---

[90]Daly is used as an example of the "rejectionist" feminists in Jacquelyn Grant, *White Woman's Christ and Black Woman's Jesus: Feminist Christology and Womanist Perspectives*, AAR Series 6 (Atlanta: Scholars Press, 1989), 151–61. Meaghan Morris thinks Daly's *Gyn/Ecology* re-creates a closed system, becoming a "reversal of the reversal" with a new "other," males and fembots. "What remains discreetly *un*-reversed by this process is the structural necessity FOR a symbol of the OTHER (who now becomes a woman as well)." We cannot simply have a reversal, Morris says, for it leads to sameness. *The Pirate's Fiancee*, 43–45.

Feminist register as graf(ph)t

Any thought that feminist theologies resist patriarchy purely and simply by virtue of their ideas is dispelled by my argument that these texts are practices with intertextual relations with certain modes of theological reflection. My reading yields something more.[91] In comparison to other regimes of reading, feminist theologies are aimed more directly at theological reflection as a system and a mode of reflection, as a way of defining knowledge and truth. This means that feminist theologies are not in any central way biblical practices, even if they may have indirect implications for biblical practice. It means also that they are not the substitute "correct" ideas for the wrong ones of critical modernist (or traditional orthodox) theologies. In their politicizing parodic register, feminist theologies raise questions about the social practices that support Christian reflection. They call attention to the temptation of pretensions to intelligibility risked by all knowledge-production. What we have still to examine are their effects on the social conditions whereby this register is graf(ph)ted on the institution of theological knowledge-production. To examine this, we must consider not only field, but tenor and mode as well, and the impact of the three together.

Read as a field–dominant genre, feminist theology is constituted not only by the ideas of these texts, but by the production of these ideas with subgenres, of which the main one is parody. This variable alone suggests that feminist theologies are about more than the sexism in Christian doctrine and symbols, and they are concerned with more than reflections of women's experience. Their targets include modern (and implicitly orthodox) theologies. They aim not only at the dominance of male symbols and hierarchical thinking in these theologies, but at their ostensible neutrality as well. In short, feminist theological discourse is politicizing parody of a certifying discourse.

The mode of feminist theology is, of course, written discourse. Feminist theology is produced as scholarly texts. These texts connect readers to other kinds of theologies. The distinctive way they make the connections is perhaps the most important feature of academic feminist discourse. The dominance of the field variable has led to a focus not only on the ideas, but on the strategies that written discourse can employ. The literary strategies of resistance are important for their transgression of the expectations associated with the civil and objec-

---

[91]Not all feminist theological writing is in the style of the Ruether and Daly texts. Some of it is written in the more muted and civil style of modern theology.

tively displayed critical modern theology. This means that the mode of this feminist practice is as important to its unique form of resistance as is its field variable, the ideas of feminism.

In addition, the character of the field variable has important consequences for the tenor of feminist theological discourse—for how we interpret the relations it evokes. Insofar as Ruether's and Daly's writings are studied as theological texts, their tenor is in some sense didactic, they inform and educate readers. My interpretation requires that they not be taken simply as didactic, however. Ruether's and Daly's texts do not simply teach or lecture; they also provoke and enrage, if read as denunciation or as literal historical description. If read as parody, they delight and effect a comradely, conspiratorial sense of community.[92]

Neither the end of intellectual profit nor private enjoyment is adequate to the tenor of feminist theology, however. By calling them certifying discourses, I not only place feminist theologies in an intertextual relation with the ideas and style of modern theologies; I indicate their graf(ph)tedness in the canonical system of theological reflection proper and the supporting conditions of that form of knowledge production. It is misleading to limit the tenor of this register to the relations between academic texts and readers/students. Because feminist theologies parody and politicize, they gesture toward practices that challenge the political and interest-laden social arrangements in which they typically function. The register of parody, in a way that no other women's discursive practice does, directs us to these practices. It is to the pleasures and parameters of these institutional supports that we must turn to develop the implications of feminist certifying registers.

Certifying discourses, we remember, are those sets of rules and normative practices that are socially endowed with the authority to define the reality of an entity. The reality for which theology is a certifying discourse is the ongoing witness of Christian community, its memory rooted in the life, death, and resurrection of Jesus Christ, its continuing faithfulness in the world to the emerging kingdom of God. Because accredited educational institutions represent social authorization in its most widely dispersed and influential sense, these institutions are the relevant contexts for theology's certifying functions. By identifying feminist theology within the parameters of the certifying genre of

---

[92]This effect is important for the texts' use outside of academic settings, namely in women's communities, consciousness-raising groups, and alternative forms of education.

the academy, we ask how feminist discourse constitutes a resisting regime of that canonical system and, at the same time, how it is caught in that system. How, in other words, are feminist resisting registers graf(ph)ted on the culture of professionalism that nourishes critical modernist theology, and how might they apply pressure to the strains in that relation?

These questions turn on how these institutions contribute to the social endowment of theology as reality-defining discourses. Critical modern theology is on record raising problems of this institutionality. The institutional production of theology as texts, according to Farley, is already shaped by a distortion brought about by the fragmenting forces of the Enlightenment that destroyed theology's unifying position as queen of the sciences. Instead of the ideal unifying and trans-formative wisdom that presides over the study of divine things in theological education, in contemporary settings theology can mean simply the study of the thought of a figure or a school.[93] Theology still exists in contemporary presentations as something that transcends a plurality of texts, however: as ecclesial reflection, reasoned faith, or a church-based form of faith seeking understanding. As such it charac-terizes some specialized form of knowledge and is reproduced in in-stitutions that pass it on, whether in the training of ministers or in the forming of educated humanists or religionists. Thus feminist resis-tance must go further.

The critical modernist critique has stopped short of its own more deeply embedded relation to this institutional culture, represented by the subject position occupied by the professional managerial class. The knowlege produced here is constituted out of certain social relations connected with that class. That professional culture is part of the dis-cursive formation of feminist theology. (Feminists typically note the failure of critical modernist theologies to socially locate themselves.)

We saw that theological texts invoke "reality" by engaging in the discourse of objectivity through devices such as the removal of sub-jects from the writing and the use of the passive voice. These literary practices draw attention away from the words and images and direct it to the supposed referents. The work of this directing discourse, however, is such that its constructed nature is muted. When we hear the language of the academy, we hear a language that foregrounds the givenness of the objects discussed; these objects appear to control the discourse. This effect may be appropriate insofar as theological dis-course needs to assume the reality of God rather than engage in its

---

[93]Farley, *Theologia.*

warranting. It is not appropriate, however, if theological discourse is to acknowledge its own complicity in social location.

Feminist theological practice is not a call for the demise of Christian faith or of theologia. By constituting a field-dominant register, feminist theology poses a challenge to the point of the field, and to the institutions in which the field is embedded—it challenges the production of knowledge. Insofar as its point is to render Christian faith intelligible in a modern world to a variety of publics and to attend to the situated and social realities of evil, there is a fracture down the middle of modern theological discourse. That fracture is a manifestation of the fact that it is driven institutionally to reproduce the culture of professionalism, which entails the education of the elite and the middle class to lead mainstream churches and to teach in the best academies. By gesturing toward this fracture, feminist theological practice exposes conflicting agendas for the field.

Feminist theological practices render theological discourse politicized, not displaced or dispelled. It foregrounds the politicization of theology because only when the social practices that are essential features of the "game" of faith are acknowledged can the full sense of theologia as a transformative wisdom be formulated. The intelligibility of a theological system and faithfulness to its sources are not adequate to reconceiving this wisdom. The politicizing parody of feminist texts points toward the unfinished task of bringing such a project into being. The first moment of that task is the incorporation of an analytic of power as essential to a display of theologia's possibilities for transformative knowledge. As much as these critical modern theologies discuss the importance of praxis, the corruption of knowledges by class, race, and gender variables, they do not recognize the embeddedness of theological rationality as such in the microtechnologies of power.

Feminists have explored some of the issues related to the production of knowledge and liberation. They have questioned the adequacy of highly authoritative, banking models of teaching, the North American forms of education that run roughshod over certain kinds of learners and favor highly linear, left-brain thinking over more creative experiential learning. They have argued that the process of theological education should model dialogical process and have justice/love as its goal.[94] But feminist criticism of the structures of patriarchy or of in-

---

[94]These issues are raised in the work of the Cornflower Collective, *Your Daughters Shall Prophesy: Feminist Alternatives in Theological Education* (New York: Pilgrim Press, 1980), and the Mudflower Collective, *God's Fierce Whimsy: Christian Feminism and Theo-*

justice of any kind — racism, classism, heterosexism — cannot move us to new strategies. They ignore the powers that traverse and produce *our place* in these structures.

When feminists discuss power as an oppressive force located in certain people and arrangements, they imply that as soon as the patriarchal, racist structures (literatures, people, pay scales, hierarchies) are removed, then justice and liberation will be in place. Power thus conceived as an end to external prohibitions has the problems attendant to liberal constructions of the subject. This conception is inadequate not only to a Christian grammar of sin, but to our own place in the game. Liberal analyses that locate power in the hands of men and misogynist structures fail to respect the instability of subject positions and the discursive production of subjects. It is these productions that channel desire, not the inner protected "self" of a subject. To return to the dichotomy between liberal subjects and social structures would be to make the fatal mistake that occludes the complicity of all in the dispersion of sin/oppression by ignoring the connections that signifying provides in the production of "objects." Isofar as conflicting discourses intersect in the academy (and church), they produce intersected/conflicting subject positions.

By insisting that power is dispersed and produced through these discourses, I refuse to separate transforming, liberating subjects and structures from oppressive and patriarchal subjects and structures. Subjects who produce in the academy *are produced by the academy and its stipulations of relevance.* Feminist theology may exist on the margins. As such, it may indeed flower as Daly says into a "ludic cerebration" that somehow reverses the creativity-killing methodolatry of patriarchal disciplines.[95] The margins do not escape, however, the overlapping of domains where certain kinds of occlusions will always occur, regardless of our good will.

To complete this sketch of the feminist resisting regime in which parody is the dominant register, the production of feminist theologian-scholars must be reviewed like that of nonfeminist scholars. In the poststructuralist subject, we cannot look for the constituting agent, but for the ways that subjects are constituted by what they are

---

logical Education (New York: Pilgrim Press, 1985). They are raised as well in more recent feminist articles in collections of essays on a variety of theological education issues. See the contributions of Elisabeth Schüssler Fiorenza and Rebecca S. Chopp in *The Education of the Practical Theologian: Responses to Joseph Hough and John Cobb's Christian Identity and Theological Education,* ed. Don. S. Browning, David Polk, and Ian S. Evison (Atlanta: Scholars Press, 1989).
    [95]Daly, *Gyn/Ecology,* 22–24.

not—by the exclusions. The category of interest handles the workings of occlusion, a set of rules that arises out of a larger canon, reproducing some of its occluding features yet contesting them as well. I have suggested that occlusions are the nether side of pleasures. Thus the possibilities for resistance and strategies that move out of the oppressive outcomes of the canonical theological system emerge when we look at the kinds of pleasures and constraints attached to the location where certifying discourses are produced.

When professional women rise in the academy, they are constituted into subject positions that may resolve the de-skilling visited on the U.S. housewife: feminist scholars are constituted as skilled professionals. They are overdetermined, however, by other processes rife with ambiguous power dynamics. Those dynamics produce a number of pleasures. First, the genre of feminist theology itself offers a pleasure not bound to the educational institution. As incendiary as they may be, Daly's and Ruether's texts offer noetic pleasures, as well as the pleasures of laughter constructed out of wild and grotesque parodies. It is not misogynist or destructive laughter when read in light of the position of dispossessed readers. This high-intensity parody opens up the possibility of a destabilizing of oppressive structures as a pleasurable idea.

The community of feminist theologians who read and write these texts, we who experience their pleasures, are graf(ph)ted onto the subject positions of educated professionals. The pleasures of this mode of discourse (written academic texts) are strikingly different from the pleasures highlighted in Pentecostal women's practices, those of intense affective performances. The former are predominantly mental pleasures and pleasures that characterize certain kinds of social locations. It is not that other social locations do not allow for mental pleasures, or that other women might not enjoy parody, but that these are not construed as valuable labor for them.

The graf(ph)t here is the codes that construct us as the professional managerial class, the aspirations inscribed in what we are and their sustenance by the practices of the university or seminary. As defined by the production of ideas, the danger in the pleasures of this discourse is precisely that relation of domination at the heart of its historic formation. If it is true that the U.S. higher education system is the primary institutional support for the values represented by professional competence, then, even though this picture is mitigated by the other goods provided by the universities of a democratic society, the production of theologians or ministers is a graf(ph)t, nurtured by social relations of benevolent domination. It is so nurtured as long as that knowledge-producing matrix is not differently conceived outside of the ideologies of merit and reward that came out of nineteenth-century middle-class notions of the successful person.

The point here is that the production of these pleasures may come at the expense of other graf(ph)tings that nurture other sensibilities. The pleasures of expertise may serve to produce a corporate habitus that cannot know or respect the other. It may serve to produce feminists who can point to the constructed and patriarchal character of theology, who can spot the inadequacy of stitching together the concern for the marginal with the respect for reasonable publics, but could not recognize an alternative wisdom. Part of the problem of respecting difference, then, is our subject position.

How can the conditions be developed for resisting—for making the commitment to the other, the excluded, the marginalized (particularly women of color, poor or working-class women and lesbians)? This commitment has generally sustained feminist theologians in resisting the accommodations that are likely in our subject position. What can support and build up these conditions of resistance? What does it now mean to respect difference? How does the intersection of "remembering Jesus" with our location make this support possible? We turn to these questions in the final chapter.

7

Chapter

Beyond Inclusion: A Feminist Theology of Difference

When a sufficient number of specialists are assembled on a college faculty, the subject of which each knows only a small part is said to be covered, and the academic department to which they all belong is regarded as fully manned. In ancient Ireland, if legend is to be trusted, there was a tower so high that it took two persons to see to the top of it. One would begin at the bottom and look up as far as sight could reach, the other would begin where the first left off, and see the rest of the way.

—John Erskine

Summary of the argument thus far

I began this project with the question: Can feminist theology rise to the challenge represented by women who occupy different social locations, and can it do so without the minimalist outcome of liberal inclusionary politics? I have pressed the question of differences among women through the examples of groups of women who do not share ostensibly feminist agendas and who occupy social locations other than liberation academic feminists. These women signify a challenge to a feminist theological method dependent on women's experience as a stable term. "Woman" includes many differently constructed subject positions, and therefore is not an identity on which theologies can be based.

This does not mean that the various debilitating configurations of gender cannot serve as sites for feminist theologizing, however. I have proposed a feminist model of discourse analysis to initiate an alternative to experience-based theology. My quarrel with some feminist

355

method is not a quarrel over whether issues of gender, class, and racial oppression should be central to contemporary Christian life and the academy. They constitute the irruptions of what Michel Foucault calls subjugated knowledges around which liberation theologies develop.

I have argued that these issues are not successfully posed around notions of subjects and their experiences in the discursive systems of academics. Appeals to experience have provoked criticisms in the academy, but they do not supply the complex grids connecting language to social practice, nor do they connect knowledge to desire and power, and these connections are necessary to avoid inclusionary positions. Appeals to experience have tended to define interest too thinly. Simply to say that theology expresses or is based on a particular experience of oppression does not get at the way theology, like any discourse, is a material process of meaning production embedded in a social location (in this case academic institutions).

The line of continuity I have developed from feminist liberation theologies is the insight crucial to any liberationist theology that rejects conventional liberal inclusion of the outsider. The insight that all knowledge is fallible and interested, for good and ill, has been developed in relation to the material character of discourse. Interest turns out to mean configurations of social codes that are supported institutionally and get produced out of the discourses, desires, and fears of the social formation at a number of levels. Because interest is socially activated, it is (ultimately) not a private or individual bias. The site of fracture, the possibility for sin, is in socially defined realities. The need for confession-transformation is, minimally, an institutional need.

I have also reconfigured the central elements in feminist theological thinking about women and Christian faith, biblical texts and interpreting subjects, as intertextual relations, suspending their ostensibly natural boundaries. By situating women's faith practices in this field of textuality or discursive processes, I have read them in light of the codes of their particular religious tradition—its constructions of gender, the constraints and pleasures of social location, and the conflicts and possibilities thereby engendered. This approach does not dissolve everything into an undifferentiated mass of signifying, but it shows that women, their biblical practices, and their redemptive outcomes are all temporary stabilizations of deeply entrenched (and different) but nonpermanent ways of dealing with sin, oppression, and Christian biblical traditions.

My account moves beyond the view that the feminist experience of certain texts and practices as oppressive is adequate to describe all forms of gendered subjectivities. The more complex grids that connect language to other signifying processes and, particularly, to social practices have shown other women's sense of the texts to be contradictory to feminists'. Such discrepancies do not discredit liberation feminist readings; but they do suggest that if we are to take seriously difference in location, we must recognize that subjects and biblical texts have less in common than we might have supposed.

On the basis of the litmus test of my own feminist theological lexicon about empowerment of women, for example, the submissive-dependence and self-denigrating language of Pentecostal women looks to be a discourse of utter misogyny. Read intertextually and as socially graf(ph)ted on their situation, however, their practice appears different. For Pentecostal women the pleasures of their canon's reading of the Holy Spirit and the ecstasies afforded in their intimacy with God produce a place of well-being, in stark contrast with the marks of marginalization in their lives. It is not a place immediately compatible with liberationist practices, which are directed toward resisting socioeconomic marginalization, but it is a place of God-sustained integrity. The gospel for these women, it seems to me, cannot be extricated from the texture of their place, their performance, their antiworld posture. To isolate their belief in divine intervention in worldly events from the discursive networks that make up their position would violate the work that belief does in their situation; similarly, we cannot isolate their dependence-submission without violating its meaning.

Feminist theology, then, cannot look only at the presence or absence of certain ideas about gender as a test of how women fare in a community. Judgment regarding what counts as women's oppression and resistance to oppression requires more respectful attention to the *how* and *what* and *where*. It requires connecting every practice with the discursive possibilities available to women, the way in which being "woman" is part of their oppression, and the distinctive scripture they hear as good news. Openings for emancipatory or liberating possibilities are found at the intersection of canonical codes and practices with the sufferings and desires of women's social location. These openings can look alien to the ideals of liberation feminism.

In addition, recognition of the inseparable connection of knowledge to desire and power takes us to a deeper issue than who is "right." It exposes the naturalized definitions of "woman" (and "man") that still cling to our theologies and remain to be challenged in ways not considered here. In short, it is important to destabilize "woman," to "textualize" all of reality, not to do away with feminist thinking but to get at the knowledge/power relations that constitute all thinking. We must acknowledge the relations in order to know what it will mean to respect difference from the site of academic practice.

The argument that difference is a matter of social construction leads to the most obvious implication of my analysis: the need for more complex feminist theological categories for language, interpreting subjects, and biblical texts. This complexity is a result of the employment of poststructuralism to extend the meaning of fallibility in support of liberationist concerns. Such a project invites another look at the theological part of feminist theology. Several questions remain. First, if feminist theology is an embedded social practice—a certifying discourse, to be precise—in what sense is it appropriate to continue to call it theology? This poststructuralist approach leaves a second matter unresolved: In what way does nonidentity theology continue to be feminist? Just what is the gain of respecting the "other" if we must problematize the notion of "woman" so completely? Finally, what difference does respecting difference make after all? Has the employment of discourse theory accomplished anything more than simply providing a display case for the exotic, asking that we admire the strange nature of women who are not like progressive academic feminists? If this is really a radicalizing of inclusion, my proposal must imply something else.

Feminist theology as theology? Certifying practices, destabilization of scripture/tradition, and other transgressions

To situate this work as a theological project is to assume, as I have, that liberation theologies emerge from particular gaps in faith's reading of reality—the "fissures and cracks," as Rebecca Chopp puts it.[1] This means that theological discernments do not arise from a foundational knowledge, a certain truth, or a system applied. Feminist theological practice comes from the judgment that historical subjects "women" are not yet fully produced as creatures of God and that such is a wrong to be redressed. To say this much is to admit that these practices erupt in relation to the canonical system of a particular faith. But it also means that one does not begin with systematic theology in doing feminist theology. One does not really "begin" theology in any linear way. Something new is cobbled together out of the necessities of the time read with the practices of faith, and it is not possible to say that one precedes the other.

---

[1] Rebecca S. Chopp, *The Power to Speak: Feminism, Language, God* (New York: Crossroad, 1989), 15–21.

The liberationist version of this insight is often described as the inseparability (or priority) of praxis from reflection. I avoid the separation by identifying feminist theology in terms of its intertextual relations and graf(ph)ted location of utterance—my subject position as a Euro-American academic feminist theologian. Of those intertextual relations, I will highlight four of the terms of critical modern theological discourses that are implicated by my proposal for feminist theology as certifying discourse.

Crucial designation of "certifying."   First, the choice of the designation "certifying" is crucial to feminist theology's liberation interests. The theological reason to designate theology as certifying discourse is to make its located and interested character constitutive. That allows us to develop the notion of fallibility beyond the recognition that our writings are historical and transient, which is the best account that critical modern theology offers. Certifying, the socially authorized practice that distinguishes between what is "real" and what is not for mainstream Christian communities, offers a thicker account of fallibility. It ties knowledge production to a particular regime of power, that of the professional class of which we academics are members. In short this designation indicates the synchronic, material character of finitude. It is a sobering reminder that the feminist theology practiced as political activism with grass roots connections and relations to other classes is incidental to any officially recognized version of "real" knowledge.

Theological definitions are attempts in a particular setting to practice Christian faith to the glory of God, to understand God truly, as David Kelsey says, and not just to describe social realities. I do not dispute that. Theological definitions are social realities, however; there is no getting around it. It would be docetic to consider that practices might refer only to God and not simultaneously be social practices implicated in specific matters and power dynamics. No one is served (except perhaps the professional theologian) by theologians' authorizations that appear to excuse theology from the other work it does at the same time that it (sometimes) honors God. This other work includes sponsoring careers, justifying failures, putting premature closure on the messiness of reality, and qualifying as ideology.[2]

---

[2]David Kelsey, *To Understand God Truly: What's Theological about a Theological School* (Louisville: Westminster/John Knox Press, 1992). As Wesley Kort puts it, theologies are not authorized by their referent or by their authors. Thus to say, "I do theology for the church," or based on the Bible, or whatever, does not *eo ipso* extricate a position from the ideological work such voice warranting can do. Wesley A. Kort, *Bound to Differ: The*

Liberation epistemology requires this refusal of typical theological dichotomies—reflection, conceived as ideas existing prior to language, or as linguistic discourse, conceived apart from material relations. Having asserted this liberation epistemological conviction in chapter 1, however, my account of discourse theory has shown that multiple signifying with accompanying occlusions does characterize ordinary processes of meaning. The same must hold for theological discursive practice, too. The fact that its work as a social practice is part of the very definition of theology is not reductive. Unless we are to except theological discourse from the processes of ordinary semiosis, the unavoidable multivalence of its signifying processes has to be acknowledged.

I have indicated the importance of social relations of theological practices by referring to the graf(ph)ted relation between discourse and social location. Academic theology is, on these terms, that socially authorized practice which distinguishes between what is "real" and what is not "real" for mainstream Christian communities. While there is certainly more to say on what constitutes this process (what counts as "academic," different kinds of institutional supports and challenges for those who qualify as certifiers, among other things), my intent here is to make it impossible to conceive of theology or any ostensible theoretical practice as something intelligible outside of the social practice that makes it real. I wish to mark our reflection as nourished and constrained by certain institutional realities.

If we fail to incorporate this mark, the constraints on our own formation as subjects go unthematized. Insofar as we can bring these constraints into view—and we cannot bring them all—the pleasures and containments of social relations will have much to do with making certain kinds of questions and inquiries unthinkable. It is just these realities that two other typical approaches to theology cannot make available. The liberal view of theology as the expression of human experience, for one, turns out to be inadequate in relation to my account of the multiple functioning of theological discourse. A notion of experience typically cannot recognize a complex web of signifying processes and the material embeddedness of those processes that makes up the blind side of our thinking. It is not within the purview of my "experience" to worry about threats that never impinge on my life or interrupt my capacity to reflect. When it assumes raw experience is the origin of meaning, an experience-based theology is not able to thema-

Dynamics of Theological Discourses (University Park: Pennsylvania State Univ. Press, 1992), 12–14.

tize how a position is itself a produced reality. The social effects of a certifying discourse are simply not "experiences" that theologians have.

The notion that theology is second-order reflection on the more primary language of faith is another unsatisfactory option. It is also not amenable to the recognition that theology does institutional and cultural certifying work. This is not to deny that theological discussions *are* frequently abstract and done in a generalizing mode that differs from liturgical or personal confession (although some theologians write in these modes). The point is not that all abstractions are bad, or that critical and reasoned arguments are not useful and needed. This project itself employs the field-dominant register of theology as a technical discipline of sorts for a regime of resistance. I clearly do not judge abstractions to be the problem; my own writing is an example of critical and abstract reasoning. Rather, the problem comes when defining theology as second-order reflection implies that theology achieves a clarifying distance from which to assess critically the rush and lived everydayness of faith in the world.

The problem is the suggestion that theoretical discourse is distanced and thereby not impacted by power. Defining theology as second-order reflection can suggest that its abstractings, even when they are posed as transient and modified universals, are disembodied, not graf-(ph)ted on social position and not constructed by desire and pleasure. The point is not infrequently made that abstractions and critical leverages themselves are contingent. They vary from one social formation to another, and therefore cannot be universal discourse, as Foucault has demonstrated so well. Most importantly, as I have argued, theological reflection and its distanced critiques are the thought forms of certain kinds of subjects. They (we) are subjects whose problem is not that intentions or private whims are biasing our thought, although that may happen. It is that we are produced in social processes that legitimate experts and create effects that are more serious than anything we individually intend.

Speaking of the appeal to ontological or universal categories of thought, Sharon Welch describes the graf(ph)t of subject position more specifically: "Universal discourse is the discourse of the privileged."[3] This does *not* mean that only the discourse of the nonprivileged should be counted as theology; my refusal of experiential

---

[3]Sharon D. Welch, *Communities of Resistance and Solidarity: A Feminist Theology of Liberation* (Maryknoll, N.Y.: Orbis Books, 1985), 80. This whole chapter is greatly influenced by Welch's work. I depart from her only insofar as I hazard a definition of truth that is not totally Foucaultian; I find a place for a kind of theo/acentric transcendence as

expressivism rules that out. Rather, Welch is on to something because in the most graphic sense the "space for universalizing" is a space whose pleasures and constraints produce biases. It would be false to think of the scholar's study as removed from the thick of things; it is simply in the middle of a different kind of thick of things than the reflection of the parish worker or Christian social activist. We whose pains are not a matter of our very survival are not likely to view the theological landscape as one that requires urgent responses to human suffering.

The certifying practice of theology is not its only work; we must take up the implications of this account of fallibility to theology's relation to its ultimate subject matter, the God of Christian faith, as well. But first, other changes from the marks of critical modern theologizing fill out my definition of feminist theology in relation to the issues of theologia as discipline (knowledge) and habitus (wisdom). The impact of discourse theory entails the dissolution of the clear distinctions between types of discourse; and it requires adjustments in the normalizing role of the past (as authoritative tradition) and the systematizing of truth. With these transgressions the nature of theological truth takes on a particular shape.

Blurring of "disciplines."   On the terms of liberation feminism, what counts as a habitus or formation of the subject is shaped by what counts as rigorous pursuit of the realities of the world—that is, by our sense of what an adequate transformed subject might look like in the contemporary situation. Theology as "discipline" is neither the study of revealed truths, nor the correlation of the sciences of modernity with the contents of Christian faith. If there is one clear lesson from the turn to discourse, it is that the project of separating out the signifiers of theology from the signifiers of other disciplines—of culture, of secular knowledges—is a fundamentally ill-conceived one.

The turn to a theory of meaning as use in my argument gives feminist theology a respect for networks of beliefs such as the grammars of a Christian community, an important alternative to foundationalism (the analogue to the notion that language is representational). The move of intratextualists to maintain the closed character of the discourses that make up these networks, however, proved to be problematic for a theological economy that opens up meaning processes to

---

she does not; and I find more in Christian practices than she does. Her vision, however, is enormously persuasive and articulated with great clarity and power.

scrutiny.[4] Recognition of the power/knowledge relation makes the desire for closure even more suspect. Theological grammars allow us to think of the way Christians order practices, but the theoretical distinctiveness of that ordering cannot be made to depend on its nonintersection with other (potentially dissonant) discourses. Other grids of analysis taken up by feminist (as well as other) theologies are not potential distortions of strictly or inherently theological realities; they are part of it. The very choice of discourse theory and Foucault in this analysis, for example, is not the corruption of theological categories. I will argue that it is a result of a theological sensibility.

Because meaning processes are always intertextual, as I have argued, inside/outside kinds of judgments no longer serve a helpful purpose where theological versus secular discourse is concerned. These discourses are always intersected; subjects are produced by, are players in, numbers of discursive practices. Any Christian practice or the grammar that orders it are already implicated in the discourses about gender or any number of seemingly ordinary things that are part of its location. I used these intersections of discourses earlier to account for subversive or counter-readings of a text within an ostensibly holistic communal network of belief. Here I conclude that they grant the feminist theologian a different take on the relation of so-called "theological knowledge" and "secular knowledge" than that typical of the holism of postliberal theology, which acknowledges that particular vocabularies may change, but grammars do not.

Recognition of the instability of discourses is, of course, not the claim that all meanings have the same force or recognition. While all discourses are constitutive (we cannot appeal to the natural over the constructed), not all are equal. "We are always," as Wesley Kort says, "in some social/cultural situation, some discursive context, that will tend to make the "referents" of some discourses appear normal and even unquestionable and others to be dubious."[5] This is an opening for criticism of hegemonic discourses by the silenced discourses, but it is also

---

[4]The network of beliefs is used by such theologians as Lindbeck and Thiemann. Philosophical holism in epistemology and theories of meaning (W. V. Quine, Ludwig Wittgenstein) form its background. These theologians, as I have indicated in a different way earlier, do not explore the structuralist problems raised by their reliance on holism. George Lindbeck, *The Nature of Doctrine: Religion and Theology in a Postliberal Age* (Philadelphia: Westminster Press, 1984); Ronald Thiemann, *Revelation and Theology: The Gospel as Narrated Promise* (Notre Dame, Ind.: Notre Dame Univ. Press, 1985).
[5]Kort, *Bound to Differ*, 32.

the admission that some beliefs in a community can be granted—need
to be granted—more force than others.

My point can be made if we ask what is protected by the appeal to
an inner biblical logic that is to dominate or correct an outside theological or secular discourse. A good example of this is found in the
postliberalist wish to protect the integrity of Christian grammar with
the notion of intratextuality. Postliberals construe meaning as imma-
nent in scripture; the core narrative of scripture must form the world
to correct for the way in which the world (or extratextual realities)
shapes persons' readings of scripture. Thus biblical forming must have
priority over world-forming. The intratextual form of postliberalism
wishes to commend itself precisely because it refuses cultural accommodation. However, I have located a form of antimodernism in the
Pentecostal community, which would also claim that the biblical text
is utterly formative of lives. This antimodernism reads women's
lives as inscribed with the agency of God's miraculous work and
consistently refuses to take up the intellectual or cultural ways of modernity.

The postliberal distinction invoked with intratextuality between
being formed by world discourses versus being formed by scriptural
discourse does no explanatory work in my example. This distinction
will not serve successfully to identify indisputable "normative" discourses. The Pentecostal women identify different biblical texts from
intratextualists. To make sense of George Lindbeck's or Pentecostal
women's different graf(ph)ts of scripture we have to go to the discursive formation in which the privileging of discourse is done. I suspect
that the lack of force of these women's discourses has more to do with
their social location than with their accommodation to culture. It is the
interplay of socially graf(ph)ted discourses that helps us see this. The
test for postliberalism as a serious refusal of the accommodations of
modernity might be its capacity to recognize any saints in the Pentecostal community. What is protected by intratextualism, to return to
my earlier question, is the need to acknowledge social location as integral to a construal of scripture.

I conclude that there simply is no absolute distinction between the
signifying processes that constitute different knowledges. A grammar
does its work in a setting. Theological rules and languages have no
meaning except in a material intertextual or even dialogical relation
with other discourses. To treat a theological conviction as a norm in
itself, outside of its work in a social practice, is to treat it as a monologue, to use Mikhail Bakhtin's terms. The final determinant of its semantic work occurs when its intertextual or dialogical character is

recognized.[6] This does not mean that distinctions cannot be made between theological and secular discourses. It is a grave error, however, to find them completely disjunctive.[7]

Let me suggest how traditional theological discourses intersect with other analytical frames in my account. The emergence of feminist theology is a first example. A feminist theological account attends to suppressed discourses, or, more accurately, the conflicts created by the several social practices that construct women and eventually produce new discourses. These emerge as dissonances with the normal discourse because of intersecting knowledges (ostensibly secular with religious). For example, it was not simply the biblical or doctrinal tradition that produced feminist judgments about needed liberation practices. These insights required the intersections of cultural texts with the religious tradition. Cultural texts such as liberal democratic justice and Enlightenment discourses created conflicts with the male-dominant terms for subjects and the obedience and submission discourses of Christian tradition. Such dissonances lead the theologian to resources in other analytical frames. Analytical grids for gender—not, strictly speaking, theological—are *necessary* then to feminists' discernments about the Christian tradition.

Cultural texts such as liberal democratic justice and Enlightenment discourses created conflicts with the male-dominant terms for subjects and the obedience and submission discourses of Christian tradition.

This intersection of so-called other knowledge grids and theological discourses also defines theologia as habitus—the salvific or formative character of theology. A feminist vision of redemption encompasses symbols of God's realm that call forth refusals of domination. Its sense of the profundity of actual forms of domination makes feminist theology incompatible with accounts of evil that entail Enlightenment notions of reason or with the uncritical appropriation of social science as neutral description. This incompatibility accounts

---

[6]Any theology can be analyzed as a monologue rather than a dialogue, or co-constitutive discourse, in the Bakhtinian sense. Any discourse can be studied as a monologue, a self-contained set of meanings. This is to repress the double-voiced or dialogical character of any piece of writing, however. See Appendix 2 in *Problems of Dostoevsky's Poetics*, 283–302.

[7]To take this seriously is to see that identifying something as Christian (or not) abstracted from its intertextual, dialogical meaning is utterly problematic. One simply has to rely on the claim of a community about what it is doing in order to distinguish what is Christian and what is not. (Clearly this is not the same thing as approving it.) The only defense a position such as mine can give that it is theology or that it is Christian is that it confesses. Not only does that confession occur within a broad range of discourses, but it commits feminist or any theology to a radically situational judgment about meaning.

for the attraction of Foucault's categories of power/knowledge. Even if his agonistic ontology is not satisfactory theologically, Foucault provides more compelling accounts of finitude than those in anthropologies characteristic of modern theologies, where a historical-temporal vector defines the possibility for sin by means of the insecurity of located self-transcendence.[8]

These intersections of a poststructuralist power/knowledge analytic with theological grammar show that a feminist theology of finitude is a tragic account. Michel Foucault's more compelling accounts of the inseparable knowledge/power connection and the productive technologies of disciplinary power help display the synchronicity and weight of finitude—it is spatial and bodied. It also displays the inescapable corruption that comes with finitude. Finitude presents itself as networks that are not permanent features of history, but technologies and apparatuses of particular epistemes. Individual subjects are not outside of these apparatuses, they are produced by them. It is impossible to separate power and its effects from any aspect of creaturely reality. Thinking about the finitude/power connection in this way makes it impossible to exclude ourselves, the privileged who produce knowledge, from this realm of fallibility so as to mark as inevitable our complicity as subjected subjects—a complicity that accords with a feminist theo/acentric grammar of sin.

A tragic sense of finitude and its fallibility are not all that draws a feminist theology to an analytics of omnipresent power. To identify the disciplining of women as diminishing and oppressive is to already participate in a discursive practice of grace, or a promise of one. Here I depart from Foucault. It is not a practice that is free from power, of course, but it transgresses certain of power's technologies. Thus Friedrich Schleiermacher is correct when he argues that it is the determination of communally shaped self-consciousness by the antithesis of sin and grace that provides the grid for a theological view of creation as God-dependent. That account of grace and redemption, however, is consonant with feminist sensibilities of the problem. Our connectedness and our helplessness in this post-Holocaust world is overwhelming, but a taste of alternatives to domination is all that is

---

[8] I cannot make the case for these as constraints insofar as for Foucault they are simply productions; there is no human nature to be constrained. The possibility of appropriating Foucault's acccount of power/knowledge and rejecting his agonistic view of reality may be more complex than I have shown here. My brief defense is that his undefended assumption that "madness, death, and sex underlie discourse and resist linguistic appropriation" is paralleled by mine with regard to the God Christians worship. See Hubert L. Dreyfus and Paul Rabinow, *Michel Foucault: Beyond Structuralism and Hermeneutics*, 2d ed. (Chicago: Univ. of Chicago Press, 1983), xii.

required by feminists. With that we can be guided by a theological grammar that indicates the need for redemption of the creation, a redemption that is neither complete nor fully known. An account of power/knowledge does not exclude practices of resisting domination; in fact it includes the constant transgressings of particular technologies of power. This power analytic also opens up a way to think theologically about resistance. In the place of a move to a place of total liberation, resistance can be figured as the grace of being situated so as to name domination.[9] Feminist theology knows that the practices of grace are never pure and simple escapes from false consciousness; they simply keep us able to name and resist new forms of sin—places where the created goodness of the other is not honored.

Another place where the discourses intersect is in my account of feminist theology as a transformative habitus. The subject to be formed by this habitus is conceived in light of a feminist vision of God's realm—but as co-constituted by the discourses of poststructuralism and power/knowledge. Consequently, the most superficial way to conceive the subject is as a discrete individual. The "who" that is transformed is only an individual in the sense that she or he is connected to the social practices of particular locations and to the larger fate of the creation.[10] The judgment that subjects are radically social and indeterminate comes from a pursuit of scientia, the "things of the world," but with a theological sense as well. Sensibilities already constructed out of faith are drawn to the categories of Foucault and poststructuralism. These categories do not legitimate theological claims to ostensible publics, save those with a faith that conceives of sin as historically socially complex and redemption as unfinished, fragile, and pertaining to all life as an interconnected web.

In sum, feminist theology seeks to unite ancient notions of a transformative habitus with accounts of the way things are that is adequate to a liberation perception of the state of a world devastated by wars, racial and ethnic hatreds, nuclear capabilities, and massive, entrenched

---

[9]Sharon Welch has expressed a similar feminist sensibility about sin/evil and redemption. I assume she might have some of the same reasons for being attracted to Foucault. See her *Communities of Resistance and Solidarity* and *A Feminist Ethic of Risk* (Minneapolis: Fortress Press, 1990), where she rejects the potentially paralyzing cynicism that might come with such a view.

[10]This addition of a global reach to local subjects is a choice for Gramsci over Foucault, because the latter's notion of a specific intellectual prevents thinking outside the local. I clearly depart from the notion of a traditional intellectual, but I find Gramsci's "organic intellectual" to have more promise for a theologian. See Antonio Gramsci on intellectuals in *Selections from the Prison Notebooks*, ed. and trans. Quintin Hoare and Geoffrey Nowell Smith (New York: International Publishers, 1971), 3–23.

systems organized to reproduce profit rather than well-being for the planet. The difference between a position like mine that acknowledges the co-constituting of all grammars by the discourses of "culture" and one that insists on their separate, oppositional existence is *not* a difference between a liberal and a postliberal position. It is a difference between two accounts of redemption and subject position. Whether acknowledged or not, the discourses of "culture" construct both positions.

Reconstructing tradition.   A third implication of my account is a striking departure from more traditional kinds of theological rhetoric. Given the usual notion that theology is reflection on the traditional authorities of the faith and the systematic exposition of this tradition, my proposal may appear quite backwards. Not only do I refuse the a priori distinctions between discourse that is essentially theological and discourse that is not; my theological appropriation of views of capitalist patriarchy and its work on women's subject positions may seem to drive my appropriation of the tradition. I have focused on its work as a hegemonic reproduction of dependencies in the various locations available for "women" and as the disciplinary production and enticements for subjects to occupy these positions. I have defined their liberating practices as the graf(ph)ts on tradition/scripture that resist these situations.

But if I am correct that the holism of theological convictions inevitably breaks apart to incorporate the dissonances of a particular cultural-theological intersection, then it is misleading to find fault with my project by claiming it works backwards. It is not legitimate to critique a position because it ostensibly allows contemporary categories of intelligibility to "control" theology's distinctive sources. My argument from discourse analysis precludes there ever being a theological discourse free from contemporary signifying processes. Again I have argued that "theological" or faith discourses and those of "culture" come into being at the same time. The Foucaultian analytic is compelling out of theological judgments about the depth of the problematic and the comprehensiveness of the hope.

I do acknowledge, however, that the effects of the contemporary refusal of modernity that shapes my project make it more difficult to use traditional metatheological discourse about the ability of the past and the tradition to "correct" and have priority over our contemporary constructions. In fact, it will sound to some like I grant priority to a contemporary analysis of social sin. If we recognize the nature of semiotic process according to poststructuralist (or structuralist) accounts of meaning, however, we must acknowledge that contemporary social practices have a constructive role in the way we construe the past. There is no simple way that an appeal to some unconstructed past—to the events of Jesus, to scripture, to historic dogmatic decisions—can serve a univocal critical role, inasmuch as constructions of the past are just that, constructions.[11] While I cannot take up the important work of discussing how we make distinctions between good and bad stories about the past, the position I work from makes distinctions between fiction and reality inadequate to this task.[12] As always, the terms for telling the difference between good and bad renderings are lodged in communities.

My feminist theological position, like any other, is constructed out of the communal convictions and creative dissonances that produce me. These include convictions that Christian faith converges with human situations to emancipate, to create good news for the broken-hearted, to proclaim release for the captives. My position, too, entails a distinctive orientation toward the function of the tradition, for a redemptive outcome is not guaranteed. The warrant of a redemptive traditioning process is not located in a discourse of the past waiting like a hidden treasure to give us permission to respond to the new. By exposing the differential character of meaning, poststructuralism once again emphasizes the fact that the signifying processes by which we read texts or have access to Christian origins have effects on those texts and events.

The role of our interests in the appropriation of scripture is constitutive: without our interests and their conflicts with hegemonic discourses, there *is* no scripture. This does not mean we make up the tradition or indulge in eisegesis, as my argument has made clear. It is the important point that *who we are*, including the regime and its dissonances that produce us, are of fundamental significance to any judgment we make about Christianity as an authoritative tradition. This point also includes the freeing methodological conviction that a "new

---

[11] Thus I disagree with Ronald Thiemann's proposal that grants agency to the scriptural narratives, which "ask to be excepted from (the) general rule" that "context most often functions to control our interpretations and construals of text." A reverse procedure occurs where this narrative of a promising God is prior to the context. My point is not to deny this as a good and helpful construal of the text, but to insist that it *is a construal*. *Revelation and Theology*, 46–47.

[12] The best argument destroying the intuitively held notion that fact and fiction have to (or can) be clearly distinguished is found in Didier Coste, *Narrative as Communication*, vol. 64 in *Theory and History of Literature* (Minneapolis: Univ. of Minnesota Press, 1989), 105–8.

past" is there to be re-membered, reconstructed. The ostensible richness of tradition is not a fixed set of gems, but shifting and open-ended source of possibilities.

What my feminist liberation position suggests for scripture and its traditional canonical authority is not the refusal of the scripture-shaped community, to use Richard Hays's phrase, as some feminists would. Nor do I commend the view that scripture as some pregiven whole will guarantee a certain outcome if rightly read. I have located the productive character of scripture not only in its use (a use that cannot exist without other discourses), but also in a certain kind of stabilization. Instead of locating the stabilizing authority of scripture in its canonical form as a written discourse, I point to practices that create spaces for well-being. Scripture will continue to be a living Word in these (temporary) stabilizations of gospel practice.

Problematizing systematics. In addition to refocusing on the co-construction of the tradition as our authoritative past by the contemporary discourses that produce us, my account reads feminist theology as generated out of certain of the tradition's grammatical rules at the expense of others. What has been distinctive about feminist theology is that on the basis of the conviction that women have not been accorded the status of fully human (*imago dei*) in the Christian tradition, a critical posture emerged that refuses absolute status to any traditional locus of truth. I began by arguing that this critical posture is generated out of a configuration of traditional grammatical convictions: the theo/acentric character of a feminist theological logic is its extension of what it means in this age for a theologian to confess that God alone saves.[13]

Once the instability of discourse is explored, the consequence is to problematize the genre of systematics when it is conceived as a closed and finished project. I will draw the implications of the poststructuralist critique even more stringently. Feminist theology invokes a particular fracture, gender oppression, around which its theological practice develops. Such a theological response is not done outside of traditional theological loci, but it only invokes pieces of a theological grammar rather than a total system. Certain theological loci are prominent grids for feminist thinking, such as the goodness of creation in

---

[13]For feminist theologians, such a confession requires the positioning of woman-church in the cracks between institutional Christianity and secular communities. Not only is Christianity not an essential thing due to its historical plurality (a plurality that liberal theologians such as David Kelsey and David Tracy want to celebrate), but Christianity is threaded with the ideological sins that birthed the protest, feminist theology.

relation to resistance to the deconstructive idolatry effected by sexism. The vision of woman as *imago dei* has been a privileged theme. Other themes, such as Christology, are muted grammatical conventions viewed in light of these primary theological interests.

Similarities can be seen in this theological practice with the move away from the structure or fixed grammar of a language to the site of utterance (or discourse) in linguistics and literary theory. A system or entire grammar is not the origin of actual meaning, and proves unable to account for the changes in meaning that occur in speaking or in particular literary discourses. It may be that, like discursive utterances, no theological position ever truly requires or assumes all the rules of its grammar, just as ordinary language use may never employ all the rules of its grammar. The liberation assumption that theological insight erupts in responses out of situations of social duress is more compatible with an open, discourse-driven account of feminist theology than with a complete systematics.

This is no call to dismantle permanently the riches of the systematic tradition. It is rather the view that attention to the cracks and openings and meaning effects of such systems is part of good theological work and therefore pertinent to the theological task. The truth of a theological position cannot be adjudicated in terms of whether it corresponds to a total system—that is, in terms of its achievement of closure. Another twist on this closure is found in Mary Daly and Rosemary Radford Ruether, whose works can be read as politicizing parodies of the civility of critical modern theological systematizing. The outrage of these works displays the inadequacy of civil discourse. Liberation theology insists that the riches of our heritage are to be put to work for concrete situations of history: as Johann Metz puts it, "After Auschwitz, every theological 'profundity' which is unrelated to people and their concrete situations must cease to exist. Such a theology would be the very essence of superficiality."[14]

What we learn from poststructuralism in the service of liberation theology adds to the rationale for feminist theology's fracturing role. Totalities created by systems create closures, and closures come with "outsiders" by their very nature. As long as there is a need for feminist theology, its engendering logic has the outsider as its special interest. Thus feminist theology will employ and deploy pieces of a theological grammar, but will be long gone before it has even contemplated an entire and finished structure.

---

[14]Johann Baptist Metz, *The Emergent Church: The Future of Christianity in a Post-bourgeois World*, trans. Peter Mann (New York: Crossroad, 1987), 22.

I have also interpreted the feminist theological task beyond the question of whether there is a Christianity hospitable to women through my liberation reading of poststructuralism and the insistence on the material-semiotic character of theological work. The repudiation of the theological tradition does not follow from either (1) the acknowledgment of the hostility to women that appears in it, or (2) the fact that some poststructuralists insist that theology must be done without God. With regard to the first point, attention to the located character of discourse suggests to me that any totalizing judgment about Christianity is the reverse side of the coin of essentialist judgments about the absolute truth of its doctrines. With regard to the second point, I can respond with less thoroughness but have chosen to side with liberationists who say that feminist discourse does not enter the lists over the question of God's existence. More specifically, I employ the critique of the transcendent signified of certain poststructuralisms as an intervention. Tradition-based belief in God already shapes human communities, including mine, and does so redemptively. Just as the deconstructionist move is always deployed within existing structures, so a theological position only emerges within a discourse of belief; whatever destabilizing occurs can never produce the positive claim that there is no God.[15] Thus I began with theological commitments and continue to invoke them as good reasons for positions—not with the view that these are incorrigible truths.

But is this claim—that feminist theology does not enter the lists over existence questions—adequate? What about the incipient nihilism in my turn to poststructuralist discourse? A final comment on the possibility of "truth" in feminist theology must detain me before I take up the implications of my position for the "feminist" in feminist theology and the difference that respecting difference finally makes.

The possibility of truth: theology as testimony

Of several forms of nihilism, some are incompatible with theology, but not all. I suggest that one can be an epistemological nihilist—that is, problematize knowledge—without simultaneously being an alethi-

---

[15]This is why most of these are negative theologies. Mark C. Taylor states that for theology to continue, we must "speak of God godlessly and of the self selflessly." These arguments are endless; they will not be resolved by those deconstructions. What we can learn from them, I think, is to attend to the practices of theological discourse and to question our disciplinary tactics. *Deconstructing Theology*, AAR Studies in Religion 28 (New York: Crossroad; Scholars Press, 1982), 89.

ological nihilist—that is, denying that there is truth.[16] Inasmuch as I have already refused the idealist-realist options as an accurate portrayal of the terms of the discursive constitution of reality, I have refused a nihilist position with regard to whether there is reality outside of discourse. I have simply argued that reality only becomes intelligible as discourse. It remains for me to clarify the way in which I deny our access to "truth" with my position.

The option I refuse is one that distinguishes knowledge and truth in such a way that truth is accessed outside of our communally based practices. These communally based knowledges are sufficient, as non-foundationalist Richard Rorty says, for justified belief. They are, as it were, all that we have; it is communally based discourses "all the way down." This position, one that is inevitable from my account of discourse, does not lead to vicious relativism (the conclusion that one thing is as good as another). Nor does this position require the absolutizing of our communal values and beliefs. The loss is not of values, but of a God's-eye view of discourses. As Donna Haraway says, "relativism and totalization are both 'god-tricks' promising vision from everywhere and nowhere equally and fully." Constructively, then, Haraway is right that "only partial perspective promises objective vision."[17] The fear that "mere" communal values will be absolutized is misplaced when the restriction to communal discourses simply allows us as Christians to commit passionately to a particular, finite situation that is God's.

There is, then, a Christian practice that makes sense of this approach to the availability of truth in the terms of communally justified belief.[18] This is so, not because I agree with Rorty's thin and elitist

---

[16]In an argument that poststructuralism (Jacques Derrida) and Richard Rorty espouse a form of nihilism that undermines its constructive value, Karen Carr distinguishes between existential/religious, epistemological, and alethiological nihilism. She argues that Karl Barth's early period of no-saying is an example of epistemological nihilism (e.g., knowledge is worthless) but not alethiological nihilism. Rorty, on Carr's terms, is an alethiological nihilist but not an epistemological nihilist. Although a definition of nihilism is obviously a subject of debate (which I will not take on), I do wish to contest this separation on the basis of a Christian account of God. Karen L. Carr, *The Banalization of Nihilism: Twentieth-Century Responses to Meaninglessness* (Albany: State Univ. of New York Press, 1992).

[17]Donna J. Haraway, "Situated Knowledges: The Science Question in Feminism and the Privilege of Partial Perspective," in *Simians, Cyborgs, and Women: The Reinvention of Nature* (New York: Routledge, 1991), 189–90.

[18]One of Rorty's early books dismantles the epistemological project as traditionally conceived. Richard Rorty, *Philosophy and the Mirror of Nature* (Princeton, N.J.: Princeton Univ. Press, 1979). His specification of a kind of pragmatism comes in *Consequences of Pragmatism: Essays (1972–1980)* (Minneapolis: Univ. of Minnesota Press, 1982). Richard J. Bernstein is a helpful interpreter of Rorty. See Bernstein, *Beyond Objectivism and Rel-*

notion of "community," but because the discourses that *can* define
Christian communities themselves provide a kind of self-criticism — a
healthy epistemological nihilism — that has an impact on what "truth"
looks like. The counterargument to this would require an account of
truth that is distinguishable from those reasons, rules, values, and beliefs that have their only foundation in communities and their traditions. Such a separate site of access, as I have argued, seems to beg the
problematic question of who occupies it — the issue I find most important. That, as I have implied all along, is some kind of "community"
not exempt from the productive work of power.[19]

A liberation feminist theology refuses to concede that there is a subject position from which the terms of truth are distinguishable from
the terms of justification. The temptation to articulate the former
always invites the proposal of a theoretical space — "publicness," ecclesial universals, objective revelation — that is ostensibly not occupied
by a desiring socially located thinker. While I have argued that theoretical abstractions are not false, I deny that they qualify as a space
where something distinct from communally based justification goes
on. What characterizes such judgments is simply a community that is
not easily recognized as shaped by power, desire, and social location
and in which it is more difficult to commit to a particular (disruptive)
good.

What distinguishes any situation of Christian communally shaped
practice from one such as Rorty's is not that Christians have beliefs
that are true because they are not-human (i.e., authorized by God and
therefore not subject to scrutiny), or because their claims to truth are
confirmed by a second-order level of reflection. The distinction is
found in the recognition that the truthfulness of these reasons, rules,
and values is tied to the visions of the good (however temporary) that
come from communities, their traditions, and the practices they produce. The distinctiveness of my feminist theological proposal comes
from the *kinds* of communal discourses that order feminist theological
practices and the practices they support. As I have said, feminist theology selectively appropriates accounts of social sin and certain Christian narratives of redemption as God's radical care for the outsider that
have helped produce the judgment that gender hierarchy is sinful. For

---

ativism: Science, Hermeneutics, and Praxis (Philadelphia: Univ. of Pennsylvania Press, 1983), 197–207.

[19]My preference for thicker communities does not align me with the position of Alasdair MacIntyre, whose notion of the unity of a tradition and its narratives is hege-monic in a way that does not square with my poststructuralist feminist liberation posi-tion.

the terms of the "truth" of this account, however, we remember that the vision of a God who liberates is inextricably tied with the fractures and hiddenness of actual liberating events.

There is a way of thinking about truth and its modes of availability that contradicts this complex vision of the good practice. That contradictory mode is closure. Brokenness and incompleteness have been fundamental aspects of liberationist refusals of triumphalism. Liberationist respect for the world precludes a notion that the truth of Christian practices is best displayed as an unbroken metanarrative, a triumphalist ontology, or any kind of theoretical discourse. (Notice I said "best displayed.") Feminist and other liberation theologians have decidedly *not* construed Christian narratives as unbroken stories of redemption or the triumph of good over evil. This refusal is a form of testimony, however, not atheism. It is testimony that Christian stories enable some communities to live through but not be resigned to such realities. Narratives of a fragmented and broken history constitute a notion of truth, not its denial, because such refusals do not (necessarily) undermine agapic practices for change.[20] They resonate with certain images for the availability of truth and not with others.

I find that the truth of faith is like the resistance of the world: instances of this resistance as gracious and transforming are utterly inconsistent and unpredictable. The kind of resistance that metanarratives of Christian truth might suggest—clear, linear, teleological, and progressive—does not occur. But gracious resistance is desirable. It is worth a wager. Truth of this sort is, as David Toole has put it so elegantly, like the flash of a fish on your line. "Truth is not something we move ever closer to, but something that surfaces from the depths of the world from time to time, only to recede once again. Because we glimpse the flash of its passing and, at times, experience the power of its pull, the activity of living remains meaningful." That resistance is unexpected, real, alluring. It is constituted by silences, waiting, as well as urgency and fear.[21] The compulsion to say more in academics, to find another arena, that of an extracommunal subject position, violates this kind of truth.

---

[20]A feminist theology of the cross might display such a notion of truth. Although she does not offer one, Welch speaks eloquently of the combination of awareness of massive injustice with passionate love for the creation and work for justice that refuses middle-class cynicism in *A Feminist Ethic of Risk*.

[21]David C. Toole offers this wonderful set of images in his article "Farming, Fly-Fishing, and Grace: How to Inhabit a Postnatural World without Going Mad," *Soundings* 7:1 (Spring 1993): 99, 85–104. Welch speaks of truth in terms of the "particulars of a relative sublime." *Communities of Resistance and Solidarity*, 74–92.

If someone disagrees with this account, I can point to no final arbiter, no account of "real Christianity" to validate my claim. Neither my experience nor scripture will serve such a purpose. I can only point to the occasions when convergences of scripture—cultural discourse—create certain communal habits, in order to persuade others that we honor God when hegemonies give way to forms of mutuality, and that respect for the other is more agapic than manipulation of the other. I can only testify when events display the movements of agapic practice that honor God. I can also argue that my criticism of larger, metaknowledges is a response to the contemporary academic subject position, the site of production of knowledge and its temptations. My proposal for a certain way of configuring the "truth" of Christian practices is a response to situation. If someone wants to label that "reducing God to experience," I can only ask how they might display a knowledge of God that escapes the discursive and its accompaniments—place, social relations, and what Foucault calls the "effects of truth."

Theological appropriation of poststructuralist discourse theory clearly relocates what might be counted as revelation since it disallows the special privileging of any discourse—its removal from ordinary processes of semiosis. For my position the alternative—the "miracle"—is that there are persons and communities that practice forgiveness and know how to nurture and sustain the capacity for it. The miracle is that reconciliations, however transient, do occur with the telling of Christian stories and holding lives accountable to them, that evil is resisted and hope is cherished. Feminist theology is about nurturing these habits and about learning their conditions in order to extend them for women. It recognizes, too, that our judgments about the oppressive and the transformative are not grounded in some pristine origin, a construct of original human nature, or a definition that is external to the practices of particular situations. Not having such foundations does not mean we cannot believe what we confess and act on it.

Theology is, then, an odd kind of noetic practice, and it sponsors what to some will appear an odd kind of truth. Its truth is ragged, not systematic or complete; its future is literally open. I agree with John Milbank that the noetic path to the good is rhetorical, not dialectical. "Only persuasion of the truth can be non-violent, but truth is only available through persuasion."[22] Therefore truth and nonviolence

---

[22]John Milbank, *Theology and Social Theory: Beyond Secular Reason* (Cambridge, Mass.: Basil Blackwell, 1990), 398. I have not done the obvious pertinent analysis of the

have to be recognized simultaneously in that by which we are persuaded. Their test cannot be coherence or correspondence, nor can
their truth be dialectical. Dialectical truth is unfaithful to the breaks
and disruptions that characterize our knowing, and it is too similar to
the kinds of modern knowledges that are incapable of sustaining a discourse of self-criticism, much less confession.

Theology needs to be testimony, and as such it is rhetoric with political implications and the potential to dissemble. But unlike a position that would claim that truth is not situated, to say that theology is
rhetorical practice is not to say it is mere opinion, or to downgrade it
to sophistry, as did Plato. Theology can be passionate commitment to
God's work of redemption in the world. The rhetoric of theo/acentric
persuasion is, as Milbank says, "attachment to a particular persuasion—which we can never *prove* to be either true, or non-violent—
[and without which] we would have no real means to discriminate
peace and truth from their opposites."[23]

If testimony (a fundamentally situated discourse) is a more appropriate characterization of the truthfulness of theology than a foundational metanarrative or universalizing discourse, how is feminist
theology to understand itself as a certifying discourse that has its "objectivity" in its commitment to a particular? In other words, how does
feminist theology testify for the "other" woman? What does it mean
to respect difference? How do we construct the agape for the other
woman that has activated much of our thinking? At this point the
nature of the discourses and social practices that produce *us* is key to
the continued liberating possibilities of our practices. Here I believe
my position pushes us to radicalize from simple inclusion.

Difference as saming the other versus difference as letting her be

If respecting difference is rightly understood, then *our own situation*
will be the next place to look. The importance of recognizing the produced and productive nature of discourse and its inextricable relation
to power is that our (those of us who engage in certifying discourse)
portraits of the "other" are inevitable acts of violence. The point is not

---

shaping of the theological academy and its organization of knowledge by the social formation. Edward Farley's good beginning of that analysis can be greatly expanded to
include the impact of global capitalism on the production of knowledge.

[23]Ibid., 398. As sensitive as he is to complexity and difference, Milbank does employ
a metanarrative about Christianity.

that we could do a better job of representing the other if we worked harder. It is that until we understand the material nature of our discourse, we continue to be tempted to imagine that we *are representing* the other—that some true essence of the stranger is disclosed by our descriptions.

This is not a retraction of the last three chapters of this book. My point is simply that this analysis is a production; it is neither the true essence of Presbyterian women or Pentecostal women, nor is it a projection of my inner subjective consciousness. It is by now clear that the analysis is predicated on refusing both ideals. Rather, this discourse—a scholarly text employing the register of a jargon-filled field—is a convergence of the discourses and social location that produced me with those that construct these other women. The lines of interest I trace out are a function in part of my feminist grid, and the possibilities and constraints are a function of my account of Christian grace and sin as well.

The theological convictions that construct my feminist readings of these women help illustrate my production of them. I have employed a theological grammar of finitude-iconoclasm, of resisting sin, which assumes some place to stand that is grace in order to speak hopefully of women's futures and the future of a world that would honor women. My proposal for feminist theology describes a synchronically weighted liberationist practice that remembers Jesus for the sake of resisting forms of contemporary social sin. I describe a located practice, not a universal feminist theology. It is one highly aware of gender constructions and the force they have on academic (certifying) definitions of reality. Thus, my subject position activates awareness of the binary gender in the figures of the tradition in a way that shapes my reading but is not found in the other women's practices that I have read.

My faithful remembering of Jesus comes from participation in the semantic fields of grace, however dimly perceived or fancied, that construct me in church and woman-church communities. This participation is crucial for my christological affirmations, and important for the ways my position differs from the women of my book. The subject position occupied by me and others like me allows us to be highly aware of the consequences of being constructed as a woman—namely, that gender (rather than race, class, or sexual preference) is the part of this subject position that contributes to our particular dependence. As much as they were intended to move out of content-readings of the oppression of these subject positions, my accounts of Pentecostal and Presbyterian women highlighted binary gender definitions rather than racial intertextual relations in their practices. This emphasis is a function of my regime of reading and the grids that resonate with my sub-

ject position and suggest its limitations as well. We might say more
accurately that class, race, and sexual preference also construct my
subject position, but binary gender is what I attend to most directly.

This subject position also distinguishes my reading regime for remembering Jesus faithfully. That regime for honoring Jesus' role in redemption is sensitive to his construction as "male" and the role that
construction has played for women as those who do not resemble
Jesus. Given this sensibility to gender, I do not find this Jesus as an
authorizing datum for our practices. What it means for me and others
of this position to worship the God of Jesus Christ requires that we
re(as)semble this Jesus in ways that subvert the binary nature of
gender. The stories of our memory, then, are constantly being retold,
recovered, remade, and, therefore, reinvented.[24] This example of the
effects of subject position on memory does not explicate a feminist
Christology, a task far beyond this project, but displays the feminist
regime of reading that has been brought into play to produce my accounts of these women. My own sense of the different resonances that
are activated for us in relation to this central figure in Christian faith
have likely led me away from attention to this part of our grammars in
my analysis of Pentecostal and Presbyterian women.

In addition to suggesting the contributing character of my analytical regime, it is important to say that I have not given these women
voice by representing their discourses as resistances of patriarchal oppression. To give women voice is a much larger project that would
require a change in social relations certainly not effected by my production of their practices. Feminists in the disciplines of folklore and
ethnography whose fieldwork has focused on collecting stories—oral
narratives of "ordinary" women—have developed (if not fully resolved) a set of critical issues around academics' "use" of marginalized
populations of women. However well-intentioned the scholar, the
power dynamics of these relations negate the innocence of the academic as representer of women who have no access to the discourses
of certification.

There is another reason why I cannot pretend that women are given
voice by my narrating their stories or practices. To give women voice
suggests something this book is designed to contest: theories of language and knowledge which assume that univocal expression of the

---

[24]There are a number of ways to re(as)semble Jesus: for example, as androgynous, as
brother, a second coming as a woman Christ, and the location of redemption in the
emergence of a Christic community. My position identifies redemptive effects with the
forging of a relation to the outsider, the stranger, and the stranger in feminist theology
has been "women."

complexities of human experience occurs in words/language. Any narrative, even one presented with a minimal interpretive apparatus, is "double-voiced," as Ruth Behar puts it. A narrative is in some sense the woman's account of herself, but it is also inscribed with other meanings, from being framed by its lodging in a mode of communication (book, anthology, etc.), to its prior inscription by the expectation of the interviewee of what the interviewer wishes to know.[25]

What, then, *is* my discourse about these other women and what does it do? Michael Taussig's comments on the observations of anthropologists are relevant for theologians and help answer my question. Taussig insists that fieldworkers are never directly confronted by the "other" that they study, but by a contact. "This means that the anthropological text is in its very essence a text mediating difference — the shadows on the blank page formed by the Other as illuminated by Western (middle class professional) light."[26] Academic theologians' accounts of the marginalized, I suggest — feminist theologians' accounts of the "other" — are similarly texts mediating difference.

That my text "mediates difference" rather than unproduced reality does not make it a false or failed representation that has simply not achieved its goal. If that were true, I would be suggesting that there is a discourse that is *not* a production. What I wish to make room for in this analysis is a different goal than truly reflecting the other in our feminist and liberation theological projects. Accounts of discourse have to include acknowledgment of their fallibility and instability, not simply in the sense of partiality and historicality, but in their ideological potential as well, their immersion in power and inevitable occlusion of some things in a possible landscape. No "respect for difference" can occur without this admission.

But more is at stake than simply qualifying our texts as partial in a theory of texts as productions mediating difference. We have to explore the work of our texts. They help us see something about who *we* are, both in terms of the meaning effects of our academic practices — their possibilities for self-criticism and for furthering agape for the excluded. A representational account of a theology of the marginalized would suggest that our descriptions were translations, more or less, of

---

[25] Ruth Behar's point is made with regard to the narratives produced by feminist academics' interviews with "ordinary" women. See "Journeys of the Heart," Behar's review of *Songs My Mother Sang to Me: An Oral History of Mexican-American Women*, by Patricia Preciado Martin (Tucson: Univ. of Arizona Press, 1991), in *The Women's Review of Books* 10:6 (March 1993): 18. See also Sherna Berger Gluck and Daphne Patai, eds., *Women's Words: The Feminist Practice of Oral History* (New York: Routledge, 1991).

[26] Michael Taussig, "Rise and Fall of Marxist Anthropology," *Social Analysis* 21 (August 1987): 101–113, 105.

the identity of the other. By contrast, the proposal that it is discourse and its social production that need to take the place of the appeal to experience requires more of our own discourse. First, its intertextual relations must be identified. But we also must look at the effects of instability, which means that we must chase down the violence done by conceptual closures. For Ferdinand de Saussure, the closure of the system did not work; the destabilizing pressure always comes from an outside that is never totally outside. By employing a liberationist appropriation of poststructuralism, I suggest that a primary effect of the search for closure, the creation of an identity, is not just the creation of an inside-outside, but a domestication of the outside.

If we are to pursue liberation academic theologies that speak about the other, the outsider, we cannot avoid this effect simply by understanding our writing the other as partial and incomplete. We must be able to see the ways our discourse *produces* the other as a result of where *we* are. The criteriological privileging of the destabilizing other must stand as a marker to warn us. It will not guarantee academic institutional confession/repentance, but it will at least remind us that our continual efforts at closure are never innocent.[27]

The difference difference makes

Let me review in order to suggest the role of this account of discourse in the definition of difference. It is not just that we (women) are different, and that the variety of subjects who represent different races, classes, and sexual preference need to be assembled in the creation of theologies that will reflect a rainbow of multiplicity. This liberal narrative implies that I can tell what difference is by looking at other women and judging them on the basis of my experience as an oppressed woman who finds liberation through certain strands of the Christian tradition. The processes of recognizing and respecting difference are more subtle and problematic than that, and the inclusionary logic does not get at these complications.

The problem in connecting difference with pluralism is that defini-

---

[27]The problematic nature of liberal notions of the subject has been sketched by postliberal theology, but never grasped in terms of the power dynamics entailed in this construction of the subject. What it fails to address is that fractures and conflicts and power are never kept outside of belief systems. When it refuses to see this, Christian faith tries to have an identity by sealing that identity off—at its peril. Strategic definitions of Christian aptness and Christian practice may be unavoidable, but they are not enough to get at the embodied, power/knowledge relations of Christian theologizing.

tions of the "other" that do not take seriously the radical instability of discourse and the intimate connection of power/knowledge are tempted to ignore the ways in which our definitions of the other do not allow us to really have an "other." Our definitions continually domesticate that which is outside and give it a name that may appear to be other, but is actually a process of objectifying or saming. As Barbara Johnson says, "difference is not engendered in the space between identities; it is what makes all totalizing of the identity of a self or the meaning of a text impossible."[28] Differential relations, not representation, account for meaning; every definition of the "other" is made differentially or relationally, and it is inscribed with power. Someone "owns" more of that supposed "space between identities."

A clear illustration of the different form of difference to which Johnson appeals is the man-woman binary, which feminists have used to suggest that "woman" is not a reality except as it comes into view differentially, as "not-man." If we extend this notion, not only are there no extradiscursive referents for defining "woman" — Anglo woman, woman of color, poor white woman — but one also does not define the other woman accurately by virtue of a prior knowledge of what a real woman is. The meaning of the privileged or base notion of "woman" is constructing of and constructed with the proposal about the other. The impulse to define the contrast out of one's own privilege is overwhelming.

The only way out of this dynamic of saming is to resist the impulse to allow the construction of the other to simply consolidate our own identity. Yet the liberal impulse to include everyone is precisely the "generous" impulse that appears to open the doors wide, while it continues to set the terms on which one is allowed in. Liberalism has no discourse to disrupt the prevailing definition of "woman" or "human being." My account of Pentecostal women is a mediation of difference — it displays the meaning of their practices through a feminist theological grid. This is positively productive, in that it honors these women from my position and uses their difference to relativize our feminist categories. Further, my theo/alogical reading of Pentecostal women's practices is undoubtedly more positive with regard to the integrity of those practices than a secular feminist reading would be. My impulse to connect with the Pentecostal woman, however, even as I believe it displays respect, is inevitably a domestication of her practice. The empowering of the other from a theo/acentric

---

[28]Barbara Johnson, "The Critical Difference," *Diacritics* 8:2 (1978): 3.

grammar requires more than writing about the other, even the "other" that is in the academy. It requires us to be transformed by the other and to resist, where we recognize it, our domestication of the other.[29]

If this were not true, we would be able to live with that which is truly not-us and resist the impulse to make it be like us as we connect. The impulse of care for the other is inevitably shaped by the impulse to control, and the process of domestication is the most obvious feature of rendering that which is strange susceptible to control. The feature of academic confession entailed in the recognition of our complicity is the public realization/acknowledgment that we cannot easily include the other without either relinquishing our own power and privilege or hiding it more successfully.

Yet the proposal that we relinquish power cannot remain in the sphere of the mental or attitudinal for feminist theology. I close by proposing two theological implications that follow if we would begin to learn about respecting difference.

Respecting difference: affinities rather than identities

My first proposal is that there is a peculiar, theo/acentric agape to which feminist theologians are called. This agape confesses that little is known about the nature of human being, even as it stumbles toward working for the conditions of well-being for us and the other woman. These are theological, not secular, projects, because they are invigorated by an iconoclastic criticism capable of supporting a passionate agape for the creation that sees the impulse to control in our class location. A passionate agape is essential, insofar as we remain unconvinced that all care for the other is will-to-power. If we act on this wager, there are two ways to think about representing the other. First, we must concede how our discourse about the other does not in the philosophical and cultural sense "represent" the other, but mediates difference. Second, we are called to represent (as in "speak for") the

---

[29]By staying in conversation with the Pentecostal women she interviewed and getting their reactions to her books, Elaine Lawless has pursued some of the implications of writing about the other. For the problems and conflicts of differences, see her " 'I was afraid someone like you . . . an outsider . . . would misunderstand': Negotiating Interpretive Differences Between Ethnographers and Subjects," *Journal of American Folklore* 105 (1992): 302–14.

outsider to well-being because of a vision of God's care for the creation.[30]

Theo/acentric iconoclasm must shape our grammar so that we can
be called to account when we mistake our discourse for the first kind
of representation. Worshiping God truly requires recognition that sometimes the nonutilitarian character of our practices is liberating.[31] Our
goal is nonutilitarian, not in the sense that we do not have political
goals, but that we recognize that our political goals may not be for
everyone. In this sense feminist theology is a theology of exile. Every
concept has its own violence, and it is only in the ironic commitment
to our projects that we can insist on concrete and specific practices.[32]

To indicate women's social locations and our distances, I propose a
feminist theology of affinity rather than identity or solidarity with the
other. Affinity acknowledges love's inability to know the other, to
resist domination of the other. Affinities rather than shared identities
are the best we can hope for in developing feminist theology toward
the respect for all subjects now defined as women and support for the
end of dominations that texture their lives. To paraphrase Donna Haraway, feminist theology "must negotiate the very fine line between
appropriation of another's (never innocent) experience and the delicate
construction of the just-barely-possible affinities, the just-barely-possible connections that might actually make a difference in local and
global histories."[33] They put into our practice what I have indicated in
defining the truth of theology and its status as rhetoric and testimony:
We do not have a "God's-eye view."

---

[30]Gayatri Chakravorty Spivak makes this distinction in a critique of Foucault's failure to make it. "Can the Subaltern Speak?" in *Marxism and the Interpretation of Culture*,
ed. Cary Nelson and Lawrence Grossberg (Urbana: Univ. of Illinois Press, 1988), 275.
See also R. Radhakrishnan, "Toward an Effective Intellectual: Foucault or Gramsci?" in
Intellectuals: Aesthetics, Politics, Academics, ed. Bruce Robbins, Cultural Politics 2 (Minneapolis: Univ. of Minnesota Press, 1990), 57–99.

[31]Kelsey, *To Understand God Truly*, 256. In distinction from Welch, I do not find that
such a belief (which includes God's transcendence in some form) works only to support
disdain for the finite and the bodily. Thus I do not substitute the community for a heretofore transcendent God. A transcendent Father God was an essential element of emancipation in Clady Johnson's story about escaping domestic violence; meaning is always
negotiated in a differential set of discourses. As theologians produced as the professional
managerial class, we need the iconoclastic work of a theo/acentric grammar as it relates
to our discourse of care and concern for the other. Welch does talk about kinds of transcendence, but these are not what Clady Johnson means. Welch, *A Feminist Ethic of Risk*,
172–79.

[32]This is Meg Gandy's phrase. I thank her for many helpful conversations on these
issues.

[33]Donna J. Haraway, "Reading Buchi Emecheta: Contests for 'Women's Experience' in Women's Studies," in *Simians, Cyborgs, and Women*, 113.

A theology of affinity is not a result of loss of political will. It is the combination of recognition that theological discourse is material–productive and a poststructuralist seriousness about sin. As a certifying discourse, we have the power to say what the other is in a way that the other does not have. Do not get me wrong. This is a request that feminist theology risk a great deal by acknowledging the problems of the identity "woman," for it is not in the position of a hegemonic discourse but in the complex situation of testifying against the universalizing discourse of other kinds of theologies. Feminist theology must risk, however, in order to avoid becoming (or trying to create) another hegemonic account of women and their oppression-liberation.

The product of my project, then, is not clearer understanding of the other women I have discussed. I have not "helped" these women. I feel a certain presumption even to say that I have learned a lot from them. There is, however, a longing in my work to hear from them, to be taught by them, without indulging in what Haraway speaks of as a "tourism of the soul."[34] What I think is accomplished is a beginning sense of what can be known about who *we are* in academics. These discourses point us *to us* and the context out of which we are produced. The conditions of hearing these women in speech, as Nelle Morton would put it, are not what is at stake in this analysis, because such conditions do not exist, and that is part of what we need to explore.[35]

The stories of the Pentecostal woman, the Presbyterian woman, and the academic feminist are cautionary ciphers — warning spaces about the dangers of academic discourse. Clady Johnson's story about the transcendent Father God as her way out of domestic violence is combined with some notion of what I would call immanence — "God lives inside our bodies." It is not my sense of the work of a transcendent Father God, and it reminds me of our different pains. These contradictions must remain; we must resist the temptation to translate them. They stand as iconic reminders of the blunderings and harm that we do as objectifiers who veil our projects with good will and intentions. As icons these stories will remind me of the face of the woman leader at a conference on grassroots projects in Appalachia, who, when asked about "the poor mountain women," turned out to be one of "them."

There is, then, a certain irony in this call to affinities. Respect for difference might be read as a new chapter in a story about hospitality

---

[34]Haraway quotes this from poet Wendy Rose, "Reading Buchi Emecheta," 115.
[35]Nelle Morton, *The Journey is Home* (Boston: Beacon Press, 1985), 202–210.

for the stranger. Written by virtue of the dissonance feminists discovered around the failure of historic Christianity to recognize women as fully *imago dei*, it continues to impel new forms of self-criticism as new "outsiders" are "discovered," as the "insider" turns out to be strange. Feminism, however, is a position not shared by the other women I have considered, and whether they would ever wish to be aligned with it is a real question. Feminist theology's commitment to the marginalized is complex at this point, not only because it will inevitably be difficult to say who the marginalized might be in any situation, but also because my identification of the marginalized is the act of the privileged that is inevitably bound to fail.

Feminist theology is a certifying discourse as well as a discourse about the marginalized. This truth commends certain practice to further our affinities. Lest it reproduce Christianity in its own image, feminist theology beyond liberalism requires an iconoclasm that refuses to say what a "real" woman is, even as it testifies to possibilities of liberation. Feminists have often remarked that a contradictory identification is lodged at the heart of feminist academic practice. Many have called it the contradiction between being oppressed and being the oppressor. Susan Thistlethwaite sees that contradiction particularly in being a white woman of privilege in relation to African American women.[36]

I propose that we learn from this contradiction. Discourses, like faces, are not windows into some innocent prepolitical reality, but they can provide reflectors of "us." They are productions that may not aspire to be the truth about the other—even our reflections are not who we really are—but they are not, for that reason, no-knowledge, simply projections. They remind us to ask, "Under what conditions of duress can we legitimately testify to a liberating God?"

Producing the theologian: who really knows?

Recognition of the call for affinity gives us a second proposal: to explore the conditions for relinquishing power, for institutional confession and transformation. This topic has to do with the formation of subjects and the defining of qualifications for the production of certifying discourses. If the academic site for the production of certifying discourses is to combine the agendas of publics that vary as widely as

---

[36]Susan B. Thistlethwaite, *Sex, Race, and God: Christian Feminism in Black and White* (New York: Crossroad, 1989), 1–10.

"the church," "the academy," and "marginalized populations," as the critical modernist theologians wish, we have to face the conflicts between our rules for what counts as knowledge. The conflicts are located at the site we cannot see, the place where speaking to contemporary publics becomes mutually exclusive with giving primacy to the voices of the marginalized.[37]

Is there wisdom among those culturally and economically marginalized who do not have a handful of representatives who make it to academia? Is there wisdom among the "saints" to whom George Lindbeck appeals in his idealization of the grammatical competence of lived faith? If so, it is not a competence that would appear to require advanced education. Were we to assume that saintly competence required education, we would be advancing a liberal progressive notion that higher education was directly correlated with maturity in faith. Those whose interest includes the marginalized and the saints would surely not agree with that notion. Nor is it a competence that correlates with access to wealth/affluence, surely another disqualifier for maturity in faith.

If Kelsey is right about the continuing dominance of *Wissenschaft* in theological education, however, and if I am right about the construction of the academic's subject position out of the forces that produced the professional managerial class, then we must conclude that theologia as formation or transforming habitus is in need of some work. Insofar as we tie theologia to a situation—recognize its graf(ph)tedness—it is dominated by certain definitions of knowledge and by certain pleasures of a class position. We need a material recognition of the obscuring disciplinary power that continues to reproduce *our* subject positions if we do any kind of theology that wishes to hear the voice of the marginalized. Theologia as a formative habitus is diminished and pinched even in the ideal as long as it cannot be formulated to resist the class blindnesses it continues to produce.

Our subject position is constructed by the culture of professionalism; it partakes of the heritage of Foucault's "traditional intellectual." One of the outcomes of affinities with other women is serious attention to our formation as rigorous seekers of *Wissenschaft*, for which the aim is "to shape 'reason'—the capacities to solve problems by asking how to answer the right questions 'formed' by acquiring 'disciplines' that keep its question-asking and question-answering rigorously self-

---

[37]In his book *Plurality and Ambiguity*, Tracy privileges the hermeneutics of the oppressed. I am arguing here that this comes into greater conflict with the other ideals of academic theology espoused by him than he admits. David Tracy, *Plurality and Ambiguity: Hermeneutics, Religion, Hope* (San Francisco: Harper and Row, 1987), 103–8.

critical."[38] Like the critical modernists of chapter 6, Kelsey wishes to see Enlightenment reason modified by theological ends. He, like they, does not wish to continue the kind of capitivity to "science" that currently characterizes theological disciplines.

If Kelsey is right, however, that "the overarching end or goal of theological schooling is to understand God, and 'to understand' is to come to have certain conceptual capacities, *habitus*, that is dispositions and competencies to *act*, that enable us to apprehend God and refer all things including ourselves to God," then how can our formation as persons who cannot recognize the wisdoms of poverty or anticulture be adequate?[39] How can we have wisdom on these matters if our very existence requires that we be trained as the professional managerial class and assumes that the deforming aspects of that training—its built-in compulsion to control—will be solved intellectually? Or that to grant primacy to the interpretations of the oppressed is to include books about them in our reading lists? Taussig's warning is pertinent. The temptation of the academic mode is the resolution of contradiction, difference, and anarchy with closure.

The civility of our ideal—making intellectual wholes—should make us nervous. Foucault's question, slightly rephrased, speaks to the heart of this:

> Even before we can know the extent to which something such as [theology] can be compared to a [rigorous] practice in its everyday functioning, its rules of construction, its working concepts . . . even before we can pose the question of a formal and structural analogy between [theology and *Wissenschaft*] it is surely necessary to question ourselves about our aspirations to the kind of power that is presumed to accompany such a [*Wissenschaft*]. It is surely the following kinds of question that would need to be posed: What types of knowledge do you want to disqualify in the very instant of your demand: "Is it a [*Wissenschaft*]?" Which speaking, discoursing subjects—which subjects of experience

---

[38]Kelsey, *To Understand God Truly*, 228.

[39]Ibid., 228. For interesting criticisms of professionalism related to clericalism, see Beverly Harrison: "We pious, white middle-stratum people in this nation are dangerous to those who share the planet with us. Professing ourselves particularly blessed and truly free, when we are neither, robs us of the capacity to fight for our own lives and also to see and respect the courage, creativity, and transformative power of those many others who struggle for theirs." Beverly Harrison, "Toward a Christian Feminist Liberation Hermeneutic for Demystifying Class Reality in Local Congregations," in *Beyond Clericalism: The Congregation as a Focus for Theological Education*, ed. Barbara G. Wheeler and Joseph C. Hough, Jr., Studies in Religious and Theological Scholarship (Atlanta: Scholars Press, 1988), 144–45. See also Stanley Hauerwas, "The Ministry of a Congregation: Rethinking Christian Ethics for a Church-Centered Seminary," *Beyond Clericalism*, 131, also notes 5 and 14.

and knowledge—do you then want to "diminish" when you say: "I who conduct this discourse am conducting a scientific (theological) discourse, and I am a scientist (theologian)"?[40]

My judgment is that the kinds of knowledge we disqualify are precisely the knowledges of poor women, of women of color, of lesbians. What we are clearest about refusing is the Enlightenment, as indicated by the great interest in Edward Farley's notion of habitus out of the desire to rejoin the knowledge of faith with the wisdom of love. The desire to nurture theologia, or a formative habitus in theological education, is widely expressed, but with the exception of feminist critics, never connected to the social practices and blindnesses of class, race, and gender that construct us as knowers.[41]

If, as Taussig says, theological texts about the marginalized are mediations rather than direct confrontations with the other, what can these shadows (or productions) do for us? The other woman as a text must serve as a mirror held up to our own practice, allowing us to focus on the unsaid, the excluded, of our practices if we are to employ them to move away from consolidation of things as they are. At the very least the texts invite questions about the elements of wisdom that our social location obscures. Although institutions vary in the closures they create—the pieties and resistances they disqualify—I will hazard some suggested exclusions that are entailed in the compromise between modernism and liberal (or orthodox) Christianities.

The reading practices and performances of Pentecostal women are not, as far as I know, legitimate knowledges in the academy. They may be read as sect-communities to be studied in religious studies courses. The Pentecostal "method," however, is not an option in an institutional production of knowledge that privileges the critical disciplines in biblical studies. The point is not simply to add on a new method; it is to ask what is occluded by the interests of critical method. The Pentecostal faith is (or was) antimodern. Is there, consequently, no wisdom there? Why should we assume it would

---

[40]Michel Foucault, *Power/Knowledge: Selected Interviews and Other Writings, 1972–1977*, ed. Colin Gordon, trans. Colin Gordon et al. (New York: Pantheon Books, 1980), 84–85.

[41]See Mary McClintock Fulkerson, "Theological Education and the Problem of Identity," *Modern Theology* 7:5 (October 1991): 465–82. Also Rebecca S. Chopp counters the unsituated character of Farley's theologia, in "Situating the Structure: Prophetic Feminism and Theological Education," in *Shifting Boundaries: Contextual Approaches to the Structure of Theological Education*, ed. Barbara G. Wheeler and Edward Farley (Louisville: Westminster/John Knox Press, 1991), 67–89. *Shifting Boundaries* takes up context in some interesting ways, although not with regard to the pleasures and enticements that construct us.

have helped Pentecostal women to "modernize" even as much as postliberalism? In fact the move of the Pentecostal community into the middle class has diminished women's access to preaching ministry.

One rejoinder to my inquiry might be that theological education is not aimed at training ministers for marginalized communities. Even so, my point is how theological education is institutionalized around certain material relations, the organizations of knowledges that created fields to be covered, as Gerald Graff notes of the university.[42] These organizations have been criticized of late for their fragmenting of theology as wisdom, but I ask a different question here. How does the organization of field knowledges contribute to the production of thinkers trained so as to find it difficult if not impossible to recognize how practitioners of faith who deal with life's conditions on the edge might "know" something that we do not? If this difficulty is the result of our production, the mediating text of the other puts a hard question to us: To what kind of liberating God can we testify, given our social location?

One way in which we can respect such others is to locate such dissonances inside our communities in order to destabilize our identity as theologians. This would mean we refuse to define the "forming" of Christians as the shaping of generic, individual subjects, unlocated (save for a religious tradition). Our definition of subjects must begin with the historically created situations of disparity and subjugation; it must place subjects in relation to the social formation and must articulate the complex relations of the religious discourses that shape them and the neighbor, the horizon of accountability in relation to which transformation might be assessed.

The most immediate question, however, regards how the production of academics as subjects is configured around the production of experts. Currently this expertise is not conducive to forming our capacities to honor the expertise of the other woman. The glimpses of Presbyterian women's skills, their production of expanded domesticity and circles of care, are other sites of wisdom that are difficult to square with the expertise born of professional activists, but at least the class and educational worlds are within some proximity. For the

---

[42]Gerald Graff's criticisms of the institutional production of knowledge include the interesting point that with "field coverage" as the organizing principle of departments, conflicts are forever avoided. New approaches (feminism, gay studies, etc.) get added as courses and are not allowed to surface as fundamental debates. See Gerald Graff, "Teaching the Conflicts," *South Atlantic Quarterly* 89:1 (Winter 1990): 51–68; and *Professing Literature: An Institutional History* (Chicago: Univ. of Chicago Press, 1987).

Pentecostal woman, whose formal education may have ended with third grade and whose wisdom is honed by living on the edge—the edge of poverty, submission, and ecstasy—the convergences with most of us in the academy are much farther apart. What are the losses with respect to affective pleasures in the production of the feminist scholar?

For anything like affinity, we must rely on our production by other communities—families of origin, churches, volunteer work, activist groups, Third World experiences—to give us sensibilities of the other. While many women of color may have non-middle-class communities and histories that give them such sensibilities, many of the rest of us do not. Even though feminist theology rooted in activism works to highlight such relations, the point is, these constructions of us are incidental to qualifying as a theological scholar. The formation of "thinkers"—theologians who produce certifying discourses—would require a very different set of processes if our qualifications were judged in relation to our capacity to hear or receive from the other. The continued approbation of reality as God's requires from us the capacity to see grace in the lives of those who speak of God's way under the adverse conditions we rarely or never live in. It may well be that our graf(ph)t as professional certifiers will provide less and less sustenance, and the theological realities we define will be increasingly rarefied and withered as our definitions of knowledge and their material formation continue to be treated separately.

The truth is, a Foucaultian take on power/knowledge means that "we cannot fully separate the existence of an object of knowledge from the various practices through which we encounter and deal with it, perhaps especially from the forms of constraint through which it is simultaneously enabled and compelled to show itself in specific ways."[43] The production of the expertise of the academic theologian is a process that invites normalization and standardization. While normalization and standardization seem to be the commonsense conditions for knowledge, we remember that if power is productive it can discipline us in ways that may be antithetical to knowledges of grace.

I can only suggest the implications of this production. The features of normalization and standardization are striking and need to be pursued with regard to the production of theological knowledge, where it is shaped by surveillance in the production of knowers and around the

---

[43]Rouse's application of this account of power to the production of laboratory knowledge is a helpful example. See Joseph Rouse, *Knowledge and Power: Toward a Political Philosophy of Science* (Ithaca: Cornell Univ. Press), 216.

fact that new subjects are really produced. For an educational process, the notion of surveillance has intelligibility as a function of the creation of a knowledge, its division into parts, and the mastery of these parts. What is key in transferring this analysis to scientific experimentation, Joseph Rouse points out, is that something is produced that can be assessed. In a scientific lab, order is introduced "into the phenomena it describes; it does not just find order there." This order creates new fields of disorder. These patterns can then become standards. If we do not see the productive normalizing process at work, then "garbled or randomly scattered data plots often indicate an unsuccessful experiment rather than an effect that needs to be accounted for scientifically."[44]

The conditions under which this scientific knowledge is produced, in many cases, are the conditions under which it is true, or under which it "works." Rouse offers examples outside the lab where the desire to get more knowledge and control of natural environments required the complexifying of that environment and increased need for intervention to support the conditions under which the procedure could be successfully performed. Thus even though they represent knowledge processes designed to "help," growing a new hybrid product or introducing hospital birth technologies actually increases the dependence of the environment or the patient on technologies of intervention.[45] Something is produced in these cases, but the knowledge that results is saturated with power effects.

Theological disciplines include criteria for assessment and procedures for judging what a "good" thinker is and what it means to master a field. Recall that David Tracy wants more compact disciplines to deal with the residue of ambiguity still clinging to such a "loose" one as theology. Were we to take apart the way in which normalizing creates the grids for what is meaningful knowledge, however, we would find that our equivalent of "garbled or randomly scattered data plots" is not true ignorance but itself a production. Our processes of validating mastery actually work to reconsolidate the rightness and trustworthiness of our judgments. According to a productive account of power, they work to create the categories they "find" — distributing subjects around a norm (good thinkers, mediocre thinkers, poor thinkers). A second implication of Rouse's analogy should give us pause as well. In science the knowledge/power relation

---

[44]Ibid., 225.
[45]See Rouse's detailed analysis of these knowledge productions and their power relations. Ibid., 209–247. A tight coupling of technical and/or organizational subsystems in natural environments leads to disciplining nature as well as bodies.

means that the conditions under which knowledge is produced are part of its reality. We find ourselves faced again with the question of how rarefied our discourse is. What kinds of interventions and dependencies are necessary for it to be transportable to other places?

The factoring of disciplinary power into the production of academic subjects does not require a liberal response—for example, that there are true and natural knowledges being repressed by our standards. This would require simple reversals—all marginalized, powerless people are wise and elites are blind. Nor does it invalidate all knowledge and direct us to look for a kind that is not invested with incitements of power. Both responses ignore the fact that occlusion is to be found in all knowledges. The point is to examine the particular problems of our production. The current proposals by critical modernists to simply combine care for the marginalized with the procedures of theologia as discipline do not take with sufficient seriousness the knowledge/power relation. In particular they do not acknowledge Rouse's second point: that the conditions of certain kinds of knowledge are both inextricable from their truth and too complex and harmful to other systems to be valuable in other settings. To put it another way, our production as academics may be at odds with the notion of theologia, a habitus that would form the faithful with a wisdom honed by a capacity for agape for the world neighbor. The capacity or habitus for such wisdom is not gained by our processes. Feminist theology must develop its alternative settings for education even more vigorously and loudly than ever if it is to alter the production of the "intellectual."

Still feminist?

What about the possibility of feminist theology being feminist? My position calls for modesty about the status of our claims. But if the possibility of this self-criticism requires the "outside" discourses calling the "inside" into question, there is another implication for current feminist theological thinking. Elizabeth Clark is right to point out that poststructuralism has implications for feminist theology and its typical invocation of the grammar of image of God to justify the inclusion of women. The destabilizing of the subject has consequences for this appeal. The critique does not simply refer to finitude and the instability of the creature before God as these have always been understood. Instead, the implication of poststructuralist destabilizing is the loss of a fixed notion of human nature.[46] Taken strictly, this means that it is no longer the province of Christian theology to make universal claims that put conditions on what it means to be human.

The call to destabilize the subject is a feminist project, but a theo/alogical one. Our conviction that gender hierarchy is sinful does not require that we appeal to being woman or human; after all, we do not know yet what that might mean. The opposite to a fixed *imago dei* is not the refusal to envision a possibility. We can support a vision of a social subjectivity that is a result of Christian faith and its intersection with the late twentieth-century capitalist world order. The vision is one of a socially connected ideal for creation, which responds to the pain and suffering of the distant neighbor and asks how our practices are connected to that fate.

For feminist Christians, the capacity to make claims that faithfulness involves resisting the evil of sexism is based on the practices of a community that knows the valuing of women has transformative effects. This kind of feminism is based on nothing else. There is no authorization that escapes the particular discursively constructed situation out of which subjects are produced. Neither telling stories about Jesus nor about an essential woman will guarantee that these sensibilities will develop, but they have developed in many communities that worship the God of Jesus Christ, and we must try to proliferate such communities. Feminist theology is a theology that testifies—testifies to the conditions under which those with hegemonic power give it up, those with no hope obtain it.[47]

We make our testimony in tension with the urge to universalize our claims because even in the name of theological truth we may deploy hegemonic notions. Here is where I commend our vocation to worship God truly, to paraphrase David Kelsey's term for the purpose of theological education. We must incorporate such a vocation in order to make space for self-criticism. But it will be self-criticism by virtue of a theological politics of difference.

This theological politics of respect for difference is included in the vision of our call to be part of communities that transgress gender hierarchies. That task is certainly more complex than I have suggested.

---

[46]Elizabeth A. Clark, "Women's Studies in Religion: Appropriating the Spoils of Theory," paper presented at a regional American Academy of Religion/Society of Biblical Literature meeting, Atlanta, March 1992.

[47]Feminists know too well the story of how the criteria for being human excluded women for centuries; the stories of what counted as human in Nazi Germany are chilling reminders of the dangers of normative anthropology. There are, then, important reasons to put a question mark beside our vision of "woman" if it comes to occupy the role of a newly essentialized *imago dei*.

Minimally, it means that we must actively seek to be constructed as theologians by multiple communities of practice. Such a project requires more than conversations, and it entails painful risks. The inevitable fragmenting feel of many commitments may be a good if it can destabilize the negative aspects of our production as a professional managerial class, of our identity as those who "know better." Beyond this minimum, however, the way is uncharted.

If changing the subject is to proceed beyond inclusion, it must go forward as a change that has no subject to ground itself in. I suspect that none of us can quite grasp that future. It holds the promise of kinds of joy that we miss under the reigning discipline. The terms of good news we might receive if we were formed to receive from the other will surprise even those of us who tell stories about the oppressed.

Index

Academic theologians, 320-21, 390-91
Accountability
  global, 237
  moral, 236-37
  personal, 235
  social, 223, 227, 232
  theological, 312n
Affectivity
  Christian, 212
  feminist, 391
  Pentecostal, 257, 274, 283, 289-90,
    295
Affinity, feminist theology of, 384,
  385-88
Agape, xii-xiv, 3, 11, 25, 375, 383-84,
  393. *See also* Care for the stranger
Alliaume, Karen T., 24
Anderson, Robert Mapes, 256-59
Anointing, 270-71, 277, 280
Apostolic faith, 286
Archimedean principles, feminist
  criticism of, 131n
Assemblies of God, 247
Authoritarian patriarchy, 217, 220-23
Authority
  Pentecostal, 253, 259, 263-69, 276,
    278, 288, 289
  Presbyterian Women, 193, 195, 231,
    233
  See also Certifying discourses
Authorization

social, 349-50
strategies of, 336-43
See also Certifying discourses

Bakhtin, Mikhail M., 364-65
Bal, Mieke, 131, 132-33
Baptism, of the Holy Spirit, 245-48,
  249, 254-55, 269
  See also Speaking in tongues
Bartky, Sandra Lee, 101
Behar, Ruth, 380
Belsey, Catherine, 73, 79n, 86
Benhabib, Seyla, 3
Bennett, Katherine, 1
Benveniste, Emile, 80
Berger, Peter L., 53
Bernstein, Richard J., 80n
Bias, 33, 38-40, 42, 138-39, 362
  of theology toward the oppressed, 33
Biblical discourse, 326-27
Biblical interpretation
  methods of, Presbyterian church,
    194-95
  political-ethical rhetorical practice, 125
  dialectical, 34-35
Biblical performances, 154
Biblical practice, 231
Binaries, 83-84, 347, 378-79, 382
Bledstein, Burton J., 318
Blumhofer, Edith L., 243n, 247, 249n,
  285n